Ceramics
A Potter's Handbook

Holt, Rinehart and Winston, Inc.

New York   Chicago   San Francisco   Atlanta
Dallas   Montreal   Toronto   London   Sydney

Ceramics
A Potter's Handbook
third edition

Glenn C. Nelson
University of Minnesota, Duluth

Editor Dan W. Wheeler
Production editor Rita Gilbert
Picture editor Joan Curtis
Designer Marlene Rothkin Vine

Library of Congress Catalog Card Number: 70-145911
College ISBN: 0-03-078835-8
Trade ISBN: 0-03-086000-8
Copyright © 1960, 1966 by Holt, Rinehart and Winston, Inc.
Black-and-white offset printing: Kingsport Press, Kingsport, Tenn.
Four-color gravure printing: Les Presses Centrales Lausanne S.A., Lausanne, Switzerland
Binding: Kingsport Press, Kingsport, Tenn.
2345 108 98765

Preface

Almost everyone has had some pleasurable experience feeling and forming the plasticity of moist clay, if only in the childhood acts of making mud pies or treading through rain-soaked paths, with pliant earth oozing up between the toes of bare feet. Ceramics, the art of clay and glazes, is an appealing medium, one that has attained immense popularity in our time, both as a craft to practice and as a tradition to appreciate. In its fired state clay is among the most ageless of materials. Its three-dimensional qualities, plus the effects of glaze, color, and texture, make ceramics potentially the richest of all art forms.

Commanding and irresistible, ceramics is also a fickle mistress. Not only do novice potters have many difficulties with clay, but even the experienced potter opens the kiln much as if he were coming downstairs on Christmas day—not really knowing quite what to expect. An old story has it that the ancient Chinese habitually formed a figurine to be placed in the kiln door to ward off evil spirits. While acknowledging with full respect the mystical and irreducible elements in the creative endeavor, the purpose of this handbook is to diminish the frustrations of the potter and endow him with greater control of his work, perhaps even help lead him to the artistry he seeks, by providing in systematic order the essential information about the ceramist's technology of transforming raw, wet clay into a fired and finished piece. Ceramics is the most technical of the forms artists work in, and to realize more than limited results the potter must acquire a good, basic understanding of the materials and processes of his medium. *Ceramics,* therefore, has been written in an effort to develop a reliable guide for the amateur potter as well as a reference volume for the more accomplished craftsman.

Singular as art history may seem in a handbook intended to serve the needs of working potters, the reader may well find the survey of traditional and contemporary ceramics, delineated in the first three chapters, the most rewarding part of the book. After all, the finished product—here the final potted form—is the paramount concern of most artists and conoisseurs. All technique is subservient to it, and many cultures have produced lasting works of art with a minimum of facilities. Readers familiar with previous editions of *Ceramics* will find this section considerably expanded both in coverage and in the quantity and variety of illustrations. The reproductions alone bear witness to the extraordinary vitality of the ceramist's art in our time.

Following the introductory survey chapters begins the main body of the book, a sequence of chapters dealing with the characteristics of clay, its properties and preparation; with the means of forming clay, in pots, sculpture, even architecture; with ceramic form and design; with the challenge of surface, of decoration and glazing; with the activity of the professional potter, in his studio as well as in industry; with kilns, their operation and construction; and, finally, with equipment, from wheels to the complete ceramic studio. Concluding the book is an appendix offering more technical and tabular data, sources of supplies, and a bibliography of published references. In addition, there is a glossary of ceramic terms.

Fresh to this edition are the particular attention given to the role played by the professional potter in the studio, in education, and in industry and the new ideas, materials, and equipment presented and illustrated throughout the book, especially in the chapter on kilns.

The chapters on forming, decoration, and glazing all take up problems and concepts in design, but the subtle aspects of design have been mentioned only in indirection. So elusive and individual are the qualities of form and decoration, they hardly lend themselves to verbal exposition but develop naturally in the studio as the student, the teacher, and the clay interact in an ill-defined way that is uniquely their own. There are no formulas and absolutes in design, for its secret and its truth lie in the craftsman's potential for growth and for developing diversity in his experience.

The illustrations for this edition of *Ceramics* have been selected and treated as elements fully as substantive as the text itself. Numbering over 500 in black and white and 22 reproduced in full color, they play an expressive role throughout the discussions pursued in the book. Now printed by gravure, a process especially sympathetic to the physical characteristics of textural, relief, and three-dimensional works, the illustrations suggest the immense range of forms and functions in ceramics, from the utilitarian teapot to the "one-of-a-kind" museum piece.

The acknowledgments of the many contributions made to the realization of *Ceramics* must begin with the potters already cited in the legends accompanying the illustrations. Without their photographs and the permission to reproduce their works, such a handbook as this could not have evolved. Museums and collectors have also been generous in granting rights to the materials they own. Special mention must be made of contributors outside the United States, who endured with grace and patience the difficulties of international communication. Among these are Asgar Fischer, of Bing and Grøndahl Studios, and Ivan Engle of Den Permanente, both in Copenhagen; Stig Lindberg, of the Gustavsberg Studios, and Carl-

Harry Stålhane of the Rörstrand Studios in Sweden; O. H. Gummerus, at the Finnish Society of Crafts and Design, and the Arabia Studios in Helsinki; the Norwegian Society of Arts and Crafts and Industrial Design; Murray Fieldhouse, editor of *Pottery Quarterly,* and Bill Read, both English potters; J. W. N. van Achterbergh of the Dutch Ceramic Society; Hildegard Storr-Britz of the ceramic school at Höhr-Grenzhausen, Germany; Kostas Panopoulos at the National Association of Hellenic Handicrafts in Athens; Tonito Emiliani, director of the State School of Ceramics in Faenza, Italy; the Japanese potter Hiroaki Morino of Kyoto; Wanda Garnsey of the Potter's Society of Australia; and Jack Sures, respondent for the Canadian Craftsmen's Association.

The manufacturers of ceramics and ceramic equipment have been cooperation itself, especially Syracuse China, Interpace Corporation, Pacific Stoneware, and the Bennington Potters. Peter A. Slusarski, of Kent State University, was most helpful in furnishing a series of illustrations on product design.

Ken Moran gave professional advice and practical assistance in the preparation of the process photographs. Richard Leach's color enlargements (Pls. 21–22) are both technically intriguing and beautiful in the abstract.

A large debt of gratitude must be acknowledged for the improvements and corrections made by Karl Martz, professor of ceramics at Indiana University, and Ed Traynor, member of the ceramics faculty at the University of California, Los Angeles, who read the entire manuscript and gave to the task the full range and depth of their knowledge and experience.

Thanks are also due to the staff at Holt, Rinehart and Winston for their skill in managing the monumental problems of producing a heavily illustrated art book—to Dan Wheeler, the editor of the series, to Rita Gilbert, who edited the manuscript and coordinated production, to Marlene Rothkin Vine, the creator of the book's stunning design, and to Joan Curtis, for her assistance with illustrations. To the author's wife, Edith, goes his last and warmest expression, in appreciation of her genius for deciphering an unintelligible scrawl and of her cheerful acceptance of endless changes in copy.

Duluth, Minnesota   G. C. N.
January, 1971

Contents

Ceramics
A Potter's Handbook

1 Ceramics of the Past

Prehistoric, Middle Eastern, Minoan, Mycenaean, Chinese, Greek, Etruscan and Roman, Islamic, Hispano-Moresque, and Italian Ceramics

THE PREHISTORIC WORLD

The origins of man are shrouded in mystery and subject to much speculation. It may have been as long as 500,000 years ago that an apelike creature first used a stone to break open a nut, thus beginning the critical tool-making process. By 100,000 B.C. early man was burying his dead with rudimentary stone tools and a supply of food included in the gravesite. Man's discovery of a means for making fire provided him with a vital asset. In an effort to explain and propitiate the great forces of nature and the mysteries of life and death, man slowly developed his religious beliefs and practices.

A small limestone carving with exaggerated female features (Fig. 2) discovered at Willendorf, Austria, (c. 15,000–10,000 B.C.) is one of the earliest known of the fertility fetishes that are found among the remains of all primitive cultures. The Cypriote statue in Figure 3 is also representative of this type of cult image. The animal cave paintings of France and Spain and the paintings and rock carvings of Africa (c. 15,000–8000 B.C. and perhaps earlier) reveal rare powers of observation and, certainly, an artistic ability equal to that of modern man.

As the glaciers of the last Ice Age retreated, much of Europe and Asia became heavily forested. The once plentiful mammoths, elk, and bison disappeared. Early man now found better hunting and fishing in the more temperate and fertile valleys of the Nile and the Tigris-Euphrates Rivers in the Middle East and of the Yellow River in China. The gathering of wild fruits, nuts, and wheat seeds gradually assumed a greater importance. About 8000 B.C. far-reaching changes occurred: a primitive type of wheat and barley came under cultivation, and sheep and goats and, later, cattle and pigs were domesticated.

The discovery of pottery making was crucial to this development, for primitive agriculturists needed cooking and storage containers. The prevalence of

opposite: 1. Vase, China. Sung Dynasty (960–1279). Tz'u-Chou stoneware, height 15 ½″. Victoria & Albert Museum, London. The crisp sgraffito design adds a touch of spontaneity to the bulbous form of this vase.

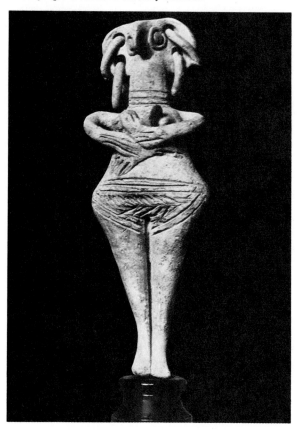

left : 2. *Venus of Willendorf.* c. 15,000–10,000 B.C. Stone, height 4 ³/₈″. Museum of Natural History, Vienna. This carving is one of the earliest known fertility fetishes.

below : 3. Female figure (fertility image ?), Cyprus. c. 1500–1200 B.C. Terra cotta, height 8 ³/₈″. Metropolitan Museum of Art, New York (Cesnola Collection; purchased by subscription, 1874–76). This rather fantastic statue is typical of fertility figures found in all early cultures.

a corded basketlike design on all early ware—whether in the Middle East, China, or the Americas—has led to the theory that baskets were first coated with clay to enable them to hold small, wild grain seeds. The accidental burning of one of these baskets led to the discovery that a clay vessel baked in the hot coals of the fire would become hard and suitable for such use. It is probable that this important breakthrough occurred independently in many areas of the world.

All early pots are black in color, having been fired in a primitive kiln or bonfire. They are all round bottomed, which may reflect the use of a gourd or round stone as a partial mold. Because they were low fired and subject to constant use, none have survived to this day, except as isolated fragments. It was a universal custom to bury pottery and other artifacts with the dead. Thanks to the imperishable quality of clay, these pottery objects often constitute the only surviving record of many ancient civilizations.

In the following pages we shall trace the development of pottery form and decoration among these early cultures. Perhaps more by chance than by determination, preferences for certain shapes and decorative motifs arose in different parts of the world, and these were refined through the ages. Influences occurred as one culture reacted upon another. But such was the persistence of custom and religion—as well as the tradition of the craft as it was transmitted from father to son—that age-old preferences were often retained. Thus, we can say that certain shapes are peculiarly Chinese or Greek or that decorative styles reflect a Japanese flavor.

MIDDLE EASTERN CERAMICS

Pottery was made at an early date (c. 5000 B.C.) in Egypt, Palestine, and the Tigris-Euphrates area. Like most early ceramic ware it was black, round bottomed, and usually had an impressed, corded surface. In time it was discovered that if the clay body was burnished with a bone or a flat pebble while half dry, it would acquire a smoother surface that was harder and more impervious to water. One such burnished ware was made in Egypt (Fig. 4). Termed *red-and-black ware*, it was fired upside down on its rim. The smoke and ashes in the primitive kiln reduced this portion to a glossy black, while the balance of the pot retained the red color of the clay. In time, a proper kiln with a chamber and fire box allowed for a clear, oxidizing atmosphere and made possible the use of clay slips to cover the red earthenware body or to decorate it (Fig. 5) with slips or metallic oxides in hues of white, cream, red, brown, and black and, at a later date, in pale yellow or blue.

At first all pottery was made by the women as part of their regular household chores. But, as the early settlements grew, a market developed in which a skilled craftsman could trade his produce for grain, leather, or other items. The earliest craftsmen were the metalsmith and the potter.

The uniformity of many of the early hand-built coiled pots would suggest that a spinner was used to scrape and refine the form. Pottery with a turned foot rim dating from about 4000 B.C. has been found in northern Iran, and this may well indicate the first use of the potter's wheel. The use of the wheel spread slowly, and larger vessels continued to be hand built in a coil-and-paddle technique. It is likely that at this period pottery making had become both a predominantly masculine and a full-time occupation. By 3000 B.C. the potter's wheel was in common use in the Middle East.

above : 4. Vase, Egypt. Predynastic (4000–3200 B.C.). Red-and-black earthenware. Victoria & Albert Museum, London.

right : 5. Jar, Egypt. Predynastic (c. 4000–3500 B.C.). Earthenware with slip decoration. Brooklyn Museum. The figures depict the journey of the soul across the Nile.

6. *Ushabti of King Seti I*, Egypt, from Thebes. 1313–1292 B.C. Alkaline-silica paste, height 11 ¾". Metropolitan Museum of Art, New York (Carnarvon Collection, gift of Edward S. Harkness, 1926). Ushabti are small, mummylike tomb figures which accompanied the dead in the afterlife.

The earliest dated glaze is on a tile fragment from the tomb of the Egyptian King Menes (c. 3000 B.C.). The initial discovery of glaze probably derives from the accidental melting of potash and sand deposits under a bonfire. All early Egyptian glazes have an alkaline flux. These early glazes were not used on pottery, however, but rather on wall tiles or for decorative furniture inlays. Glazed fig-

urines and small animal sculptures were popular, especially the turquoise Ushabti figurines (Fig. 6). The dearth of important Egyptian ceramics after a promising beginning may be explained in part by the wealth of the priesthood and the royal family. Pottery was for the poor and never developed into an art form, since the wealthy used eating vessels of gold and silver and had vases laboriously made of alabaster and even harder polished stone.

MINOAN AND MYCENAEAN CERAMICS

During the period between 3000 and 2500 B.C. a culture quite different was evolving on the island of Crete, about 600 miles northeast of Egypt. Without an oppressive priesthood and protected by the sea from invaders, the Minoans enjoyed a prosperity unique in its time. The cities and the palaces of merchant princes were unfortified, and the trading vessels of Crete were to be found in all parts of the eastern Mediterranean. The palace at Knossos (Fig. 7), home of the legendary King Minos of Homer's epic tales, was both a royal residence and a religious center, but large areas were given over to living quarters for the court, storerooms, and workshops. The principal structures rose to four and possibly five stories and were equipped with light wells and sanitary drains. The palace at Knossos and other palace buildings in Crete were undoubtedly the most advanced living quarters the world would see until the era of the Romans.

Early pottery in Crete followed the usual sequence: first a corded black ware, then a polished red and black, and finally a polished ware with simple incised cross-hatched and dotted designs. Frequent trade with Mesopotamia introduced the spouted ewer in a birdlike form characteristic of the pottery of that area. Stone vessels in the Egyptian style have also been found in Crete, as have small sculptures in Egyptian *faience* (a low-fire body high in silica and alkaline fluxes). Bronze tools, weapons, and small bronze figures were common. Delicately made gold jewelry was worn by the nobility, and gold cups and dishes were fashioned with great skill. Colorful frescoes—processions, youths with bulls, fish and bird life—covered the palace walls, and their spirit was not so much religious as athletic and exuberant.

In the Early Minoan period (c. 2800–2000 B.C.) the prevailing style of Cretan pottery was largely a decoration in white over a black slip, occasionally in a marbled imitation of stone, but also with banded and geometric motifs. The usual cups, bowls, and spouted round vases were present, but the form, like the decoration, was a bit heavy and clumsy. The following period, which is called Middle Minoan (2000–1550 B.C.), reflects the greater prosperity of the island and the increasing skill of the potter. The potter's wheel was in common use, and forms became more graceful. The favored designs were curling plant and circular motifs in white, cream, and red on a dark body. These gradually gave way to a preference for dark designs on a light tan body.

The closing years of this period and the early part of the Late Minoan era marked the high point of the island culture (1600–1500 B.C.). The flowing motifs of plant and sea life (particularly the octopus) were superbly suited to the popular oval water bottle and rounded vase forms (Fig. 8). In quality they are doubtless equal to the ceramic art of any historical period. Especially noteworthy are

above : 7. Stairwell, Palace of King Minos, Knossos, Crete. c. 1600–1500 B.C. (destroyed c. 1450 B.C.). Reconstruction.

below : 8. Jars, Crete. 1600–1500 B.C. Buff-colored earthenware with red-and-black slip. Herakleion Museum, Crete. The free decoration is characteristic of Minoan ware.

the huge palace storage jars nearly 6 feet high used for oil and wine, with numerous carrying lugs and a vigorous banded relief decoration. Also characteristic of this period, and peculiar to the region, are the so-called "snake goddesses," small faience figures with coiling snakes in their hands or around their bodies (Fig. 9). A period of decline set in after 1500 B.C. as the "palace style" vases became rather stiff with stylized floral patterns and over-elaborate with applied clay spurs.

Meanwhile, in the valleys of the Peloponnesus, the southern peninsula of the Greek mainland, a new power was growing. Shortly after 2000 B.C. a group of warlike tribes descended from the north of Greece, conquering the local inhabitants and building their fortress palaces at Mycenae and Tiryns. These were the Achaeans of Homeric legend. By 1400 B.C. the Mycenaean princes had founded most of the Greek cities we now know from Classic times (Fig. 10) and were expanding their power throughout the islands of the western Mediterranean.

above : 9. *"Snake Goddess"* (priestess ?), Crete. c. 1600 B.C. Faience, height 13 ½″. Museum, Candia, Crete.

left : 10. Lion Gate, Mycenae. c. 1250 B.C.

The Minoans had early trade with the Mycenaeans, and it is likely that many craftsmen emigrated from Crete to the mainland, since much of the goldwork and pottery found in Mycenae has Minoan characteristics. But the Mycenaean ware did develop its own direction. The vase forms were higher footed and had a more rounded curve at the shoulder (Fig. 11). The foot rims and lips developed a more definite flange. High-stemmed and delicately formed cups were popular. The more dynamic floral and sea forms of the Minoans were subdued and conventionalized, and often only simple banded decoration was used (Fig. 12).

The eastern Mediterranean has a long history of intensive volcanic action, and the palace sites in Crete indicate a series of destructions and rebuildings. About 1450 B.C. a particularly violent eruption caused large portions of the island of Thera (San-

left : 11. Amphora, Greece, from Mycenae, found on Cyprus. Early 14th century B.C. Museum, Nicosia, Cyprus. The rather sketchy decoration shows the influence of Minoan ceramics.

center : 12. Amphora in sub-Minoan style, found in Cyprus. c. 1150–1000 B.C. Earthenware. Museum, Nicosia, Cyprus.

right : 13. Jar, China. Neolithic Period, c. 2000 B.C. Earthenware with double-spiral decoration in brown-black and purple slips. Victoria & Albert Museum, London.

torini) to collapse into the sea. Because it is only 70 miles from Crete, huge tidal waves swept the populous coastal towns of the Minoan island. Lesser quakes destroyed the palaces, which were built of timber and stone. Huge fires raged as stores of olive oil were ignited, and a thick layer of volcanic ash covered the fertile valleys of Crete. In the following years, the Mycenaeans gradually occupied Crete, and the island never regained its former importance.

In time the Mycenaeans had their own problems. During the thirteenth century B.C., new waves of Greek-speaking people descended from the North, a group now called the Dorians. Somewhat soft from long years of peace and prosperity and divided by local rivalries, the Mycenaeans were no match for the barbarian invaders. The Dorians lacked an art of their own and appreciated but little that of

the conquered land; their coming brought about a period of dark ages in which only the crudest peasant crafts survived. But it was from this background that, Phoenixlike, Classical Greece arose.

CHINA AND THE FAR EAST

As in Europe and the Middle East, bands of hunter-fishermen inhabited the fertile valleys of China after the passing of the Ice Ages. The cultivation of wheat, the smelting of copper, and pottery making may have occurred there slightly later than in the Middle East (c. 3500 B.C.), but the dates are rather uncertain. As elsewhere, the early pottery was black, round bottomed, and had an impressed cord decoration. This gave way to a polished ware and, finally, when true kilns developed, to a pottery decorated with clay slips colored with various metallic oxides. A popular form was the oval jar with a small base, a large opening with a collar, and loops for tying down a cover. A circular double spiral design was common (Fig. 13). The cooking pot with three hollow feet was a unique form that was later taken over for ceremonial bronze vessels.

As in other cultures, most ancient Chinese pottery has been found in tombs. Very early in Chinese

above : 14. Vase, China, from Anyang Province. Shang Dynasty (1523–1028 B.C.). Thrown earthenware with banded and incised motifs of a metallic character. Metropolitan Museum of Art, New York (Harris Brisbane Dick Fund, 1950).

below : 15. Vase, China. Han Dynasty (206 B.C.–A.D. 220). Earthenware with applied clay decoration and runny green glaze, height 14 ³/₈″. Victoria & Albert Museum, London.

history we can detect a reverence for the dead, family pride, and the beginnings of ancestor worship. Pottery, jade articles, bronze weapons, jewelry, and particularly bronze vessels intended for burial rites were common tomb objects. The bronze vessels are especially noteworthy for their excellent craftsmanship. First copied from pottery forms, they soon became quite elaborate, with numerous pictographs, fantastic stylized animals, and, finally, representational scenes. In time the pattern was reversed, and some of the pottery forms imitated the bronzes with similar impressed designs.

By the Shang Dynasty period (1523–1028 B.C.), the potter's wheel had come into common use, and a white ware was made as well as the older red ware (Fig. 14). By the Chou period (1027–256 B.C.) the ware was higher fired, perhaps an influence from bronze casters who were working in high temperatures. This pottery was generally black or gray with impressed designs similar to those on the bronze vessels. The Chou Dynasty was a period of great prosperity and enlightenment in China, and the philosophies of Confucius and Lao Tzu, written about 500 B.C., still influence Chinese thought.

In Shang and Chou times it was common for the dead ruler to be buried with his horse and servants and perhaps even his wife. By the Han Dynasty (206 B.C.–A.D. 220) this custom was felt to be too barbaric, and pottery figures were substituted. The first lead-based glazes date from early Han times and are of a green, runny character (Fig. 15). It is likely that the earlier shiny, high-fire pieces were the result of ash falling on the ware during firing. But potters were more interested in the higher-fire ware, and by late Han they were producing stoneware jars with a feldspathic glaze fluxed with lime or wood ashes. The white slips used to cover the coarser stoneware bodies have a porcelain quality, and it was only a matter of time before a true porcelain body was developed.

In the Six Dynasties period (A.D. 220–589) and the T'ang Dynasty (A.D. 618–906) a remarkable number of excellent figures were made (Fig. 16). Mythical beasts, guardian soldiers, and especially the favorite horses (Pl. 1, p. 21; Fig. 17)—as well as dancing girls and ladies in waiting (Fig. 18)—

above : 16. *Horse and Rider*, China. Six Dynasties Period (220–589). Terra cotta with red, green, and blue paint. Museum of Far Eastern Antiquities, Stockholm. This horse is typical of the vigor of Chinese clay figures.

below : 17. Horse, China. T'ang Dynasty (618–906). Terra cotta with brown-black glaze. Metropolitan Museum of Art, New York (gift of Mrs. Edward S. Harkness, 1926).

right : 18. *Lady of the Court*, China. T'ang Dynasty (618–906). Painted earthenware. Victoria & Albert Museum, London.

China and the Far East 9

were modeled with a carefree skill and vitality seldom seen in ceramic sculpture of any age.

The T'ang period was a time of great experimentation in form and technique. Trade contacts with the Middle East were common, as is reflected in echoes of Greek and Roman vase forms, impressed decorative motifs, and marbelized clay bodies. The stoneware bodies were more refined, and it becomes a matter of opinion whether to term some pots stoneware or porcelain. Most impressive are the stoneware vases and bowls with incised lotus-leaf and dragon motifs, covered with the gray-green glaze called *celadon* (see reduction glazes, p. 213). Its similarity to jade, which was treasured by the Chinese and was thought in ancient times to possess magical properties, causes it to be universally esteemed. During the T'ang Dynasty ceramics became

a major Chinese art form, and the celadon vases took the place of honor in tomb offerings formerly accorded bronze vessels.

The Sung Dynasty period (960–1279) may be likened to the western Classical era, in that it set a standard that was emulated for the next thousand years. Sung ceramics reflect a refinement of older forms, a simplification that adds to their strength. The pieces may be heavy or thin depending upon the shape. Many earlier glazes did not fit the clay body and often crazed. The Sung potter was able to control this to produce a fine or heavy crackle or none at all (Fig. 19). The white porcelain body made possible the use of delicate blue and green glazes on which a fine crackle became a decorative element. Dark glazes, such as the *temmoku* with its pale silver-like oil spots, were popular for tea bowls. The large,

below : 21. Bottle, China. Sung Dynasty (960–1279). Pale green celadon with silver-brown iridescent spots, height 10 ⅞″. Victoria & Albert Museum, London.

bottom : 22. Pilgrim bottle, China. Ming Dynasty (1368–1644). Porcelain with dragon decoration in cobalt blue, height 14 ½″. Victoria & Albert Museum, London.

small-mouthed vase forms (T'zu-Chou) are especially attractive in a brown-black glaze, which is cut away and incised in vigorous floral patterns to expose the gray stoneware body (Fig. 20). Delicate long-necked bottle and gourd forms also originated in the Sung period (Fig. 21). Buddhism had by this time traveled from India to China, and the influence of the new religion was reflected in numerous terra cotta sculptural pieces based upon the Indian Buddha and his entourage of saints.

China has suffered during its long history from invasions by the nomadic warlike tribes to the north. Of the many invasions, that of the Mongol tribes under Genghis Khan was the most catastrophic. He invaded China in 1211, and its capital fell soon afterward. But due to conquests as far west as Persia, all of China did not fall until 1280, to his grandson and successor, Kublai Khan. The short Yuan period (1280–1368), under the Mongol conquerors, was an era of stagnation in ceramics.

The Ming Dynasty (1368–1644) brought another period of peace and prosperity. It may be likened to the Western Baroque and Rococo ages in that it was time of great technical skill, and, partly because of this, both form and decoration became rather overelaborate and fussy. Of course, many fine pieces were made in the older Sung styles and cannot be distinguished from earlier prototypes. The underglaze blue-and-white decorations on white porcelain that made such an impact on Europe were common during this period (Fig. 22). Many of these—strong, full jar forms with floral, figurative, or landscape motifs—are tastefully painted and most impressive. But these were not considered elegant enough for wealthy court tastes, and soon potters were using three- and even five-color overglaze enamel decorations in gaudy patterns. A few of the pieces have forms and decorations that are harmonious, but many are almost hideous when judged by contemporary tastes.

A more enduring technical accomplishment was the development of a rich red achieved by reducing copper with an alkaline flux (see reduction glazes, p. 213). The glaze ranged from a pale "peach bloom" to a deep purple-red, and when applied to a simple porcelain form the result could be both rich and

China and the Far East   11

elegant without being ostentatious. The porcelain sculpture of the Ming period also reflects the skill of the modeler, but with some loss of the vitality characteristic of the earlier T'ang pieces.

As was common in Chinese history, dissention at home and pressure from the Manchurians to the north led to the fall of the Ming Dynasty. During the subsequent long and changing Ch'ing period (1644–1912) there were several diverse trends. The technical skill evidenced in the blue-and-white ware and the multicolored enamels continued. Colors became brighter, and gold and luster were added. There is some influence of Islamic decoration, but in general the forms are those of the Sung and Ming eras except, perhaps, for a more perfect and mechanically correct execution (Fig. 23). It is possible that some cleansing influence might have taken place were it not for the increasing trade with Europe. In the midst of an industrial revolution that destroyed their own crafts, the *nouveau riche* of Europe were hardly the ones to appreciate subtleties in either form or decoration. Only the most elaborate and decadent styles were imported, and these were mass-produced in a way that was highly injurious to local Chinese traditions.

GREEK CERAMICS

After the overthrow of the Mycenaeans by the Dorians there were no longer any large Greek cities. Trade and the crafts declined, and even the rudimentary writing that the Minoans and Mycenaeans used for their record keeping was forgotten. The surviving pottery shows a crude imitation of the older forms and decoration. Perhaps the only significant change was that the focus of community life turned from the palace to the temple. Instead of the informal and even whimsical arts of the Minoans, there was a new emphasis on the monumental and the stylized art form. Beginning about 1050 B.C., ceramics in the area of Athens showed an improvement. Although the form imitated that of the Mycenaean cups, vases, and jars, it was better thrown and higher fired. The decoration—banded lines or concentric circles in a dark slip on a light red body—was executed with care and precision (Fig. 24). In

23. *Kwanyin*, China. Ch'ing Dynasty (1644–1912). Porcelain with greenish-white glaze, height 18 ½". Art Institute of Chicago (Buckingham Collection).

time this decoration, termed Protogeometric, gave way to a more varied style.

The style that is called Geometric (c. 900 B.C.) was still a banded type, but it was enlivened with rows of triangles, zig-zags, meanders, and swastikas, with the neck and shoulder of the vase emphasized. Eventually figurative elements were introduced. First came the horse, a prestige symbol in this warrior culture, and later man and the chariot. A classic example of the style is the *Dipylon Vase* (Fig. 25), so called because it was found in the Dipylon cemetary in Athens. A funeral procession is portrayed on the

motifs. However, a very effective black-figure style of the human was used on a series of miniature bottle and vase forms.

During the period of the Oriental style (late eighth and seventh century B.C.) the Athenian potter continued to be interested in the human figure, but he was satisfied to paint it in an outline that was not too effective. Toward the end of the seventh century, he adopted the black-figure style with greater success. Corinthian ware was now made rather carelessly. This factor, coupled with the Persian wars, which made Eastern influences unpopular, again

shoulder and body of the vase, and the deceased and mourners are represented by stylized figures composed of circles for heads, triangles for torsos, and sticks for arms and legs. It was only a matter of time before such simple depictions would prove unsatisfactory.

As the Greek city-states grew, trade developed with the islands and finally with Asia Minor to the east. The older civilizations of the Middle East had a long tradition of fantasy in their art—winged monsters, gorgons, and sphinxes, often set against a background of imaginative floral patterns. Corinth, to the west of Athens, became the center of this new Oriental style, although Rhodes and other islands close to Syria were similarly influenced. Instead of simple zig-zags, the borders were decorative floral forms, and the central panel was enlarged to feature stylized birds and animals and finally figures from the Homeric legends. Clay slips were now carefully prepared of fine decanted red clay particles which, after burnishing and firing, assumed a smooth, black, glazelike surface (see slip glazes, p. 215). Details were added by incising, or, occasionally, by adding touches of white slip. In general the larger Corinthian pieces featured animal or bird

Greek Ceramics 13

above : 26. Horse and rider, Greece. 7th century B.C. Terra cotta, height c. 8″. Museum, Nicosia, Cyprus.

right : 27. EXEKIAS, Greece. *The Return of Dioscuri* (black-figure amphora). c. 540 B.C. Vatican Museum, Rome.

gave Athens the central position in the creation of Greek pottery.

In the seventh century small terra cotta figures, in human and animal forms, were made throughout the Greek islands (Fig. 26). Their forms are highly stylized, but the figures are gay and almost whimsical in character.

Due perhaps to the use of pottery in burial rites, ceramic forms had been codified into a definite series

of vase, jar, bottle, pitcher, and cup forms. The major area of the black-figure vase was given over to a figure or group representing heroes, gods (Pl. 2, p. 22), or episodes from Homeric legends, satyrs, and maenads (Fig. 27), and only later athletes and domestic scenes. It was this interest in illustration that deterred the Greeks from any attempt at a true glassy glaze, which might run and destroy their meticulous vase paintings. Perhaps their world was

right: 28. Attic red-figure kylix, Greece. 490–480 B.C. Earthenware, height 5¼". Metropolitan Museum of Art, New York (bequest of Joseph Pulitzer, 1953).

below: 29. Interior of Fig. 28, red-figure kylix.

more isolated than we suspect today, and the Greeks might have been unaware of the Egyptian glazes made over two thousand years earlier.

The black-figure style, which portrayed the subject in profile with feet flat on the ground, proved successful in terms of harmonious ceramic design, but it offered little flexibility for the increasing skill of the vase painter. After about 520 B.C. the method changed to create a background in black which left the figure in the red body color (Figs. 28–30). Details could be added more easily with a fluid brush stroke than with the older method of incising. White was employed to highlight flesh tones, as it had been in the old black-figure style, and eventually it was used to form an allover ground on which the vase painter drew his figures. This technique appeared usually in the slender *lekythoi* (oil jugs) that served as funerary offerings, and it permitted still

Greek Ceramics   15

left : 30. *A Victorious Charioteer and the Goddess Nike* (red-figure column krater), Greece. c. 460–450 B.C. Metropolitan Museum of Art, New York (Rogers Fund, 1941).

below : 31. Figure of a woman, Italy. 3rd century B.C. Terra cotta. Metropolitan Museum of Art, New York (Rogers Fund, 1913). This figure was discovered in Tarentum, in southern Italy, but it is of a type first found at Tanagra, north of Athens, and its origin is Greek.

greater fluency in the drawing. The white ground took the role of empty space, with forms—naturalistic, foreshortened, and in three-quarter perspective—emerging from this space, thus creating an illusion of depth on the planar surface of the vessel.

In Greece, for the first time in history, pots were signed by their makers, and, as specialization grew, they were signed by both the potter and the painter. This was an uneasy partnership, which would be successful only when the painter realized the need of harmony between the pot and the decoration. It was natural, however, that as the skill of the vase painter grew, he would be tempted to make more extravagant efforts. By the fourth century B.C. Greek pottery was in the same decline that affected the sculpture of the period. The original decorative quality of the pottery was destroyed by confused overlapping, by excessive foreshorting, and, eventually, by multicolored landscape effects. The very popular Tanagra statuettes of small seated or standing figures are well known (Fig. 31). But more important were the early ceramic statues used on temple pediments. Unfortunately, constant wars among the Greek city-states resulted in their nearly complete destruction. Fragments of two large ceramic figures from Olympia (c. 470 B.C.) reveal an artistry equal to the marble sculpture of the era and indicate a long period of prior development in clay modeling (Fig. 32).

ETRUSCAN AND ROMAN CERAMICS

The Etruscans are thought to have come to the eastern area of central Italy from Syria in Asia Minor in the ninth century B.C. During the period when the Greeks were setting up colonies as far west as Sicily and southern Italy, the Etruscans were expanding their influence into the valleys of central Italy, and

32. *Zeus and Ganymede*, Greece, from Olympia. c. 470 B.C. Terra cotta, height c. 43¼″. Museum, Olympia.

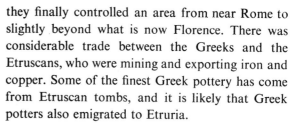

they finally controlled an area from near Rome to slightly beyond what is now Florence. There was considerable trade between the Greeks and the Etruscans, who were mining and exporting iron and copper. Some of the finest Greek pottery has come from Etruscan tombs, and it is likely that Greek potters also emigrated to Etruria.

The traditional Etruscan pottery is a black polished ware called *bucchero* (Figs. 33–34). An earlier ware has a red polished body, often incised with bands or cross-hatched motifs. Etruscan pottery is uneven in quality, for there were many influences: Villanovan black ware (Fig. 35), the Eastern Oriental style, the Greek, and embossed metalwork, none of which were completely assimilated into a coherent art form. Their work in bronze is perhaps more significant than their pottery.

It was in the field of ceramic sculpture that the Etruscans were most noted (Figs. 36–37). The earliest

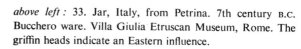

above left : 33. Jar, Italy, from Petrina. 7th century B.C. Bucchero ware. Villa Giulia Etruscan Museum, Rome. The griffin heads indicate an Eastern influence.

left : 34. *Procession to the Sphinx*, oenochoe (wine vase), Italy. 6th century B.C. Bucchero ware with metallike carved relief. Museo dell'Opera, Orvieto.

below : 35. Cinerary urn, Italy, from Vulci. 9th–8th century B.C. Black-polished Villanovan ware. Villa Giulia Etruscan Museum, Rome.

left: 36. Canopic cinerary urns, Italy. 8th century B.C. Museo Faina, Orvieto. The interest in portraiture that began with the Etruscans continued in the Roman era.

below left: 37. Maenad-head temple antefix, Italy, from Falerii Venteres. Terra cotta. Villa Giulia Etruscan Museum, Rome.

below: 38. *Apollo of Veii*, Italy. c. 510 B.C. Terra cotta, height c. 5′10″. Villa Giulia Etruscan Museum, Rome.

temples of the Etruscans were not unlike those of the archaic Greeks, in that they were built of wood with colonnaded porticoes. The Etruscan temples differed, however, in the terra cotta that was used extensively in them. The roof tiles at the eaves culminated in elaborate gorgon heads. In the more ambitious temples large ceramic figures topped the roof peaks, and an entablature in high relief filled the triangular pediment of the main façade. The life-size image in Figure 38 is one such example

Etruscan and Roman Ceramics   19

above : 39. *Sarcophagus of the Spouses*, Italy, from Cerveteri. Early 6th century B.C. Terra cotta, length 6′7″. Villa Giulia Etruscan Museum, Rome.

left : 40. Detail of Fig. 39, sarcophagus. The delicate modeling and forceful stylization of the *Spouses* represents a high point in Etruscan ceramic art.

arrangements, but they were essentially an exuberant and fun-loving people, qualities revealed by the colorful frescoes in the tombs. The wealthier families buried their dead in large ceramic coffins surmounted by portrait figures of the dead. Most famous are the couples, man and wife, who recline at their ease on couches, apparently in animated conversation with their friends (Figs. 39–40). It is this personal and informal quality that distinguishes the Etruscans from the Greeks, whose work was directed toward a predetermined ideal. Perhaps some of the freedom of expression is a result of working in the plastic clay, for the Greek terra cottas from Olympia display much the same vitality as the larger Etruscan pieces.

Shortly after 500 B.C. warlike Latin tribes in the vicinity of Rome began expanding north, into Etruscan territory, and south, against the Greek

from Veii, near Rome. Unfortunately, the Etruscan temples were later completely destroyed by the Romans. Well preserved, however, were the rock-cut tombs, many of which escaped the sporadic looting that has occurred over the centuries. One might suspect the Etruscans of a morbid preoccupation with death because of their elaborate burial

Plate 1. Horse, China. T'ang Dynasty (618–906). Glazed terra cotta, height
30¼″. Cleveland Museum of Art (anonymous gift). (See also Fig. 17.)

above : Plate 2. EXEKIAS, Greece. *Dionysus in a Boat* (Attic black-figure kylix). c. 540 B.C. Earthenware, diameter 12″. Staatliche Antikensammlungen, Munich.

left : Plate 3. Bowl, Persia, from Kashan. 13th century. Minai ware with opaque turquoise glaze and polychrome over-glaze painting and gilding, diameter 7 ¾″. Metropolitan Museum of Art, New York (gift of Mr. and Mrs. A. Wallace Chauncey, 1957).

41. Brick wall (detail) from the Procession Street, Palace of King Nebuchadnezzar II, Babylon. 6th century B.C. Terra cotta tin-lead glazed in blue, white, and yellow. Metropolitan Museum of Art, New York (Fletcher Fund, 1931).

colonies. Neither the Etruscans, a loose confederation of twelve small kingdoms, nor the Greek colonies and their mother city-states, continually quarreling among themselves, could present a united front against the Romans. During the next two hundred years all fell before the growing power of Rome, which took over not only the eastern empire of Alexander but all the lands bordering on the western Mediterranean.

Roman art is a mixture of Etruscan and Greek elements. The Etruscan interest in portraiture became a dominant Roman characteristic, and with so many captive artisans working in Rome, it is difficult to tell where the late Greek and Etruscan art left off and the Roman began. Ornate Hellenistic ceramics were popular in luxury-loving Rome. Native Roman pottery is in the polished Etruscan bucchero tradition, but with a red oxidized body. The adopted Greek forms were usually covered with a banded pressed or applied decoration reminiscent of relief metalwork. Due to the intricate detail, the pottery pieces were often pressed in bisque molds. Although the first temple in Rome is reputed to have had terra cotta sculpture made by the craftsmen of the still-flourishing Veii, the Romans soon adopted marble as a favorite medium. Terra cotta reliefs, portraits, and small ceramic sculptured pieces continued to be made, but they lacked the nervous and sometimes crude vitality of the Etruscans.

The Roman empire fell not because of invasion from the outside but from internal decay. Futile wars, excessive sums spent on temples, and ornate public and private buildings all squandered needed resources. Captured booty gave a false sense of prosperity. Perhaps the practice of slavery, which was widespread in the ancient world, was equally at fault. As an increasingly large proportion of the populace, both in Rome and in its colonies, was unable to purchase back the products of its labor, trade stagnated, and the economy ground to a halt.

ISLAMIC CERAMICS

The earliest records of pottery making come from the area of Egypt and Mesopotamia. The Middle East saw the rise and fall of many ancient civilizations—the Sumerians, the Assyrians, the Persians, and the Egyptians—and these influences, as well as its position as a meeting place of East and West, created a complex art form. But in spite of almost perpetual conflicts and invasions, certain characteristics have remained constant. One is a preference for curved forms, like those found as early as 2500 B.C. in the stylized animals depicted on Babylonian pottery. Another interest is the use of repetative patterns and a symmetrical composition. A third is a desire for color (Fig. 41), which we find in the polychrome glazed tile reliefs (c. twelfth–

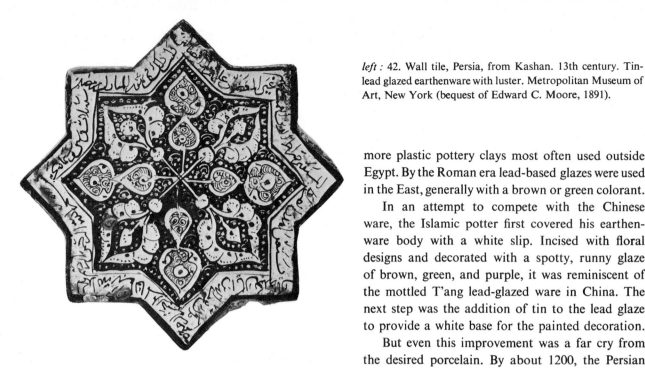

fifth century B.C.) on the walls and palaces of the Assyrians and Babylonians.

As Rome's vast empire in the Middle East declined, numerous small states emerged, which were in constant conflict with one another. The events in the life of Mohammed (A.D. 570–632), the prophet of Islam, later generated a force that was to fill this vacuum. In the century following his death the religious and political power of Islam conquered the Middle East and spread east from Arabia toward India and west across North Africa and into Spain. With this sudden outburst of energy, there also appeared a synthesis of ancient art traditions that became characteristic of Islamic art: the flowing curve of the arabesque, intricate detail and pattern, and a love of color.

The pottery of the eighth and ninth centuries is of little interest to the contemporary craftsman. Were it not that imported Chinese pottery, particularly the porcelains, excited the ruling caliphs and their courts, it is likely that Islamic pottery would never have had its great success. Local pottery was held in low regard, but the thin and delicate porcelains were treasured by the wealthy as the equal of their vessels of gold.

Early Egyptian alkaline glazes fused satisfactorily on their sandy clay bodies, but not on the more plastic pottery clays most often used outside Egypt. By the Roman era lead-based glazes were used in the East, generally with a brown or green colorant.

In an attempt to compete with the Chinese ware, the Islamic potter first covered his earthenware body with a white slip. Incised with floral designs and decorated with a spotty, runny glaze of brown, green, and purple, it was reminiscent of the mottled T'ang lead-glazed ware in China. The next step was the addition of tin to the lead glaze to provide a white base for the painted decoration.

But even this improvement was a far cry from the desired porcelain. By about 1200, the Persian potter, after continued experiments, developed a soft paste porcelain. It was rather like that used in eighteenth-century France, but somewhat coarser and sandy in texture. Composed of a powdered silica and a glass frit held together with a small amount of white clay, it was not very plastic and was probably a factor in limiting the Islamic form to rather simple dishes, bowls, ewers, and vases.

Possibly the most unique achievement of the Islamic potter was in the use of a luster glaze (Fig. 42). A luster is essentially a thin layer of metal fused onto the glaze at a lower temperature (see p. 214). It was first used on glass during the eighth and ninth centuries to produce a goldlike effect. Early ninth-century lustered pieces exhibit a variety of metallic colors in hues of ruby red, green, brown, and yellow, applied in complicated patterns. But, perhaps due to difficulties of technique, the pale golden brown became the favorite and was used in an overall pattern in connection with polychrome decoration in blue, turquoise, manganese purple, and pale green. Intricate entwined floral designs were a favorite motif, sometimes used as a background for a stylized bird, animal, or human subject. Much has been made of the Koranic ban against the pictorial representation of man, but this pertained only to the decoration of the Mosque, which was often covered inside and out with colorful tiles, largely of

above : 43. Jug, Persia. 13th century. Earthenware with Kufic script decoration in black slip, height 5 ¾″. Victoria & Albert Museum, London.

below left : 44. Drug jar, Syria. 13th–14th century. Earthenware with black slip decoration under turquoise glaze, height 13″. Victoria & Albert Museum, London.

below right : 45. Jar, Syria. 14th century. Earthenware with blue and black painted decoration under clear glaze, height 16″. Victoria & Albert Museum, London.

floral patterns and inscriptions from the Koran. The flowing and graceful quality of the Kufic script was a most satisfying decoration in itself (Fig. 43).

The *minai* decorations popular in Persia during the late twelfth century reveal great interest in everyday human life (Pl. 3, p. 22). Derived from manuscript illustrations (now lost), they represent in miniature scenes of horsemen, hunting, court life, and tales from the romantic legends. Quite different but equally impressive is the dark slip- and sgraffito-decorated ware of animals and floral patterns under a turquoise glaze (Fig. 44). For brief periods a pressed ware reflecting metal forms was popular, and continued Chinese imports resulted in a carved ware reminiscent of T'ang celadons.

Despite continued conflicts, the greatest period of Islamic ceramics came in the twelfth and thirteenth centuries, as power moved from Damascus, Baghdad, Samarkand, and Cairo under various ruling groups. The Mongol invasions directed by Genghis Khan and the assumption of power in Mesopotamia by his grandson, Hulaju, in 1258, began a decline in the ceramic arts. The fourteenth century was a period of renewed contacts with, and influence from, China. Brush decoration in black under turquoise or clear glaze (Fig. 45) gradually

left : 46. Dish, Byzantine. 14th century. Earthenware with sgraffito decoration through white slip with yellow and green, diameter 9″. Victoria & Albert Museum, London.

right : 47. Plate, Turkey, from Isnik. 1550–60. White earthenware with polychrome floral decoration, diameter 14 ½″. Victoria & Albert Museum, London.

replaced the older luster ware and minai, and the subject matter was influenced by Chinese textiles and paintings. Stylized animal and bird forms were still popular (Fig. 46). Imports of the older Islamic pottery and cobalt ores also reached China and undoubtedly led to the development in the late Yuan (Mongol) Dynasty of the first blue-and-white decorated porcelain.

Meanwhile, the Turks were again coming to power in the Middle East. A nomadic tribe living north of Afghanistan, they moved south and west during the eleventh century, and they controlled much of the Middle East when the conquering Mongols arrived. Pushed into Asia Minor by the Mongols, the Turks renewed their expansion after the collapse of Mongol power, and by 1453 they

had captured Constantinople, bringing an end to the old Byzantine-Roman empire. In 1516 Syria and Egypt fell under Turkish rule.

The fifteenth century was a confused period for the potter. Persians, imported to work on tiles for the new mosques and tombs at Bursa and Idirne (in Turkey near Constantinople), were most successful in combining Chinese and Persian floral motifs in blue and turquoise. The sixteenth and seventeenth centuries marked the high point in Turkish pottery. The initial use of blue-and-white decoration in the Chinese style gradually succumbed to the Islamic love of color. Floral decoration was still dominant, but now it took the form of distinct sprays of identifiable flowers—the tulip, the blue bell, and other garden blooms (Fig. 47). There were also attempts to imitate the carved Chinese celadons. A bright monochrome ware in blue-green and amber developed, as did a white pierced ware with the design filled in with a transparent glaze. A revival of luster ware occurred, but during the eighteenth and nineteenth centuries the decoration became increasingly rigid and mechanical. Meanwhile, to the west, Islamic pottery was taking new directions in Moslem Spain.

48. Vase, Spain, from Valencia. c. 1470. Gold and blue luster ware, height 20 ¾″. Victoria & Albert Museum, London. The overall form and wing handles on this vase are derived from the Alhambra vase style. (See Fig. 49.)

HISPANO-MORESQUE CERAMICS

Spain was invaded in 711, as the early Moslem wave of expansion spread across North Africa. In 732 the Moors were defeated at Poitiers, in the south of France, after which only the southern half of Spain remained under Moslem control. This period was one of prosperity and stimulation of the arts. Leatherwork flourished at Córdoba, metalwork at Toledo, and pottery at Málaga. The palace fortress of the Alhambra, with its pointed domes, colonnaded courts, delicate tracery in stone, and colorful tiles, remains the most distinctive architecture in Spain. Early tenth- and eleventh-century pottery of stamped or slip designs in geometric motifs or Koranic inscriptions is of little interest.

The dispersal of Persian potters following the Mongol conquests is probably the reason for the initial growth of lustered pottery. Unlike his Middle Eastern counterpart, the Spanish potter continued to use an earthenware body with a lead-tin covering glaze. The Málaga potter reflected the art of the metal engraver and textile worker in his use of a complicated overall pattern of stylized floral elements, chevrons, knotted ribbons, and Koranic inscriptions. The favorite luster was a pale gold with details in blue (Fig. 48), although occasionally a violet and a turquoise-green was also used.

In time Gothic influences from the North crept in, and a more naturalistic foliage, and even animals, birds, horsemen, and humans were used. Interested primarily in decoration, the Islamic potter, except in

the Alhambra vases (Fig. 49), never developed the more graceful style of the Chinese. His forms were rather heavy—large platters with flat rims, pitchers, and drug jars with a severe vertical shape (Fig. 50).

The luster ware of Málaga and Murcia was in great demand throughout the western Mediterranean. By the early fourteenth century Moslem potters were working at Manisis, a pottery town near Valencia, which later grew in importance. Possession of large sets of luster ware became a prestige symbol for the ruling families of the many small dukedoms in northern Spain, France, and Italy (Fig. 51). The heraldic family crest surrounded by an elaborate border became the style for large platters intended primarily for display (Fig. 52).

The local rulers in the North and the leaders of the Christian Church were moved by the same spirit of gain and conquest that characterized the seventh- and eighth-century Moslems. By 1212 only the small kingdom of Granada was under Moslem rule, and that fell in 1492 to Ferdinand and Isabella. In the same year the Jews were expelled from Spain. The infamous Spanish Inquisition began, and in 1502 the remaining Moslems were forcibly converted to Christianity and, in 1609, finally expelled. The flow of gold and treasure from the looted Indians of Mexico and Peru temporarily concealed the tragedy of the expulsion of the Moors and Jews, but southern Spain never recovered its former prosperity in agriculture or in trade.

As silver and gold plate became accessible to the now-wealthy ruling families, luster ware lost its appeal. Imitative attempts to shape the raised metallic bosses and designs in a pottery form were not successful. Perhaps the association of luster with the Moors was a factor in its flagging popularity. As luster ware became increasingly scarce, the pictorial majolica of Renaissance Italy was gaining in favor. A small local market for luster remained until the seventeenth century, but its great days were past.

above : 49. Alhambra vase, Spain. Late 13th–early 14th century. Olive-green luster ware with floral and Kufic script decoration, height 5′6″. Museo Nazionale, Palermo.

left : 50. Drug jar, Spain. c. 1440. Opal and blue luster ware, height 15 1/8″. Victoria & Albert Museum, London.

ITALIAN CERAMICS

Little pottery of interest was made in medieval Italy. Roman and Etruscan ware had been long forgotten. By 1400 the typical Italian functional earthenware bowls, pitchers, and jars were covered with a white slip incised with a free rendering of

birds and animals with simple geometric borders (Fig. 53). The sgraffito decoration and the runny lead glaze with areas of green and yellow were not unlike the Islamic ware of the ninth and tenth centuries. It was natural that the early luster ware of Spain became highly prized in Italy. Trading vessels from Spain stopped frequently at the island of Majorca en route to Pisa and Genoa. Thus, the new tin-glazed Italian ware in the Spanish style became known as *majolica*.

By 1450 the Hispano-Moresque pottery was being extensively copied, both in form and in decoration, in Faenza, Sienna, Orvieto, Florence, and other pottery centers. But only at Deruta was luster ware made with any great success (Fig. 54). The

Italian Ceramics 29

typical majolica decoration was painted in hues of blue, purple-black, green, or yellow. More naturalistic floral motifs gradually superseded the intricate and stylized Islamic motifs. By 1500 foliage decoration became a minor interest as figurative elements took over, first portrait heads on pitchers or plates (Figs. 55–56) and, finally, whole figures and groups. This trend might be attributed to a lingering Roman influence, as well as to the greater stress on personality in the Renaissance. The major strides made by mural painters were reflected in pottery, as the decoration became increasingly crowded and illusionistic, with scenes from classical mythology, occasional biblical themes, and genre topics (Fig. 57). Like late Greek vase painting, it is hardly a successful merger of form and decoration.

In some provinces extensive use was made of architectural friezes and decorative moldings in

above left : 54. Drug pot, Italy, from Deruta. c. 1500. Majolica ware with decoration in blue, green, and yellow; height 10 ¾". Victoria & Albert Museum, London.

above right : 55. Drug jar, Italy, from Faenza. c. 1475. Tin-lead glazed earthenware with majolica decoration featuring a portrait of a young man, height 11 ½". Metropolitan Museum of Art, New York (Fletcher Fund, 1946).

right : 56. Plate, Italy, from Deruta. c. 1520. Blue and gold luster, diameter 15 ¾". Victoria & Albert Museum, London.

terra cotta. As glazes were perfected, colorful tile work became more common. But perhaps the most significant ceramic contribution of the Italian Renaissance was in the field of clay sculpture. Since clay is universally used as a sketch material for sculpture, many of these were subsequently fired. A number of sculptors, including Donatello and Michelangelo, made specific works in terra cotta, but these have received little recognition beside their major works in marble.

Of the many sculptors working in glazed terra cotta, the workshop of Luca della Robbia (1400–82) is best known. The soft white glazes on his

simple, modeled madonnas were most successful (Fig. 58). The pale blue backgrounds and unobtrusive floral borders were not in conflict with the sculpture form, as was often the case with the work of his followers. Glazed terra cottas were very popular (Fig. 59) and included, besides the lunettes and madonnas, figures in the round, baptism fonts, and even entire altarpieces of great size. Unfortunately, by the third generation of the della Robbia family, the same overcrowded and confused illustionistic effects occurred that characterized other later majolica pottery, and the early elegance was lost.

right : 57. *The Calydonian Boar* (decorated plate), Italy, from Urbino. c. 1542. Polychrome majolica ware, diameter 10 ¾". Victoria & Albert Museum, London.

below left : 58. LUCA DELLA ROBBIA, Italy. *Madonna and Child with Scroll.* c. 1450. Glazed terra cotta, height 31 ¼". Metropolitan Museum of Art, New York (bequest of Benjamin Altman, 1913). This graceful madonna is modeled in Renaissance tradition and decorated with a lead-tin glaze.

below right : 59. LEONARDO DA VINCI (?), Italy. *Ginevra de' Benci.* c. 1500. Glazed terra cotta. Private colllection, Italy.

2 Ceramics of the Past

*Later European; African;
South, Central,
and North American;
Korean;
and Japanese Ceramics*

LATER EUROPEAN CERAMICS

Northern Europe lagged far behind the Middle East and the Orient in its ceramic development. It was the misfortune of this region to be overwhelmed by foreign influences before strong native traditions could emerge and take form. As a result, European ceramics, like American, are forever eclectic. Just as life quickened in thirteenth-century Italy, trade increased and small handcraft industries began in the North. During the late thirteenth and fourteenth centuries some very freely thrown and forceful pitchers, jugs, and mugs were made in England and France (Figs. 60–61), especially in the monastery workshops of the Cistercians. Incised, applied clay, and slip decoration, with a thin lead glaze in a mottled green and yellow, are typical of the style of this early period (Fig. 62). Little change took place during the fifteenth century (Fig. 63). But during the sixteenth and seventeenth centuries an interesting development occurred in slip-trailed and combed decoration (Fig. 64). The new floral, animal, and human motifs seem related to tapestry or embroiderywork, but this doubtless was due to method. The unique slip technique was snuffed out in the eighteenth century as imports increased and as industrialization accelerated.

Although high-fire stoneware was made at an early age in China, its development was very late in the West. This probably was due to the lack of high-fire and stoneware clays in the older civilizations of the Mediterranean. But during the thirteenth century (and perhaps as early as the twelfth century) a red polished pottery was being made in the Rhineland area near Cologne which had the characteristic hardness of stoneware. By the fifteenth century there were many small pottery towns near the Rhine—Höhr-Grenzhausen, Siegberg, Cologne, and Raeren in Flanders—producing a salt-glazed stoneware (see salt glaze, p. 214). This was a discovery unique to the area. The favorite shapes were the

opposite : 60. Jug, Normandy, from Rouen. Late 13th century. Thrown clay with applied clay decoration and thin yellow glaze, height 9 ½″. Guildhall Museum, London.

above left : 61. Ram's head jug, England. 14th century. Buff ware with applied clay decoration and thin yellow-green glaze, height 14″. Guildhall Museum, London.

above right : 62. Jug, England. 14th century. Red ware with yellowish green glaze, height 14″. Guildhall Museum, London.

utilitarian round jug with a small neck and a loop handle, and various vase and mug forms, including the well-known beer tankard with a pewter lid. The influence of metalwork is evident in the applied and stamped medallion decoration, which is revealed under the salt glaze. The glaze may be a near white to a chocolate brown, depending upon the body color, and it shows the pebbly surface characteristic of the salt glaze. Blue remained the major colorant applied to the raw ware before firing,

although in later periods polychrome effects appeared. Salt-glazed stoneware was made extensively during the sixteenth and seventeenth centuries (Fig. 65), and its practice spread to England.

Imported Chinese porcelain reached Northern Europe shortly after the Renaissance, and it created just as much interest with the Europeans as it had among Islamic potters many centuries earlier. Late in the fifteenth century attempts were made in Venice to produce porcelain by adding a powdered glass and flux to white earthenware. Further efforts were made near Florence, but the ware was brittle and warped badly. During the late seventeenth century, a slightly similar but more successful soft-paste porcelain was made in France and later in Germany.

By 1715 a true high-fire porcelain, using local supplies of kaolin and feldspar, was made near

above left : 63. Jug, Germany, from Siegberg. 15th century. White stoneware, height 10 ³/₈″. Guildhall Museum, London.

left : 64. Posset pot, England, from Staffordshire. c. 1700. Buff earthenware with white and brown slip decoration under yellow glaze, height 6″. Victoria & Albert Museum, London.

above right : 65. "Gray beard" jug, Germany, from Frechen. 17th century. Gray stoneware with mottled brown salt glaze, height 8 ⁵/₈″. Victoria & Albert Museum, London.

Meissen by Johann Böttger, a German alchemist working for the Elector of Saxony. Prior to this discovery a majolica-type earthenware (also called faience), influenced by Italian imports, had been made throughout Europe. The hard porcelain gradually supplanted this majolica ware in Germany and then in Scandinavia. After some experimentation the English developed their bone china, which

right : 66. Jug, England, from Staffordshire. c. 1740. Salt-glazed stoneware in the form of a bear hugging a dog, height 8 $^1/_8$″. Metropolitan Museum of Art, New York (gift of Carlton Macy, 1934).

below : 67. Platter, England, from Staffordshire. 18th century. Red earthenware with combed white slip decoration, length 20 $^1/_2$″. Victoria & Albert Museum, London.

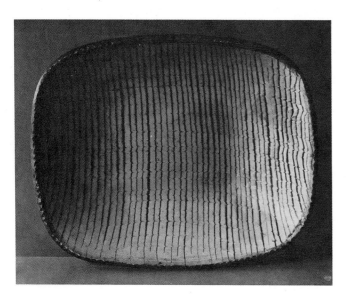

was fired at a slightly lower temperature. France clung to its early soft-paste porcelain, and the Dutch, perhaps due to their profitable import trade of Chinese porcelains, remained wedded to their popular majolica Delft ware, which was largely a low-fire imitation of the Chinese blue-and-white porcelain.

During the eighteenth century European ceramics became increasingly industrialized. A growing quantity of pottery was mechanically made by casting, pressing, or jiggering (see Chap. 10). The German stoneware and English slipware in the local tradition (Figs. 66–67) lost favor before both the imports and the production ware based on classical forms and decoration in the Chinese or Italian manner (Fig. 68). The Rococo taste, with its emphasis on elaborate detail and decoration, prevailed (Fig. 69). While eighteenth- and nineteenth-century ware is valued by the collector, it is, for the most part, of little interest to the serious student except as a history of industrial techniques. An appallingly large quantity of bad pottery was made, and its presence continues to distort public awareness of what constitutes ceramic art.

below left : 68. Vase, England, from Wedgwood. c. 1785. Green and white Jasper ware, height 10 ¾″. Victoria & Albert Museum, London. The fussy decoration exemplifies the tendency to borrow inappropriate classical motifs.

below right : 69. RALPH WOOD FACTORY, England, Staffordshire. Toby jug. 1770–80. Earthenware, height 11 ½″. Victoria & Albert Museum, London. This jug, with its excessive detail, lacks the strength of earlier English wares.

AFRICAN CERAMICS

Our knowledge about African pottery suffers from the same lack of historical data that, until recently, has characterized all study of ancient African cultures. Prehistoric man lived in Africa as early as did his counterpart in Europe and Asia. Skillful stone engravings and rock paintings (c. 7000 B.C. or earlier) in North, Central, and South Africa reveal a gradual change from a hunting culture to a pastoral one. It is likely that the descendents of the earliest civilizations are the Pygmies of the Congo area and the vanishing Bushmen of the South.

Prehistoric Africa was very sparcely settled. Present speculation is that a series of migrations, originating perhaps in India, began about 6000 B.C. and moved across the Straits of Aden into northeast Africa. This first group spread across North Africa,

which was not as arid as it is now. Their Hamitic descendents are the Berbers of North Africa and the ancient Egyptians of the upper Nile. Next came the Bantu tribes, which presently occupy forested equatorial Africa. Finally, a third group moved into the grassland area from the Sudan to the west coast, which lies between the desert of the North and the forests of the South. In general, the movement was westward and southward.

Continual trade and at times warfare between Egypt and the ancient African kingdoms of Kush (Sudan) and Punt (Ethiopia and Somaliland) exposed Africa to all the developments in the Middle East. At Meroë, the Kush capital on the upper Nile, there was an extensive iron industry by the first century. But the technique of iron making

had earlier spread westward to Darfur and finally to northern Nigeria, where the Nok culture was working in iron as early as 300 B.C. This use of iron gave rise to many cultures in West Africa, which in material prosperity soon equaled the northern areas of Europe. Life-size terra cotta heads and figure fragments dating from about 500 B.C. of the Nok culture (900 B.C.–A.D. 200) have an impressive realism that is unique. This large and fertile area of the Niger River valley later saw the rise of many stable kingdoms: Ghana, Mali, and the Shonghay.

While trade continued between the Niger region and the Sudan and Egypt, there was also contact across the desert to the Mediterranean coast. Although this trade may have existed to a slight degree in Roman times, its greatest expansion occurred as Islam spread across North Africa. By A.D. 1000 Arab trading settlements appeared in Timbuktu and other northern Nigerian cities. The local rulers were converted, and by 1050 the first pilgrimages to Mecca had been made. This area has remained Islamic to the present.

The well-known African wood sculptures are seldom more than 150 years old, if that, but they represent an ancient tradition, and, due to their ceremonial and religious nature, they are probably similar to those made for countless years. Hundreds of seated stone figures about 2 feet high and dating between 700 and 1100 have been found near Esie in northern Nigeria. Some have bearded Mediterranean features, while others display African facial types.

Bronze casting was well established along the Niger River between 600 and 950, and from there it spread south to Ife and later (c. 1280) to Benin during the reign of the Benin Oba Oguola. A seated bronze (Fig. 70) from the village of Tada on the Niger River is unusual for its realism, yet it lacks the stiffness we associate with Egyptian or Roman sculpture. The Ife preference for realism, seen in the

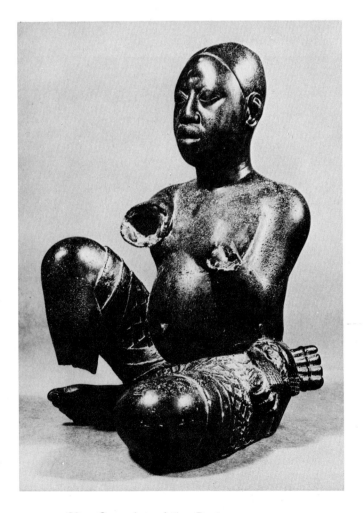

left : 70. Ife figure, Nigeria, from Tada. 10th–11th century. Bronze, height 20 ½″. Department of Antiquities, Nigeria.

opposite : Plate 4. *Seated Ball Player,* Nayarit figure, Mexico. 8th–10th century. Clay with polychrome slip decoration, height 13″. Minneapolis Institute of Arts.

opposite : Plate 5. CHONIU, Japan. Tea bowl. c.1760. Raku ware, height 3 ½″. Metropolitan Museum of Art, New York (Howard Mansfield Collection; gift of Howard Mansfield, 1936).

left : 71. Ife portrait head, Nigeria. 13th–14th century. Terra cotta, height 6″. Brooklyn Museum (lent by Mr. and Mrs. Alastair Bradley Martin). This clay fragment is similar in character to the portrait heads in bronze.

below : 72. Benin head, Nigeria, from Bini. 1560–1680. Terra cotta, height 8 ½″. Museum of Primitive Art, New York.

numerous royal portrait heads (1000–1400), gradually died out in the Benin bronzes (1400–1900), which reached a high point between 1575 and 1625. These bronzes exhibit a more emotional approach common to wood carvings, as exemplified by the exaggerated features, oversize heads, and costume detail. Since clay is a common study material for sculpture, it is not surprising that we find many terra cotta portrait heads in both the Ife and Benin styles (Figs. 71–72). They have the same plastic feeling for form and the sensitivity that characterize the bronzes made by the lost wax casting process.

As in other tribal cultures, most pottery is made by women, often by the wife of the metalsmith. However, in some cases whole villages make pottery and trade their surplus to other areas. Except in a

few Moslem-influenced regions in the North, all pottery is hand built in a combination coil-and-paddle technique. The gourd so commonly used as a container has influenced many forms. Large oval vases with collar rims serve for food and water storage. Textural decorations are often applied in a basketlike weave (Fig. 73) or painted in iron oxides to produce a red or black design. Since most

above : 73. Mangbetu bottle, Congo. 19th–20th century. Paste and sand temper with stirrup handle, height 9 ³/₈″. Brooklyn Museum.

above right : 74. *Flute Player,* Ivory Coast, from Krinjabo. Before 1911. Terra cotta, height 10 ³/₈″. Museum of Primitive Art, New York. This figure reveals the same expressive modeling that is found in the gold and bronze castings of the area.

left : 75. Mangbetu portrait bottle, Congo. 19th–20th century. Terra cotta, height 11 ³/₈″. Museum of Primitive Art, New York.

right : 76. Ashanti head, Ghana. Terra cotta, height 12″. Museum of Primitive Art, New York. This stylized form, with its contrasts of smooth and textured surfaces, is not unlike the traditional wood-carved artifacts.

77. Remojades head, Mexico, from Veracruz. Classic Period (A.D. 600–900). Clay, height 7 5/8″. Museum of Primitive Art, New York. The plastic and emotional quality of Pre-Columbian ceramics is exemplified in this head.

pottery is fired in the open with straw and twigs, it is not very hard, and little early ceramic ware has survived.

In addition to the large and rather formal terra cotta sculpture of the Nok, Ife, and Benin kingdoms, many tribes made small figures (Figs. 74–75). The figurative pottery of the Mangbetu is best known. These effigy heads, like those of the Peruvian Mochica, have an elusive stylization that is quite satisfying, a form in which the late Greek portrait vases and the English Toby pots often fail. Perhaps, with our present stress on written and verbal communication, we in the Western world have forever lost the plastic inventiveness that characterizes so much of African art (Fig. 76).

CERAMICS OF THE NEW WORLD

While the Middle East was a meeting ground for the exchange of ideas among Europe, Africa, and Asia, the Americas had an entirely separate development. Though they never used iron, and rarely bronze, and had no beast of burden such as the horse or the ass, the American Indians attained a relatively high civilization. Their ceramics, made without the potter's wheel or a true glassy glaze, is of special interest (Fig. 77).

During the Ice Ages, perhaps as early as 25,000 years ago, small groups of nomadic hunters and fishermen crossed the Bering Straits and entered the North American continent. This mass migration continued intermittently for thousands of years; by 7000 B.C. the wandering hunters had traversed both continents to the tip of South America. As in the Old World, settled communities and agriculture first began in the more temperate regions. These were the fertile valleys of central Mexico, the coastal plains of Peru, and the highland plateaus of Colombia and Bolivia. Agriculture of a sort began as early as 2500 B.C. By 1000 B.C. the cultivation of maize (corn), which is thought to have begun in Mexico, had spread to Peru, and the potato was grown in many areas. Other domesticated plants were the lima and the kidney bean, squash, yams, peanuts, peppers, the chocolate bean, and fruits such as the avocado and the pineapple. Cotton was raised in both Mexico and Peru, which also had wool from the llama and the alpaca. Long before the era of the Spanish conquest gold jewelry was worn by the wealthy. Alloys of copper, gold, silver, and even platinum were not uncommon. Unfortunately, most of the jewelry, vessels, and small statues of gold, formed by either hammering or the lost wax casting process, were melted down by the Spaniards and lost forever. Although some copper was used for tools and weapons (and even bronze was used by the Mochica in Peru), stone was more universally employed for both tools and weapons. Step pyramids of adobe brick, faced with stone or polychrome stucco and surmounted by small temples, were traditional in both north and south.

right: 78. Naxca bottle, Peru. c. A.D. 500. Earthenware with burnished polychrome slip decoration, height 5 $^9/_{16}$". Art Institute of Chicago (Buckingham Fund).

below: 79. Naxca bowl, Peru. c. A.D. 500. Earthenware with painted polychrome decoration in a tapestrylike design, height 3 $^1/_2$". Museum of Primitive Art, New York.

below: 80. Mochica stirrup bottle, Peru. c. A.D. 500. Clay, height 8 ⁷/₈″. Museum of Primitive Art, New York. This bottle shows the Mochicas' overriding interest in form.

bottom: 81. Mochica stirrup bottle, Peru. c. A.D. 500. Earthenware with painted decoration depicting a hunting scene, height 8 ⁷/₈″. Museum of Primitive Art, New York.

South America

The first pottery, dating from about 2500 B.C., was gray or black from the primitive firing, round bottomed, and had a corded and later a simple incised geometric design. As settlements grew in the Andean highlands and coastal areas (c. 1200–400 B.C.), a jaguar motif, evidently of religious significance, appeared on jewelry, weaving, and pottery. The pottery of this Chavín period has a burnished black surface with incised and dotted geometric and circular designs and often takes a feline form. In addition to functional bowls and jars, a unique form —the stirrup bottle, with its hollow-handled spout— developed in this era.

Gradually the ware became thinner, and better kilns permitted slip decoration. In the Experimenter Period (c. 400 B.C.–A.D. 1) the feline motif disappeared, and a red-on-white slip and a negative

clay-resist technique evolved. As the forms became more varied, sculptural additions were made, and the pots began to assume human, bird, or animal form.

The period of the Master Craftsman (c. A.D. 1–900) is best typified by the Mochica and Naxca cultures in the irrigated coastal valleys of Peru. The Naxca were highly skilled in both weaving and embroidery, and their elaborate textile designs were reflected in their slip-decorated pottery motifs. The ware was quite thin, often made in partial bisque molds, and carefully fired. Clay slips in hues of red, yellow, black, violet, and white were carefully prepared and burnished to a glossy surface. The popular Naxca bottle form has twin spouts with a connecting strap handle (Fig. 78). Bowls and tall goblets, which provided a good decorating area, were also favored (Fig. 79). In contrast to the stylized figures, animals, and plant designs favored by the Naxca, the Mochica potter to the north was interested in sculptural form. His favorite stirrup bottle might be a portrait head of a chief, a bird, a figure, or even a group of people on a mountain-top (Figs. 80–81). The portrait heads are forcefully modeled and are remarkable for their depiction

Ceramics of the New World   45

82. Mochica effigy jar, Peru. c. A.D. 500. Earthenware, height 4 ⁵/₈″. Museum of Primitive Art, New York. The depiction of personality in this head is striking.

of character (Fig. 82). Also interested in figurative form were the Chancay, another coastal group (Fig. 83).

Among the numerous tribal cultures of the Expansionist Period (c. 900–1200) were the Tiahuanaco of the south Peruvian highlands, whose culture grew after the peak of the Naxca and Mochica had passed. The characteristic pottery forms of the Tiahuanaco are flaring goblets, open bowls with wide rims, and oval and modeled vessels with twin spouts and a strap handle. The slip decoration may be multicolored, but the usual decorative designs are in white on a red base color outlined in black. The puma is a favorite motif both in painted and modeled form (Fig. 84).

The Tiahuanaco culture was short-lived, and local patterns again evolved in the coastal areas, north and south, and in the divided highlands. The population increased, and towns and temple areas were enlarged. As wealth and social distinctions grew, the potter was no longer the free artisan of

earlier cultures. The dominant pottery style of the City Builder Period (c. 1200–1450) was the Chimu of the northern coastal area. Chimu ware shows the older Mochica influence in its stirrup spout bottles (Fig. 85), but the southern double spout and strap was also used. Painted decoration was rare, and the usual Chimu body was red or smoked black, reflecting the decline in craftsmanship. The use of clay bisque molds with geometric designs and bird or fish motifs also resulted in decreased individuality. Double whistling bottles with small animals modeled on the handle bases were among the most common Chimu forms.

The Incas began their expansion from the central highlands. In the period before the Spanish conquest (c. 1450–1532) they were the only unified state in the vast area of western South America. Reflecting their own origins, their pottery was quite different from that of the more subdued cultures. Their favorite form was the aryballoid jar with a pointed base, long neck, flaring collar, low side handles, and

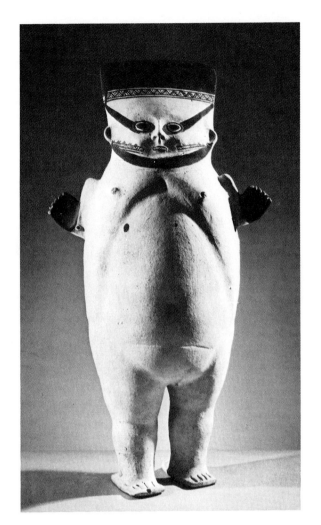

left : 83. Chancay figurative vessel, Peru. c. A.D. 800. Painted clay, height 25″. Museum of Primitive Art, New York.

below : 84. Tiahuanaco incense burner, Bolivia. c. A.D. 1000. Painted clay with applied clay handle in the form of a puma head, height 10 $\frac{1}{8}$″. Museum of Primitive Art, New York.

85. Chimu effigy vessel, Peru. City Builder Period (c. 1200–1450). Burnished black ware with stirrup handle and puma, height 10 $\frac{5}{8}$″. Museum of Primitive Art, New York.

right : 86. Inca aryballoid jar, Peru. c. 1438–1832. Earthenware with painted geometric slip decoration, height 8 ¼″.
Museum of Primitive Art, New York.

below : 87. Tlatilco figure, Mexico. c. 900–300 B.C. Clay,
height 4 ¼″. Museum of Primitive Art, New York.

applied small animal heads (Fig. 86). Shallow plates
with bird handles, straight goblets, pedestal
beakers, and pitchers with one or two handles were
also common. Except for occasional bird or animal
designs, the decoration was geometric with banded
elements and triangular, cross-hatched, and dotted
motifs in red, white, yellow, orange, and black slips.
While craftsmanship was far improved over that of
the Chimu, it hardly equaled the quality of the more
imaginative Mochica or Naxca ware made a thousand years earlier.

Mexico and Central America

By 1500 B.C. farming communities had grown up in
the fertile valleys of central Mexico. At Tlatilco,
near present-day Mexico City, large quantities of
small figurines, mostly female, have been found,
which indicate a fertility cult of some sort (Fig. 87).
Many are quite charming, lacking the grotesque and
fearsome quality that characterized much of Mexico's later religious art. The Tlatilco pottery was a
burnished black or red ware with simple incised
designs. In addition to conventional bowl or bottle
shapes, we find modeled pots in a bird or fish form.
This early interest in modeled forms continued,
partly because the potter's wheel, which dictates
a symmetrical, rounded form, was never introduced
in pre-Columbian Mexico.

The first major culture to emerge in Mexico was
that of the Olmecs, who lived southeast of the Gulf
of Campeche. The Olmecs (800–400 B.C.) had their
major religious center on the small island of La
Venta. Its stepped pyramids and large stone sculptures were repeated in most of the Mexican cultures
that followed. The Olmecs were a highly sophisticated culture who used a calendar and astronomical
observations to regulate sacrifices to the gods for
successful crops.

left : 88. Olmec style seated figure, Mexico, from Puebla. 1200–400 B.C. Kaolin with red pigment, height 13 ³/₈″. Museum of Primitive Art, New York. This figure is typical of the rounded and fleshy form preferred by the Olmecs.

above : 89. Tripod urn, Mexico, from Teotihuacán. A.D. 200–600. Painted clay, height 9 ³/₄″. Museum of Primitive Art, New York.

Olmec sculpture is noted for its rounded, plastic forms and the fleshy, pouting, baby-faced character of its figures (Fig. 88). Its influence was wide and easy to separate from the rather stiff art of many later cultures. The large stone head of La Venta is 8 feet high, but the Olmecs made many smaller carvings and hollow pottery figures.

The extensive ruins of Teotihuacán (c. 50 B.C.–A.D. 600), near modern Mexico City, reveal that, unlike La Venta, it was both a temple area and a large city. The elaborate building complex is dominated by the famous Pyramid of the Sun. Its many sculptured reliefs of a feathered serpent, which continued in other cultures, reveal that the temple's modern name is inaccurate. Teotihuacán pottery is unlike that in other areas. The favorite shape, a straight or slightly concave low cylinder on three raised legs, is metallic in concept (Fig. 89). The body is usually brown with incised or carved areas in red. Reflecting the stucco temple and pyramid decorations are a few rare pottery pieces covered with stucco and painted in red, yellow, white, blue-green, and black with stylized depictions of the gods, chiefly the rain god, Tlaloc. Small clay figurines with elaborate headdresses were also common. Some have movable arms and legs and might be children's toys.

South of Mexico City near present-day Oaxaca rises the large mountaintop temple complex of Monte Albán, built by the Zapotec culture. The Zapotecs inhabited Mexico at a very early date, but the high point of their civilization was reached between 200 and 800. They are noted for their immense stone pyramids, temples, and ball courts, and their sculptured terra cotta pots are of equal interest. Perhaps misnamed funerary urns, the earliest examples show a head modeled on a vase form. In time a full figure evolved, usually seated, with an oversize head and a slightly open mouth. The most striking feature of the urn reproduced in

above : 90. Zapotec urn, Mexico, from Oaxaca. c. A.D. 1000. Clay, height 14 ¼″. Museum of Primitive Art, New York.

right : 91. Mixtec xantile figure, Mexico, from Puebla. 1250–1500. Clay, height 23″. Museum of Primitive Art, New York.

Figure 90 is the elaborate feathered headdress of the god or chieftain portrayed.

By the year 900 the temple site of Monte Albán was largely abandoned, and during the following century much of the Zapotec territory was taken over by the invading Mixtecs from the North who built their own temple complex at Mitla. The popular Mixtec pottery forms were a rounded vase with long tripod legs and a bowl with a flared pedestal base. The decoration (repetitive geometric designs in yellow, brown, red, blue-gray, orange, and black slips) is reminiscent of Peruvian textile designs. The Mixtecs were skillful jewelers, and it is likely that much of the gold and jadework attributed to the later Aztecs was made by captive Mixtec craftsmen.

Indicative of this interest, their stiff potlike seated figurines, unlike the more plastic work of the Zapotecs, have a wealth of detail revealed in bracelets, sandals, earrings, and tattoo markings (Fig. 91).

The Mexican culture popularly known as Tarascan—located in the western states of Michoacán, Nayarit, Colima, Jalisco, and Guerrero—is unique in many respects. There are no temple areas that required an immense and serflike labor force for construction. Nor are there the fearsome gods who demanded continual human sacrifice to ensure ample crops. The pottery figurines were made for tombs and, like Chinese figures, were intended for companionship in the hereafter. They are the products of a relaxed and fun-loving people (Fig. 92).

left : 92. *Seated Hunchback*, Colima figure, Mexico. A.D. 1–600. Clay, height 13 ⁵/₈″. Museum of Primitive Art, New York.

above : 93. Colima acrobat effigy vessel, Mexico. A.D. 1–600. Clay, height 9 ¹/₄″. Museum of Primitive Art, New York.

below : 94. Nayarit seated figure, Mexico. A.D. 1–600. Clay, height 15 ³/₈″. Museum of Primitive Art, New York. Nayarit figures have animated poses and alert expressions.

Although regarded as good fighters and never defeated by the fearful Aztecs, the Tarascans were as apt to depict a ball player as a warrior in their ceramic sculptures (Pl. 4, p. 39).

While small fertility figurines with elaborate hairdos were made several centuries before Christ, most of the pottery figures that survive are dated between 800 and 1300. Most depict single figures, but dancing groups are not uncommon, and the round, pot-bellied dog is a favorite motif. Pottery vessels are often shaped like a gourd or a human figure or, at the very least, have sculptured additions. The Colima figures are distinctive for their rounded, plastic style, which imparts a feeling of energy and movement (Fig. 93). Details usually are added to the polished red clay body by incising. Nayarit pottery tends to emphasize a straight torso with rather thin, flat arms. The features are animated and expressive in caricature fashion (Fig. 94). The elaborate tattooing and costume are rendered in polychrome slip, which time has weathered to an attractive speckled surface (see Pl. 4). The Jalisco

style is equally interesting but hard to define, since it has characteristics of both Colima and Nayarit (Fig. 95).

Perhaps the most advanced culture of Mesoamerica was the Mayan, located in the Yucatán Peninsula, Guatemala, and Honduras. This jungle region with its poor soil was an unlikely area for the development of what was perhaps the world's greatest stone-age civilization. Even today, hitherto unknown stone temples continue to be unearthed from the growth and debris of centuries. Exhaustion of the soil, with its porous limestone base, is thought to be responsible for the abandonment of old temple pyramids and the building of new ones in other areas. Of the early Mayan era (1500 B.C.–A.D. 317) little is known. Most of the sculpture and temples date from the classic period (A.D. 317–889).

Mayan art is serene and confident, as one might expect from a peaceful culture whose temple areas and cities display no fortifications. The priests also functioned as astronomers and astrologers, which explains in part the absence of the barbarism and excessive human sacrifice practiced by many other Mexican cultures. Both their calendar and their mathematical system, which used a zero, were a thousand years in advance of Europe. The small ceramic figures of the classic period are doubtless the most plastic and well articulated of the Americas (Fig. 96); they have a repose which has caused the Mayans to be called "the Greeks of the New World." Mayan pottery was simple in form, with straight-sided bowls and footed vessels showing, perhaps, a Teotihuacán influence. Decoration consisted of incised hieroglyphs or multicolored slip patterns and ceremonial figures similar to those in the temple murals (Fig. 97).

In the late ninth century the great temples at Copán, Quirigia, and Palenque were suddenly abandoned; some Mayans moved west, while others traveled farther east in the Yucatán Peninsula. In the following century much of the Mayan territory was invaded by the Toltecs, a warlike tribe from Tula, north of Mexico City (Fig. 98). The Mayan Chichén-Itzá was transformed into a new

left : 95. Jalisco effigy vessel, Mexico. A.D. 1–600. Clay, height 17½". Museum of Primitive Art, New York. The figurative and vase forms are skillfully combined.

below : 96. Maya figure, Central America. 900–1200. Terra cotta, height 14 ½". Museum of the American Indian, New York. The fluid, plastic modeling of this figure is characteristic of Mayan art.

above : 97. Maya jar, Guatemala. 600–900. Clay with polychrome decoration, height 5 ⁷/₈″. Museum of Primitive Art, New York. The motifs are reminiscent of temple murals.

above right: 98. Toltec funerary urn, Mexico, from Hidalgo. Clay, height 12 ¹/₈″. Museum of Primitive Art, New York. This Toltec piece is typically grotesque.

right : 99. *Girl on a Swing,* Remojadas whistle toy, Mexico, from Veracruz. c. A.D. 750. Painted clay, height 9 ³/₄″. Museum of Primitive Art, New York. This delightful toy evokes the lighter, more tender aspects of Indian life.

and larger Tula. After 1200 Mayapán became the center of this merged Toltec and Mayan culture. After an initial upsurge, the arts and building skills deteriorated. Relative to the Mayan era, ceramics were crudely made. The new religion demanded captives for human sacrifice. Continual strife with neighboring groups led to the sack of Mayapán in the mid-fifteenth century, and in 1541 Yucatán fell, with little difficulty, to the Spaniards.

The gulf coast area near Veracruz is the site of several ancient civilizations. Of special interest is Remojadas ceramics, with its smiling faces and swinging dolls, which displays another aspect of the Indian cultures (Fig. 99). But there is little of

above : 100. Aztec tripod vessel, Mexico, from Mexico City. 1327–1481. Clay, height 9 ¾". Museum of Primitive Art, New York. Teotihuacán influence is evident in this bowl.

below : 101. Water bottle, Louisiana, from Ouachita Parish. 1300–1700. Gray burnished clay with incised decoration, height 5 ¾". Museum of the American Indian, New York.

this lighthearted character to the Aztecs (Fig. 100). Like the Incas, they were a conquering, imperialistic power. The Aztecs were the last of a succession of warlike tribes who invaded the fertile valley of Mexico from the north. In 1168 they evicted the Toltecs from Tula and forced them to move south into Mayan territory. By intrigue and constant warfare, they soon controlled most of central Mexico. Like the Romans, they were builders of roads and aqueducts, efficient administrators and tax collectors. The much admired Aztec gold, jade, and featherwork were actually the products of captured Mixtec and Zapotec craftsmen. While their capital of Tenochtitlán, on the island of Lake Texcoco, was splendid with its temples, pyramids, palaces, and marketplaces, it festered underneath with the barbarism of the priesthood, whose continual demands for human sacrifice to the Aztec gods resulted in perpetual warfare. Without the eager help of the subjected tribes, the small group of Spaniards who arrived in 1519 would have been unable to overthrow the Aztecs.

North America

European settlers arriving in North America found the area thinly populated. The natives were primarily hunters and fishermen with a limited cultivation of indigenous vegetables. Corn, dispersed from the valley of Mexico, was grown by many tribes. The Mississippi Valley area was the site of several large earthen temple and burial mounds, perhaps influenced by the Mexican pyramids. The pottery of this region was a burnished black ware with incised scrolls and geometric patterns (Fig. 101).

A more advanced culture developed in the Southwest, above the Mexican border. The high point of this Pueblo culture dates from A.D. 800 to 1100. With extensive irrigation of crops and multistoried apartment dwellings, the settled life of the Pueblo Indians allowed more leisure time to develop crafts than did the nomadic ways of the tribes to the north. The Pueblo Indians were skillful weavers whose geometric designs were often reflected in their red, brown, black, and white slip-painted pottery (Fig. 102). The pottery of the nearby Mimbres Valley in

New Mexico was unlike that of the Pueblos in that the usual stylized, decorative patterns were combined with sensitive and realistic paintings of birds and animals (Fig. 103). The Casas Grandes culture to the south, in the Mexican state of Chihuahua, shows Mimbres characteristics, as well as a more southern influence in the shape of the effigy jars (Fig. 104).

The first pottery made in Colonial America was produced by the settlers of Jamestown in about 1611. Of this early ware, mentioned in *The True Travels of Captain John Smith*, nothing remains. Essex County in Massachusetts became a pottery center in mid-century; among its resident craftsmen in 1641 were John Pride and William Vinson of Salem. The first individual potters of record in New York were Derick Claesen in 1657 and Derick Benson and William Croylas in 1698. Historical reference is also made to a pottery located in Burlington, New Jersey, in 1684. It is no wonder that nothing of this early ware has survived, since it was a low-fire, lead-glazed pottery made for kitchen use. Not surprisingly, these immigrant potters carried on the old English slipware tradition in decorating their functional platters, pitchers, and jugs. The preferred style for teapots employed a brown-black glaze colored with manganese or dark Albany slip clay. When the red clay body was covered with a cream

above : 102. Pueblo pitcher, New Mexico. 1100–1400. Earthenware with painted black decoration over a white slip, height 6 ¾″. Museum of the American Indian, New York.

left : 103. Mimbres bowl, New Mexico. c. 1100. Clay with stylized fish decoration in black over white slip, diameter 10 ½″. Museum of Primitive Art, New York. Mimbres bowls were "killed" by having a hole punched in the bottom before they were buried with the dead.

below : 104. Cases Grandes bird effigy jar, Mexico. 1300–1450. Yellow clay with stylized decoration in black and red, height 6 ½″. Museum of the American Indian, New York.

slip, the colorless lead glaze took on a yellow hue. Pennsylvania potters, reflecting their German background, usually combined a sgraffito technique with slip decoration for their popular tulip and other floral designs (Fig. 105).

Potters in England were experimenting with stoneware and higher-fire white ware bodies, and examples of this ware were exported to the New World, where they were much prized. It was natural, then, that the Colonial potter would attempt to reproduce the technique. The first native stoneware of record is that made by General James Morgan at Madison, New Jersey, in 1775. Due to the abundant supplies of good stoneware clays in New York and New Jersey, this region took the lead as the higher-fire ware gradually supplanted red ware.

The first known pottery produced west of the Alleghenies was made in 1784 at Morgantown, West Virginia. This early red ware was cumbersome and fragile, so potters gradually moved westward in search of new clay deposits and better methods of transportation. A pottery was operating in Detroit as early as 1820; in Ripley, Illinois, in 1836; and in Sargents Bluff, Iowa, in 1838. However, it was along the Ohio River, where there were good deposits of stoneware clays and water transportation was available, that the major potteries developed. Stoneware potteries had been established in Steubenville, Zanesville, East Liverpool, and Cincinnati, which in time supplied a large part of the Middle West and the area along the Mississippi River as far south as New Orleans with its needs of crocks, jugs, dishes, and platters.

Although there were red ware potteries in the South, the plantation philosophy never encouraged them to compete with the imported ware desired by the wealthier classes. These small family-owned and isolated mountain potteries have continued to this day, producing simple lead-glazed ware for local sale, although in recent years the tourist trade has provided the major outlet.

The Colonial red ware and much of later stoneware were coarse in body and hand thrown. In an effort to compete with the imported ware, American potters gradually developed a finer body, termed *brown ware*. It was actually a cream- or buff-colored

above : 105. DAVID SPINNER, U.S.A., Bucks County, Pa. Pie plate. c. 1800. Red earthenware with sgraffito decoration. Brooklyn Museum (gift of Mrs. Huldah Cail Lorimer in memory of George Burford Lorimer).

below : 106. D. GOODALE, U.S.A., Hartford, Conn. Jug. 1818–30. Salt-glazed stoneware with incised American eagle decoration, accented with cobalt; height 15″. Brooklyn Museum (gift of Arthur W. Clement).

earthenware with a lead or alkaline glaze, higher fired than the old earthenware, but not vitrified like the stoneware. After about 1830 brown ware supplanted the earlier red ware, and stoneware, usually salt glazed, was used only for the more utilitarian jugs and crocks (Fig. 106). This development marks the transitional stage between hand-thrown pottery and that which was mechanically produced by jiggering, press molds, and, later, slip casting.

Although there were regional variations, early nineteenth-century American potters generally followed the lead of the English potters who first developed mass-production techniques. Unfortunately, not only the methods were copied, but also the form and decoration. The latter had in turn been inappropriately lifted from Baroque and Classical models. It is interesting to conjecture about the direction American pottery might have taken had it not been continually subjected to a flood of imported styles which, however technically competent, were of little esthetic merit.

Perhaps no pottery better illustrates the trend during the late eighteenth and nineteenth centuries than that of Bennington, Vermont. Founded in 1793 by Captain John Norton, a Massachusetts potter,

the Bennington pottery first produced red ware and, later, under Norton's sons, Luman and John, a yellow ware in imitation of the English "Queen's Ware" and a utilitarian stoneware. The pottery continued for three more generations until 1894. The greatest innovator in the firm was Christopher W. Fenton, brother-in-law of Julius Norton (a grandson of the founder). Fenton became a partner in 1844, then separated from the firm in 1848 and operated his own pottery in Bennington until 1858. Perhaps the best-known ware produced by Bennington was the mottled brown-glazed cream ware called Rockingham (Fig. 107). Although it originated in England, it became more popular in America and was produced everywhere, from New York through the Middle West, during the second half of the century. By employing English potters such as Daniel Greatback, and by constant experimentation, Fenton was able to duplicate most of the imported English ware. A Parian ware, copied after that of the English firms of Minton and Copeland, used a semisoft bisque porcelain for figurines, as well as for pitchers and vases with elaborately modeled figures and floral decorations (Fig. 108). Many of these pieces had a blue slip background, an

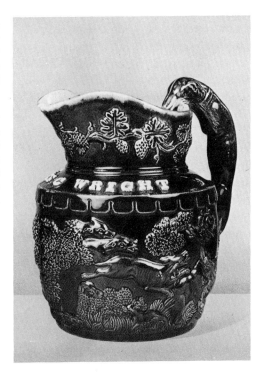 

right : 107. Salamander Works, U.S.A., Woodbridge, N.J. Hound-handled pitcher. c. 1845. Brown-glazed Rockingham cream ware. Brooklyn Museum (gift of Arthur W. Clement).

far right : 108. United States Pottery, U.S.A., Bennington, Vt. Pitcher. 1852–58. Parian porcelain in "Paul and Virginia" design (copied from Wedgwood), with Jasper technique. Brooklyn Museum (gift of Arthur W. Clement).

obvious imitation of Wedgwood jasper ware. Other innovations included the "croddle ware," made of different colored clays to give a marbled appearance, and the "Patent Flint Enamel," in which wet glaze was peppered with different coloring oxides to give a multicolored mottled effect. The Bennington styles were widely copied and, with the English imports, spread the Victorian gospel of elaborate and arbitrary decoration. For a frontier people striving for middle-class values it had a stifling influence from which American ceramics is still suffering.

The first known white ware dates from 1738 and was made in Savannah, Georgia, by the Philadelphia potter, Andrew Duché, who used local kaolin clays. Although this preceded the discovery of china clay in England, the pottery was unsuccessful, as were many early experiments conducted by other potters. The first true porcelain was made in 1826 by the short-lived Jersey Porcelain and Earthenware Company. In all these ventures American potters had difficulty competing with imported ware, which the public deemed superior (as indeed it often was). Occupying a position between the frail and somewhat heavy cream ware and expensive bone china and porcelain was a new white body, called variously ironstone, white granite, or stone china, developed early in the nineteenth century by the English Staffordshire potters. The names reflect the quality of hardness and durability of the new body, which was essentially a high-fire white earthenware with sufficient additions of Cornwall stone, feldspar, or powdered iron foundry slag to enable it to fuse into a body resembling porcelain but fired at lower temperatures. Most of the English ware was highly decorated in Chinese or Japanese motifs, often by the new engraved print transfer process. But exports to America were generally plain white or had a simple striped decoration, similar to the white granite ware commonly made in the United States after 1850. This body was the forerunner of modern "hotel china," and much American dinnerware today is of the same character. It was not until some years after the upheaval of the Civil War that commercially successful porcelain or vitrified china was made, first in Trenton, New Jersey, and soon after in Syracuse, New York, and East Liverpool,

Ohio. But such was the appeal of the imported item, even though no longer superior, that it was not until 1918 that the White House bought, from Lenox, Inc., its first domestic porcelain.

The industrialization of American potteries to meet the competition of mass-produced foreign imports was inevitable (see Chap. 10). As elsewhere in the world, it interrupted the age-old patterns of internal growth and change, since design decisions were now placed in the hands of a managerial entrepreneur, whose major interest was to produce a profit. The increasing use of plaster of paris for models and molds was not bad in itself, but it usually led to the copying of forms intended for metal, wood, or basketry. For the hand potter economical considerations had had the effect of limiting elaborate and fussy decoration. But once a model in plaster was made, the most intricate form could be reproduced by the press or slip-cast process. Fashion set the day, and the taste of the socially aspiring new bourgeoisie was for a conspicuous display of their recently acquired material wealth.

KOREAN CERAMICS

The ceramics of Korea and Japan are historically related to that of China. However, since both of these styles have had a great influence on modern potters, it is fitting that they should be considered as a prelude to our discussion of contemporary ceramics. While Korea is geographically adjacent to China, the mountainous character of the land enabled Korea to evade direct Chinese control and so develop its individuality, although Chinese influence has always been present.

After a period in which only crude, round-bottomed ware was produced, an earthenware with combed patterns and later a red burnished ware developed during the pre-Christian era. Three small kingdoms arose: Koguryo (c. 37 B.C.–A.D. 668) in the North, partially controlled by, and in continual conflict with, Han China; Paekche (c. 18 B.C.–A.D. 668) in the Southwest, which provided the contact between China and Japan; and Silla (c. 57 B.C.–A.D. 935), which was the most independent and typically Korean of the three.

Koguryo pottery shows continual Chinese influence. The ceramics of the Paekche kingdom—a red polished earthenware, a glazed earthenware, and a gray stoneware—also reflects Han influences in form, glaze, and occasionally in the pressed mat decoration. Silla gray or reddish stoneware was fired at a higher temperature and, though unglazed, developed a glazelike surface from the free ash in the kiln. A large bowl or covered jar set on a high foot with rectangular cutouts was a popular shape (Fig. 109). Incised geometric patterns were also common during this early period. The tomb mounds

of the Silla Dynasty contain terra cotta sculptures, but they differ from those made in Han China. Of particular interest are the horse-and-rider figures, which have a strange archaic quality. They are too dignified to be comic, yet they have a droll air.

Buddhism was introduced to Korea in the fourth century, and by the seventh century it had become the dominant religion. Funerary customs changed from burial to cremation. The urns used for ashes were low, footed vases, with swelling shoulders, short collar rims, and low covers. The decoration was pressed rather than incised as in the earlier style. Because the vases were wheel thrown, the pressed motifs of circular and angular patterns were of a banded nature. In 668 Korea was united for the first time, when the entire area came under Silla rule. The yellow-brown and green glazes used thereafter were doubtless due to the Koguryo influence.

The porcelains and celadons of the Chinese Sung Dynasty made a tremendous impression on nearby Korea. As a result of this influence the Koryo Period (918–1392) represents the high point of Korean ceramic art. The tenth century brought a gradual change from the gray stoneware to a crude celadon. During the next century Sung forms and glazes were widely copied, but by the twelfth century unique Korean variations evolved. The blue-green hue of celadon, which is typically Korean, became common, as did an inlayed decoration called *mishima* (Fig 110). Chinese brushed decoration, often floral, was used in a white or black slip

above : 109. Covered stem cup, Korea. Early Silla Period, after A.D. 668. Stoneware with olive-green glaze, height 9 ¼″. Seattle Art Museum (Eugene Fuller Memorial Collection).

right : 110. *Sanggam* bowl, Korea. Koryo Period, 14th century. Porcelain with inlayed mishima decoration under pale celadon glaze, diameter 7 ¾″. Seattle Art Museum (Eugene Fuller Memorial Collection).

with a red iron or copper oxide under the celadon glaze. The latter, when reduced, produced a reddish or plum-colored glaze. The prunus vase, derived from the Chinese T'zu-Chou, was a popular form, which, when adapted to the fuller curve of the Korean style, took on more graceful proportions. More elaborate were the lobed vases, wine pots, and ewers derived from the melon form and the wine cups patterned after the lotus bud. Footed dishes similar to the Chinese T'ing porcelains, with their delicately incised floral patterns, were made, but in Korea mishima techniques were used.

Like China and the Middle East, Korea was upset by the Mongol invasions. The Korean capitol, Seoul, and most of Korea, was occupied from 1231 to 1260. Independence came again under the Yi Dynasty (1392–1910), which must be divided into two periods separated by the invasion (1592–98) of the Japanese warlord, Hideyoshi. Although pottery making prospered during the early Yi period, it had lost the delicate craftsmanship of the Koryo potter. The forms were heavier, and the celadon color deteriorated, because the firing of the kilns was not carefully controlled. However, the production of porcelain, which began in the late Koryo era, was widespread. Whenever possible, stamped patterns replaced hand incising in the inlayed mishima, which inevitably led to a rather mechanical style. More successful were the slip-covered wine bottles, which were incised in a vigorous floral sgraffito style.

The invasion by Hideyoshi was a great blow to the Korean ceramic industry. Many kilns were destroyed, and a number of potters were taken to Japan. Celadon production ceased after the invasion, and porcelain, decorated in Ming blue and white, became the major style. More Korean in character and more satisfying were the porcelain and stoneware bowls and vases with free brush decoration in an underglaze of iron brown and copper red. Japanese influence became stronger, and, after victorious wars against China (1894–95) and Russia (1904–05), Korea was annexed in 1910. Korea was free again in 1945, but, with rapid communications and trade, it is doubtful that Korea (or any modern nation) can ever again develop a truly unique and national character in her ceramics.

JAPANESE CERAMICS

The islands of Japan, stretching in thousand-mile arc from Korea to Siberia, were in prehistoric times joined to the mainland. The Ainu aborigines of northern Hokkaido are descendents of the original inhabitants, but the vast majority of Japanese are of ancient Korean and Chinese stock, which, over a long period, migrated from the south and by the fourth century B.C. occupied all the islands except Hokkaido.

The pottery of the early Jomon Period, which lasted until about 250 B.C., was characterized by an overall decoration of cord impressions or by incised and applied clay strips in vigorous patterns of abstract angular and circular motifs. In addition to simple cooking and storage pots, there were spouted vessels, incense burners, and effigy figures. Accompanying this ware is a group of strange, cord-marked figurines. Some are small, intended perhaps as charms (Fig. 111). Others are larger (up to 20 inches in height) and are modeled around a hollow core.

111. Head of a Dogu, Japan, probably from Kamegaoka. Jomon Period (c. 100 B.C.–A.D. 100). Clay, height 2″. Seattle Art Museum (Eugene Fuller Memorial Collection).

Although made over a span of several thousand years, they are all of a type, with heavy, widespread legs, rudimentary arms, and flat, upturned faces with goggle eyes. Most of the pieces have been found in the northern section of Honshu. Those from the south have less of the almost frenzied detail of costume and hairdo. Perhaps reflecting outside influences they are more plastic and naturalistic in concept.

The Jomon Period was a time of stagnation and of isolation from the many cultural advances occurring on the mainland. But pressure from an expanding China encouraged migration into Japan from Korea. In the second century B.C. the tempo of life changed, as primitive Japan moved into the bronze and iron ages. A significant factor in Japan's progress was the introduction of rice growing, for food gathering and fishing had provided a rather precarious existence. The pottery of the Yayoi Period (c. 250 B.C.–A.D. 250) was, unlike the Jomon ware, simple in form, thinner, and higher fired. Much of the change was doubtless due to the introduction of the potter's wheel. The clay body had a light brown color and was occasionally painted in a red design, but shallow incised geometric bands were the more common decoration. The popular vase form—a small flared base and a full, rounded midsection which contracts and then expands into the rim— relied more upon its graceful shape than upon decoration for effect. The form reminds one somewhat of certain Han vases. These pieces are definitely not the work of a primitive people but reveal the influence of a long ceramic tradition.

The increase in population and agricultural prosperity can be seen in the appearance of huge burial mounds. That of the Emperor Nintoku (A.D. fifth century) near Osaka was 1574 feet in length and 114 feet high. Of special interest to the potter are the rows of terra cotta figures called *Haniwa*, which encircled the crest of the burial mound. The earliest Haniwa were simple clay cylinders about 2 or 3 feet in height. These were probably

derived from libation urns and funeral pottery traditionally placed in or upon graves. In time they evolved into guardian figures. The fact that hundreds or even thousands of such figures might be required for a single grave led to a simplified technique. Often a round head on a cylinder, with quickly cut holes for eyes and mouth, sufficed. More elaborate were the warrior figures in padded armor and skillfully carved helmets (Fig. 112). Most of these are about 3 feet tall, but the largest are almost life size. Another favorite subject was the horse, which was

a prestige symbol (Fig. 113). Costumed ladies were not neglected, nor were dogs, birds, domestic animals, and even house models. What has impressed today's sculptor is the extreme simplicity of form of the Haniwa figurines, which creates a greater impact than would a more realistic interpretation. The competition between local rulers in the construction of the huge tomb mounds was a drain on the local economy and may have been a factor in the transition to the Buddhist rites of cremation. After a short period the Haniwa figures were no longer made, and the old tomb mounds were overgrown and forgotten.

During the late Haniwa Period (c. 400–552) many Koreans migrated to Kyushu from the Paekche kingdom, perhaps because of wars with Silla. Among them were potters who began to make a gray stoneware that was much harder than the Japanese earthenware. The greater heat was achieved by using a long, single-chambered kiln built on a sloping hillside. Called an *ana-gama* kiln,

above : 113. *Haniwa* horse, Japan. Haniwa Period (A.D. 200–552). Clay, height 26 ½″. Seattle Art Museum (Eugene Fuller Memorial Collection). This horse, like most Haniwa figures, is constructed in simple, tubular form.

below : 114. Medicine jar, Japan. Nara Period, Tempyo Era (710–94). Sue ware, height 9 ¾″. Seattle Art Museum (Eugene Fuller Memorial Collection).

it was the predecessor of the multichambered climbing kiln still used in Japan today. The new ware, called *Sue*, was similar to the Korean forms of the period and used a green, runny ash glaze (Fig. 114).

Continual contacts with China led to the adoption not only of new materials and techniques but also of philosophy, religion, and the use of Chinese characters to express the Japanese language. Along with Buddhism came the influence of Indian temple and pagoda styles and Indian religious sculpture —together with their Chinese variations—which were gradually absorbed into Japanese traditions. During this period of cultural exchange, the Japanese capital was located first at Asuka (552–646) and subsequently at Nara (646–794). Due perhaps to this early stimulation, the Nara-Kyoto area remained a major artistic center through the centuries. Chinese influence continued during the following Early Heian Period (794–898), when the capital moved to Heian-kyo (modern Kyoto). T'ang-influenced pottery was made in the typical two- and three-color lead-glazed ware, as well as in the older Sue style.

At the beginning of the Late Heian Period (898–1185) contacts with China were cut off due to political turmoil in the closing years of the T'ang Dynasty. This was a period of introspection for the Japanese, during which the many Chinese influences were digested and revised to suit the Japanese temperament. It was an age of great temple building, for an accommodation was made between the older Shinto faith and Buddhism. Painting and literature prospered, but the growth of pottery making was hampered by the amazing quality and variety of the lacquer ware, which, among wealthy Japanese, inspired the same high regard that the Chinese accorded their fine porcelains and celadons.

During the Kamakura Period (1185–1333), named after the site of the new capital near modern Tokyo, contacts were renewed with China. The latter was at the height of the great Sung Dynasty, regarded as the golden age of Chinese ceramics, and the pottery that was imported into Japan had a lasting effect upon Japanese ceramic art. Seto, near the old centers of Nara and Kyoto, became and remained a major pottery center. An effort was made to reproduce the Korean and Chinese celadons, and a greater variety of forms were created than in earlier periods: vases, bottles, pitchers, tea bowls, and incense burners. Incised and impressed designs in bold floral patterns characterize the Kamakura ware.

Perhaps more important to the later philosophy of ceramics was the growing influence of Zen Buddhism and its connection with the uniquely Japanese cult of the *tea ceremony*. As originally practiced by the Zen monks, it was merely a pause in a long period of religious meditation during which a cup of tea was served. Gradually it became a standardized ritual, first among the monks and a few members of the ruling family, then among the Samurai warrior class, and finally expanding to include the wealthy merchant class. The origin of the tea ceremony is officially dated in the Muromachi Period (1392–1573), but it was formalized during the Momoyama Period (1573–1615). Eventually all Japanese claiming to be cultured participated in the tea ceremony.

The character of the tea ceremony stresses simplicity and thoughtful contemplation. It is held in a small room or in a simple structure in a garden, for no more than four or five persons are involved. The room is bare except for the tea utensils and a slight alcove, which may contain a small wall painting or a vase with perhaps a single flower. The importance of the tea ceremony to the potter lies in the fact that, apart from an iron kettle and an occasional lacquer piece, all of the tea paraphernalia is ceramic. The prescribed accouterments include, first, the tea bowls and the jar in which the powdered tea is kept, then the large water jars and bowls for washing, and finally the trays or cake dishes.

As the tea master prepares each bowl individually by beating the powdered tea into a froth with a bamboo whisk, the guests are expected to make appreciative comments upon the beauty of the pottery, the artistry of the flower arrangement, or the substance of the poem that usually accompanies the wall painting. At first rare Chinese celadon and temmoku tea bowls were used, and a cult of extravagance arose. But many tea masters preferred the simple strength and directness of the Korean ware over the sophisticated Sung porcelains. Given this philosophy, it was only a matter of time before the common pottery used by the peasant would be prized for its naturalness, the asymmetrical quality of its freely thrown form, and the uneven run of a thickly applied glaze. This predilection for an unbalanced design is an underlying characteristic of Japanese painting, prints, house and garden design, and, of course, ceramics. Japanese woodcuts had great influence on Western painters of the Impressionist school, and Japanese ceramics has had a similar effect upon Western potters in recent years.

Partly to fulfill the demands of the tea ceremony, the Seto kilns improved the quality of their traditional yellow and black glazes (Fig 115). The nearby Mino kilns produced the Shino and Oribe pottery, which was especially prized by the tea masters for its free and colorful brush decorations (Figs 116–118). Also popular was Karatsu ware, produced by immigrant Koreans in northwest Kyushu, who used their native forms but combined them with a typically Japanese brush decoration. In their search for the simple and unaffected, the tea masters discovered several isolated potteries producing a functional ware for the local trade, oblivious to the foreign celadons and porcelains. One such center

above : 115. Bowl, Japan. Momoyama Period (1573–1615). Yellow Seto ware with green decoration, diameter 6 ³/₈″. Seattle Art Museum (Eugene Fuller Memorial Collection).

below : 116. Cake plate, Japan. Momoyama Period (1573–1615). Nezumi-shino stoneware with gray glaze over mishima slip decoration in "wind-blown grasses" design, length 9″. Seattle Art Museum (gift of Mrs. John C. Atwood, Jr.).

was Bizen near Okayama, which made an unglazed pottery in the old Sue tradition. Accidental and random markings characterize this style, for the vessels were wrapped in a salt-soaked straw prior to firing. An even more primitive pottery was made on the shores of eastern Honshu at Iga and Shigaraki. The coarse clay used was suitable only for larger containers. The clay body of the Iga ware was poorly prepared, with the result that the usual green glaze is pitted and scarred from impurities and often sags out of shape. The Shigaraki also was often carelessly thrown. Its incised banded patterns and thin runny ash glaze are hardly noticed due to the pitted surface and the blotchy red and black discoloration from the kiln fire.

Many of these old Shigaraki and Iga pots, as well as the more skillfully made ware from Bizen and Tokoname, are now in museums or are highly

right: 117. Cake plate, Japan. Momoyama Period (1573–1615). Oribe stoneware with green glaze over brown slip decoration in "half-submerged wheels" design, 7 ³/₄ × 8″. Seattle Art Museum (Eugene Fuller Memorial Collection).

treasured by individual owners. By technical standards—perfection of thrown form, quality of decoration, understanding of clay bodies, and glaze and firing skills—most old Iga and Shigaraki pots are inept and poorly made. But within the context of the philosophy of the tea ceremony they take on those qualities that we find interesting in a beach pebble or a weathered piece of driftwood, and they inspire, as it were, the respect accorded natural beauty, without the critical judgment we reserve for man-made objects. This esthetic has had considerable influence upon the contemporary potter, whether he is aware of it or not. For the most part, it has been beneficial, for it is all too easy to admire a skillful technique which might, in fact, be rather sterile. However, the influence can be destructive if nothing remains of the potter's art but the "accidental effect" so that the material itself becomes all important.

Of course, all Japanese were not satisfied with the more austere ware of the tea ceremony. As trade increased Korean Yi and Chinese Ming porcelains were greatly admired and sought after. In 1616 a Korean potter working for Lord Nabeshima discovered a kaolin clay, essential for making porcelain, near Arita in northern Kyushu. Within a few years this area, with its many Korean potters, became a center of the Japanese porcelain industry. Generally termed Imari ware, the porcelains were made first in the Korean blue-and-white style, but later the Chinese spirit prevailed, with the usual subject matter of landscapes, flowers, birds, and figures. The Westerner usually associates the term Imari with the garish multicolored enameled porcelain later exported in great quantity to Europe and related in character to the Chinese Ch'ing enamels.

Of finer quality were the Kakiemon and Nabeshima porcelains, which were each produced in a single workshop. The Kakiemon enameled ware was in the Chinese style, but the color and painting was done with more restraint and a greater feeling

118. Teapot, Japan. Momoyama Period (1573–1615). Oribe stoneware with green and transparent glazes over brown slip decoration in tortoise-shell design, height 7 ⁵/₈″. Seattle Art Museum (Eugene Fuller Memorial Collection).

Japanese Ceramics   65

above : 119. Plate, Japan. Edo Period (1615–1868). Kakiemon ware porcelain with floral design, diameter 7 ³/₈. Seattle Art Museum (Eugene Fuller Memorial Collection).

below : 120. Teapot, Japan. Edo Period, mid-18th century. Nabeshima ware porcelain with pale celadon glaze in "plum blossoms and buds" design, height 6″. Seattle Art Museum (gift of Mrs. Charles E. Stuart).

of openness (Fig. 119). Nabeshima porcelains (Fig. 120) were, like the Kakiemon, more delicate than the usual Imari ware, but decorated in a more Japanese fashion with motifs from textile designs or landscapes in the Kano manner. Kutani, on the west coast of Japan near Kanazawa, was the site of another early porcelain kiln (c. 1660). Kutani ware is heavier and more vigorous than most Japanese porcelains, and the brushed decorations of birds, fruit, and landscapes are boldly executed in darker tones of green, blue, yellow, and a blackish purple, quite unlike the Imari style.

For the most part, porcelain followed the tradition of the imported wares, and, while of great commercial importance, it does not quite reflect the unique quality of Japanese artistic feeling as does the pottery. For example, there is no place of honor in the tea ceremony for the highly decorated tea bowl. Even more appropriate to the tea ceremony than the Karatsu stoneware was raku ware (see p. 216). It is thought to have been made first by an immigrant from Korea who settled in Kyoto and married a Japanese woman. Raku ware is particularly suited to the Zen philosophy, since the typical

bowls are formed of a coarse clay (Fig. 121). The importance of the accidental effect, the irregularities of the rim and form, plus the runny, uneven quality of the glaze, give it a natural charm, while the insulating quality of the porous body makes it a perfect container for hot tea (see Pl. 5, p. 40).

The first raku potter's son, Chajiro (1515–92), made tea ware for the famous tea master Sen-no-Rikyu, and so began a line that lasted into the twentieth century, for the thirteenth of the line, Seinu Kaju, died in 1944. In sixteenth-century Japan, as in other cultures, pottery began to be signed by the maker. Because of the association with the tea ceremony, many cultivated Japanese began making pottery as a sort of hobby, much as the calligrapher and painter also wrote poetry. One such educated tea devotee was Honami Koetsu, who became friendly with the third raku potter, Doniu.

Best known of historical Japanese potters is Ogata Kenzan (1663–1743), who was distantly related to Koetsu and much influenced by him as well as by his older brother, Ogata Korin, a famous painter. Kenzan was not so much a potter as a painter and decorator of pottery. Trained as a calligrapher and painter, he evolved a highly personal style which was characteristically Japanese in its color and brushwork (Figs. 122–123). More than two centuries later, in 1911, the English potter, Bernard Leach, then a young painter in Tokyo, studied pottery with the sixth Kenzan. Through his work, his many students, and his writings, Leach is largely responsible for the present interest in Japanese and Korean ceramics.

top : 121. DONYU, Japan. *Tamamushi (Golden Beetle),* tea bowl. Early Edo Period, 17th century. Black raku earthenware with lead glaze, diameter 5″. Seattle Art Museum (gift of Dr. Masatoshi Okochi).

center : 122. OGATA KENZAN, Japan. *Bellflowers,* fan-shape cake tray. Edo Period, 18th century. Stoneware with enamaled decoration on cream-colored glaze, length of sides 6 ⅝″. Seattle Art Museum (Eugene Fuller Memorial Collection).

right : 123. OGATA KENZAN, Japan. *Camellia,* cake tray (one of a set of four). Edo Period, 18th century. Stoneware with creamy transparent glaze over brown slip, 5 ¾″ square. Seattle Art Museum (Eugene Fuller Memorial Collection).

3 Contemporary Ceramics

*Potters in Europe,
the Far East,
and North America*

For the past fifty years there has been a slow but steady growth of public interest in ceramics and in the actual craft of pottery making. Contemporary potters whose work is illustrated in this text comprise a rather mixed group, both in background and in goals. A very few grew up in pottery communities and early accepted ceramics as a natural life occupation. Most contemporary potters, however, drifted into ceramics after training in other fields. Many have attended various art and craft schools, but in most cases they studied, originally, painting or sculpture. Some art school graduates have served as apprentices in small hand potteries.

Much of the variety and strength of contemporary ceramics doubtless lies in the diverse backgrounds of these practitioners. The initial lack of skill and knowledge has proved to be a great handicap to some, for traditional workshop training teaches the beginning potter how to avoid many pitfalls. On the other hand, this very absence of systematic instruction has often led to greater vitality and experimentation.

Modern ceramics is tremendously varied. Though its diversity is, perhaps, not greater than in the past, it is remarkable in that everything is happening all at once, not over a span of milleniums. The ease of travel and the proliferation of visual materials have made the contemporary potter decidedly eclectic. We have in ceramics today an international school much like that of painting, and the great body of work that it produces is very stimulating. Variations of form and decoration are infinite, and these variations may be compared to the words in a dictionary, which, lifeless in themselves, can be combined to make a beautiful poem. It is how they are put together that matters. Not having grown up in a pottery tradition, the ceramist of today must learn both from the past and from his fellow potters in order to develop a dictionary of forms from which to select the nuances that reflect his own feelings. The student cannot help but lean

opposite : 124. ROBERT TURNER, U.S.A. Vase. 1968. Stoneware with speckled blue and cinnamon glazes, height 24″. The contemporary potter seeks the unusual form, contrasts of texture and color, and even the runny quality of a glaze.

69

above : 125. NORMAN SCHULMAN, U.S.A. Teapot. Red stoneware with cone-9 barium mat glaze. The pulled handle adds an individual touch to this rounded, functional teapot.

below : 126. DONALD FRITH, U.S.A. Covered jar. Stoneware with sgraffito decoration through light slip. Although this graceful jar can obviously serve as a container, its form and details would suggest a more decorative function.

upon others until the time when his own personality dictates a direction.

The explosion of communications today has made it difficult to categorize the potters of the several countries discussed in this chapter as being of specific national groups in the sense of their having distinct regional styles or similar methods of working. On the contrary, a modern ceramist may have more in common with a craftsman in another country than with the potter down the street.

Exhibitions and magazine articles to the contrary, the largest group of potters still follows what might be called the *traditional* style and produces a functional pottery (Fig. 125). Most of them cannot quite be classed with the old folk potter, since their ware is made for a rather sophisticated group. The desire to possess and to use an object bearing the imaginative touch of the human hand represents a natural reaction against the sterility of industrially produced products, and this is responsible for the recent widespread interest in all the crafts. The work of the second group of potters is what we might call *decorative* and indicates a direction that has also been with us through the ages (Fig. 126). Although derived from a functional form, often the size, decoration, or delicacy of a piece makes practical use unlikely. There is a fine line dividing the two groups, for, ideally, all functional ware should have a certain refinement of form and decoration. However, many would consider the extremely decorative ware to be decadent and not a desirable trend.

One phenomenon that is attracting much attention on the contemporary scene is what might be termed *nonpot* ceramics. Although occasionally reflecting a potlike origin, these works generally stress abstract form and the textural qualities of clay. They are as unrelated to the more traditional ceramic sculpture as the work of David Smith differs from that of Donatello. The so-called *pop-pots*, as well as the nonpots, depend not on form but on rather literary ideas or on an incongruous assembly of shapes made simply for effectiveness (Figs. 127–128). They are more closely related to a revived Dada movement than to any area of ceramics.

Many potters today hold teaching positions, and this has naturally had an effect upon their work.

right: 127. PHILLIP GEARHEART, U.S.A. *Self-portrait*. Height 18". This work is a personal fantasy in which traditional sculptural forms serve as props to express an idea.

right: 127. PHILLIP GEARHEART, U.S.A. *Self-portrait*. Height 18". This work is a personal fantasy in which traditional sculptural forms serve as props to express an idea.

below: 128. RICHARD PEELER, U.S.A. *Beautiful Love*. 1969. Stoneware, string, chain, and artificial flower; height 20 ½". This sculptural creation exploits the contemporary interest in mixed media while making a social comment. A tape recorder in the base mumbles poetry.

There is no fast rule, but, in general, potters in crafts or ceramic schools tend to be more traditional; those in art schools often compete with their avant-garde colleagues in painting and sculpture, and, as a result, their work is usually more experimental and influenced less by pottery traditions than by new developments in painting and sculpture.

There is a much smaller group of potters oriented toward industrial design. Ideally, these designers ought to combine some of the talents and experience of the hand potters with a knowledge of production techniques. The management of industrial plants plays a key role in establishing a balance between handcraftsmanship and technology. Only in the Scandinavian countries has it been a common policy to have a design staff composed of creative potters. Since designs do not have the patent protection accorded mechanical devices, American factories have long been content to copy imported patterns and to steal designs from each other. European porcelain factories have always copied from the Chinese, so it is not really shocking to learn that the Japanese do the same with current Scandinavian designs. Unfortunately, this situation has discouraged many able potters and students from entering the industrial design field.

ENGLAND

The commercial success of industrialized ceramics in late eighteenth- and nineteenth-century England caused the demise of the English hand pottery. The few hand potteries that remained in the twentieth century survived in rural areas and specialized in making flowerpots and crocks for the local trade. The prevailing Victorian taste saw little merit in the special qualities of a hand-thrown piece when

left : 129. BERNARD LEACH, England. Plate. Before 1920. Raku ware with slip-trailed decoration, diameter c. 13 ½". Leach made this plate during his stay in Japan.

Oriental manner of life, it was simultaneously beginning to adopt an Eastern esthetic philosophy.

The work and teachings of William Staite Murray (1881–1962) and Bernard Leach (1887–) were significant in the revival of English pottery after World War I. Although they had much in common, they held divergent views about the direction ceramics ought to take. Murray was more committed to the unique one-of-a-kind piece, whereas Leach advocated a cooperative workshop approach aimed at producing functional ware at a reasonable price, with only an occasional "show" piece. These differences of opinion are easily understandable, for while both men came from an art school background, their later experiences were quite different. Having studied at the Camberwell School of Art, Murray, after World War I, set up his own workshop, where he experimented with glazes and firing techniques. He is reputed to have built the first studio-size oil-burning kiln in England. Contacts at St. Ives with Shoji Hamada may have influenced Murray toward a looser style. His characteristic pieces are large bottles and vase forms, dynamic and freely thrown, with a vigorous decoration. Murray spent the last part of his life in Africa, but his influence has been continued by the students he taught at the Royal College of Art from 1925 to 1939. Among these were Heber Mathews, Henry Hammond, Constance Dunn, and Sam Haile.

After returning to England from Japan in 1920, accompanied by his friend Hamada, Bernard Leach established a pottery at St. Ives in Cornwall. Here he encountered the usual problems of building a kiln and becoming accustomed to the local clays and materials. Early sales in England were disappointing, but pots shipped to and sold in Japan provided an income. Sensitive as he was to all the persuasive strength of tradition of the Oriental potter, it was natural that Leach would seek his own identity as a European. Even while in Japan he had experimented with early English slipware techniques (Fig. 129). These were continued at St. Ives with

mechanically perfect ware was available in unlimited quantities and at very low cost.

The writings of John Ruskin and the efforts of William Morris and his followers to revive traditions of integrity in materials, design, and workmanship were based on a romantic idea that would ultimately fail. However, these men did bring into focus the dissatisfaction of late nineteenth-century England with the poor quality of its contemporary design. The Art Nouveau movement of the 1890s and early 1900s in England and France and the *Jugendstil* in Germany had quite different goals, but both were a reaction against the prevailing criteria of worn-out academic design. Meanwhile, isolated experiments were being carried out by potters such as Theodore Deck, Ernest Chaplet, and Auguste Delaherche in France, and the Martin brothers and William de Morgan in England, who sought to rediscover some of the lost pottery secrets of an earlier era. At first interest centered primarily on decorative techniques, such as the Islamic luster ware, and later on glazes, such as the Chinese sang-de-boeuf. The Victorian taste for the more ornate wares of the Ch'ing Dynasty slowly changed to an appreciation of classical Sung pottery, as well as that of Korea and Japan. It is ironic that while Western industrialism was undermining the ancient

right : Plate 6. VICKI READ, England. Covered jar. Stoneware with elmwood ash glaze over red iron slip, height 9 ½″.

below : Plate 7. GEOFFREY WHITING, England. Teapot. Stoneware with carved decoration and semimat wood-ash glaze, fired in saggers in coal-burning and wood-burning kiln.

greater intensity, and most early work at St. Ives was in this vein. Later, medieval ware, such as the forceful Cistercian pitchers, exerted a greater influence on his work, and production was changed to stoneware (Fig. 130). To this day medieval English and Korean ware, rather than Japanese, have been the major factors in shaping his style, although they have been merged into a genre typically his own.

Leach's workshop approach—producing a quality functional ware at reasonable prices, with only an occasional unique piece—had a widening influence in the 1930s. Among early apprentices at St. Ives were Michael Cardew, Norah Braden, Katharine Pheydell-Bouverie, Dorothy Kemp, Harry Davis, and Leach's son, David, who since 1956 has had his own pottery near Bovey Tracey (Figs. 131–133). Among his former students are the

above left: 130. BERNARD LEACH, England. Vase. 1931. Stoneware with brushed fish decoration in brown, height 14″. Victoria & Albert Museum, London. The influence of oriental design in Leach's work is reflected in this vase.

above center: 131. MICHAEL CARDEW, England. Covered jar. Stoneware with incised decoration.

above right: 132. HARRY DAVIS, England. Jar. Stoneware with wax resist and oxide decoration.

133. DAVID LEACH, England. Covered casseroles. Clay with dark temmoku glaze.

American Warren MacKenzie and Canadian John Reeve, who is now working in England (Fig. 134).

The publication of *A Potter's Book* in 1940 further spread Leach's philosophy, as did his lecture tours to the United States in 1950 and 1960. Encouraged by his old friend Soetsu Yanagi, founder of the Japanese Craft Society, Leach has returned to Japan on numerous occasions. The several publications that have followed *A Potter's Book* have continued to spread the ceramic traditions of the Orient, as well as invoking an interest in the preindustrial pottery heritage of Europe.

Although Bernard Leach has been a major influence in the rebirth of English ceramics as a creative craft, it does not follow that all potters subscribe to his functional workshop approach. With the contemporary pressure on the artist for extreme individuality, the avoidance of tradition becomes a virtue in itself. A majority of today's studio potters came from an art school background, and they are, perhaps, little inclined to make mugs or teapots. The thrown form dictates certain limitations, and its long but varied tradition makes it difficult to be strikingly different. Therefore, it is natural that the more inventive young potters would turn to coil and slab techniques to achieve greater individuality in the form of their work or a style that is wholly sculptural in nature.

above left : 134. JOHN REEVE, England. Covered jar. Stoneware with wood-ash glaze and incised decoration, height 7 ½".

above : 135. LUCIE RIE, England. Bottle. Stoneware, sgraffito decoration. Collection J.W.N. van Achterbergh, Amsterdam. This flaring bottle is characteristic of Lucie Rie's work.

left : 136. HANS COPER, England. Bottle. Thrown and pressed form with dry mat textured glaze in off-white and brown-black. Collection J. W. N. van Achterbergh, Amsterdam.

There are many small potteries in England producing a varied and often excellent functional ware at moderate prices. Even those potters whose inclination is toward the unique piece find that some semiproduction ware is necessary in order to meet expenses, because the market for higher-priced ware is limited. For this reason many potters teach part time in art schools. Lucie Rie, originally from Austria and a former pupil of Michael Powelny of Vienna, and Hans Coper from Germany are among the best known of the potters in England who have developed a unique style (Figs. 135–136). The work of several others is shown in the text (Pls. 6–7, p. 73; Figs. 137–142).

above : 137. BRYAN NEUMAN, England. Set of matching pitchers, covered jar, soup bowl, and plate.

above right : 138. BILL READ, England. Tankard. Stoneware with cone-10 elmwood ash glaze over iron slip, height 6″.

right : 139. CHRISTOPHER CHARMAN, England. Salt jar. High-fire earthenware with lead glaze over slip, height 10 ½″.

above : 140. CHRIS HARRIS, England. Plate. Earthenware with slip-trailed decoration under lead glaze, diameter 12″.

above right : 141. IAN AULD, England. Containers. Slab-built stoneware, height of largest container 17″.

right : 142. MURRAY FIELDHOUSE, England. Bowl. Brown-ribbed body with smooth Bristol glaze on the interior surface.

below : 143. JAN VAN DER VAART, Holland. Architectural form. Stoneware with bronze-black manganese glaze.

right : 144. HANS DE JONG, Holland. *Cry Baby.* Stoneware with ash glaze, height 12″. Collection J.W.N. van Achterbergh, Amsterdam. Modern Dutch ceramics are often whimsical.

below right : 145. HELLY OESTREICHER, Holland. *Cylinders and Arcs.* 1965. Unglazed stoneware, height 19″.

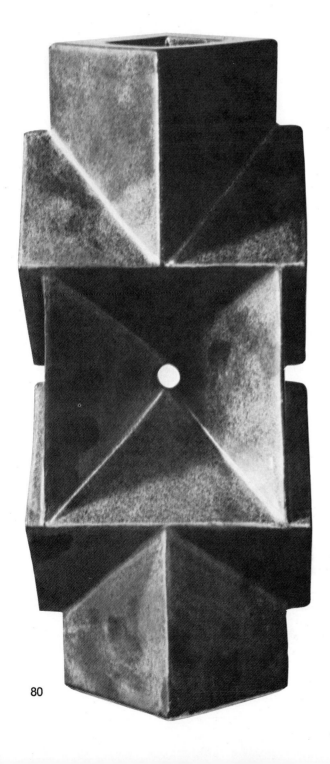

80

HOLLAND

Holland has had a long history of extensive trade with the Far East, and to this day her fine museums and many antique shops have excellent collections of Oriental ceramics. The blue-and-white porcelains imported from China and Japan became immensely popular in Europe, and the Dutch were quick to capitalize on this interest. By the early eighteenth century a number of potteries were producing a majolica-type ware in the Chinese blue-and-white style, although there were elements of an Italian pictorial tradition. This ware, in a higher-fire version, has continued to be made to the present day and is popularly called Delft after the major factory.

Perhaps in reaction to the all-pervasive blue-and-white tableware, the contemporary Dutch ceramist produces little functional pottery. There is less interest in thrown form than there is in England. Most pieces are hand built, and the trend is toward architectural form, sculptural whimsy, or textural qualities of clay (Pls. 8–9, pp. 74, 91; Figs. 143–148).

left : 146. JAN DE ROODEN, Holland. *Composition in White and Black*. 1968. Stoneware with mat glaze, height 24″.

top : 147. MARIANNE FRANKEN, Holland. *The Fairy Ring*. Stoneware. Collection Kyuken-Schneider, The Hague. Even with thrown pieces, Dutch ceramists explore their preference for applied decoration and unique textural effects.

above : 148. JAN DE ROODEN, Holland. *Form in White and Black*. 1968. Stoneware with mat glaze, height 6″. The purposeful eruptions caused by internal pressure, together with the strong glaze patterns, are the dominant features of this pot.

Many of the Dutch potters whose work is illustrated here have small studios in the vicinity of Amsterdam. They are, for the most part, in their early thirties and have quite varied backgrounds. A few have art school training, some have studied in England or Scandinavia, and others are largely self-taught, having had initial experience in other professions.

Some of these potters are or were members of the experimental group at the Porceleyne Fles at Delft, which was established in 1956 and patterned in part after the studio sections in many of the Scandinavian factories. The studio at Delft is under the direction of Theo Dobbelmann, a noted sculptor, glaze chemist, and a teacher at both the Art Academy and the Craft School in Amsterdam (Figs. 149–150). Perhaps because of their art school training, the Porceleyne Fles group, mostly female, has tended to emphasize a sensitive, linear, sgraffito-type decoration (Figs. 151–154). An informal workshop has developed, and often one person throws the pot while another does the decoration. Another interesting feature at the Delft factory has been the cooperation and technical help given to architectural designers in the execution of large ceramic mural projects for various schools and public buildings.

above and above right : 149–150. THEO DOBBELMANN, Holland. Ceramic forms. 1965. Height 36″, 14″. Excerpts from French poems enrich the surfaces of these constructions.

151–154. The work of several former members of the Porceleyne Fles experimental group reveals a common interest in
incised decoration on a reserved, often organic, form.

above : 151. ELS BOONE, Holland. 1967. Height 6 ¾″.

right : 152. KEES VAN RENSSEN, Holland. 1966. Height 15″.

below : 153. ANNEMIEKE POST, Holland. 1966. Height 9 ³/₈″.

below right : 154. LEIS COSIJN, Holland. 1966. Height 16 ¾″.

FRANCE AND BELGIUM

Historically, Belgium has always been dominated by French styles in art and by the Delft pottery styles in ceramics. The noted painter, designer, and architect Henry Van de Velde was a leader in the Belgian Art Nouveau movement, but he was more popular and influential in France and especially in Germany. The soft-paste and porcelain factories of the eighteenth and nineteenth centuries regarded the pottery form primarily as a space for pictorial decoration in an elegant court style. In spite of the early success of Art Nouveau in France, public support for ceramics never grew to the same extent as in England or Germany. French taste prefers ornate decoration, and consequently the work of traditional French stoneware potters was regarded as having little merit. The more conven-

above : 155. PABLO PICASSO, France. *Le faune barbre.* 1952. Painted ceramic, diameter 14″. Courtesy Galerie Louise Leiris, Paris.

right : 156. PABLO PICASSO, France. *Red and White Owl.* 1953. Painted ceramic, height 13 ¾″. Private collection, New York.

tional work of French potters such as Jean-Bertrand Tessier, René-Louis Dauchy, and Francine del Pierre has received little recognition relative to the renown of the plates and sculptural pieces decorated by Joan Miró and Pablo Picasso. Picasso's ceramic works (Figs. 155–156) are not nearly as well known as his painting and sculpture, but they display the same fresh inventiveness. Made in collaboration with his potter friend Artigas, Picasso's ceramics anticipated by several decades much of the nonpot work that is being done today.

The Belgian ceramist Pierre Caille was originally a painter, but he turned to ceramics in 1937 (Figs. 157–158). Although he occasionally makes pottery, Caille's major interest is in figurative pieces and panels, often grotesque, but with a very personal style and a sociological impact that reminds one of the later paintings of his countryman James Ensor.

right : 157. PIERRE CAILLE, Belgium. Ceramic form. c. 1958. This powerful study, with its simplified form and dramatic intensity, is characteristic of the work of Pierre Caille.

below : 158. PIERRE CAILLE, Belgium. *Grinning Faces.* c. 1958. This ceramic panel has a rather medieval, macabre quality.

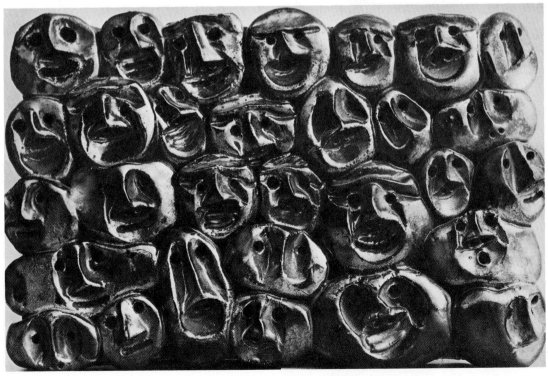

SPAIN

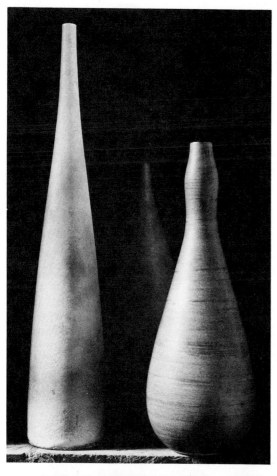

After the great period of the Hispano-Moresque luster ware of the fifteenth and sixteenth centuries, Spain slipped gradually into a ceramic doldrum. Seen against the background of the popular and rather gaudy majolica ware, the austere stoneware of Antoni Cumella comes as a surprise. Born in 1913, Cumella lives in Granolles, near Barcelona, where he has been potting since 1936, developing a severe personal style quite unlike that of his contemporaries in Spain. His typical bottle and vase forms have a stony sculptural quality (Fig. 159). Although his more recent panels have cut-out and textured surfaces (Fig. 160), Cumella's pots are unrelieved by any decoration except for the mat glazes with subtle color variations. Perhaps more in the Spanish tradition is the work of Maria Bofill, instructor at L'Scala Massana in Cataluña (Figs. 161–162).

left: 159. ANTONI CUMELLA, Spain. Bottles. Stoneware with off-white mat glaze, height of tallest bottle, 19 ½".

below left: 160. ANTONI CUMELLA, Spain. Tile (detail of wall at Spanish Pavilion, New York World's Fair, 1964). Stoneware with blue, pink, and ochre glazes, 35 × 19 ½".

below: 161. MARIA BOFILL, Spain. Multispout jar. Stoneware with decoration in wax resist and iron oxides, height 7 ½".

above : 162. MARIA BOFILL, Spain. Covered jar. Stoneware with white glaze and decoration in wax resist and iron oxides, height 14 ½″. The elaborate decoration on this jar is somewhat reminiscent of old Spanish pottery styles.

below : 163. CARLO ZAULI, Italy. Sculptural form. Stoneware with white wood-ash glaze, 43 × 39″. Even in Italy, with its craft tradition, the accidental effect has assumed esthetic importance for contemporary potters.

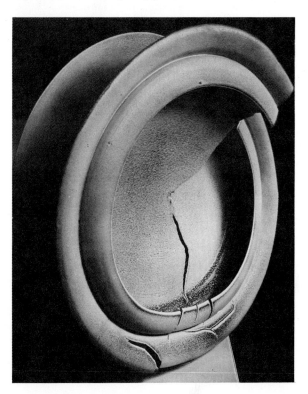

ITALY

Indigenous crafts survived longer in Italy than in the more industrialized areas of northern Europe. Unlike glass, pottery is made in all areas of Italy, but it generally follows a low-fire majolica tradition. In keeping with the Italian temperament, the ceramic ware is colorful and exuberant, often fantastic, and sometimes sentimental. But, like any art form that feeds upon tradition, the majolica potteries have long lost their reason for being, and they find their principal audience in the tourist trade.

Italy is truly a living museum of the great periods of Etruscan, Roman, Renaissance, and Baroque art. It has been extremely difficult for the modern Italian artist and craftsman to throw off the weight of this tradition. Gio Ponti—a Milanese architect, influential designer, and founder of *Domus* the excellent magazine on architecture and decorative arts—has been a leader in bringing the craft ideas of William Morris and the functional aspects of the German Bauhaus movement to Italy. The large ceramic firm of Richard-Ginori has slowly veered toward contemporary design. The Triennale Exhibition of Decorative Arts, which was started in Milan prior to World War I, has also been a great influence in spreading new ideas, for it has become the finest international exhibition of its kind. (Unfortunately, the American contribution typically ignores crafts in favor of industrial superproducts.)

In the last few years Italian ceramics has shown a dramatic departure from the older concentration on low-fire ware to a new interest in stoneware. The many new art and crafts schools in every major city have certainly had a part in this trend. Many of the pieces shown here (Figs. 163–168) are by faculty members in these schools, chiefly from the State School of Ceramics at Faenza, which has for centuries been an Italian pottery center and where the Ceramic Museum conducts a yearly international exhibition. Architectural and sculptural ceramics follow an ancient Italian tradition, and it is not surprising that the modern Italian potter should work in this vein, but in a very contemporary manner (Figs. 169–170). Even the functional pieces are in this modern style.

top left : 164. ANGELO BIANCINI, Italy. *The Annunciation,* sculptured panel. 1963. Majolica with polychrome and luster decorative details, height 31 ½″. Vatican City.

top right : 165. LEONI ALFONSO, Italy. Ceramic assemblage. Thrown forms in deep bowl with green glaze, diameter 15″.

above : 166. GUIDO GAMBONE, Italy. Hanging wall sculpture. 1964. Manganese and white glazes, height 18″.

left : 167. FULVIO RAVAIOLI, Italy. Vases. 1964. Mat and crackle glazes, height of larger vase 13″.

top left : 168. CARLO ZAULI, Italy. Sculptural form. Thrown and slab stoneware with wood-ash glaze, height 16″.

above : 169. GUIDO GAMBONE, Italy. Wall panel. 1967. Stoneware slab forms with white glaze, height 44 ⁷/₈″.

left : 170. LEONI ALFONSO, Italy. *Machine 11111112.* Ceramic with white and black majolica glaze, 24 × 20″.

GREECE

The Greek potter, even more than his Italian counterpart, is submerged under the legends and glories of an ancient past. The tourist trade, while adding immeasurably to the economy of Greece, subsidizes mainly the hotelkeeper and the souvenir shop. There are many potteries in Greece, but most are turning out copies of antique black- and red-figure ware. The imitative decoration is usualy stiff and stilted, but a few pieces have such a delicacy of line one wonders if the chipped, clay-encrusted ware offered as "classical" originals might have come from the hands of the same talented copyists.

The skill of the traditional Greek potter is evident, but the importance of the tourist trade and the conservatism of the Greek middle class have made it most difficult for the craftsmen of modern Greece to explore a contemporary direction. The situation is further complicated by the fact that kiln materials are difficult to obtain, and most glaze chemicals and colors must be imported. Greek ceramics, unlike those of Germany and Scandinavia, shows little interest in glaze effects, and this may be due to the influence of older traditions or to a more contemporary trend toward textural surfaces. In addition to study in Greece, most of the potters whose work is illustrated (Pl. 10, p. 92; Figs. 171–176) have studied at art or craft schools in France or Italy. It is encouraging to note that each seems to have developed a.very personal style. There is not yet an identity of interests such as is found in many other areas, but it will undoubtedly occur as the contemporary trend continues to develop in Greece. This will depend more on public acceptance than on the interest of the individual craftsman. In this regard the Greek potter is not unlike the Italian glass blower at Murano, who continues to make Baroque forms because that is what the public expects.

top: 171. KOSTAS PANOPOULOS, Greece. Bottle. Red clay with cream glaze wiped off to expose body, height 18″.

left: 172. PANOS VALSOMAKIS, Greece. Cubistic relief panel. Terra cotta with polychrome crackle glaze, height 26″.

opposite: Plate 9. HANS DE JONG, Holland. *Two Birds*. Stoneware with oxide colorants and thin glaze.

left : Plate 10. MARY HATZINICOLI, Greece. Bottle. Hand-built low-fire porcelain with brushed colorants, height 12″.

below left : Plate 11. HILDEGARD STORR-BRITZ, Germany. Wall tile. Stoneware with stamped decoration, partially glazed; height 13″.

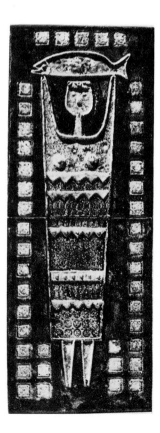

above left : 173. MARY HATZINICOLI, Greece. Vase and bottle. Hand-formed earthenware with tracing in blue and brown on a white ground, height of vase 13″.

above right : 174. KOSTAS PANOPOULOS, Greece. Vase. Hand-formed earthenware partially glazed with blue-gray and pink, height 14″.

right : 175. ATHANASE PAPAVGERIS, Greece. Relief panel. Terra cotta with polychrome stylized design, height 33″.

far right : 176. ATHANASE PAPAVGERIS, Greece. Low-relief panel. Terra cotta with polychrome glaze decoration, height 29″. The design suggests the levels of a terraced Greek village.

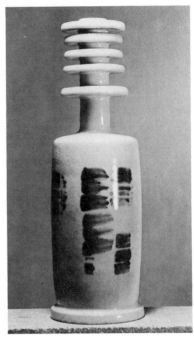

GERMANY

German potters have long been interested in higher-fire ceramics, perhaps because they are influenced by the old salt-glazed stoneware tradition of the Rhine and the efforts of the early eighteenth-century potteries, which developed the first porcelain in Europe. The vast amount of porcelain produced on the Continent during this era, which might be typified by that of Meissen, grew not from a long and natural ceramic tradition but from an effort to copy Chinese form and decoration. In later years Baroque paintings in the Italian or French style became the models for decorative motifs, and by the end of the nineteenth century it was obvious to forward-looking architects and designers that this ornate and derivative ware did not fit modern needs.

Influenced by the ideals of Morris and the anti-academic philosophy of Art Nouveau, as well as by their own *Jugendstil*, German architects, artists, and designers of the pre-World War I era laid the basis for the modern design movement that culminated in the Bauhaus. The craft and trade schools which were established in the major cities, along with

several magazines, exhibitions, and organizations like the Deutsche Werkbund—whose members included architects, designers, craftsmen, and manufacturers—all played a role in developing new design concepts related to the vision and function of contemporary life.

The war periods, of course, were times of retreat. The conservatism of the British prevented their accepting modern ideas of functional design in industry. In 1933 the reactionary ideals of Nazism closed the Bauhaus and drove most of its staff and its sympathizers abroad. A great many of these innovators emigrated to the United States, which, with its mass markets and large industry, was a fertile ground for the Bauhaus concept of functionalism. The principle of "form follows function" —that the design of any object must be faithful to its purpose and that integrity of materials must be respected—had been promulgated in the late nine-

top left : 177. BEATE KUHN, Germany. *Spiny Creature.* 1965. White stoneware with coffee-brown mottled glaze, height 16".

top right : 178. WALTER POPP, Germany. Bottle. Stoneware with white glaze and brown and green accents, height 11".

teenth century by the American architect Louis Sullivan and subsequently refined by his disciple Frank Lloyd Wright. Interestingly, both architects employed much ceramic for the decorative details with which they embellished their buildings. Although the work of the two men was highly acclaimed, their philosophy did not, for many years, have any significant effect on American design. Wright's ideas and conceptual drawings, however, received European publication in 1910–11, and these had considerable influence on the formation of what became the "International Style," which approached its fullest expression during the 1920s in the teaching, design, and art of the faculty at the Bauhaus. It is ironic that, because of the migration of Walter Gropius, Miës van der Rohe, Josef Albers, Marcel Breuer, and László Moholy-Nagy to the United States, the Bauhaus functionalist esthetic had greater eventual impact in America, where, through the philosophy of Sullivan, it, in part, had its initial inspiration.

There are at present several fine craft and ceramic schools in the major German cities. Many train ceramic engineers and production designers as well as hand potters. A few are located in old pottery centers such as Höhr-Grenzhausen, a small Rhineland town where there are still dozens of salt-glaze potteries producing ware in a centuries-old tradition. Although some potters have had workshop training, most of those whose work is illustrated here (Figs. 177–189) attended craft schools, and many are teaching as well as maintaining their own studios.

Given the technical aptitude attributed to the Germans, it should not be surprising to find a concentration on rich glaze effects. The pieces tend to be designed and have little of the thrown feeling characteristic of English pottery. Nor is there the delight in texture that intrigues the Dutch potters. Continuing the early interest of such sculptors as Ernst Barlack (1870–1938), who illustrated the pioneering *Die Jugend* magazine, and Gerhard Marcks (1889–), director of the ceramics program at the Bauhaus, many contemporary potters have turned to sculpture and architectural decoration. In fact, most of the German work shown here exhibits a preference for sculptural qualities, rather than for traditional pottery forms (Pl. 11, p. 92).

above : 179. WILHELM and ELLY KUCH, Germany. Bottles. Stoneware with beige, brown, and black glazes; height 11″.

below : 180. GÖRGE HOHLT, Germany. Columnar vases. Stoneware with intense reduction glazes in clear blue, oxblood red, and titanium blue; height of tallest vase 16 ½″.

below left : 181. ULRICH GÜNTHER, Germany. Bottle. Thrown stoneware with semimat brown glazes, height 7 ½".

below right : 182. HILDEGARD STORR-BRITZ, Germany. Vase. Stoneware with banded impressed decoration and gray-brown salt glaze, height 12 ½".

right : 183. INGEBORG and BRUNO ASSHOFF, Germany. Bottle-shape figures. 1960. Stoneware with blue earth glaze.

bottom left : 184. WALTER POPP, Germany. Bottle. Stoneware with white and blue black reduction glazes, height 6 ½".

bottom right : 185. WILHELM and ELLY KUCH, Germany. Bottle. Black, brown, and blue glazes; height 22".

above : 186. HILDEGARD STORR-BRITZ, Germany. Bottle. Stoneware with stamped and applied decoration and mottled dark gray-green salt glaze, height 10″.

right : 187. SABINE NASKE, Germany. *Tree of Life*. Stoneware with blue-green and dark brown glaze, height 21″.

below : 188. SABINE NASKE, Germany. *Garden Cock*. Groggy clay with brown-red and green glazes, height 21 ½″.

below right : 189. INGEBORG and BRUNO ASSHOFF, Germany. Double vase. Stoneware with thick ash glaze, height 30″.

SCANDINAVIA

Although the Scandinavian countries have their individual characteristics, they also have much in common. After centuries of Viking raids against the British Isles and, later, intermittent wars among themselves and with Germany and Russia, the Scandinavians long ago turned inward. Except for Sweden, the northern countries lack the mineral resources of Germany, France, and England. Until recent years their population was largely rural, and industrialization came later than elsewhere in Europe. Native crafts survived longer than in most parts of the Continent, much as they did in Italy. With the decline of the medieval guilds, craftsmanship also deteriorated, and a new system of training was needed. Architects, designers, and small manufacturers banded together in the late nineteenth century to offer design training in each of the capital cities. At first the instruction consisted of little more than drawing classes in which historical patterns were copied. Later, full-fledged craft schools emerged that were rather like those in Germany. During the eighteenth and early nineteenth centuries, Scandinavia was greatly influenced by late Rococo and Neoclassical French styles in furniture and interior decoration. Upper- and middle-class taste was influenced from abroad, while in the rural areas the more simple handcrafts prevailed.

The Morris movement, Art Nouveau, and finally the Bauhaus—each in turn had its impact upon Scandinavian designers, craftsmen, and manufacturers. However, these three successive influences, though significant, do not completely explain the sudden upsurge in design excellence and craftsmanship in furniture, silver, glass, weaving, and ceramics during the thirties and forties. Rather, it is likely that certain philosophies arising from the emergence of socialism in these countries provided the catalytic agent. Under a slogan of "beautiful ware for everyday use" designers, craftsmen, manufacturers, schools, and trade unions, with government support, were united toward a common goal of quality. Very gradually the combined efforts of these groups—through formal teaching, exhibitions, and craft societies—had an educational effect upon the public. The rights of the designer were protected, and today one finds his name listed on price tags along with that of the manufacturer. In addition to the few special retail outlets run by craft societies, all the larger cities have many shops carrying handmade items. Major department stores, such as Nordiska Kompaniet in Stockholm and Stockmans in Helsinki, have splendid displays of contemporary designed items. The large Danish craftsman's store, Den Permanente, is now world famous, and the revival of the craft workshops in the old medieval town of Fredrikstad reflects Norwegian involvement. All these elements have contributed to the wide influence of "Scandinavian modern" design.

Traditional medieval Scandinavian pottery was a dark red burnished earthenware, usually unglazed. The early pottery factories—the Royal Copenhagen (founded in 1779) and Gustavsberg in Sweden (1827)—first produced a majolica ware and later switched to porcelain and stoneware. Their products were inspired by German porcelain, Dutch majolica, and English bone china, all of which derived their decorative styles from Chinese prototypes, although the forms were often Neoclassical. Contemporary influences did not occur until the 1920s, when artists whose training was not in the traditional ceramic arts joined the staffs of several factories. The latter direction continues and is doubtless responsible for much of the success of the Scandinavian factories. The situation is not completely idyllic; conflicts do arise between the design and studio staffs and between sales and management personnel. Nevertheless, the Scandinavian design philosophy is far more progressive than that which prevails in most parts of the world. Some members of the studio staff work only on mass production, while others concentrate on one-of-a-kind pieces or on limited-production items. Their presence is bound to have a stimulating effect. Many of the early designers had painting or sculpture backgrounds, and the transition to the pottery medium proved difficult. But, as the craft schools have gradually turned to a designer-craftsman point of view, many talented people have begun to enter industry from the schools. There is a close association between the two, with many of the professional designers teaching part time.

Denmark

For years the commercial success of the traditional dinnerware patterns and figurines made by the Royal Copenhagen factory has perpetuated a conservative policy on the part of its design staff, although some contemporary patterns have been produced. Axel Salto, Royal Copenhagen's design head, has a most individual style derived from the organic bulblike growths that typify his personal work. The second large Danish porcelain factory, Bing and Grøndahls, also produces a line of conservative patterns, but in recent years it has sought a more contemporary outlook (Fig. 190). In the experimental studios at Bing and Grøndahl a group of young potters, under the direction of Asgar Fischer, are working with complete freedom in a variety of directions (Figs. 191–196). Fischer, for years the director of the craftsman's store, Den Permanente, and a brother of sculptor Adam Fischer,

below: 190. Erik Magnussen for Bing and Grøndahl, Denmark. Thermo casserole with lid. White porcelain. The cross-section shows the ingenious heat-saving construction.

bottom: 191. Sten Lykke Madsen for Bing and Grøndahl, Denmark. *Fantastic Animal*. The staid functionalism of Scandinavian ceramics is increasingly enlivened by whimsical and delightful creations.

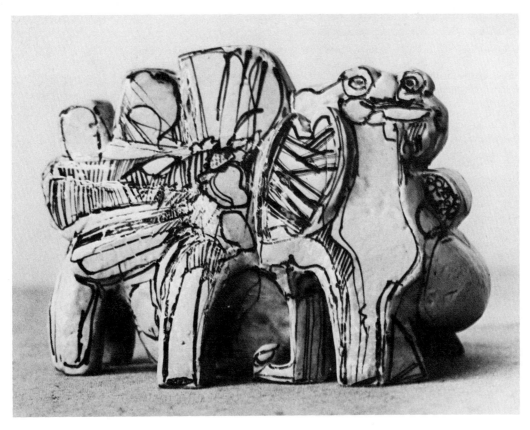

left : 192. URSULA MUNCH-PETERSEN for Bing and Grøndahl, Denmark. Vase. 1964. Stoneware with assembled thrown sections, glazed in green on the interior only; height 11 ³/₈″.

below : 193. BENTE HANSEN for Bing and Grøndahl, Denmark. *Fantasy.* Stoneware sphere, altered, with partial glaze and oxide decoration. This piece captures the quality of accidental charm that is often found in a beach pebble.

below : 194. ERIK MAGNUSSEN for Bing and Grøndahl, Denmark. *Abstract Sculpture.* Stoneware with lava and luster.

right : 195. STEN LYKKE MADSEN for Bing and Grøndahl, Denmark. *Fantasy Hen.* Applied and incised decoration.

has been an enthusiastic proponent of Danish crafts since the modern movement began.

Several smaller factories and Danish workshops are also producing contemporary and distinctive patterns. In general, Danish ceramics emphasizes a sturdy, solid form with an inclination toward functionalism (Figs. 197–200). Textural effects have gradually replaced glaze perfection as the main area of concentration (Figs. 201–204), and interest in purely sculptural—even nonobjective—pieces is growing. In addition to the several larger workshops, there are many small private potteries in Denmark where apprentices may train.

top : 196. EDITH SONNE BRUUN for Bing and Grøndahl, Denmark. Vases and platter. Stoneware with crystalline glaze.

right : 197. CHRISTIAN POULSEN, Denmark. Vases and lidded jar. Stoneware with light blue, dark brown, and white glazes.

top : 198. NIELS REFOGAARD for Dansk Designs, Denmark. *Generation Mist* dinnerware. Stoneware with grayish glaze and brown decoration. (Executed by Eslau Keramik.)

above : 199. DORTHE MØLLER, Denmark. Mug and teapot. Stoneware with light gray glaze and brushed blue decoration.

left : 200. MYRE VASEGAARD, Denmark. Bowl. Stoneware with gray glaze and blue-green brushed and wiped decoration.

left : 201. HELLE ALLPASS, Denmark. Lidded jug. Stoneware with gray-green glaze and iron red spots.

below left : 202. GUTTE ERIKSEN, Denmark. Jar. 1962. Stoneware with off-white variegated and runny glaze.

below : 203. HANS and BIRGITTE BÖRJESON, Denmark. Tureen and bowls. Stoneware with light brown speckled glaze.

bottom : 204. CONNY WALTHER, Denmark. Bottles. 1961. Groggy stoneware with blue-green glaze, height of each c. 5″.

Sweden

The porcelain factories of Gustavsberg and Rör-strand (founded in 1726), which recently merged with the Upsala-Ekeby firm, dominate the Swedish scene. Sweden has numerous small studios and individual potters, but these three large factory groups enjoy major contact with the public. Wilhelm Kåge of Gustavsberg and Gunnar Nylund of Rörstrand were most influential during the 1930s and afterward in urging the rejection of traditional styles based on German porcelain and English bone china. Today Carl-Harry Stålhane and Stig Lindberg head the large staffs at Rörstrand and Gustavsberg, which design mass-production ware and also produce one-of-a-kind pieces (Pl. 12, p. 125; Figs. 205–212).

The austere and streamlined designs of the 1950s are still reflected in Swedish functional ware, but even this is becoming more colorful. As in Denmark, the esthetic of simple form and perfect glaze has given way to an interest in textural complexity and a more sculptural approach to form (Figs. 213–217). Stig Lindberg heads the ceramic

above : 205. CARL-HARRY STÅLHANE for Rörstrand, Sweden. Mural. Stoneware. Collection AB Volvo, Göteborg.

below : 206. MARIANNE WESTMAN for Rörstrand, Sweden. Plate. Stoneware with freely brushed circular glaze decoration.

program at the Konstfackskolan in Stockholm and Carl-Harry Stålhane at the craft school in Göteborg, and for this reason there is perhaps greater cooperation in Sweden between school and industry than anywhere else in the world. While the situation might not be a true heaven on earth for the ceramic designer in Sweden, it is nevertheless remote from the distinctly earthbound conditions that prevail in the United States, where potters teach teachers how to teach and the advertising departments of some major potteries are largely content to pirate designs from their competitors at home and abroad.

left : 207. STIG LINDBERG, Sweden. *Ting* (lamp, gong, birdhouse, and flower holder). 1969. Unglazed bone china. The same globular shape is used to create four different items.

below left : 208. STIG LINDBERG, Sweden. Mural (detail) for Nacka Hospital, Gustavsberg. 1967. Cast clay, length 130′.

below : 209. CARL-HARRY STÅLHANE for Rörstrand, Sweden. Sculptural form. Stoneware with red and brown-black glaze.

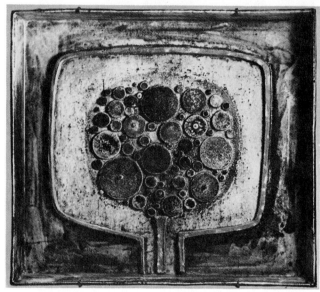

top left : 210. INGER PERSSON for Rörstrand, Sweden. Vase forms. Stoneware with freely brushed glaze decoration.

top right : 211. OLLE ABERTIUS for Rörstrand, Sweden. *Forma* table service.

above : 212. SYLVIA LEUCHOVIUS for Rörstrand, Sweden. Wall plaque. Stoneware with stylized plant and polychrome flowers.

left : 213. BERTIL VALLIEN, Sweden. Sculptural form. 1969. Swedish potters have turned increasingly to fantasy.

below: 214. BRITT LOUISE SUNDELL-NEMES, Sweden. Vase and plate. 1969. Stoneware with glossy crystalline glaze.

bottom: 215. ULRICA HYDMAN-VALLIEN, Sweden. *Bomb Number 6314.* 1969. Unglazed white stoneware, painted with blue, black, and brown enamels. Although the inscription suggests antiwar sentiment, the effect is of a stylized ballet.

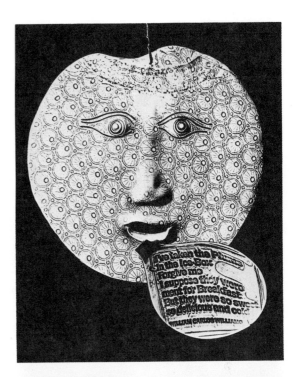

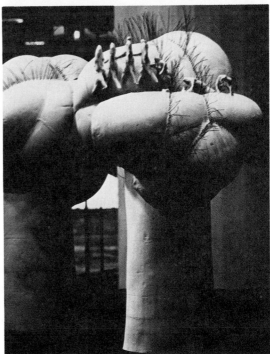

top: 216. BENGT BERGLUND, Sweden. Wall plaque. 1969. The stamped technique is used here very effectively.

above: 217. BRITT INGRID PERSSON, Sweden. *Line Drawings.* White unglazed stoneware molded in a mushroomlike form.

Scandinavia 107

Norway

Norway is a long, mountainous country, cut by numerous fjords and sparsely populated. Forestry, fishing, and shipping have for generations been major industries. Of the native crafts, weaving is perhaps the most important, as befits a cold northern country. The long dark winters have encouraged a taste for colorful patterns, and these characterize much of the weaving, the glassware, the popular majolica pottery, and the enameling on silver in which the Norwegians excell. Among early proponents of contemporary design in Norway were Thor Kielland, who later became director of the Art Industry Museum in Oslo, and Jakob Prytz, owner of the Tostrup silver firm and a teacher of silversmithing in the local craft school. In more recent years Per Tannum, whose large furniture store in Oslo has often carried craft items, has been a leading advocate of modern design. In cooperation with many others in the crafts and industry, Per Tannum

formed the Plus organization, which has developed a series of craft workshops in the old medieval town of Fredrikstad. The shops have proven to be quite a tourist attraction and are educational in an unobtrusive manner. As in the other Scandinavian capitals, there are display stores in Oslo, such as Forum, run by the various craft and design societies. The Norwegian commercial potteries have not supported studio staffs to the degree that the other Scandinavian countries have. There are, however, a number of talented individual potters. Until recent years most of them have worked in a decorated majolica pottery style, but the trend now is toward stoneware, with an emphasis on solid form and pressed or carved decoration (Figs. 218–224).

top left : 218. RICHARD DUBOURGH, Norway. Teapots. Unglazed body with rough, textured surface and cane handles.

top right : 219. ERIK PLØEN, Norway. Vase. Stoneware with pressed stamp decoration.

top : 222. DEGNY and FINN HALD, Norway. Bowl. Stoneware with cut decoration heightened by opaque glaze.

above : 223. ROLF HANSEN, Norway. Deep bowl with handles. Stoneware with stamped decoration and olive-green glaze.

below : 224. ERIK PLØEN, Norway. Square vase. 1960. Stoneware with pressed decoration and thick, viscous glaze.

top : 220. ROLF HANSEN, Norway. Bowl and vases. Thrown stoneware with brush and sgraffito glaze decoration.

above : 221. ERIK PLØEN, Norway. Vases. 1966.

Finland

The Finns migrated from central Europe to their present area before the eighth century, bringing a language distantly related to an ancient Hungarian dialect. Finland became a Duchy of Russia a hundred years before the Bolshevik revolution, but prior to that and since the twelfth century it had been a part of Sweden. Therefore, the Finns, despite

top left : 225. ANNIKKI HOVISAARI for Arabia, Finland. Covered bottle. Engraved decoration and gray glaze.

above : 226. TAISTO KAASINEN for Arabia, Finland. *Virgo* (one of a series depicting the signs of the Zodiac).

left : 227. OLLI VASA for Arabia, Finland. Flasks and tumblers.

their adherence to old customs and their unique language, share many attitudes with the Swedes.

The surprising realization of excellence in contemporary Finnish design that began in the 1930s may in part be explained by the outpouring of spirit of a people suddenly freed from centuries of foreign rule, but it still remains a baffling phenomenon. Isolated from the main currents of European life, the Finns had to turn inward, perhaps to the age-old legends of the ancient national epic, the *Kalevala*, for inspiration and survival.

Eliel Saarinen, who came to the United States in 1923, and later Alvar Aalto were among the pioneering architects and designers to influence the direction of Finnish design. As in Sweden, craft societies, schools, and industry cooperated in an attempt to produce a well-designed product for common use. The Ateneum, the School of Arts and Industrial Design administered by the Society of Industrial Design in Helsinki, has played an important role in this program. Many of Finland's outstanding designers, such as Kaj Franck and Tapio Wirkkala, have studied and later taught at the Ateneum. The Finns are particularly skilled and inventive in the design and production of fabrics, glassware, laminated furniture, and ceramics.

The huge Arabia porcelain factory in Helsinki has dominated Finnish ceramics for many years. Although founded by the Swedish Rörstrand firm in 1874, it came under Finnish control in 1916. At the turn of the century A. V. Finch, a potter and painter of Belgian and English descent, had begun teaching ceramics at the Ateneum, and most of the Arabia designers were trained under him or his former pupil, Else Elenius, who succeeded him. Kurt Ekholm, who later left to head the craft school in Göteborg, was an important design leader at Arabia. Maija Grotell, known for her teaching at Detroit's Cranbrook Academy, studied under Else Elenius, as did Kyllikki Salmenhaara, an excellent potter now an instructor at the craft school.

The present Arabia design supervisor is Kaj Franck, a versatile artisan in glass and ceramics and a noted teacher, whose esthetic philosophy has great influence in Scandinavia. Most of the ceramics illustrated here (Figs. 225–230) were made by the

above : 228. RAIJA TUUMI for Arabia, Finland. Bowl. Stoneware with perforated design and mat gray glaze, diameter 18″.

below : 229. LIISA HALLAMAA for Arabia, Finland. Vase and egg cups. Stoneware.

Arabia staff, some of whom design solely for production while others create only one-of-a-kind pieces and a few work in both fields. The pieces are extremely varied and quite personal in expression, ranging from the fantasies of Birger Kaipiainen (Fig. 231) through the colorful decorations of Rut Bryk (Fig. 232), the thrown pottery of Anja Jaatinen (Fig. 233), and the textural constructions of Francesca Lindh (Pl. 13, p. 126; Fig. 234). The publicity and exibition facilities enjoyed by the Arabia potters have made it difficult for smaller potteries to compete, and, therefore, there are few unaffiliated potters (Fig. 235) such as are common in Sweden, Denmark, and the rest of Europe.

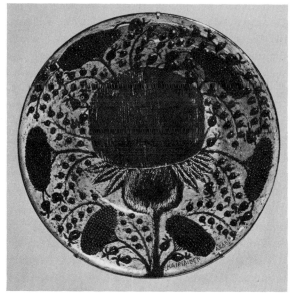

left : 230. HELJÄTUULIA LIUKKO-SUNDSTRÖM for Arabia, Finland. *Torpedo.* Stoneware with white mat glaze (metal base).

top : 231. BIRGER KAIPIAINEN for Arabia, Finland. Wall plate. Earthenware with gray-green and black decoration on gray background, beads cemented in place; diameter 18″.

above : 232. RUT BRYK for Arabia, Finland. Decorative tile. Engraved and stamped design, turquoise and other glazes on gray-white background; 9″ square.

above left : 233. ANJA JAATINEN for Arabia, Finland. *Samurai* vases. Stoneware with mat blue glaze.

above right : 234. FRANCESCA LINDH for Arabia, Finland. Vase. Slab and thrown stoneware with pressed decoration and blue glaze, height c. 19″.

left : 235. LEA HAGMAN, Finland. Vase forms (intended for lamp stands). Stoneware with gray, blue, and brown glazes.

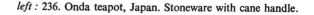

JAPAN

Ceramics has long been an integral part of Japanese culture, developing in the era of Jomon and Haniwa terra cottas and continuing through the centuries when Chinese and Korean influences were being absorbed into the Japanese tradition. The tea ceremony and the resultant high esteem for the necessary ceramic pieces are uniquely Japanese (Fig. 236). However, the changes that followed the overthrow of the Shogunate in 1868 and the subsequent restoration of the imperial house under Emperor Meiji were catastrophic for the Japanese potter. The industrialization of the old pottery centers at Seto and Arita not only destroyed the craftsmanlike manner of working but, with the introduction of new mass-produced and cheap porcelains, also doomed the many small hand potteries that were scattered throughout Japan. Only a few—the family-owned potteries with generations-old reputations and those in remote areas, such as in Onda and Koishibara in Kyushu, where potters of Korean descent continued their combined farming and potting way of life—managed to survive.

The recent revival of folk pottery is largely due to the efforts, during the 1920s and 1930s, of the late Soetsu Yanagi and his Mingei (folk art) society, aided by the now-famous potters Shoji Hamada and Kanjiro Kawai (Fig. 237). Through constant lectures, exhibitions, and encouragement of young potters, Yanagi was able to renew interest in the native crafts, which were all but destroyed by industrialization and the disappearance of the old ways of life. Today, with craft museums, exhibitions, and sales rooms in some of the finer department stores, the traditional hand crafts are again high in public regard.

By a happy coincidence, Bernard Leach, the English potter, became acquainted with Yanagi, Hamada, Kawai, and the young architect Kenkichi Tomimoto (1886–1963) during his stay in Japan from 1909 to 1920. Hamada and Kawai were trained as engineers, but, along with Tomimoto and Leach, both were influenced by Dr. Yanagi's interest in the strength and naturalness of the neglected folk arts. Kawai in Kyoto, Hamada in Mashiko, and, later, Leach at St. Ives in England went on to gather sympathetic groups around them. Tomimoto, however, was drawn toward a more personal expression, one not within the "Mingei tradition." Applying the concept of the artist-craftsman, he explored new techniques and directions (Fig. 238). After encouraging the growth of several craft societies fostering these aims, Tomimoto established, in 1949, the first college-level ceramics program in Japan, at the Kyoto Municipal College of Fine Arts.

Japanese ceramics continues to follow diverse trends: rural potters influenced by Korean styles; the continuation of old Japanese traditions, such as Bizen; and the newer "Mingei" potters, such as those at Mashiko (Figs. 239–244). Finally, there is a younger group of potters, many of them trained as painters or sculptors, who view ceramics as a personal expression and conceive of it in sculptural terms only incidentally related to the functional use of pottery (Figs. 245–251).

left : 237. SHOJI HAMADA in his studio at Mashiko, Japan.

below : 238. KENKICHI TOMIMOTO, Japan. Covered jar. 1958. White porcelain with clear glaze and red, gold, and silver decoration; height c. 7 ¼". The superb craftsmanship of Tomimoto is evident in this intricate design.

left : 239. MASAYUKI IMAI, Japan. Bottle vase. Stoneware with line decoration, stained with slip but unglazed.

below left : 240. YAICHI KUSUBE, Japan. Vase. Stoneware with cut-out sections and green "fern sprouts" glaze, height 10″.

below right : 241. TOSHIO KATO, Japan. *Swellfish.* Thrown stoneware, compressed and altered, oxidation fired; height 18″.

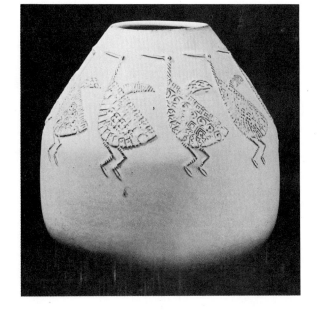

above : 242. KAKO MORINO, Japan. Vase. Stoneware (reduction fired with wood) with salt glaze and cobalt decoration.

above right : 243. MUTSUO YANAGIHARA, Japan. Vase. 1968. Stoneware with wax-resist design and umber glaze, height 8″.

right : 244. KANZAN SHINKAI, Japan. *Birds in a Circle.* Applied and stamped relief decoration.

left : 245. Hiroaki Morino, Japan. Slab sculpture. 1967. Textured stoneware with dark green stain, height 20".

below : 246. Heihachiro Hayashi, Japan. Sculptural construction. Unglazed, oxidation fired; height 13".

right : 247. Shin Fujihira, Japan. *A Guide Post*. Textured slab-built stoneware with contrasting light and dark areas.

below : 248. Yoshitaka Yasuhara, Japan. Garden sculpture. Slab-built with wood-ash glaze and cut-out sections.

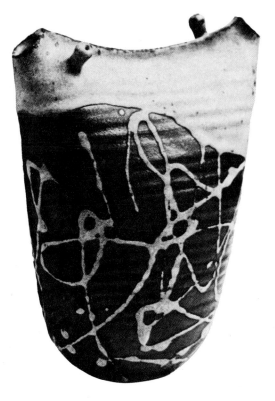

above left : 249. KIYOYUKI KATO, Japan. Vase. Stoneware with iron glaze.

above right : 250. HIROAKI MORINO, Japan. Vase. Thrown stoneware, compressed and joined, with mat gray slip-trailed decoration.

left : 251. SHIN HATTA, Japan. *Harmony.* Stoneware, altered, reduction fired, with blue mat glaze; height 16″. The accidental cracking becomes a decorative element.

AUSTRALIA AND NEW ZEALAND

As was the case in America, European ceramic imports dominated Australian taste during the early history of that country, especially since industrialization in England was proceeding at a rapid pace during the era of settlement. Early Australian ceramics was at first limited to the manufacture of bricks, tile, flowerpots, storage jars, simple dinnerware, and other utilitarian objects, most of which were low fired, although some salt stoneware was made.

Merric Boyd (1888–1959) was the first Australian to work in the studio art tradition. His early interest was in clay modeling in an Art Nouveau style, so it was natural that, when he turned to pottery, he preferred to use convoluted, writhing, and organic plant, animal, and human motifs to embellish his forms. His son, David, also a potter, has continued the family interest in decoration. Other ceramic pioneers were Peter Hall, Paddy Walsh, Jim Landison, and Alan Lowe.

Most early Australian work was in earthenware, but in recent years the trend has swung to stoneware (Figs. 252–254). Since World War II, there has been a tremendous increase in public interest in ceramics. Most colleges and art schools have pottery courses, exhibitions are frequent, and many small and sucessful workshops are in operation. A similar situation prevails in New Zealand. The Leach preference for the freely thrown, functional pot has been influential (Figs. 255–257), and many of the younger potters whose work is illustrated here have traveled or studied in England. Michael Cardew's work has also had an effect, and his recent extended stay in Australia and the impact of his personality and philosophy will certainly influence the course of Australian ceramics. Museum collections of Oriental ware, as well as the relative proximity to Japan, have caused the same echoes of Japanese and Korean form that are found elsewhere in the world. While a few potters are inclined toward a sculptural and decorative approach, rather than the more functional (Figs. 258–263), they have rejected the neo-Dada, avant-garde tendencies so common among American potters.

above : 252. CARL McCONNELL, Australia. Wine jug. Stoneware with trailed decoration in black and rust red, height 12″.

below : 253. MOLLIE DOUGLAS, Australia. Teapot. Stoneware with off-white glaze and rust-red accent at base, height 5″.

left : 254. Peter Travis, Australia. *Cathedral*. Slab and coil construction, height 18″.

above : 255. Derek Smith, Australia. Flanged cooking pot. Stoneware with brown and black ash glaze, diameter 16″.

left : 256. Peter Rushforth, Australia. Jug with large handle. Stoneware with runny ash glaze, height 14″.

above : 257. Les Blakebrough, Australia. Flower container and small box. Mittagong blue porcelain, reduction fired, with free brush decoration in cobalt and iron oxides.

above : 258. IAN SPRAGUE, Australia. Vase. Coiled stoneware, unglazed, with iron oxide to accentuate texture; diameter 20″.

below : 259. MARGARET TUCKSON, Australia. Covered casserole. Groggy clay with clear mat glaze on exterior, diameter 8″.

right : 260. BERNARD SAHM, Australia. *Anthropots*. Slab and partially thrown stoneware with mat glaze, height 28″ each.

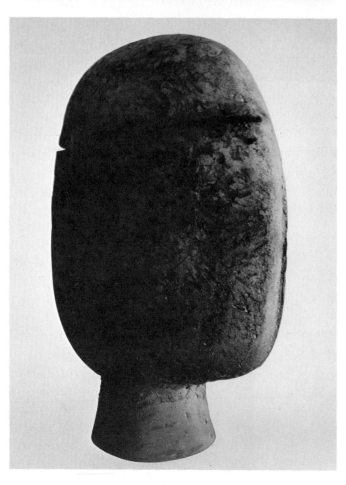

left : 261. WANDA GARNSEY, Australia. Vases. Stoneware with dolomite glaze and reduced specks, height of larger vase 8″. The applied "fins" give the vases an asymmetrical quality.

below left : 262. MAREA GAZZARD, Australia. *Dials.* High-fire coiled earthenware, unglazed, with coloring oxides; height 22″.

below : 263. IVAN ENGLUND, Australia. *Celebration.* Thrown and modeled stoneware with oxide decoration, height 19″.

opposite: Plate 12. STIG LINDBERG, Sweden. *People Bottles.* Stoneware with iron-red glaze.

CANADA

The first historical mention of pottery making in Canada dates from 1686 and relates to bricks, tile, and earthenware pottery being manufactured in Quebec. Early ware followed the French and English lead-glazed slip ware traditions. By the late eighteenth century numerous small potteries were supplying local needs. However, as the English ceramic industry grew in the early nineteenth century, the hand potters in the colonies could not compete with the inexpensive, mass-produced product, which was often technically superior, even though it lacked the unsophisticated charm of the local wares.

In North America generally the growing interest in handcrafts is in no way a continuation of colonial Old World traditions, but rather a twentieth century reaction against the sterility of industrial products. Although the idea may seem romantic, it has been suggested that modern man longs for that which displays the irregularity of the human touch as an antidote to an ordered and mechanized way of life.

Formal Canadian instruction in pottery began in 1915 at the Central Technical School in Toronto, later joined by the Ontario College of Art and the Fine Arts School in Montreal. The Canadian Guild of Potters, organized in 1936, has been, along with regional groups, an important influence in spreading interest in ceramics through its numerous exhibits and workshops. In the Maritime Provinces the Danish potters, Kjeld and Erica Deichmann, contributed to public interest from 1935 through the fifties. Among the many active potters before World War II were Molly Satterly, Bailey Leslie (Fig. 264), Bobs C. Haworth, and Gaetan Beaudin. Since the War there has been a tremendous growth in public interest in ceramics, as well as in the number of active potters and schools offering instruction. A few

potters have succeeded in their own workshops, but most do some teaching in addition. The influence of Bernard Leach was great during the 1950s, especially as potters generally shifted from earthenware to stoneware (Figs. 265–266).

Present influences are quite diverse, and Oriental elements now derive more from Japanese than from Chinese styles. As elsewhere in the world, many Canadians have begun to think of clay in terms of sculptural form, free from the traditional restrictions of functional pottery (Figs. 267–272). The work illustrated gives some idea of the variety of expression found in Canadian ceramics (Figs. 273–280). It hardly represents a unified national trend, but its quality is both vigorous and experimental.

opposite : Plate 13. FRANCESCA LINDH for Arabia, Finland. Wall plaque. Stoneware with suspended clay bells and barium copper-blue glaze.

right : 264. BAILEY LESLIE, Canada. Bottles. Slab-built porcelain with wheel-thrown necks, textured with copper oxide rubbed under white mat glaze; height of largest bottle 17 ½″.

above : 265. ALLAN CRIMMINS, Canada. Bottles. Stoneware with feldspathic and wood-ash glazes, height of bottle at left 8″.

right : 266. MAYTA MARKSON, Canada. Planter. Stoneware with free brush decoration and mat copper glaze, height 14″.

below : 267. MIMI CABRI, Canada. Vase. Slab-built stoneware with brushed brown engobe over white mat glaze, height 10 ¼″.

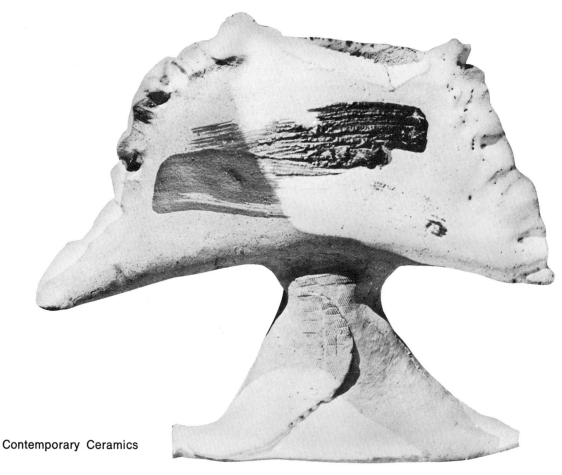

below : 268. ROBERT BOZAK, Canada, Sculptured pot. Slab-built raku ware with gray body and poured glaze, height 9″.

right : 269. MARION LEWIS, Canada. Abstract sculptural form. Accented areas of glaze and color.

below : 270. JACK SURES, Canada. *Ric's Planter.* Multicolored stoneware clays with fiber glass, unglazed; 14 × 49 × 6″.

left : 271. YOLANDE ROUSSEAU RIOUX, Canada. *Terre des hommes* (made for exhibit at Expo 67). 1967. Red clay.

below left : 272. DOROTHY MIDANIK, Canada. Vases. Slab-built stoneware with applied decoration glazed in white and yellow, with coloring oxides of black, brown, and ochre rubbed into unglazed body; height of largest vase 22″.

below : 273. CHARLIE SCOTT, Canada. Jar. Stoneware with reduced feldspathic glaze and zipper, height 13 ⅛″

bottom : 274. MARILYN LEVINE, Canada. Vase. Stoneware, 18 × 10″. The torn rim imparts tension to a placid piece.

above : 275. JOAN BOBBS, Canada. Jar. Coiled stoneware with texture formed by joining, orange-brown glaze; height 18″.

right : 276. WILLIAM NORMAN, Canada. Cylindrical bottle. Thrown stoneware with applied clay decoration and black slip accent under a reduced clear white glaze, height 10″.

below left : 277. JULIEN CLOUTIER, Canada. Vase. Stoneware with freely poured glaze, height 20″.

below right : 278. JOHN SHAW, Canada. Bottle. Stoneware with mottled blue glaze over iron-oxide decoration, height 10″.

above : 279. MAURICE SAVOIE, Canada. Five bottles. Coiled stoneware with feldspathic glaze, height of largest bottle 16″.
below : 280. JACQUES GARNIER for Céramique de Beauce, Canada. Tea set. Earthenware with dark mat glaze.

THE UNITED STATES

As discussed in Chapter 2 (pp. 57–58), the Industrial Revolution had a devastating effect on American handcrafts. One exception to the prevailing trend of commercial production in the late nineteenth century was the Rookwood Pottery. It was founded in 1880 by Maria Longworth-Storer, a wealthy Cincinnati woman and an art school graduate, who, with several friends, had long been interested in china painting, then a popular pastime. Mrs. Storer eventually learned to throw on the wheel and, with a small factory staff, experimented with various glazes and types of decoration. Rookwood's well-known vase forms were influenced by the Chinese, their decoration by the Japanese and by Art Nouveau floral motifs. While we might question today the several international awards won by the Rookwood Pottery, the work was far superior to that of its more commercial competitors during the forty years of the company's operation (Fig. 281).

Another pioneer in ceramic design was Adelaide Robineau of Syracuse, New York, who also began as a china painter, then learned to throw and experimented with high-fire bodies and glazes. This was the era of Art Nouveau and Tiffany glass, both of

which are reflected in her work (Fig. 282). In addition to her own ceramic production, Adelaide Robineau founded the Ceramic Studio magazine in about 1903, which popularized an elementary idea of craftsmanship and Art Nouveau principles among a wider audience.

More influenced by the philosophy of Morris and the reserved forms of the Chinese was the English potter, Charles Binns, who became in 1900 the first director of the New York State College of Ceramics in Alfred, New York. Through experiments in high-fire stoneware and porcelain, Binns and his many students, such as Charles Harder and

below left : 281. Rookwood Pottery, U.S.A., Cincinnati, Ohio. Mug. 1882. Earthenware with blue glaze and figurative decoration. Brooklyn Museum (gift of Arthur W. Clement).

below : 282. ADELAIDE ROBINEAU, U.S.A. Vases. Late 19th– early 20th century. Porcelain with decorative crystalline glazes in floral design. Everson Museum of Art, Syracuse, N.Y.

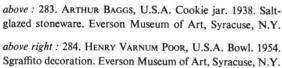

above : 283. ARTHUR BAGGS, U.S.A. Cookie jar. 1938. Salt-glazed stoneware. Everson Museum of Art, Syracuse, N.Y.

above right : 284. HENRY VARNUM POOR, U.S.A. Bowl. 1954. Sgraffito decoration. Everson Museum of Art, Syracuse, N.Y.

right : 285. MAIJA GROTELL, U.S.A. Vase. 1946. Stoneware with slip-trailed design. Everson Museum of Art, Syracuse, N.Y.

Arthur Baggs (Figs. 283), laid much of the technical foundation that underlies the present ceramic programs in American colleges. Also prominent during the 1930s was the California potter Glen Lukens, who developed some unusual glazes from local minerals. Henry Varnum Poor was the first well-known painter to become interested in pictorial and figurative decorations for pottery, based on the majolica tradition (Fig. 284).

Much as American architecture and design were enriched by the arrival of the Bauhaus expatriates, so also did American ceramics profit from such European potters as Marguerite and Frans Wildenhain, Gertrud and Otto Natzler, and Maija Grotell (Fig. 285), most of whom came to the United States during the 1930s.

The National Ceramic Exhibition, first organized at the Syracuse Museum of Fine Arts as a memorial to Adelaide Robineau in 1932, has played an important part in uniting potters and spreading ideas from one section of the country to another. Craft exhibitions, which were rare in the 1930s, are now common, due to the efforts of various local groups and the American Crafts Council, which maintains the Museum of Contemporary Crafts in New York, and which established the School for American Craftsmen in Rochester, N. Y. The Council also publishes the magazine *Craft Horizons* and formerly operated America House, once a leading craft sales outlet. A recent outgrowth of the Council is a World Crafts Council, an organization formed to facilitate an exchange of ideas among craftsmen everywhere.

After the war years there was a tremendous growth in all the crafts. A new prosperity which allowed for increased leisure time, coupled with an inarticulate distaste for the impersonal products of the modern plastic genre, evoked a greater fascination for handcrafts in both the hobbyist and the professional. As college and art school programs grew, the prewar preference for earthenware and decorative techniques changed to a concentration on stoneware and higher-fire glazes. Chinese ceramics of the earlier period were studied with increasing interest. The writings and several lecture tours by Bernard Leach also had great influence.

Pots were better thrown, and glazes were more suitable and varied than ever before in American history. But the situation of the potter had also changed. Most were not producing functional pottery or even decorative ware for a local market but more often were teachers in art schools or college art departments. Under these conditions the exhibition piece assumed greater importance. If it were to stand out, it must necessarily be larger, rougher, or in some way bizarre. Thus during the 1950s there was a gradual shift toward interesting texture, asymmetrical coiled pieces, and combined slab and thrown forms. This new variety created a more excit-

ing exhibition and provided a different challenge to the potter. Symptomatic of the change, he now preferred to be called an "artist-craftsman." This is not surprising, since in the traditional university structure the crafts were always subservient to the "fine arts," but with the trend toward mixed media, the old categories are breaking down. It is now difficult to label some works as either painting or sculpture; similarly, the distinction between pottery and ceramic sculpture is ever more nebulous.

A leader in this drastic change in the ceramic arts was the West Coast potter, Peter Voulkos. An expert craftsman, he was producing in the early 1950s a variety of thrown pieces in a more-or-less functional tradition (Fig. 286). But, possessing an exuberant and

right : 286. PETER VOULKOS, U.S.A. Covered jar. 1950s. Stoneware with sgraffito, height 17". Museum of Contemporary Crafts, New York (gift of Mrs. Vanderbilt Webb).

left : 287. PETER VOULKOS, U.S.A. *Cross.* 1959. Stoneware with polychrome low-fire glaze, height 30 ½". Johnson Collection of Contemporary Crafts. This piece illustrates Voulkos' complete break with traditional ceramic form.

below : 288. PETER VOULKOS, U.S.A. *Aratsa.* c. 1968. Stoneware with black mat glaze, height 26 ¼". Johnson Collection of Contemporary Crafts. The black glaze emphasizes the stark, almost brutal explosion of form.

competitive personality, Voulkos was soon pushing the traditional forms into new directions, and by 1957 he had abandoned the functional aspect for sculptured pots and, ultimately, for large clay forms which were completely sculptural in nature (Figs. 287–288). Although in recent years Voulkos has confined his work almost exclusively to cast-bronze and metal sculpture, his radical departures from traditional pottery forms during the fifties have had a continuing influence on American ceramics.

Expressionist painting has also had its effect in developing a more vigorous decorative style totally unlike the usual glazed ceramic surface, even to the extent of replacing glaze with brilliant acrylic paints and cemented fabrics in a collage technique. Pop Art has encouraged this trend, often creating an assemblage of objects primarily for their shock value. Impressions from type faces and photographic decals have introduced literary and associative images in a neo-Dada fashion which is new to the ceramic medium. Even the recent popularity of the old Japanese raku pottery is primarily due to its firing process, which has the character of a "happening," for the patterns and colors that evolve are unpredictable and often accidental.

Contemporary ceramics is in a state of flux, and traditional values are under attack. A great deal of experimentation occurs, both in form and in materials, but the larger question is one of direction. Undoubtedly most of the present work will eventually go into the dust bin, as it has in other eras, but it is doubtful that ceramics will soon, if ever, return to anything approaching the esthetic that existed thirty years ago. There certainly is no concensus about what this direction should be, as the many illustrations of American pottery in this volume will demonstrate. If any quality can characterize this work, it is that of an iconoclastic attitude which is dynamic and vital, even if offering neither the constants nor the solutions that our confused society, at the same time pragmatic and idealistic, so desperately desires.

4 Clay and Clay Bodies

Most people confuse clay with soil, and this is quite understandable, since the two are related. Garden soil is a combination of clay, sand, and humus (partially decayed vegetable matter). Compared with other materials in the earth, this layer of soil is extremely thin, usually only a few inches —seldom over a foot—thick. There are, of course, large areas without soil, such as most desert and mountain regions. Between the soil proper and the rocky mantle of the earth there is a subsoil—composed of clay, sand, or gravelly mineral deposits in either a pure or a mixed form—that may vary from a few inches to hundreds of feet in thickness.

After a fiery genesis, the earth cooled for billions of years before water vapor and an atmosphere formed. The slow march of the seasons began. Erosion from wind and water, as well as expansions and contractions from heat and ice, gradually crumbled the rock that comprised the earth's surface. The initial composition of this rock varied from place to place. Minerals that were relatively water soluble broke down much more quickly. The evolution of plant and, later, animal life hastened this process, for organic acids contributed their decomposing action. In certain locations, the movement and melting of the ice cover during the glacial ages had considerable effect on the mixture and breakdown of minerals composing the surface rock.

Clay derives from the disintegration of granite and other feldspathic or pegmatite rocks which, as they decompose, deposit alumina and silica particles. The latter two minerals, combined with water, form pure clay, whose composition is expressed chemically as $Al_2O_3 \cdot 2\,SiO_2 \cdot 2\,H_2O$. This is an ideal formula, however, for nearly all clays contain some impurities, and it is these impurities and variations in the basic formula that account for the different characteristics of the numerous clay types.

A unique and valuable quality of clay is its plasticity; unless a clay will hold its shape while being formed, it is useless (Fig. 290). This factor depends on the fineness of particle size. In the geological forma-

opposite : 289. LYLE N. PERKINS, U.S.A. Vase. Slab-built stoneware with some glazed areas, height 26″.

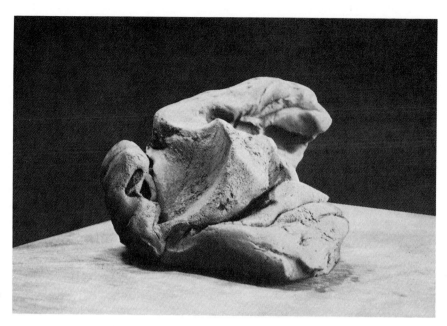

290. A unique and valuable quality of clay is its plasticity.

tion of clay it is the softer, more soluble feldspar in granite rock that decomposes to leave alumina and silica particles, and for this reason clay particles are very tiny. A fine grain of sand is 1/500 inch in diameter. Even this is huge compared with a clay particle that is only 0.7 microns in diameter and 0.05 microns in thickness. (A micron is about 1/25,000 inch.) The natural structure of a clay particle is a flat, shinglelike shape, and the particles tend to slide together and give support to one another, whether in a plastic state or after a formed piece has dried. By comparison, even the finest ground minerals have large, granular crystals with no ability to adhere.

CLAY TYPES

All clays can be classified first as either *residual* or *sedimentary*. Residual clays have remained more or less at the site of the original rock formation. They are less plastic than sedimentary clays and contain many larger-size particles. Sedimentary clays are those that, by action of wind or running water, have been transported far from the site of the parent rock. This action usually affected only the clay particles of the finest size, and therefore sedimentary clays are the more plastic of the two types.

Kaolin

Kaolin is a very pure form of clay, approaching the ideal formula on page 139. Although never used alone as a body, it serves as a standard with which to compare other clays. It is white in color and can be fired to an extremely high temperature. Kaolin provides a source of alumina and silica for glazes and is an important ingredient in high-fire white ware and porcelain bodies.

The wide variety of kaolin types available is indicative of the difficulty in classifying clays. In the United States the major commercial deposits are in the Southeast. North Carolina produces a residual-type kaolin with many coarse rock particles, while the deposits in South Carolina and Georgia are of the sedimentary type. Florida deposits are even more plastic and are termed ball kaolin. No kaolin, however can truly be termed plastic in comparison with ball clay.

Ball Clay

Ball clay is chemically similar to kaolin after firing. In its unfired state, however, the color is dark gray due to the presence of organic material. Although weathered from a granite-type rock much like that which produced kaolin, the ball clay particles were deposited in swampy areas where the organic acids and gaseous compounds released from decaying vegetation served to break down the clay particles into even finer sizes than those of the sedimentary kaolins.

Ball clay imparts increased plasticity and dry strength when used as a body component. If a clay body contains 10 to 20 percent ball clay, its throwing qualities are greatly improved. Like kaolin, ball clay has a high maturing temperature. It can be used as a source of alumina and silica for glaze, as well as a binding agent. However, when they are stored for long periods, such glazes tend to form gas leading to glaze defects. In this event the glaze can be dried out and reused, or a few drops of formaldehyde can be added to discourage fermentation. Tennessee and Kentucky have the largest deposits of ball clay in the United States.

Stoneware Clays

Stoneware clays are of particular interest to the potter, because they are generally plastic and fire in a range from cone 6 to cone 10.* Depending upon the atmospheric conditions of the firing, the color will vary from buff to gray. Stoneware clays are found in scattered deposits from New York and New Jersey westward to Illinois and Missouri and also on the Pacific Coast. The clays differ in composition; in comparison with kaolin they contain impurities, such as calcium, feldspar, and iron, that lower the maturing temperatures and impart color to the clay.

It is quite unusual today for a single clay to be used as a throwing body. To the principal clay, which may be either stoneware or fireclay, portions of ball clay, flint, feldspar, and even earthenware clay are added to obtain the desired plasticity, firing temperature, color, and texture.

---

* See Appendix for temperature charts giving cone equivalents in degrees Fahrenheit and centigrade. Cones indicated in the text refer to the Orton series. Note that Seger cones have a slightly different range.

Fireclay

Fireclay is a high-firing clay commonly used for insulating brick, hard firebrick, and kiln furniture. Its physical characteristics vary; some fireclays have a fine plastic quality, while others are coarse and granular and unsuitable for throwing. Fireclays generally contain some iron as an impurity but seldom have calcium or feldspar. The more plastic varieties, like some stoneware clays, are sometimes found adjacent to coal veins. They can be high in either flint or alumina and therefore have special industrial uses. Fireclays of one type or another are found in most states, absent only from a few mountainous regions and the southeast and northeast coasts.

Earthenware Clays

Earthenware clays constitute a group of low-firing clays that mature at temperatures ranging from cone 08 to cone 02. They contain a relatively high percentage of iron oxide, which serves as a flux (a substance that lowers the maturing temperature of the clay), so that when fired they are rather fragile and quite porous. Unlike stoneware bodies, which are almost completely vitreous, the usual earthenware body, after firing, has a porosity between 5 and 15 percent. Because of the various fluxes it contains, earthenware cannot be made vitreous, for it deforms and often bloats and blisters at temperatures above 2100°F (1150°C). All of these factors limit its commercial use to building bricks and tiles.

Earthenware clays of one type or another can be found in every part of the United States, although commercial deposits are most abundant in the lower Great Lakes region. Many such clays, available commercially, are of a shale type. Shale deposits are clays laid down in prehistoric lake beds. Time, chemical reactions, and pressure from overlying material have served to cement these clay particles into shale, a hard, stratified material halfway between a clay and a rock. Shale clays are mined and ground into a powdered form similar to ordinary clay. The small lumps that remain can be troublesome if they are not screened out, for they will absorb moisture, expand, and rupture much like a piece of plaster.

Some earthenware clays are of glacial origin and therefore are quite varied in composition. They frequently contain soluble sulfates that are drawn to the surface during drying. When fired, a whitish film appears on the surface. This defect can be eliminated by the addition to the clay body of 2 percent barium carbonate.

Slip Clay

Slip clays are those clays that naturally contain sufficient fluxes to function as glaze without further additions. Although white and even blue slip clays exist, the most common are tan, brick red, or brown-black. Most slip clays fire in a range from cone 6 to cone 10. The best-known commercial slip clay is Albany, mined in small pits near Albany, New York. There are many small deposits of glacial clays scattered throughout the northern states that will make satisfactory slip glazes with little or no addition. Slip glazes are easy to apply; they usually have a long firing range and few surface defects.

Bentonite

Bentonite is an unusual clay that is used in small amounts as a plasticizer. Deposits are found in most of the western mountain states, the Dakotas, and in several Gulf states. It has the finest particle size of any clay known.

Bentonite was formed in prehistoric ages from the airborne dust of volcanic eruptions. It is composed largely of silica. A nonclay glaze may include up to 3 percent bentonite in order to assist adhesion without noticeably changing the glaze. When used in nonplastic (short) clays, one part bentonite is usually equal to five parts ball clay. It should be mixed dry, since it becomes quite gummy when mixed alone with water.

CLAY BODIES

An earthenware, stoneware, or porcelain body that is completely satisfactory in all respects seldom occurs in nature. It may not be plastic enough, nor have the right color, nor fire at the desired tempera-ture. Even clays from the same bed will vary slightly in chemical and physical qualities. Thus it is usually necessary to mix clays in order to achieve a workable clay body.

In making up a clay body, one generally begins with a clay that is available at a reasonable price and that has no major faults, such as an excessive amount of sand or grit. No clay should be considered unless it is moderately plastic. The plasticity can be improved by additions of ball clay or bentonite. In rare cases, a clay may be so fine that it will not dry easily without cracking. In this event, a less plastic clay, a silica sand, or a fine grog (coarse, crushed, fired clay), can be added to *open up* the clay body and make it more porous so that it will dry uniformly. This treatment is often necessary to make an extremely fine or *fat clay* throw and stand up better.

Occasionally a clay will lack sufficient fluxes to fire hard enough at the desired temperature. When this occurs, inexpensive materials containing fluxes, such as feldspar, talc, dolomite, nepheline syenite, bone ash, and so on are usually added. If color is no problem, iron oxide can be used. In some cases a small amount of lower-firing clay can be added, which has the advantage of not cutting down on plasticity, as additions of any of the above materials will do. If, on the other hand, there is too large a proportion of fluxes and the clay body deforms at a relatively low temperature, the potter must either begin again with a different clay or add clays that are higher in alumina or in silica and alumina. Either a Florida kaolin or a plastic fireclay of a high maturity can be used for this purpose.

Porcelain bodies are more commonly used for commercial ware that is mechanically produced in plaster molds or by jiggering (see Chap. 10, pp. 261, 264), since the hand potter usually prefers the reduction effects and the plastic qualities of gray or reddish stoneware. Porcelain bodies are compounded principally from kaolin, feldspar, and flint. If greater plasticity is desired, some ball clay is used, resulting in increased shrinkage. For a throwing body, the ball clay may be as much as 25 percent of the body. (See Appendix, pp. 321–323, for suggested clay bodies.) Chemically, there is little difference between a stoneware and a porcelain body, except for the presence of small quantities of iron and other impurities that color the stoneware and fireclays. Bone china is similar to porcelain, with the exception that bone ash has been added to the body as a flux to increase translucency and to reduce the temperature needed for maturity to about 2275°F (1250°C). Like porcelain, bone china is very hard, white, and translucent when thin. Its greatest faults are a tendency to warp in firing and the lack of sufficient plasticity for throwing.

The term *chinaware* is used rather loosely to designate a white body usually fired between cone 4 and cone 8. Some types, such as restaurant china, are very hard and durable. However, they should not be confused with the even harder and more translucent porcelain bodies fired at cone 10 to cone 16. A white body in the cone 4 range often uses nepheline syenite, rather than feldspar, as a flux. White earthenware clay rarely occurs in nature. The low-fire white bodies often used for gift pottery contain large amounts of talc to reduce their firing temperatures to cones 08 to 04 (1750°F–1950°F, 955°C–1065°C).

TESTS FOR CLAY BODIES

Before a new clay or clay body is purchased or used a few simple tests should be made.

Plasticity

Plasticity is essential to a throwing clay. A standard, simple test for plasticity is to loop a pencil-size roll of clay around one's finger. If the coil cracks excessively, it probably will not throw well. The ultimate test, however, is to throw several pieces. In comparring bodies, the potter should make sure that all samples have been aged for equal lengths of time. Three weeks in a plastic state usually is adequate for a clay to improve appreciably in throwing qualities. In this time the finest particles become thoroughly moist, and the slight chemical breakdown caused by the organic matter contained in all clays can occur. The increase in plasticity brought about by aging is more pronounced in acid than in alkaline clays. If

it is necessary to use an alkaline body, the addition of a small amount of vinegar to the throwing water will prove helpful.

Wedging, a process by which the clay is kneaded by hand to remove air pockets, has a considerable effect in increasing plasticity. In a coarse clay, the realignment of particles by the wedging action can also prove beneficial (see p. 147).

Water of plasticity refers to the amount of water needed to bring a dry, powdered clay into a plastic state suitable for throwing. The finer the particle size, the more plastic a clay will be and the more water it will absorb.

Porosity

The porosity of a fired clay body is directly related to the hardness and the vitrification of the clay. To make a porosity test, an unglazed fired clay sample is weighed. After an overnight soak in water, the sample is wiped clean of surface water and weighed a second time. The percentage gain in weight will be the porosity of the clay body.

Most bodies used by the hand potter can be fired with a variation of at least 50°F (10°C) from the optimum firing temperature without proving unsuitable. As a general rule, fired clay bodies fall within the following porosity ranges: earthenware, 4 to 10 percent; stoneware, 1 to 6 percent; porcelain, 0 to 3 percent (see Chap. 11, pp. 278–279). A higher firing will reduce the porosity, but normally a specific firing temperature will already have been chosen. Adjustments in the flux ratio will affect the firing temperature and, thus, the relative porosity.

Shrinkage

Shrinkage of the clay body occurs first as the clay form dries in the air and then again as the form is put through the bisque (preliminary) firing and the glaze firing. The more plastic clays will always shrink the most. The test for shrinkage is quite simple: first, a plastic clay slab is rolled out and either cut or marked to a measure; when the slab is totally dry, a second measurement is taken; a final measurement is made after firing.

Clay shrinkage rates generally range from 5 to 12 percent in the drying stage, with an additional 8 to 12 percent shrinkage during firings. Thus, the potter can expect a total shrinkage of at least 13 percent and an extreme of 24 percent, with a median of 15 to 20 percent between the wet clay state and the final glazed ware. These normal shrinkage rates apply to plastic throwing clays. Special white ware bodies using spodumene in place of feldspar and only small amounts of clay have a greatly reduced shrinkage and can even be compounded to develop a slight expansion in firing. Wollastonite as a replacement for silica and flux in a body will also decrease firing shrinkage.

Because of shrinkage strains placed upon large sculptural forms, it is often necessary to include a grog in amounts of 20 to 30 percent of the body. Since this material is already fired, little further change occurs. There is also a tendency in drying for the clay to pull away slightly from the grog and thus open air channels that facilitate the drying out of thicker portions that would otherwise crack.

QUARTZ INVERSION

A major problem in the successful compounding of ceramic bodies is quartz inversion. During the firing of a ceramic body, silica (quartz) changes its crystalline structure several times, with a rapid expansion in size. This is especially true of free silica that is not in a chemical bond with other body components. The most pronounced change occurs when the firing temperature reaches 1063°F (575°C). At this point the quartz crystals change from alpha to beta quartz, with a resultant expansion. At about 1850°F (1010°C) tough, interlocking mullite crystals composed of alumina and silica begin to form, and this chemical combination gives the fired body its strength. In the cooling process the situation is reversed; when the kiln temperature drops to 1063°F, the free silica in the body contracts. Quartz inversion is one of the reasons why a slow cycle of firing and cooling is essential. If a ceramic piece is heated or cooled too quickly, or if the distribution of heat is uneven, the piece will crack. Special precautions are required for ovenware, which must be able to withstand, with minimal thermal expansion, the heat to which it will be exposed in use.

In preparing a clay body several things can be done to control the effects of quartz inversion. A combination of pyrophyllite and talc substituted for part of the feldspar will reduce thermal expansion, as will the addition of petalite ($Li_2O \cdot Al_2O_3 \cdot 8\,SiO_2$). Spodumene ($Li_2O \cdot Al_2O_3 \cdot 4\,SiO_2$) in a clay body creates an irreversible expansion, while the inclusion of wollastonite ($CaSiO_3$) also reduces firing shrinkage and aids in developing a tougher body that is more resistant to heat shock.

Rhodesia has been a major source of petalite, but at present the political situation has made shipments uncertain. Three parts of spodumene and one part of feldspar can be substituted for four parts of petalite. The amounts needed will depend upon the alumina-silica ratio of the body and the fluxes present. A 5 to 10 percent addition of any of the suggested chemicals will often make an appreciable difference in reducing the problems of quartz inversion encountered in developing an ovenware body. The precise amounts can be determined only by testing a number of different body compositions, since the character of various stoneware and fireclay bodies, as well as the firing temperatures, precludes the setting of any arbitrary percentages.

CLAY PROSPECTING AND PREPARATION

There are few sections of the United States in which a suitable pottery clay cannot be found. Digging and preparing one's own clay is seldom an economic proposition, but it can be rewarding in other ways. If one is teaching in a summer camp, a hike can easily be turned into a prospecting trip. In commercial clay mining, the soil overburden is removed by power shovels, and the entire operation is quite mechanized. For the few hundred pounds of clay the individual wishes to obtain, he must depend upon the accidents of nature to reveal the clay bed. A river bank, a road cut, or even a building excavation will often expose a deep bed of clay that is free of surface contamination (Fig. 291). If the clay contains too much sand or gravel it may not be

291. Digging clay in the local hills at Mashiko, Japan.

worth the trouble. A few tree roots will not disqualify a clay, but any admixture of surface soil or humus will render it unusable.

On the first prospecting trip it is advisable to take samples of a few pounds of clay from several locations. These samples should be dried, pounded into a coarse powder, and then soaked in water. Passing the resultant clay slip (liquid clay) through a 30-mesh sieve is usually sufficient to remove coarse impurities. If the clay proves too sandy, one can allow the heavier particles to settle for a few minutes after stirring and then pour off the thinner slip. This slip is then poured into drying bats and tested as described earlier.

In most localities, surface clay is likely to be of an earthenware type. The samples should also be tested as possible slip glazes. It is surprising how many pockets of glacial clay work nicely as glazes, either alone or with a small amount of flux added. In some areas, the river-bank clay may be of a stoneware or fireclay type. All in all, clay prospecting can be profitable, but it is mostly fun. In this day of the super-processed item, starting out from "scratch" gives one a rare feeling of satisfaction.

5 Forming Methods

Pottery, Sculpture, and Architectural Ceramics

A ball of plastic clay and our fingers are all that we need to form a pot. The survival and continued popularity of ancient methods of hand construction (Fig. 293) are clearly a reaction to the impersonal nature of modern industrial society. Perhaps no other endeavor represents such a link with the past and reflects the continuum of human life better than ceramic art. It rejects the nineteenth-century ideal of rational progress in favor of a more natural sequence of change, forgetting, and rediscovery.

POTTERY

Early man used a natural object, such as a shell or a gourd, as a container for countless ages before he learned to fabricate a more efficient receptacle. It is probable that a gourd or round stone served as the first mold over which a layer of clay was pressed and allowed to harden, then removed to form a hollow bowl. The accidental burning of a clay-lined basket is thought to have been the means by which man learned to make pottery (see p. 2).

Preparation of Clay

Whether clay is prepared in small amounts or in large quantities in a pug mill, it should be mixed with slightly more water than is needed for forming consistency. This is because some evaporation will occur both in storage and in *wedging*. In order to achieve proper control in the forming processes, the plastic clay must be perfectly uniform in consistency and free of air bubbles. Therefore, it must be thoroughly wedged (kneaded) before any of the forming methods described in this chapter can proceed. As illustrated in Figure 294, firm pressure from the heel of the hand compresses the clay and forces air pockets to the surface. This is accomplished with a rocking motion and with a slight twist at the end of the action. The resulting spiral eventually exposes all portions of the clay mass and

opposite : 292. WARREN MacKENZIE, U.S.A. Vase. Porcelain with clear glaze, height 14″. The finger marks and slight irregularities add spontaneity to this vase, which might have been dull if it had been thrown mechanically.

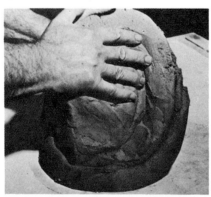

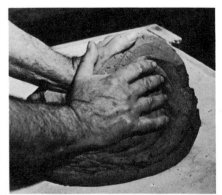

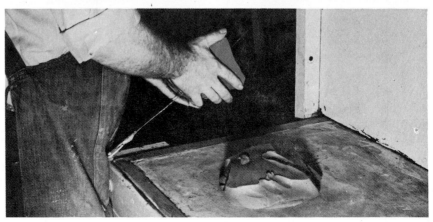

left: 293. DON FINEGAN, U.S.A. Planter. Thrown and hand-built stoneware with glaze and polyester resin, height 18″.

294. In wedging, the plastic clay is kneaded with the fingers and the heel of the hand in a rocking spiral motion (*below*, *left* and *right*). A wedging table (*bottom*) can also be used.

allows the trapped air pockets to escape. Proper wedging is vital, for if any air bubbles remain in the clay after it has been wedged and formed, the finished piece may very well explode in the kiln.

Occasionally the potter will have two batches of clay that are of a slightly different composition or moisture content. The process of wedging them into a uniform body can be hastened by first cutting the clay into thin sections with a wire and then forcibly throwing the sections edgewise onto a plaster wedging table. After a few such operations, the clay can be kneaded in the usual manner.

The Pinch Pot

The pinch method is perhaps the easiest way of forming a small bowl, and it requires no apparatus whatever (Figs. 295–298). A hollow is formed with the thumb in a small ball of clay. With careful pressure between the fingers, the wall is gradually thinned, and the form is developed. If the clay is too moist, the piece will sag, while a stiff clay will crack excessively. By pressing the fissures together and smoothing with the fingers, any small cracks can be healed. It is not a good practice to use water on the surface in an attempt to seal cracks in too-dry clay. Instead, one should soak the clay, knead it into a ball, and begin again. Legs or a coiled foot can be added when the piece is leather hard (see p. 195).

296. The wall is gradually thinned, and the form develops.

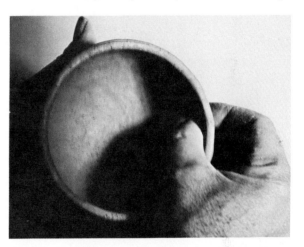

297. The interior is smoothed with the thumb to heal cracks.

295. A hollow is formed with the thumb in a ball of clay.

298. A coiled foot rim is added to the completed pot.

The Hump Mold

Solid plaster of paris molds of various shapes can be used to form a vessel (Figs. 299–301). Plastic clay is pounded or rolled with a rolling pin to the desired thickness on a piece of light canvas. The resulting slab is then draped over the mold and pressed to conform to it. The excess clay is trimmed away. If a moistened paper towel is shaped smoothly over the mold, the clay form, after drying slightly, can be removed without sticking. The hump mold process, while hardly creative, is a good beginning project, especially for children, who need a bit of early success to maintain their interest. In a summer camp, rounded beach stones are a readily available source of varied and interesting forms (Fig. 302).

299. A slab of clay is draped over the mold and pressed down.

300. Moist paper towels separate the clay from the mold.

301. Decorative additions are applied to the drying clay.

302. Rounded beach stones can make excellent hump molds.

The Coiled Pot

The coiling method, employed for thousands of years before the invention of the potter's wheel, has continued in use by many cultures until the present. Needing no equipment except a simple turning device, it is an ideal method for beginners. Since the potter's wheel produces only a symmetrical form, many contemporary ceramists have returned to the coil method—either alone or in combination with slab and wheel-thrown forms—because of the free sculptural constructions possible. In the past very large pieces have usually been coiled and later refined on a slow-turning wheel.

The technique is simple (Figs. 303–306). A round slab of plastic clay is pounded out to the desired size and thickness to form a base and then placed on a turning wheel with a plaster bat. A lump of plastic clay is squeezed into a ropelike form and rolled with the flat of the hand on a level surface. The clay should not be so moist that it sticks to the fingers or so dry that cracks develop. Slip can

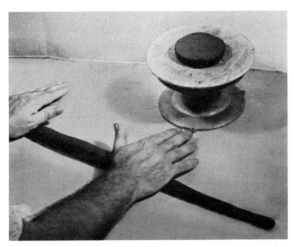

303. A rope of clay is rolled out to the desired thickness.

304. The first coil is laid upon the prepared slab base.

305. The coils are joined on the inside with a wiping motion.

306. The finished coil pot is smoothed with a metal scraper.

be used to join the coils, but it is a messy and time-consuming procedure; if the clay is of a proper consistency, no slip is needed. Not all forms are practical in the coil method. Flat, platterlike shapes can best be made from a slab on a plaster supporting mold, while small, symmetrical objects are more efficiently thrown on the wheel. However, coarse, groggy clays, which are almost impossible to throw, can be coiled.

Unless a piece is exceptionally large, it is usual to roll out a coil long enough to lay about three circles on the base. The coils are joined inside and out with a vertical wiping motion of the fingers. Squeezing or pinching should be avoided, for either will stretch and distort the form. The inside must be smoothed as the coiling proceeds, but as long as the coils are completely joined, a perfect outer surface is not needed. When the form is finished it can be refined with a flexible scraper, and applied, pressed, or carved decorations can be added.

Some shapes will sag if they are coiled too rapidly, so it may be necessary to let a portion of the work dry slightly (with the top edge protected by a damp rag) before continuing to build up the form. Interrupted work can be covered with a plastic bag to prevent its becoming too stiff, for if the clay dries beyond the leather-hard state, damp coils cannot be

applied, nor can handles and other additions be made. When work is resumed on a partially dried piece, the topmost joint must be scored (roughened and slashed with a sharp tool) and slip applied to facilitate joining. The finished piece is covered with plastic or placed in a damp box to allow moisture content to equalize, for otherwise cracks will develop. If it is dried in the open air, small appendages, such as handles, should be wrapped in damp paper toweling to prevent too-rapid drying.

Thick Coil and Paddle

A variation on the coil method is the paddled pot (Figs. 307–312). In this technique the heavy coil shape should be tall and narrow, for paddling stretches the clay. A curved block of wood is held against the inside of the pot for support, while the outside is struck repeatedly with a wooden paddle to thin and shape the coils. The paddle may be textured or wrapped with cord to prevent sticking. The coils should be of a slightly stiffer clay than is used for normal coiling. It is possible to pull the form in, but not so much as on the wheel. Smaller coils can be used to complete the form, and applied or carved decoration added later.

307. Thick coils are laid upon a prepared slab base.

308. A curved piece of wood and a paddle shape the form.

309. The walls have been thinned by beating with a paddle.

310. The exterior surface of the finished pot is smoothed.

311. Small coils are added at the top to form a rim.

312. Carved and applied decorative textures are added.

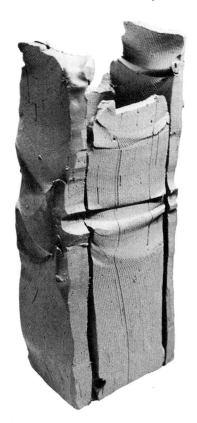

The Slab Pot

In addition to the very simple mold-draped form described at the beginning of this chapter, many other forms can be made by the slab method (Pl. 14, p. 159; Figs. 313–314). The slab can be pounded with the heel of the hand or rolled to the desired thickness with a common kitchen rolling pin (Figs. 315–320). To prevent the clay from sticking, it should be rolled out on a piece of canvas, which also allows for easy transfer. A dry plaster slab or grog dusted on a table top will serve the same purpose. If the proposed form is rather flat, the clay pieces must be leather hard before assembly begins. The joints should be scored and covered with clay slip. Since flat, horizontal sections tend to sag in construction and firing, it may be advisable to insert clay partition walls. These must have cut-out openings to allow for drying.

above : 313. STEPHEN POLCHERT, U.S.A. Bottle. Slab-built stoneware with thrown additions, height 36″.

below : 314. ED TRAYNOR, U.S.A. *Slab Form.* 1969.

right : 315. A clay slab is rolled out with a rolling pin.

below right : 316. The ends are scored and joined.

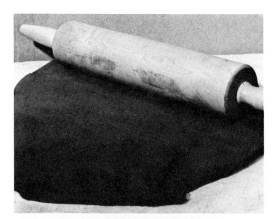

317. The upper edge of the slab is scored with a tool.

318. A carved slab is added to form the top of the pot.

319. Spouts and legs can be thrown or pinched separately.

320. Decorative lines are incised in the finished piece.

Throwing on the Wheel

People generally think of wheel-thrown ware when they speak of pottery. For most potters, throwing is the most enjoyable aspect of the ceramic craft. Coaxed by the skillful fingers of the experienced potter, an expanding form seems to acquire a life of its own. One must learn to throw quickly and efficiently, for clay softens and sags from the water used in the throwing process. Throwing, when done by an experienced craftsman, looks deceptively easy, and the beginning potter should not be discouraged by his initial difficulties and failures, or let himself be put off by virtuoso, "show-off" demonstrations, often staged for students, in which the spinning form is made to change rapidly from one shape to another. This may make a good show at a crafts fair, but it is not useful instruction for the novice potter. To develop skill at throwing on the wheel demands much practice, even for the experts.

The first task for the student is to learn to throw the largest piece possible from the ball of clay on hand. He should have in mind a rough idea of the form he wishes to achieve, and each change in shape should be directed toward this end. Every form begins with a cylinder, but the proportions of the cylinder will depend upon the final shape desired. For example, a bowl shape requires a low cylinder with a thick lip, so that the rim can be expanded; it must be taller than the finished size that is wanted, for as the form is pulled outward, it will settle.

In throwing a tall vase or bottle the potter should not try to develop the desired form with thick walls and then attempt to make them thinner. Instead, he should throw a cylinder to the maximum height possible; neck in the top if necessary, allowing room for the hand or arm; flare out the bottom and mid-section to the desired shape and thickness; then quickly pull in the top and finish the rim. Speed is essential, for the longer one works on the neck area, the more the bottom sections will sag and settle.

In the beginning the student should confine himself to throwing simple cylinder shapes, as tall and as uniform as possible. Since the cylinder is the basis for all pottery forms, it is pointless to attempt anything else until this first step has been mastered.

As work progresses, the student should concentrate on throwing a series of similar forms, discarding the bad ones (Fig. 321). He will thus develop naturally both technique and a feeling for design. Designing forms on paper is of little use to the beginner. Only when he acquires a feeling for a clay form and a knowledge of what forms can or cannot be thrown conveniently will a meaningful design evolve.

By working with one particular form for a while the student will learn to sense subtle variations, to which earlier he was oblivious. With practice he will throw taller and thinner shapes from the same amount of clay and, eventually, will develop a dynamic quality in his throwing that comes with greater freedom and ease in handling the clay. It is a poor practice for the student to attempt to throw a different shape each time, for he thus learns nothing from previous errors and misses the most natural method of developing form and design.

Centering

Perfect centering on the wheel is essential to the success of any thrown form (Figs. 322–326). A clay ball is placed on a freshly moistened bat, and, with the wheel turning, the clay is forced down with the right hand. Bracing the elbows at the sides will increase strength and accuracy in centering. When the clay has been centered perfectly, it is opened out with the thumbs into a thick bowl shape.

321. Facility in throwing is attained by throwing a number of similar shapes and then discarding the awkward ones.

322. A ball of plastic clay is placed on a freshly moistened plaster bat.

323. While the wheel is turning, the clay is forced down.

324. With his elbows braced, the potter centers the clay.

325. When centered, the ball is opened with the thumbs.

326. The clay ball is gradually opened into a bowl shape.

327. The clay must be perfectly centered on the wheel.

328. With the hands joined, the cylinder is pulled up.

329. If the rim is uneven, it can be trimmed with a needle.

330. The walls are thickened and pulled up by necking.

right : 331. Even pressure forces the clay wall upward.

The Cylinder

As with any other form, the throwing of a cylinder begins with the clay perfectly centered on the wheel. With the hands joined for better control, the walls are gradually pulled up to form a cylinder. If the top is uneven, it can be cut off with a needle. The walls can be thickened and pulled up by necking (drawing in gently at the neck of the cylinder). Even pressure forces the wall upward (Figs. 327–331).

Plate 14. KENNETH GREEN, U.S.A. Lidded vessel. Slab-built stoneware with stamped and carved decoration, Barnard slip under a mat dolomite glaze; height 13 ½″.

Plate 15. JOHN MASON, U.S.A. *Cross.* Height 5′. The size, the stark geometric quality, and the vivid color all contribute to the excitement and impact of this piece.

332. Pressure from the inside flares out the cylinder.

333. The top of the cylinder is necked in and thickened.

334. The top is pulled up farther, and the walls are thinned.

335. Thinning continues until the desired height is reached.

right : 336. The lip is finished with a soft leather.

The Bottle Form

To create a bottle form, the potter begins with a cylinder thrown as in Figures 327 to 331. This cylinder is flared out by pressure from the inside, and the top is necked in and thickened. The top is then pulled up and thinned. This process is repeated until the desired shape or height is reached. Finally, the lip of the bottle is finished with a piece of soft leather (Figs. 332–336).

The Bowl Shape

From the basic clay form begun as in Figure 326, any number of shapes can be made. The bowl presents the fewest problems (Figs. 337–340). As always, the opened ball must be perfectly centered. The potter should throw as quickly as possible, for otherwise the clay will become too wet. The clay should not be pulled too thin where it flares up from the bat, and the concave form must be maintained as the walls are pulled up, for any flatness of the curve will cause the piece to sag. Unevenness in the outer rim is trimmed with a needle, then the rim is moistened and finished with a piece of soft leather.

337. The centered clay is opened to form a bowl shape.

338. The walls are carefully pulled up and thinned.

right : 340. The rim is finished with a soft leather.

339. Unevenness in the rim is trimmed with a needle.

341. A rib is used to thin the wall and smooth the surface.

342. The knuckle can be used to lift and shape the form.

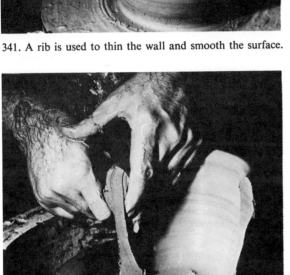
343. Hands are interlocked, and the knuckle exerts pressure.

344. As the form rises, the knuckle and hand thin the walls.

right : 345. Pressure is exerted from inside and outside.

A slightly different technique is illustrated in Figures 341 to 345. A rib (a flat oval of hardwood) is used to thin out the wall and smooth the surface. Since the pressure is concentrated, it creates less torque and not as much water is needed as when working with the fingers alone. Use of the knuckle is common in the preliminary shaping of a form and when throwing larger pieces. The partially cut-away forms (Figs. 343, 345) illustrate how the clay is both thinned and pulled up in the forming process.

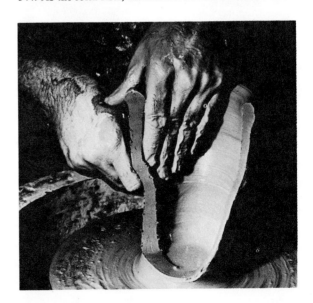

left : 346. A small piece is cut from the wheel with a wire.

below : 347. After cutting, the pot is lifted from the wheel.

Problems in Throwing

An initial error many students make is to start with a clay ball that is too soft, too stiff, or improperly wedged. It takes considerable pressure and ample water to center the ball on the wheel head. Only when the ball is perfectly centered should it be opened with the thumbs. To do otherwise will create an uneven wall thickness, which usually results in the eventual collapse of the piece.

As throwing progresses excess water will cause the clay to soften too rapidly. The slurry that forms on the hands should not be washed off but used on the pot as a lubricant. Some potters use a thin slip instead of water. The walls should be pulled up evenly without deep finger grooves, which may create a weak spot in the wall. In throwing large pieces a sponge can be used to eliminate the grooves that are caused by firm pressure on the large mass of clay.

The palms and fingers are used when centering or when necking in a large vase or bottle, but for normal throwing only the fingertips are required. They create a greater pressure with less friction and are more sensitive in revealing the action of the clay. Whenever possible one elbow is braced at the side and the thumbs are joined for better support.

It is important that the inside curve of the pot be formed when the cylinder is quite low, for it is impossible to shape it easily when the walls are higher. The clay should not flare out at the wheel head but should be pulled up as the cylinder rises. Students often leave this base section too thick.

Throwing Aids

While large bowls must be thrown on a plaster bat and trimmed later, most pieces can be thrown more conveniently on the metal wheel head, then cut off with a twisted wire (Figs. 346–347). A hinged, adjustable pointer is a handy guide for throwing sets (Fig. 348). Small pieces, such as egg cups (Figs. 349), are best thrown "off the hump" (a 50-pound ball of clay). To remove the thrown form from the mass of

348. A pointer assists in making a number of uniform pieces.

349. Small pots and cups can be thrown "off the hump."

350. With the wheel turning, a string cuts the pot free.

351. Excess clay is trimmed from the foot of the pot.

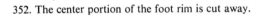

352. The center portion of the foot rim is cut away.

clay, the potter cuts a groove at the bottom and inserts one end of a piece of string. With the wheel revolving slowly, the string cuts through the pot at its base (Fig. 350).

Trimming the Foot

Excess clay on the bottom of a thrown form can be trimmed while the pot is still on the wheel head. Small pieces are cut off with a twisted wire immediately after throwing. Larger pots are allowed to dry slightly, cut off the bat with a ground-down hacksaw blade, then trimmed as illustrated in Figures 351 and 352. A needle will serve to indicate the bottom thickness.

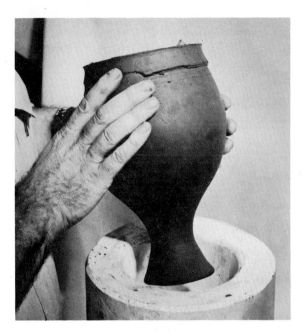

353–354. A large piece can be trimmed by setting the neck inside a plaster cylinder.

Small bottles can be trimmed by setting them inside a large-mouthed glass jar, which is held in position on the wheel head by a coil of clay. For larger pieces a hollow plaster form serves the same purpose (Figs. 353–354). After trimming, large bowls should be placed upside-down on a flat surface to dry evenly and to avoid warping.

The Foot and Lip

Because of the emphasis on form as a whole, the details of the foot and lip are often neglected. The most common error is to make the base area too large, thus imparting a heavy and clumsy feeling to the pot, which, instead, ought to suggest a form in space, resting lightly on its foot rim (Fig. 355).

It is quite satisfactory for a small, functional pot to have a flat base, showing the slight ridges left by the cutting wire. Generally, however, the center of the base is trimmed out with a looping tool (Fig. 352) in order to lighten this area, as well as to give a feeling of the continuing curve of the form. There are many types of foot rims—low and high, thin and broad, flat and delicate—and the kind that is used should relate to and complement the character of the pot form (Fig. 356). The foot rim may be the result of the trimming operation, or, in the case of a high foot, it may be a cylinder thrown separately and joined to the pot with slip. Because the potter's name is usually incised or stamped here, and also because it is an inconspicuous area, most pot lovers look immediately at the foot for what it reveals about the attitude and craft of the potter. Regardless of the type of foot that is used, the base of the pot should be perfectly smooth and have a slight bevel at the edges.

A small pot can have a simple, rounded rim, but a larger piece may appear weak without some accent at the lip. Apart from esthetic considerations, a slight thickening is desirable to strengthen the rim, to reduce warpage in drying, and, in the case of a very large bowl, to make lifting more convenient. Unfortunately, we can too easily become creatures of habit and, during a day's throwing, put a similar rim on all our pots. It is far better to analyze the form as it develops and plan the rim to harmonize with the total design. Occasionally just a finger depression in a flat rim or a simple impression from a roller will add distinction and emphasis.

Covers, Handles, and Spouts

Teapots and covered jars present a greater problem in design and technique, for the various parts must be thrown separately but form a unified whole when assembled (Fig. 357). This is one instance when it is desirable to make a few sketches beforehand in order to develop the form of the cover and its relationship to the body. In the case of a teapot, the type of handle and its balance with the spout should be worked out in advance.

Commercial teapots are slip cast in one piece, and the model is carved from a solid block of plaster. Students, unfortunately, tend to be influenced by such industrial products. A much more exciting and individual form will result if the character of the clay and the imprint of the finger are revealed in the joining of handles and spouts, rather than having them modeled and sponged to an impersonal smoothness.

It is imperative that the vessel and the cover be thrown at the same time and of clay with a similar moisture content. Accurate measurements should be taken with a caliper and the cover thrown to

above left: 355. HARRISON MCINTOSH, U.S.A. Compote. Stoneware with blue-green and black glazes, height 6½″.

left : 356. ANGELO GARZIO, U.S.A. Oval vase. Stoneware. In this vase, as in the compote by Harrison McIntosh, the treatment of the lip and foot is in perfect accord with the form and the decoration of the entire piece.

below : 357. ANGELO GARZIO, U.S.A. Teapot. Stoneware with rust glaze. The spout and handle are sensitively balanced.

size (Fig. 358). There can be no trimming on the rim, because drying rates are so different that a proper fit would be most unlikely.

There are many types of covers. Perhaps the easiest to make is a flat disk form with a knob thrown in place. The cover must be slightly thicker than needed, so the round rim can be formed with a soft leather. If the lid is small, it can be cut off the wheel with a twisted wire; larger lids are thrown on a plaster bat and allowed to dry slightly before removal. When a flat cover is used, the vessel must have a depressed inner flange, which can be used as a chuck (an edge support) when trimming the underside of the lid.

A domed cover is thrown like a simple dish or bowl (Fig. 359). After trimming, a knob can be thrown on top or a modeled knob can be attached with slip. A teapot lid is also thrown like a dish, with enough clay left on the rim to create a deep flange that will prevent the cover from falling out when the teapot is in use.

Teapot handles, like covers, take many forms. Pulled clay or hollow thrown handles are quite satisfactory, but the most common are made of bamboo or cane and attached to two or three clay loops on the pot. The loops must be sturdy and affixed securely to the pot, with an ample opening for the cane. Dry cane can be purchased in many

left : 358. The measurement for the lid of a pot must be perfectly accurate. A caliper is used to determine exact size.

hobby shops. It must be soaked overnight in water and then boiled for several hours. After the appropriate length is determined, half of the cane is cut away on the ends that are to fold over the clay loops. Nails driven into a board will assist in bending it to the desired curve. When dry, the cane is inserted into the loops, and the ends are whipped.

A teapot spout must be thrown at the same time as the body and cover, and the base must be broad enough and long enough to allow for loss of length in fitting it to the pot (Fig. 360). The pieces are joined as soon as the teapot is trimmed and while the spout base is damp enough to be pinched rather than cut to fit the pot. Strainer holes should be ample in size, because some filling with glaze is likely. A strainer placed low on the pot is less apt to become clogged with tea leaves. The spout should reach to the height of the teapot rim and be rather sharp in profile at the pouring edge, since a

below : 359. CHARLES LAKOFSKY, U.S.A. Jar with domed cover. White porcelain with light gray to pearly blue-violet glaze, height 7″. Adding a knob to this cover would have been redundant and would detract from the form and decoration.

left : 360. A spout must be thrown at the same time as the pot, so that both pieces will dry at the same rate.

361. Pitcher spouts are formed with a wiping motion.

362. A pulled handle is made by impressing with the thumb.

rounded edge is bound to drip. If a sharp edge on the pouring lip is not feasible, a small groove cut in it and left unglazed will also discourage dripping. A large spout is not necessary for proper pouring and may give an awkward appearance to the teapot or pitcher. Pitcher spouts are formed as in Figure 361 with a simple wiping motion of the fingers.

A properly pulled handle, revealing as it does the fluid quality of clay and the impression of the fingers, adds a note of spontaneity to any pot (Fig. 362). The clay must be very plastic but a little stiffer than that used in throwing. Starting with a thick coil of clay and ample water, the potter extends the clay with a stripping motion of the fingers and thumb, gradually thinning it to a diameter natural and comfortable to hold. The heavy upper section is pinched off, and the remaining butt end pressed firmly against a roughened area of the pot. The clay is flared around the joining for maximum support. After the proper curve is formed, the bottom of the handle is attached to the pot. The finger marks created in joining can be left if desired. Beginners invariably take too long to complete this process, and the clay handle becomes soft. If this happens, the butt end can be stuck on a shelf edge to dry slightly before joining. Smaller handles, such as those on mugs, can be attached directly to the pot and pulled in place.

New Techniques

Relatively few changes have occurred in ceramic techniques over the centuries, although attempts at refining methods and materials are made continually. For several years the Kansas potter Sheldon Carey has tried to find an acceptable substitute for water in the throwing process, one that eliminates the inevitable softening of the clay. The most successful of the many substances tried is Separan 20, a synthetic material manufactured by the Dow Chemical Company of Midland, Michigan. About 2 percent of this granular material is dissolved in hot water. The clay ball is centered with water, and throwing proceeds in the customary manner, with a small amount of Separan used as a lubricant. Since the clay does not soften, very thin walls can be thrown. This technique is especially suited to porcelain, which is much less plastic than ordinary throwing clay. It is not recommended for the beginner but could be of use to the experienced potter.

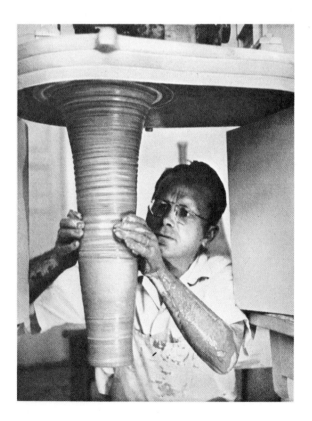

The Separan solution cannot be kneaded into the clay, for it is rather oily and will make the clay nonplastic. Hands are best cleaned with a plastic choreboy, rather than a sponge.

Another innovation by Sheldon Carey is an "upside-down" wheel (Fig. 363). The wheel is attached to a heavy shaft so that it can be raised and reversed after the basic cylinder is begun. As the illustration reveals, extremely tall cylinders and bottles can be thrown with this device. An air bubble, however, is disasterous, for the whole pot will collapse.

A further aid to the experienced potter is the inclusion of 1-inch lengths of fiber glass kneaded into the clay body. This should be done just before throwing. By increasing the strength of the clay one can throw flaring forms, such as bowls, much larger and with a thinner wall. Since the fiber is of a silica composition, it melts in firing with no apparent change in the clay body.

CERAMIC SCULPTURE

Terra cotta sculpture can be constructed in many ways (Pl. 15, p. 160; Figs. 364–365). The clay body should contain at least 20 percent grog to reduce shrinkage in firing and to allow for more rapid drying of thick sections.

If the form is relatively simple, such as a small, blocky figure or a head study, it can be modeled solid. When it has dried slightly, it is cut into two or more sections with a fine wire, and these sections are hollowed out to form walls of a uniform thickness. Then the joints are scratched and coated with slip, and the whole structure is reassembled.

Elongated forms or figures are usually constructed from hollow clay sections modeled over wooden dowels or fiber tubes. Surface additions are made after the structure has been assembled (Fig. 366). A continuous air passage must be provided to allow for uniform drying and to avoid an explosion in firing. Protruding forms will usually

left : 363. The " upside down " wheel for throwing very tall forms was developed by SHELDON CAREY.

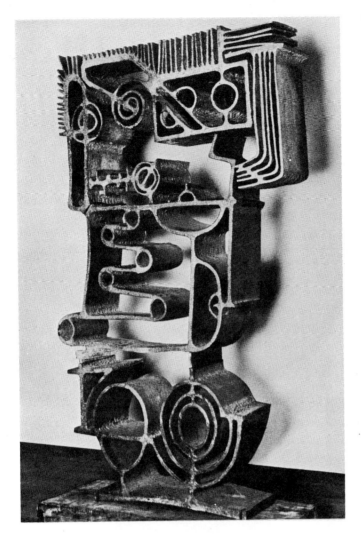

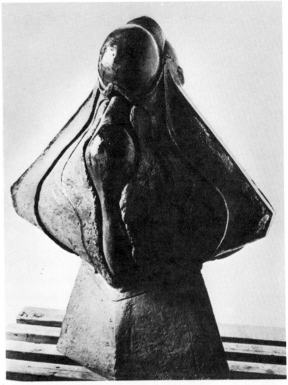

above left : 364. DIRK HUBERS, U.S.A. *Figure*. Medium high-fire clay (fired in several sections), height 6'.

above right : 365. JERRY ROTHMAN, U.S.A. Sculptural form. Hand-modeled clay with red and green glazes, height 30".

right : 366. TOM SOUMALAINEN, U.S.A. *Reinvention of Tula*. Slab and modeled clay, reduction fired; height 4'2". Collection Mr. and Mrs. Ira Julian, Winston-Salem, N.C.

below : 367. EARL HOOKS, U.S.A. *Fruit Forms*. Wheel-thrown and hand-molded clay with white mat-satin glaze, diameter 16″. Collection Fisk University, Nashville, Tenn.

right : 368. DANIEL RHODES, U.S.A. *Stoneware Form*. Stoneware and fiber glass, height 48″.

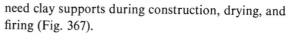

need clay supports during construction, drying, and firing (Fig. 367).

Fiber glass fabric, like that used in boat repairs, is helpful in adding strength to the clay during construction (Fig. 368). For use in slab pieces, the fiber must have an open mesh like a common window screen. The fiber glass is cut to size and placed on a rolled-out slab; then a thin layer of softer plastic clay is worked across the fabric to join it to the slab. Fiber glass gives a remarkable stiffness to the clay, allowing the construction of forms that would

369–371. Sculptor Narendra Patel has experimented with several methods of modeling over a styrofoam core.

right : 369. Clay slip is brushed onto the styrofoam surface.

center : 370. The completed sculpture is allowed to dry slowly.

bottom : 371. Vermiculite provides support for the hollow sculpture when the styrofoam is drained out through a hose.

otherwise be very difficult. If the clay is not too stiff, there is also a certain amount of "give" to the material, which permits some manipulation of the form. As mentioned earlier, fiber glass, when cut into 1-inch pieces, separated, and kneaded into the clay, will also increase the wet strength of clay used in slab, coil, and throwing techniques.

Sculptors accustomed to the usual methods of modeling clay upon a wood or metal armature are always frustrated by the need to model hollow if the form is to be dried and fired. Several new materials, if carefully used, eliminate this problem. The commercial insulating material, styrofoam, can be used as a core around which to model the clay. It is available in different shapes and sizes, which can be cemented together to create an armature. The form of the sculpture should be realized rather completely before the application of the clay. A clay slip brushed on the styrofoam surface will cause the plastic clay to adhere to the armature as the form is modeled (Fig. 369). The completed piece (Fig. 370) is allowed to dry slowly until the first crack occurs, at which time the crack is carefully filled with stiff clay. A small hole is then cut in the top of the figure, and a styrofoam solvent is poured in. If the piece is small, it can be upended when the styrofoam is completely dissolved, but for a large construction a small hole is made near the base to permit the dissolved liquid to run out. The studio must be well ventilated, because the mixture is quite volatile. When the sculptural form is such that the removal of the armature might cause the partially dried clay to deform, a hollow box can be placed around it and filled with vermiculite to furnish support (Fig. 371). A small rubber hose is used to drain off the dissolved styrofoam. The piece is then allowed to dry completely, and firing proceeds as usual.

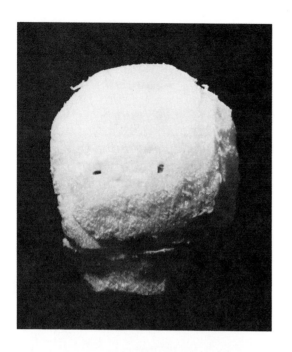

The Wisconsin sculptor Narendra Patel has experimented with several types of combustible armatures. The method illustrated uses a styrofoam core (Fig. 372). This is covered with a layer of cellulose sponge (Fig. 373), which compresses as the modeled clay form shrinks. The sponge is coated with clay slip, and, when dry, this creates a base for modeling the form (Fig. 374). If the layer of sponge is sufficient, the completed sculpture will dry and shrink without cracking. The core material burns out in firing.

372–374. When used as a base for modeling sculpture, styrofoam can also be burned out during the firing.

left : 372. A rough styrofoam core is cemented together.

below left : 373. Cellulose sponge covers the styrofoam.

below : 374. When the piece is fired, the styrofoam burns off.

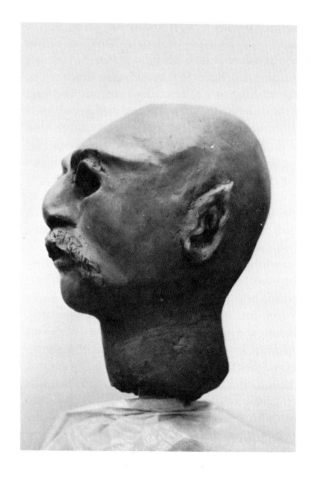

375. JOHN MASON, U.S.A. Sculptured wall mural. 1964. Black and brown stoneware, 7 × 14′. The exciting plastic and textural qualities of this mural provide a great contrast to the cast concrete of the architecture.

ARCHITECTURAL CERAMICS

When one considers the drab, factorylike atmosphere of many contemporary buildings, it would seem logical that the ceramic mural—with its possibilities of color, texture, and durability—would be relatively popular (Figs. 375–379). Its use abroad is much more common than in the United States. The customary requirement in many European countries that a certain percentage of the construction costs of public buildings be spent for art works is a factor in the widespread use of murals. A less fortunate situation prevails in America, where most buildings are financed by speculators primarily concerned with the optimum utilization of space for the maximum return of profit on their investment. There are, nevertheless, a few innovative and imaginative architects and clients who are willing to commission ceramists.

The medium-size wall panel is no problem to the potter, either in conception or in relation to studio facilities. A large decorative pot demands the same attention for a central design motif and the use of textural patterns and color accents. However, a truly large mural must be conceived on a broad scale for it may have to "carry" effectively for several hundred feet. Perhaps just as important to the potter as the design aspect are the factors of sufficient kiln space and a large and efficient work area in which to lay out and complete the project.

left : 376. RUTH DUCKWORTH, U.S.A. Sculptured reliefs. Clay, height 11′. University of Chicago.

below : 377. Detail of Fig. 376, sculptured reliefs.

right : 378. JERRY ROTHMAN, U.S.A. Sculptured triptych. Brick-red stoneware, height 8′ (figures later glazed black).

below : 379. JERRY ROTHMAN, U.S.A. Sculptured wall reliefs (detail). Clay with red, green, and blue glazes, height 8′.

6 Ceramic Form and Design

The examples of ceramics from the past illustrated in Chapters 1 and 2 are unquestionably a source of interest and inspiration for all students, reflecting as they do the efforts of countless generations of potters. There is a danger, however, in uncritically accepting them as models to emulate. When social and economic conditions change, the function of ceramics within a culture also changes. Much of the variety found in historical ceramics is the result of the different needs experienced by the cultures that produced them.

In this respect our own era is drastically unlike earlier periods. Technological advances have produced glass, metal, fiber, and plastic containers, completely eliminating the need for many of the standard forms. Never again will man make the huge earthenware oil containers of the Minoans or the stoneware storage crocks of Colonial America (Fig. 106). Nor is it likely that a modern aristocracy will collect, as status symbols, delicately decorated luster-ware plates, as did the Islamic caliphs (Fig. 47).

The Industrial Revolution, which began to change the basis of pottery making as early as 1750, severed the age-old pattern by which form and design, nurtured by a local market, evolved in the transition from father to son. With no guidance from the past, the contemporary potter is most eclectic, absorbing influences from hither and yon. Many theories have been proposed regarding ceramic design, and they serve a comforting and guiding role, much as did the older traditions. But like all theories, they can become self-defeating if applied in a didactic manner.

FORM AND FUNCTION

A generally accepted tenet of contemporary design is that the *form* of an object is largely dictated by its *function* (Fig. 381). About this there can be little debate, for if a spout on a pitcher does not pour

opposite : 380. JOHN MASON, U.S.A. Sculptural form. 1963. Brown clay with polychrome glazes, height 5′. The different glazes and varied textural areas soften only slightly the almost brutal explosion of form.

well or if the handle on a vessel is difficult to hold or is in poor balance, the value of the entire design is in question, regardless of its appearance.

The importance of this observation is somewhat obscured by the diminished need for ceramic containers in our culture. In recent years ceramic pieces have tended to fill a decorative and sculptural role (Fig. 382), which is just as valid an expression of the material as were the earlier functional wares. This transition from pottery to sculpture has produced

above: 381. ANGELO GARZIO, U.S.A. Pitcher. Stoneware. The accents of spout and handle and the flaring rim add interest to this functional pitcher.

right: 382. CARL PAAK, U.S.A. Sculptural pot. Clay with gray and cobalt glazes, height 25″. The assembled sections in this sculpture create a compatible organic unity.

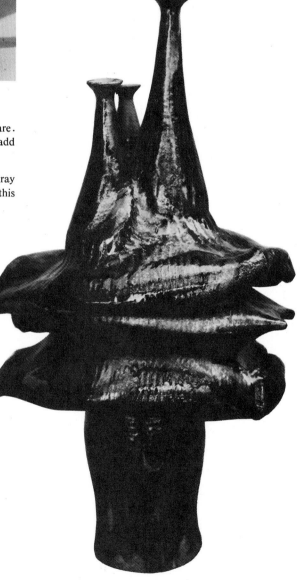

many decorative works embellished with nonfunctional spouts and handles, a device that can be incongruous if not used with taste and skill.

There is a trend among some contemporary potters deliberately to make pots that are patently useless. This Pop Art or Dada approach has had the effect of shaking us loose from conventional design stereotypes. Its greatest value is usually in the idea it presents, rather than the resulting form. The "nonpots" of a less literary nature must be evaluated from a sculptural rather than a pottery standpoint (Fig. 383). The major problem facing the ceramist who works in this idiom is his inability to free himself completely from the standard pottery forms. Once the line between a decorative pot and a fully sculptural piece has been crossed, potlike elements remaining in the work may be distracting and spoil the effectiveness of the design.

MATERIAL AND METHOD

The inherent nature of clay imposes restraint on ceramic design much as do the requirements of function. Clay in either the plastic or the fired state has unique qualities that distinguish pottery from artifacts made of wood, metal, fiber, or glass. It is logical that these characteristics be stressed in the design development (Fig. 384). While a thrown clay form and a piece of blown glass have much the same

below left : 383. PHILLIP GEARHART, U.S.A. *Untitled.* 1969. Thrown and hand-built clay with cast bronze arm, height 25″. Although the social comment in this piece is of primary importance, the form is equally arresting.

below right : 384. DANIEL RHODES, U.S.A. Sculptural form. Stoneware and fiber glass, height 12″. The plastic form emerges from a cylinder, which functions as a base.

left : 385. DAVID SHANER, U.S.A. Planter. Hand-built clay with salt glaze. A rough textural quality in this large planter becomes the major decoration.

below : 386. WARREN MACKENZIE, U.S.A. *Four Vases (for a Gynecologist's Office)*. Porcelain with celadon glaze, height of largest vase 6″. The plasticity of these expanding forms has been skillfully enhanced by the pinching and distortion of the rims.

particularly satisfying medium for the designer. One is its plasticity—its ability to respond to the touch of the finger, to be stretched, impressed, incised, and added to with ease (Fig. 385). Another is its natural color and rough texture, which are often sufficient decoration, although the addition of glazes gives a new dimension of surface effect and color which may rival the attractiveness of the form itself. These two elements, form and surface decoration, must be in harmony in order for a ceramic design to the successful.

Of critical importance to the character of a ceramic piece is the forming method used. Ancient pottery was usually coil constructed, and this technique is still employed today for very large pieces, for groggy clay, or for asymmetrical forms. Not all

effect in terms of expanding volume, attempts to achieve in clay the thinness and translucency of glass would be unsuccessful. Similarly, metal has a strength that permits the construction of apparently fragile and protruding forms which would be impossible in clay. Lacking both transparency and tensile strength, clay has other qualities that make it a

above: 387. WILLIAM DALEY, U.S.A. Planter. Stoneware, reduced and unglazed; length 24″. The slab construction is uncompromisingly revealed.

right: 388. RON GILBERT, U.S.A. Hanging weed bottle. 1969. Slab-built stoneware with thrown spouts and mat gray glaze, height 13″. The decoration stresses the plastic, textural quality of clay.

thrown pieces reveal their origin by finger-impressed throwing rings, but they have in common the tensions of expanding plastic clay and a symmetrical form (Fig. 386). Slab constructions, by their angularity, are perhaps easiest to identify (Fig. 387). It is desirable that the forming method be revealed in a clear and straightforward manner, both for the integrity of the design and for a logical economy of time and effort. It is most often pointless to laboriously coil and refine a hand-built form that might more easily be thrown on the wheel. The plastic quality of clay, which readily permits addition, encourages a combination of construction methods (Fig. 388). The contrast of expanding thrown form with angular slab can be a pleasing design element, but the potter must take care that the two elements of construction are in harmony, and not fighting each other for dominance.

ASPECTS OF CERAMIC FORM AND DESIGN

Aside from the dictates of function, and perhaps because of the unique qualities of clay, a tremendous variety of form is feasible in ceramics. The flexibility of techniques—coil, thrown, and slab or a combination of all three—permits the realization of nearly any conceivable form. A ceramic piece embodies, simultaneously, concepts of negative space and solid form. Because of the nature of the construction and firing processes, we know that every ceramic work, however heavy and solid it may appear, is hollow.

The perfect form, the sphere, when cut in half becomes a hemisphere or bowl, another esthetically pleasing form. But when we depart from these geometric absolutes, we find that some shapes are much more satisfying than others. This is because of our psychologically influenced perception. The human eye is attracted to a dominant form or color; if we are presented with two centers of interest, the effect is distracting, even psychically disturbing. A desire for order seems basic to human equilibrium.

The "stop sign" or "bull's eye" approach of advertising is useful in attracting attention, but there is little to hold the viewer after this initial and demanding contact. Pop Art, a style that began in England in the 1950s—but which, from the start, drew on such resources of American mass culture as advertising and the comic strip—had a great success in America through the 1960s and continues to

389. RUTH DUCKWORTH, U.S.A. Vase. Slab-built porcelain with crackle glaze and touch of iron oxide, height 6″.

390. THEODORE RANDALL, U.S.A. Punch bowl. Stoneware, diameter 23″. The unusual tripod feet provide a sense of lightness.

be influential (Pl. 16, p. 193). By exploiting the contemporary commercial, mechanized environment, Pop assimilates images as commonplace as flags, hot dogs, beer cans, and movie posters. In this, a new humanism or a return to recognizable forms and images, after decades during which modern art seemed to move relentlessly toward greater abstraction, has been claimed for the style. Often as amusing and trenchant in its commentary on modern experience as the biting, ironic subject matter of the paintings and prints produced by Hogarth in the eighteenth century, Pop, like Hogarth's work, is significant not only for its content but for the remarkable sureness of design and composition the Pop artists imposed upon their materials—ordinary, even debased, as the sources of Pop typically have been. Still, the billboard may be an all-pervasive element in American life, but its presence in the American living room in the form of Pop Art or Pop ceramics could be an uncomfortable one.

Geometric shapes—the sphere, the cylinder, the cone, the cube—have a strength and simplicity that make them complete in themselves. When we begin to stretch and elongate these stable forms, we develop a sense of movement (Fig. 389). Interest in a form is proportionate to the length of time needed for one's eye to travel over it, sense the movement of contours, the swelling of volumes, and enjoy subtle contrasts of color and texture. To sustain our interest, the contour must maintain this flow as the volume contracts or expands. A pot with a base and top that are similar in size or one with the greatest girth in the center is generally unsuccessful, for the equal division that results creates a feeling of monotony and little sense of movement. The most satisfying design is one conceived with a definite zest and sweep. Our senses react more favorably toward forms with unhesitant conviction of roundness or straightness, with no evidence of ambiguity. This does not rule out subtlety—only indecision.

Contrasts in the character of the form heighten our enjoyment; textural areas serve the same function, as they react against smoothly defined forms or surfaces. Elaborate embellishments and colorful glaze effects are best suited to rather simple shapes, for otherwise the form and decoration compete for attention. For the same reason a brilliant color, which might be overwhelming on a large vase, will be more satisfying on a small piece.

The foot rim and the lip of a pot are details often neglected by students. The tendency is for the base to become heavy and clumsy. Unless extreme stability is a functional necessity, the foot should serve as a pedestal for the pot, to give a feeling of form suspended in space (Pl. 17, p. 194; Fig. 390). In rare cases the shape of a pot is such that no evident

391. MARC HANSEN, U.S.A. Footed bowl. Stoneware with applied clay and brown slip under salt glaze, height 10″. The plastic decoration and throwing rings are clearly visible.

lip is necessary, but normally a thickening of the lip is desirable to strengthen the rim and to reduce warpage. Just as important is its function in closing the composition—terminating the upward movement of the form—and its role as a decorative accent.

SURFACE DECORATION

Ideally, decoration should be a part of, and inseparable from, the form, such as throwing rings or stamped and applied clay accents, which reveal the plastic nature of the clay in a simple, unobtrusive manner (Fig. 391). One of the advantages of a salt glaze is that applied and incised decorations are not obscured by the glaze but retain their crispness in a pleasing contrast to the smooth glazed surfaces. The character of a form largely determines the type of decoration that would be most effective. For example, the taut outline and idealized proportions of early Greek ware seem quite suited to repetative overall geometric patterns. By contrast, the vigorously thrown Sung forms are in perfect agreement with bold brush designs and incised slip motifs.

Intricate and delicate decoration such as was used on Islamic luster ware requires a simple and reserved form for success. These curvilinear designs in overall patterns complement the typical shallow bowl forms. Spotty panel designs of a realistic nature are usually distracting on a pottery piece, for they tend to monopolize the viewer's attention and thus overpower the form.

Skill with the brush is rather rare among contemporary Western potters (Fig. 392). It is not surprising that those cultures which traditionally have used the brush as a writing medium excel in this type of ceramic decoration. Even to make a simple bold stroke of color or slip across a plate in a way that will produce the effect of careless freedom requires a certain amount of practice. The novice potter often goes overboard, with glaze patterns that look like discarded paint cans, completely devoid of any accidental charm. But in the hands of an experienced craftsman, the chance running of a heavy glaze can become a type of decoration, intriguing because it reveals the viscous nature of glazes (Fig. 393).

above : 392. PAUL SOLDNER, U.S.A. Vase. Thrown
and compressed clay with lightly smoked raku glaze,
brushed iron engobe and sgraffito decoration;
height 10″.

right : 393. KAREN KARNES, U.S.A. Platter. Clay
with runny, overlapping glazes. Reduction brings
out the iron specks.

7 Decoration and Glazing

DECORATION

There can be no doubt that, in ceramics, creating a form is the most critical process, but the techniques of decoration and glazing must not be overlooked. As the final operation, the embellishment of a piece can be the deciding factor in its success or failure. Throwing must be accomplished with freedom and ease and must be expressive of the fluid, plastic quality of clay. The trimming and refining of a thrown form should not destroy this spontaneous quality. The throwing ridges left on the surface of a piece may well prove to be a more suitable decorative device than one that is laboriously contrived.

The decision about what decorating technique will be used should be made by the potter as soon as possible after the piece has been thrown, for there are certain types of decoration that must be undertaken while the clay is still plastic. The character of the thrown form will usually determine the type of decoration that is most suitable (Pls. 18–19, pp. 194, 211; Fig. 395). For example, a delicate brushwork is obviously out of place on a vigorously thrown, heavily grogged piece. It is essential that the decoration complement rather than overwhelm the form. As in all aspects of craftsmanship, practice is necessary to achieve freshness and fluency of execution.

Clay in a Plastic State

Immediately after removal from the wheel a pot can be pressed or pinched to change either its shape or its surface (Fig. 396). Figures 397 to 406 illustrate a few of the many possibilities for surface decoration of clay while it is still in the plastic state. These include scratching, incising, or cutting away with a tool. Sometimes additional clay is applied to form a raised design. Impressions can be made with various implements, with a cord or serrated roller, or with stamps fabricated from ceramic, plaster, and other materials (Fig. 407).

opposite : 394. HARRISON MCINTOSH, U.S.A. Covered jar. Clay with white mat glaze over dark engobe, height 10 ½″. The incised oval motifs echo the shape of the jar.

left : 395. DAN SCHAUMBURG, U.S.A. Vase. Stoneware, height 12″. Pinch marks in the plastic clay, an uneven poured glaze, and reduction specks produce a spontaneous decoration.

above : 396. DOROTHY PERKINS, U.S.A. Vase. Thrown stoneware, altered with the fingers, with thick slip; height 10″.

below and opposite page : 397–404. Incised and stamped decoration can be made with a number of simple devices or even with the fingers.

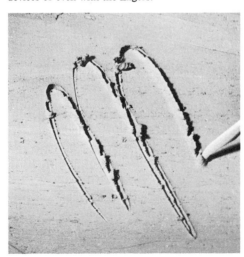

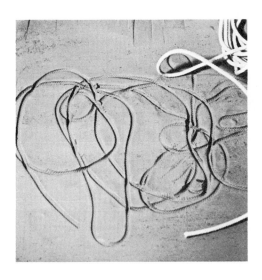 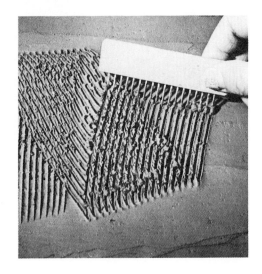

above : 405–406. Simple stamps are used to create repeat patterns.

left : 407. RICHARD PEELER, U.S.A. Bottle. Hand-built stoneware with stamped decoration and white engobe, glazed only with falling wood ash; height 14″.

Plate 16. ROY LICHTENSTEIN, U.S.A. *Head With Black Shadow*. 1965. Glazed ceramic, height 15″. Collection Mr. and Mrs. Leo Castelli, New York.

left : Plate 17. HARRISON MCINTOSH, U.S.A. Bottle. Stoneware with swirling decoration in red and black mat glazes, height 15 ¾″. Although contemporary, this bottle has an ancient, timeless quality.

below : Plate 18. KARL MARTZ, U.S.A. Bowl. Stoneware with iron-red decoration formed by a Japanese limestone glaze over brushed oxide, diameter 4 ½″.

Leather-hard Clay

The term *leather hard* refers to clay that has dried enough that it can be handled without deforming or suffering other injuries, but which contains sufficient moisture to permit handles and knobs to be readily joined and clay slips applied without flaking off. Carving and incising are more conveniently done at this stage, since the clay cuts cleanly and does not stick to the tool.

Sgraffito refers to a design produced by scratching through a layer of clay slip to expose the color of the clay body underneath (Fig. 408). Care must be taken that the slip is not too dry, for otherwise it will flake off; if it is too wet, the incision will be smudged.

Mishima is a decorative technique of Korean origin (Fig. 409). An incised area or line is filled with plastic clay of a contrasting color. When partially dried, the surface is scraped flush, revealing the design underneath (Fig. 410). A slip glaze can also be used effectively.

above : 408. Sgraffito designs are scratched through slip.

below : 409. ROBERT ECKELS, U.S.A. Bowl. Clay with mishima decoration in light clay on a dark body, diameter 10″.

right : 410. Scraping reveals the mishima decoration.

Slip trailing, using a syringe in the manner of a pastry bag, must be done before the ware has dried too much. The piece should be left in a damp room for a day after the design has been applied. Raised glaze decoration can be applied in a similar fashion (Fig. 411). This technique was popular in Colonial America and earlier in England (see p. 33).

Clay in the Dry State

Decoration on a clay surface that has dried is limited to application of engobes, coloring oxides, and stains. An *engobe* is clay slip to which feldspar, flint, and a flux have been added. These reduce the shrinkage of the engobe and increase adhesion when the ware is fired (see Appendix, p. 323).

Color oxides or stains are applied to dry clay in much the same way as one would paint a watercolor. Too thick an application will flake off or cause poor glaze adhesion. A small amount of the base glaze—or feldspar and bentonite—added to the colorant is desirable.

Wax-resist decoration generally is used in conjunction with coloring oxides (Fig. 412). The wax may be a hot paraffin or beeswax; more convenient water-soluble wax emulsions that need not be heated are now available. The wax design repels the applied stain, which then serves as a background color. Incised lines through the wax will absorb stain, thus producing a linear decoration that is difficult to achieve by other methods.

Glazes can be applied to some raw clays and fired in a single operation. The glazing must be done quickly to prevent uneven moisture absorption, which will cause cracks. Glazes with a high clay content, such as the Bristol type, work best for this process. Majolica decoration can be used on the raw glazed ware in the usual manner.

Clay in the Bisque State

The possibilities of decoration become much more limited after the pottery has been bisque fired.

above : 411. Glaze is slip trailed onto the clay surface.

below : 412. Color oxides are applied over a wax resist.

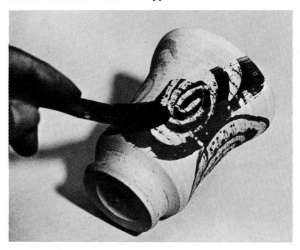

Engobe decoration can be brushed on if the clay content is low enough to reduce shrinkage and if sufficient fluxes are present to bind the engobe to the body when it is fired. It is much more convenient to apply such decoration in the leather-hard stage.

Sgraffito decoration can be applied to this kind of engobe or to a glaze. In order to execute a linear design with precision, the glaze or slip coating must not be too heavy; if it is too dry, it will flake off and leave a ragged incision. The purpose, of course, is to reveal the contrasting color of the clay.

Color oxides or stains are sometimes used as brush decoration or as an overall colorant either on a bisque body or on a glazed surface. Designs incised into plastic clay are generally brushed with oxides prior to glazing (Fig. 413). As a rule, brush decoration with oxides is more effective over a glaze, for underglaze designs on bisque ware may be obscured by an uneven glaze or damaged during application.

Wax-resist decoration is frequently used both under and over a glaze and in combination with stain and sgraffito designs. It has a tendency, however, to ball up when used on a sprayed glaze. A binder may be necessary even in a dipped glaze to provide a stronger decorating surface.

GLAZING

Glazing in the raw-clay state was mentioned briefly in the section on decoration. This method has definite advantages. By eliminating the normal bisque fire, there are savings not only in the labor needed for the extra stacking, unloading, and operation of the kiln but also in the fuel or power needed for the extra firing. A single firing also promotes a better union between the body and the glaze. There are, however, several disadvantages to the combined firing. Because of its fragility, the dry raw-clay vessel may be broken in handling. Expansions caused by the moisture absorbed into the dry clay may cause the vessel to crack. In general, only when the body of a piece is rather thick and uniform can

glaze be poured safely. Other pieces should be sprayed, since the glaze, with its troublesome moisture content, can then be applied at a slower rate. One additional precaution must be taken in glazing raw ware: alkaline fluxes must first be fritted. These compounds have a high coefficient of thermal expansion. When they are absorbed into the outer portion of the clay, their expansion and contraction rate during firing and cooling is so great in contrast to the remainder of the body that they will cause it to crack.

Glazing in the bisque state is the most common procedure (Fig. 414). Normally bisque ware is fired to about cone 010 or 1650°F (900°C). At this stage

left : 413. Color oxides are rubbed into an incised design.

above : 414. ROBERT ECKELS, U.S.A. Bottle. Stoneware with scratched motif, height 14″. After glazing, portions of the glaze were rubbed off to reveal the decoration and the contrasts between body color and glaze.

Glazing   197

415. In dip glazing the piece is plunged into a large pan of glaze and then quickly withdrawn.

416. Tongs are used for dip glazing small pieces or when overall coverage is desired.

the bisque is hard enough to be handled without mishap yet sufficiently porous to absorb glaze readily. Bisque ware that is fired at lower temperatures will absorb too much glaze; if fired too high, it is especially difficult to glaze, for the glaze tends to run off. An exception to the normal bisque firing is high-fire chinaware. Such pieces as thin teacups, which are fragile and likely to warp, are often placed in the kiln with supporting fireclay rings inside their lips, or they are stacked upside down and then fired to their maximum temperature. Later, these chinaware pieces are glazed and fired on their own foot rims at a lower temperature where warpage losses are much less.

How to Glaze

Glazing is a process that can be described only inadequately. Before the actual glazing operation takes place, there are a few precautions that must be taken. If bisque ware is not to be glazed immediately upon its removal from the kiln, it should be stored, if possible, where dust and soot will not settle on it. The bisque ware should not be handled

excessively, especially if the hands are oily with perspiration, for this will deter the glaze from adhering properly. All surfaces of the bisque ware should be wiped with a damp sponge or momentarily placed under a water tap to remove dust and loose particles of clay. The moisture added to the bisque ware by this procedure will prevent an excessive amount of glaze from soaking in and thus allow a little more time for glazing. Extra moisture also helps to reduce the number of air pockets and pinholes that form when the glaze dries too quickly on a very porous bisque. The amount of moisture required depends upon the absorbency of the bisque, the thickness of the piece, and the consistency of the glaze. Should the bisque-fire temperature accidentally rise much higher than cone 010, the ware should not be dampened at all. The glaze must be cleaned completely off the bottom of the pot and $\frac{1}{4}$ inch up the side as soon as it is dry enough to handle. Excess glaze will always run, so it is never advisable to allow a heavy layer of glaze to remain near the foot rim. The cleaning operation can be simplified by dipping the bottoms of bisque pots into a shallow pan of hot paraffin before glazing.

Dip glazing is probably the simplest glazing method. Its chief drawback is that a rather large amount of glaze is required. After the vessel has been cleaned and moistened with a damp sponge, it is plunged into a large pan of glaze (Fig. 415). It should be withdrawn almost immediately and shaken to remove the excess glaze. The object is then placed on a rack to dry, and any finger marks are touched up with a brush. Small-size pots can be dip glazed with metal tongs, which come in several shapes (Fig. 416). The slight blemishes in the glaze caused by the pointed tips usually heal in firing. A more uniform surface is produced if the glaze is thin enough to allow dipping two or three times within a few seconds.

Pouring requires less glaze than dipping, and the technique can be applied to a greater variety of shapes. For example, the insides of bottles and deep, vaselike forms can be glazed only in this manner.

In the case of a bottle, the glaze is poured through a funnel (Fig. 417), and then the vessel is rotated until all its surfaces are covered. The remainder is poured out, and the bottle is given a final shake to distribute the glaze evenly and to remove the excess (Fig. 418). Glazes that are poured or dipped must be a little thinner in consistency than those that are brushed on. The insides of bowls are glazed by pouring in a portion of the glaze, spreading it by rotating the bowl, and then pouring out the excess. This must be done rather quickly, or an overabundance or uneven amount of glaze will accumulate. To glaze the exterior of a bottle, the potter grasps it by either the neck or the foot rim and pours the glaze from a pitcher, allowing the extra to run off into a pan beneath. Finger marks are then touched up with a brush, and the foot rim is cleaned when dry. The outsides of bowls are glazed in the same manner, provided the foot is large enough to grasp. Otherwise the bowl can be placed

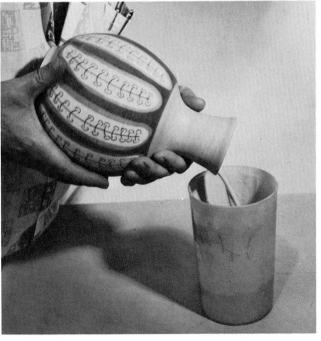

above : 417. Glaze is poured through a funnel to coat the interior of a bottle.

right : 418. The bottle is rotated to coat the entire inner surface, and extra glaze is poured off.

upside down on wooden dowels extending across a pan (Fig. 419). It is better to glaze the interior of a vessel first and the exterior later.

A brushed glaze (Fig. 420) is easiest for the beginner. It is also used for glazing large pieces that are difficult to pour or dip. A flat brush, at least 1 inch in width and possibly larger, is used. An oxhair bristle is preferred, for camel hair is much too soft and floppy. Unless a considerable amount of clay is in the glaze, the addition of bentonite or a gum binder is necessary for proper adhesion. The potter must work rapidly, using a full brush, and cover the piece with a second and third coat before the bottom layer is completely dry, for otherwise blisters will develop. The glaze must be neither too watery nor so thick that it will dry quickly and cause uneven laps and ridges.

Sprayed glazes permit subtle variations in color and more definite control over glaze thickness and coverage (Figs. 421–423). Actually, these advantages are more theoretical than real and apply more to the beginner than to the experienced potter. The finest Chinese glazes of the past, which we have difficulty in equaling today, were all dipped or poured. Gradations of color were achieved by blowing the color on separately through a lung-powered bamboo tube atomizer.

The spray method has two major drawbacks: large amounts of glaze are often wasted; and the glaze coating, because of its fragility, is easily damaged by handling during the process of loading the kiln. With practice smooth glazes can be poured, eliminating these disadvantages and saving time. In general, sprayed glazes are most satisfactory on flat, shallow bowls or for reglazing. Various effects can be achieved by grading one glaze into another and by toning down an underglaze with a second that may be more neutral or with a mat. When a viscous glaze covers one that tends to be runny, the underglaze may break through and run, causing a spotty decorative effect.

Because many glaze materials are toxic, glazes should be sprayed only in a booth with an adequate exhaust fan. In order to obtain an even layer, one should spray the glaze slowly, building up a coating with a soft, "woolly" surface. If the sprayed piece becomes too moist (Fig. 422), a shine may develop, blisters may form, and the glaze may run. In the latter event, the glaze will be uneven, regardless of how many more coats are applied. It may be advisable, under some conditions, to scrape off the glaze and begin again.

above : 421. Glaze is sprayed in a booth with an exhaust fan.

below : 422. Even coverage is vital in spray glazing.

Glaze Defects

There are usually several reasons, all logical, why a particular glaze fault occurs, but trying to deduce the cause from one piece may prove quite difficult. When there are a number of pots having the same glaze from a single kiln load or when there are several glazes on a single body, the problem of deduction is much easier. The following section outlines some of the factors that can cause glaze defects. Glaze faults may result not only from the composition of the glaze but from the improper selection or preparation of the clay body, faulty kiln operation, or, as is most frequently the case, lack of skill and care in application.

Defects Caused by the Body

1. A body that is too porous because of improper wedging, kneading, blunging, or pugging may cause small bubbles, beads, and pinholes to form in the glaze as the body contracts and the gases attempt to escape.

2. Excessive water used in forming the body can result in similar conditions.

423. The finished sprayed piece is allowed to dry.

3. A large amount of manganese dioxide used as a colorant in a body or slip may cause blisters to form in both the body and the glaze.

4. Soluble sulfates are contained in some clays and come to the surface in drying, forming a whitish scum. Pinholes and bubbles develop as these sulfates react with the glaze to form gases. This condition can be eliminated by adding up to 2 percent barium carbonate to the body. A slight reduction fire at the point when the glaze begins to melt will reduce the sulfates and allow the gas to pass off before the glaze develops a glassy retaining film.

5. If the body is underfired in the bisque and therefore very porous, it may absorb too much glaze. Soluble fluxes in the glaze, because of their higher thermal expansion and contraction rates, can cause the body to crack. In any case, a glaze applied to a very absorptive body could have a coarse, or even a sandpaperlike surface.

Defects of Application

1. Blisters or pinholes may result if the bisque ware has not been moistened slightly before glazing. The glaze traps air in the surface pores of the body.

2. Dust or oil on the surface of the bisque ware may cause pinholes or a scaly surface in the glaze.

3. If the glaze is applied too heavily, it will run and obscure the decoration, perhaps causing the pot to stick to the kiln shelves.

4. In addition to flowing excessively, glazes that have been applied too thickly will usually crack in drying. When the piece is fired, these cracks will not heal but will pull farther apart and bead at the edges. If the drying contraction is great enough, the adhesion of the glaze to the body will be weak, causing portions to flake off during the initial smoking period of the firing cycle.

5. On the other hand, a glaze application that is too thin will result in a poor, dry surface. This is especially true of mat glazes, which require a slightly thicker application than do glossy glazes.

6. If a second glaze coating is applied over a completely dry first coat, blisters will form. The wetting of the lower glaze layer causes it to expand and pull away from the body.

7. If the bisque ware is considerably cooler than the glaze at the time of application, bubbles and blisters may develop later.

8. Glazes high in colemanite should be applied immediately after mixing. If they are allowed to set, they thicken from the deflocculating effect of the colemanite. The extra water necessary to restore their consistency causes the glaze to separate and crawl in drying. The addition of .5 to 1 percent soda ash will retard the tendency of colemanite to thicken.

9. Bristol glazes require perfect surface application. Because of their viscosity, thin areas will pull apart and crawl when fired.

Defects Originating in Firing

1. If freshly glazed ware is placed in the kiln and fired immediately, the hot moisture will loosen the glaze from the body, causing blisters and crawling.

2. Too-rapid firing will prevent gases from escaping normally. They will form tiny seeds and bubbles in the glaze. For some especially viscous glazes, a prolonged soaking period is necessary to remove these gas bubbles.

3. Excessive reduction will result in black and gray spots on the body and glaze and will produce a dull surface.

4. Gas-fired kilns with poor muffles employing manufactured gas are troublesome to use with lead glazes. The sulphur content in the combustion gases will dull the glaze surfaces and possibly form blisters and wrinkles.

Defects in Glaze Composition

1. Glazes that are not adjusted properly to the body are susceptible to stresses that may cause the glaze, and at times even the body, to crack. If the glaze contracts at a slower rate than the body does in cooling, it undergoes compression. This causes the glaze to crack and, in places, to buckle and separate from the body. This defect is commonly known as *shivering*.

2. Slightly similar to shivering, and also caused by unequal contraction rates in cooling, is *crazing* of

the glaze. When this happens, the glaze contracts at a greater rate than the body, causing numerous cracks to form (see p. 210).

3. Glazes that run excessively at normal firing temperatures should be adjusted by the addition of kaolin to increase the refractory quality of the glaze or, if possible, by changing the bases. Those that have a lower molecular weight will be less fluid in the glaze melt.

4. A dull surface will result if the proportion of silica to alumina or barium is too low.

5. An excessive amount of tin, rutile, or colored spinels, which are relatively insoluble in the glaze, will also cause a dull or rough-surfaced glaze.

6. Bristol and colemanite glazes not fitted properly to the body will tend to crawl or to crack. This may be due in part to an excess of zinc, which has a very high contraction rate at greater temperatures.

7. Glazes ground too finely—thus releasing soluble salts from the frits, feldspar, and so forth— will develop pinholes and bubbles.

8. Glazes that are allowed to stand too long may be affected by the decomposition of carbonates, organic matter in ball clay, or gum binders. Gases thus formed can result in pinholes and bubbles in the final glaze. In some cases, preservatives like formaldehyde will help. If washed, dried, and reground, the same glaze can be used without difficulty.

8 Glazes

Formulation and Types

SIMPLE FORMULATION

A ceramic glaze and its formulation are not as mysterious as they seem to most pottery students. Basically, a glaze is nothing more than a thin, glasslike coating that is fused to the clay surface of a pot by the heat of the kiln. While some glaze compositions are quite elaborate and use a variety of chemical compounds, a glaze need not be complex, for it contains only three necessary elements.

Silica, commonly called flint, is the essential glaze ingredient. It is also known as quartz in its pure, crystalline state. Were it not that the melting point of silica is so high—about 3100°F (1700°C)—this single material would suffice to form a glaze. However, most earthenware clays mature at about 2000°F (1093°C) and will seriously deform if fired higher, while stoneware and porcelain bodies mature between 2250°F and 2400°F (1238°C–1315°C). Thus, pure silica cannot be used on these bodies.

Flux is a term applied to those compounds that lower the melting point of a glaze. Fortunately, many chemicals with a low melting point will readily combine with silica to form a glassy crystal. Two types of materials are commonly used as fluxes in low-fire glazes: *lead oxides* (lead carbonate, red lead, galena, and litharge) and *alkaline compounds* (borax, colemanite, soda ash, boric acid, and bicarbonate of soda). Although these two categories of low-fire fluxes have comparable fluxing power, their effects on glaze colorants and many of their other qualities are different (see Chap. 9).

A refractory element helps to form a stronger glaze that will better withstand the wear of normal use. The glaze produced solely by a mixture of silica and either lead or borax compounds is soft and rather runny and therefore suitable for only low-temperature glazes. We add a third ingredient, *alumina*, to the glaze to gain this quality. Silica and

opposite: 424. MIKAIL ZAKIN, U.S.A. Covered jar. Salt glaze on a wheel-thrown and hand-shaped stoneware form, height 4⅞".

alumina unite to form tough, needlelike mullite crystals, creating a bond more resistant to abrasion and shock.

In its final composition, then, a glaze includes its three necessary elements: silica, the *glass former*; a flux, which *lowers the fusion point* of the silica; and alumina, a refractory element that gives *added toughness* and hardness to the glaze, allows a higher maturing temperature, increases viscosity, and prevents devitrification.

It is not economically practical to use refined and pure oxides to make up glazes. The compounds used by the potter are usually those minerals that are abundant in nature in a relatively pure state. Therefore, a simple, low-fire glaze will be made from kaolin ($Al_2O_3 \cdot 2\,SiO_2 \cdot 2\,H_2O$), potash feldspar ($K_2O \cdot Al_2O_3 \cdot 6\,SiO_2$), and red lead ($Pb_3O_4$) or borax ($Na_2O \cdot 2\,B_2O_3 \cdot 10\,H_2O$) as the flux.

The silica content will be provided by both the clay (kaolin) and the feldspar. Alumina is also a constituent of both kaolin and feldspar. Feldspars are minerals that contain alumina, silica, and varying amounts of potash, sodium, and calcium. The predominant flux gives its name to the compound, such as soda feldspar. Potash feldspar, the more common type, is slightly cheaper and fires harder and higher than soda feldspar. Feldspar should be considered only incidentally as a flux in the low-fire range, since it is an important source of silica and alumina. In addition to aiding the fusion of the glaze ingredients, a flux also combines with the silica contained in the clay body of the pot to form a bond uniting the body and the glaze. This union becomes stronger as the temperature increases. Occasionally, a porous clay will absorb so much flux that the glaze will become thin and rough and require adjustments to either the glaze or the body.

Low-fire Glaze Tests

In order to gain an understanding of the qualities imparted to the glaze by silica, alumina, and the flux, the beginning student should make several tests with varying proportions of feldspar, kaolin, and borax fired to cone 04. Earthenware tiles 2 by 3 inches and ¼-inch thick make satisfactory tests. These should be bisque fired to about cone 010. The glaze samples should always be fired upright to detect a tendency in the glaze to run. The bottom quarter inch of each tile is left unglazed to catch the drips and evaluate the fluidity of the glaze.

A suggested beginning formula for an 04 glaze test is three parts borax, three parts feldspar, and four parts kaolin. Unless the scales are extremely accurate, a total sample of 100 grams is advisable. After weighing, the ingredients are ground in a mortar, and water is added until a creamy consistency is obtained. Modern ceramic materials are finely ground, so only a brief mixing is needed for a small sample. The glaze is brushed on a clean, dust-free tile in several thin coats. Experience is the only guide to the proper thickness of application. Cracks will develop if a layer is too heavy. In succeeding tests the feldspar is left constant, the kaolin is decreased by half, and the red lead is increased by the amount necessary to replace the kaolin. The total number of parts should be kept at ten, so that valid comparisons can be made. This process is repeated until the clay content is reduced to one part. The clay also functions as a binder to hold the nonplastic ingredients together; thus, if no clay is present, methocel or another binder must be added.

The fired samples will show a gradual change from a claylike white coating to one that becomes more fluid and glassy as the increased lead combines with the silica. Finally, a point is reached at which the glaze runs excessively. This tendency can be retarded by substituting additional feldspar for some of the lead. At different firing temperatures the necessary proportions of flux, alumina, and silica will vary. When the temperature exceeds 2050°F (1230°C), the low-fire fluxes must be gradually replaced by calcium carbonate (whiting), the principal high-fire flux. At temperatures above 2100°F (1150°C), the lead and alkaline fluxes run immoderately and are used only in minute quantities. A glaze can have a different crystalline surface structure because of variations in the proportion of alumina to silica. A slight excess of alumina produces a mat instead of a glassy finish; either too much or too little silica will result in a rough surface. Silica in its pure form is easily added to glaze if necessary.

After completing successful glaze tests with these three basic ingredients, we can substitute for all or part of the feldspar other materials such as nepheline syenite, spodumene, lepidolite, or Cornwall stone. Further possibilities are cryolite, talc, and dolomite, which fire at slightly lower temperatures. Although some of these compounds contain silica and alumina, their main purpose is in varying and increasing the proportion of flux. These additions can affect the color and surface quality of the glaze. The principal advantages of having several fluxes in a glaze are the extension of the firing range and the more complete fusion of the chemicals with fewer glaze defects. (See Chap. 9, pp. 231–241, for more specific details about these materials.)

Barium carbonate additions will produce a mat glaze in cases where increasing the alumina content is not convenient. Zinc oxide can be added to the glaze in small quantities to obtain more fluxing action and reduce surface defects. It is essential that the glaze and the body cool and contract at the same rate after firing. If the body is weak and underfired, a contracting glaze may cause it to crack. Uneven contractions are also responsible for crazing. If sufficient tensions exist, the glaze will eventually craze, although this may not occur for days or even years. Expansions resulting from moisture collecting in a porous body may have a similar effect (see Chap. 7, pp. 202–203). On a decorative piece, tiny hairline cracks can add to the interest of the total design. If they are intentional, such effects are called crackle glazes to distinguish them from the unexpected and undesirable crazing.

Elimination of crazing is necessary in all functional ware to prevent seepage of moisture and to avoid odors resulting from trapped food particles. Changes can be made in the clay body to increase or reduce contraction and thereby adjust it to the glaze. The addition of silica to either the body or the glaze is one method used to prevent crazing. In the body the crystal formation developed by excess silica usually increases contraction, but in the glaze's glassy state silica is more likely to produce an expansion. Generally a potter has developed a satisfactory body with desired plasticity, vitrification, and so forth, and for this reason experimental glazes are adjusted to fit the body, rather than the other way around.

Lead is popular in low-fire glazes, because it reduces surface tension to yield a smooth, blemish-free glaze. However, powdered white or red lead is highly toxic when inhaled or absorbed, and, unless properly compounded, all lead glazes are subject to attack by acids, such as those found in citrus fruit juices and vinegar salad dressings. Moreover, since lead is a cumulative poison, even slight leaching of the glaze is dangerous. For these reasons, lead should be used only in fritted monosilicate or bisilicate form. Certain chemical combinations will produce an acid-resistant glaze even with lead, while others encourage lead release from a glaze. It is essential that a lead glaze be high in both SiO_2 and Al_2O_3. Pemco lead-silica-alumina frit #316 (p. 308), which fires at cone 06, is such a stable lead frit. Combined fluxes provide minimum lead release, but the addition of a single flux—K_2O, BaO, Na_2O, and to a lesser extent CaO_2 or Li_2O_2—encourages lead release. Of the opacifiers, ZrO_2 diminishes release, while the others have a minor effect. Copper oxide should not be used in lead glazes, for it greatly increases lead release, as does a combination of Fe_2O_3 and MnO_2.

High-fire Glaze Tests

High-fire glaze tests differ from those in the low-fire range only in the substitution of calcium carbonate ($CaCO_3$), commonly called whiting, for the low-melting lead and alkaline compounds. In this experiment tiles must be made from a stoneware or porcelain body. A good starting formula for a cone 6 to 8 glaze would be four parts kaolin, four parts potash feldspar, and two parts whiting. This will produce a sample that is white and claylike in character. In succeeding tests the whiting is held constant, the amount of feldspar is gradually increased, and the proportion of the more refractory kaolin is decreased. As the kaolin is lessened, the test glazes will become smoother and glassier. Depending upon the temperature, a satisfactory glaze should be achieved at the point when the kaolin content is between 10 and 20 percent. Throughout this series of tests we have lowered the fusion point of the glaze by the addition of the active flux, potash, which is contained in the feldspar. Only at higher temperatures can feldspar be considered a flux, since it is also a major source of alumina and silica.

A successful stoneware glaze can be made using only feldspar, kaolin, and whiting. As mentioned earlier, however, it may be desirable to add small amounts of other chemicals to obtain a greater firing range, achieve a better adjustment to the body, provide a more varied color spectrum, and develop a surface free from minor defects. Flint can easily be added to supply silica if needed. The student should attempt to vary his basic glaze to produce a glossy surface, a mat surface, and one that is fairly opaque (without the use of an opacifier such as tin oxide). Substitutions of some of the feldsparlike materials with different fluxes, such as lepidolite or nepheline syenite, can be tried. Often small amounts of another flux will result in a great improvement in a glaze. Other suggested additions are zinc oxide, talc, and barium carbonate. (See Chap. 9, pp. 228–243, for more detailed information on these and other chemicals, including colorants that will be used in further tests.)

GLAZE TYPES

At the beginning of this chapter we stressed the simplicity of glaze formulation, and indeed it is so. A functional and attractive glaze can be made from only a few materials. Several glazes, however, use rather uncommon ingredients or require special firing techniques. The glaze recipes in the Appendix (pp. 313–319) will clarify the general descriptions of the glazes that follow.

Low-fire Glazes

Low-fire glazes can be grouped into two distinct categories distinguished by the major flux included in the glaze.

Lead glazes comprise the largest group, firing from cone 016 to cone 02, which is between 1450°F and 2050°F (790°C–1120°C). These glazes take their names from the fluxes used, primarily oxides of the lead compounds. The most common fluxes are lead carbonate [$2PbCO_3 \cdot Pb(OH)_2$] and red lead

(Pb_3O_4). Lead is a very active flux, melting at about 950°F (510°C), flowing uniformly, and giving a bright, glossy surface. Used alone, it may constitute 50 percent of the glaze batch; it is often combined with other fluxes. The use of more than one flux is common, since each one has slightly different qualities. In combination they tend to encourage a lower melting point and a more complex and intimate reaction than can be obtained from using a single flux.

Lead has the disadvantage of being very poisonous and requires careful handling to avoid breathing the dust or getting particles in the mouth. For this reason, lead is often converted into the nontoxic silicate form by fritting. Fritting is a procedure by which a flux and silica are melted and later ground to form a glaze addition that is both nontoxic and insoluble in water. Vessels glazed with lead should never be used to store liquids containing large percentages of acid, such as fruit juices. Merely fritting the lead and silica does not guarantee that the final glaze, which may contain other compounds, is stable and nontoxic. Two acid-resistant glazes, meant to be fired at cone 06 and cone 4, are listed on pages 314 and 315.

Alkaline glazes have a firing range similar to the lead glazes (cones 016–02) and use an alkaline flux such as borax, colemanite, or soda ash. Alkaline fluxes encourage certain color effects, particularly the turquoise-blues that lead glazes cannot produce. Because of their extreme solubility, alkaline fluxes should never be used on raw ware. When absorbed into the clay, the expansions and contractions that alkaline compounds undergo during firing and cooling will cause the body to crack.

A very soft bisque ware also reacts poorly to an alkaline glaze, for it will absorb a portion of the flux, leaving an incomplete and usually a rough-textured glaze upon firing. Because of their solubility and their tendency to become lumpy in the glaze solution, the alkaline compounds (such as borax) are often fritted into the nonsoluble silicate form. In general, alkaline glazes have a smooth, glossy surface similar to that produced by glazes in the lead group.

High-fire Glazes

High-fire glazes are generally compounded to fire in a range from cone 6 to cone 14, or 2250°F to 2500°F (1230°C–1370°C). At these extreme temperatures, common low-fire fluxes, such as lead and borax, must be replaced with calcium carbonate, which has a higher melting point of about 1500°F (816°C). Glazes are compounded to fit the maturity of the clay body. Since earthenware can seldom be fired over 2000°F (1093°C), and stoneware usually matures above 2300°F (1260°C), there is a gap between these temperatures at which little work is fired by the average studio potter. However, numerous commercial bodies are compounded between cones 02 and 6 for use on dinnerware, gift ware, and tiles. Glazes for these temperatures must contain both high- and low-fire fluxes to adjust within these limits (see Appendix, p. 315).

Porcelain and stoneware glazes are identical, except in cases where adjustments must be made to accommodate a difference in firing shrinkage. Because feldspar is a major ingredient in such glazes, the term *feldspathic glaze* is often applied to stoneware glazes. Due to the high temperature, the union of glaze and body is quite complete. The interlocking mullite crystals prevent detection of the line of junction that is easily visible between a glassy glaze and a porous earthenware body. Feldspathic glazes are very hard (they cannot be scratched by steel), and they are resistant to most acids, the exceptions being hydrofluoric, phosphoric, and hot sulphuric acids. The surfaces may be either mat or smooth, but they never reveal the excessive gloss of low-fire glazes.

Ash Glazes

Ash glazes were probably the first glazes used by man. At present they have no commercial application, but they may be of interest to the studio potter. The ash can derive from any wood, grass, or straw. Depending upon the specific source, the chemical composition can vary considerably: it is generally very high in silica; contains some alumina and calcium; moderate amounts of fluxes, such as potash, soda, and magnesia; plus iron and small quantities of numerous other compounds. Because of the high silica content, ash can seldom be used in low-fire glazes in amounts over 15 to 20 percent. This is not sufficient to make much change in the basic glaze. A suggested starting point for a stoneware ash-glaze test would be forty parts ash, forty parts feldspar, and twenty parts whiting. Fireplace ashes should be collected in a fairly large quantity and then mixed thoroughly to ensure uniformity. The ash is first run through a coarse sieve to remove unburned particles. It can then be soaked in water that is decanted several times to remove soluble portions. However, many potters prefer to run the dry ash through a fine sieve without washing (taking care not to inhale the fine ash particles), and thus retain the soluble fluxes. The latter procedure will allow a larger percentage of ash to be used in the final glaze. Liquid glaze containing ash is quite caustic and should not be stirred with the hand.

Frit Glazes

Frit glazes may be little different chemically from the two low-fire types described earlier. Fritting is a process that renders raw-glaze materials either nontoxic or nonsoluble. Lead or alkaline fluxes (borax or soda ash) are melted in a frit kiln with silica or silica and a small amount of alumina. When the glaze becomes liquid, a plug is pulled in the bottom of the frit furnace, and the contents are discharged into a container filled with water. The fractured particles are then ground to the necessary fineness. Small amounts can be made in the studio using a crucible. One disadvantage of studio manufacture is the extremely long grinding time necessary to pulverize the frit to adequate fineness.

Many different types of frit glazes are commercially available. Frit composition is complicated, for nontoxic or nonsoluble elements must be completely absorbed within a satisfactory firing range and without creating later adjustment problems. A frit glaze is seldom a complete glaze for several reasons. Since it is usually colorless, opacifiers or colorants must be added. The frit has little ability to adhere, so a small amount of plastic clay or bentonite is usually necessary. Adjustments for the final firing ranges must also be made. Frits have extensive commercial use where large amounts of standard glaze are employed. For the studio potter, frits are of most value in eliminating the lumpy quality of borax needed in crystalline, copper reds, and similar glazes. Purchased in 100-pound lots, low-fire frits might well be used in the public schools to replace the small and expensive colored glaze packets now purchased. The addition of a few color oxides and kaolin would not raise the cost substantially.

Crackle Glazes

Crackle glazes cannot be characterized by their composition, for they are merely the result of tensions that arise when a glaze and a body expand and contract at different rates. In most glazes, except perhaps the mats, a crackle can be produced. The simplest way is to substitute similar-acting fluxes for others having a different contraction rate. The reverse is true if a noncrackling glaze is desired.

A crackle is a network of fine cracks in the glaze. It must be used on a light body to be seen properly (Fig. 425). To strengthen the effect, a coloring oxide or strong black tea is often applied to the crackled area. The Chinese were able to achieve, by successive firings, a network of both large and fine crackles, each stained with a different coloring oxide. On certain shapes, a crackle in the glaze can have an interesting decorative quality. It is more practical on a vitreous stoneware or porcelain body, because a crackle on a porous earthenware pot will allow liquids to seep through and make it unsatisfactory for holding food.

Mat Glazes

Mat glazes generally are formed either by adding an excess of alumina or by substituting barium carbonate for some of the flux in the glaze. Therefore, they are often called *alumina mats* or *barium mats*. A mat glaze should not be confused with a thin, rough, or underfired glaze. It should be smooth to the touch, with neither gloss nor transparency. The mat effects sometimes observed on an underfired glaze are caused by incompletely dissolved particles, whereas a true mat develops a different surface

425. WARREN MACKENZIE, U.S.A. Vase. Porcelain with cloudy celadon glaze and crackle surface, height 5 ½″. The cut facets add a distinct quality to the form of the vase.

left : Plate 19. TOSHIKO TAKAEZU, U.S.A. Dish. 1967. Porcelain with brush decoration. The abstract brushwork on this dish evokes the quality of a misty Oriental landscape.

below : Plate 20. RICHARD LEACH, U.S.A. Jug. Stoneware with overall salt glaze; upper part coated with Albany slip, brush decoration of china clay; titania, rutile, and cobalt glazes. (See Pls. 21–22, overleaf.)

Plates 21–22. RICHARD LEACH, U.S.A. Details of a salt glaze. The base slip is 75 percent china clay, plus flint and feldspar. The light crystals are produced by 10 percent titania, the gold by rutile, the blue-green by cobalt, the orange-red by uranium oxide.

crystalline structure. An unusually long cooling time will encourage the formation of mat textures. One test for a true mat is to cool the glaze quickly to see if it will develop a shine. A mat surface caused by the incomplete fusion of particles will continue to have a mat surface, regardless of the cooling time. It is generally a bit rough to the touch and lacks the smoothness of a true mat. Mats can be calculated for all temperatures, but they are particularly attractive in the low-fire ranges, since typical lead and borax glazes are so shiny that their glare tends to obscure all decoration and form. Mat glazes are related to the crystalline group, because both depend upon the surface structure of the glaze for their effects. Therefore, mats can also be made with iron, zinc, and titanium (rutile) when properly compounded and cooled slowly.

Reduction Glazes

Reduction glazes are those that are especially compounded to develop their unique color characteristics only if fired in a kiln capable of maintaining a reduction atmosphere during certain portions of the firing cycle. The normal kiln firing is an oxidizing fire. An electric kiln always has an oxidizing fire, since there is nothing in the kiln atmosphere to consume the oxygen that is always present. To reduce the atmosphere in a gas or oil kiln, the draft is cut back to lessen the air intake, resulting in an incomplete combustion that releases carbon into the kiln interior. In a muffle kiln, some of the muffles will have to be removed to allow the combustion gases to enter the kiln chamber.

Carbon has a great affinity for oxygen when heated and will steal it from the iron and copper-coloring oxides in the glaze. It was in this manner that the Chinese produced their famous copper reds (sang-de-bœuf) and celadons. When either copper or iron oxide is deprived of its oxygen, it remains suspended in the glaze as the pure colloidal metal. Thus a normal green copper glaze becomes a beautiful ruby red with occasional blue or purple tints. The iron oxide loses its customary brownish-red tone and takes on a variety of soft gray-green hues. Because of its likeness to jade, which had religious

symbolism for the ancient Chinese, celadons of remarkable quality were developed. In a small muffle kiln, a reduction can occur if pine splinters or moth balls are inserted into the peephole. The usual reduction fire starts with an oxidizing fire, and reduction does not begin until just before the melting of the first elements of the glaze. After the reduction cycle, the firing must return to oxidization in order to develop a surface free from pinholes and other defects (see Chap. 11, pp. 279–280).

A so-called local reduction can be achieved by using a small amount (about .5 percent) of silicon carbide (carborundum) in the glaze. The effects are slightly different from the standard reduction, for the color is concentrated in little spots around the silicon carbide particles. But this technique has an advantage in that it can be used in an electric kiln, since the heating elements are in no way effected. The firing range of copper-red and celadon reduction glazes is quite wide, from about cone 08 to the porcelain temperatures.

Crystalline Glazes

There are two types of crystalline glazes. One has large crystal clusters embedded in or on the surface of the glaze; the second type, called aventurine, has single crystals, often small, suspended in the glaze, which catch and reflect the light. These are interesting glazes technically, but they must be very carefully related to the pot shape. The jewellike effects seem to float off the surface of all but the most simple and reserved forms. The crystalline formation is encouraged by additions of zinc and iron or by titanium (rutile). Borax and soda can also be used, but no lead. Possible firing ranges are wide, and, as with mat formations, the rate of cooling is most important. In order to allow the crystals to develop properly, the temperature of the kiln should be permitted to drop only about 100°F (38°C) after maturity, and it must be held at this level for several hours before slow cooling. Crystalline glazes are quite runny, so a pedestal of insulating brick should be cut to the foot size and placed under the ware. If fired high, the piece can be set in a shallow bisque bowl that will collect the excess glaze.

Bristol Glazes

Bristol glazes are very similar, in most respects, to the typical porcelain glaze, except that a relatively large amount of zinc oxide is added. In most cases, this tends to lower the melting point and to add a certain opacity to the glaze. Most Bristols fall into the cones 5 to 9 range, although formulas have been successfully developed for cones 3 to 14. The most common use of the Bristol glaze is for architectural tile and bricks.

Since a large amount of clay is normally used, the ware is generally given a single firing, and there is no problem of shrinkage. However, by calcinating part of the clay, the glaze can be fitted to double firings. The commercial single fire usually takes fifty to sixty hours, not only because of the thickness of the ware being fired but also because of the extremely viscous nature of the Bristol glaze. It is this quality of the glaze that makes it valuable to the studio potter. Interesting effects can be achieved by using a Bristol glaze over a more fluid glaze that breaks through in spots. The application of the glaze must be perfect, because its viscosity prevents any cracks that may occur from healing. Moreover, in firing the edges of the cracks will pull farther apart and bead. In general, Bristol glazes are shiny, but they can be matted by increasing the amount of calcia while reducing the silica content.

Luster Glazes

Luster glazes usually consist of a thin and decorative metallic coating fired on top of a lead-tin glaze. This coating is achieved by applying a solution of pine resin, bismuth nitrate, and a metallic salt dissolved in oil of lavender over a fired glaze. The luster is fired at a low red heat, sufficiently hot to fuse the metal and burn off the resin but lower than the melting point of the original glaze. A variety of reds, yellows, browns, and silvery-white lusters, as well as nacreous and iridescent sheens, are possible. The metals normally used are lead and zinc acetates; copper, manganese, and cobalt sulfates; uranium nitrate; and silver and gold compounds. Bismuth is generally used as a flux. Until

A.D. 1529 bismuth was thought to be an impure form of silver, and therefore the silver mentioned in old records probably was a silver-bismuth compound. (See Chap. 9, pp. 243–244, for a description of the historical method of preparing lusters.)

Usually the luster is not an overall coating, but rather it is applied in the form of a design combined with colored slips or stains. This is especially true in Islamic pottery, which, because of religious edicts against representational painting, developed an intricate and interlocking decorative motif used between the ninth and the fourteenth centuries (see Fig. 42).

Salt Glazes

Salt glazes have enjoyed a revival in recent years after a long period of neglect by the studio potter (Fig. 426). From the twelfth to the mid-nineteenth century, such glazes were common in Europe and were also used in Colonial America. Commercial applications are largely limited to stoneware crocks, glazed sewer pipe, hollow building brick, and similar products.

The salt-glaze procedure is simple. The ware is fired to its body-maturing temperature, at which time common salt (sodium chloride) is thrown into the firebox or through ports entering the kiln chamber. The sodium combines with the silica in the clay to form a glassy silicate. The studio must be well ventilated, since deadly chlorine gas is also released at the moment of salting. Occasionally, silica can be added to the clay to form a better glaze coating. By reducing conditions (incomplete combustion to introduce carbon into the kiln atmosphere), buff or red clays can be glazed either brown or black. Other colors can be obtained only by using colored slips or body stains. (Pls. 20–22, pp. 211–212).

The disadvantage of the salt glaze, other than its limited color effects, is that it coats the whole interior of the kiln. This generally renders the kiln unsuitable for other types of glaze firing. The firing range of salt glazes is wide, from cones 02 to 12, but the most common firings are from cones 5 to 8. (See Chap. 11, p. 280, for more specifics on the salting technique.)

426. MARC HANSEN, U.S.A. Bowl. Stoneware with salt glaze, brown slip, and applied clay decoration; diameter 10½″. The throwing rings and applied clay decoration are revealed clearly under the pebbly salt glaze.

Slip Glazes

Slip glazes are made from raw natural clays that contain sufficient fluxes to function as glazes without further preparation beyond washing and sieving. In practice, additions are often made to enable the slip glaze to fit the body or to modify the maturing temperature, but these changes are minor. The so-called black varnish of the Greeks and the Roman terra sigillata are slip glazes formed by decanting the finer particles of a liquid slip made from red clay. Reduction produces the black color by converting the red iron oxide into black and magnetic iron oxides. A later oxidizing fire restores the iron in the more porous clay body to its red color, while leaving the black iron sealed in the denser slip. This process does not create a true glassy glaze. Rather, it is halfway between a slip and a glaze and is not completely waterproof.

Slip glazes were commonly used by early American stoneware potteries that produced such utilitarian objects as storage crocks, bowls, mugs, and pitchers. Albany slip clay is the only commercial variety that is widely used. It fires brown-black at cones 8 to 10. The addition of 2 percent cobalt to Albany slip will result in a beautiful semigloss jet black. Wrenshall slip, mined near Duluth, Minnesota, fires to a pale yellow at cones 6 to 10 with the peculiar streaked effect characteristic of rutile. There are many slip clay deposits that are not recognized as such. Frequently earthenware clays can be used as slip clays when fired high enough and with the addition of small amounts of flux. Most slip clays fire from cone 6 to cone 12. Slip-clay fluxes are generally the alkaline earth compounds, plus iron oxide in varying amounts. A high iron content serves also to produce a color ranging from tan to dark brown.

above: 427. GENE BUCKLEY, U.S.A. Bowl. Slab-built stoneware with pitted surface and a band of lustrous green and red typical of the raku technique, height 6 ½".

The potter must be careful in using slip clays, for they are generally mined in small pits, and their composition will vary slightly. Each new shipment of material should be tested before being used in quantity. Some Albany slip is so lacking in the usual brown colorant that the resulting glaze is a pale, semitransparent tan. Studio potters should pay more attention to this group of glazes. Slip clays are easy to apply, adhere well, and fire with few, if any, defects. The composition, chemically, is most durable, and, since additions are few, much time can be saved in glaze preparation.

Raku Glazes

Raku glazes are low-fire glazes used on bodies containing a high proportion of grog (Fig. 427). The ware is associated with the Japanese tea ceremony and with Zen Buddhism. Raku tea bowls, usually hand built and irregular, are perfectly suited to the Zen emphasis on nature and the simple, unaffected way of living.

The firing procedure is an essential part of the raku technique. The clay body used is generally a stoneware containing up to 30 percent grog. The grog and the firing process tend to limit the form and size of the ware. Simple bowl shapes are most common. Since the glaze temperature never exceeds 1750°F (955°C), the glaze may contain as much as 60 percent lead or colemanite. The ware is bisqued and then glazed.

The glaze firing is most unusual and quite dramatic. In Japan the firing is generally done outdoors, using small, charcoal-burning kilns, which often contain only a single pot. The glazed piece must be perfectly dry, and it can be placed on top of the kiln to ensure that all the moisture has evaporated. When the kiln has reached glaze temperature and the bricked-up door is opened, the pot is quickly placed in the chamber with a pair of tongs. Because of the high grog content and porous nature of the body, this sudden heat change has no effect. Firing proceeds, and in a few minutes the pot begins to glow. (Most kilns in the United States are fired with a single gas burner and have a capacity for several pieces. Insulating bricks can be easily bolted together to form a top cover.) Depending upon the character of the kiln, the glaze should begin to melt and develop a liquid shine in 10 to 15 minutes. Before running occurs, the pot is removed with tongs. The tong marks on the glazed surface are regarded as a decoration. Generally the glowing pot is placed in a covered metal container filled with sawdust, which

gives a smoked and accidental quality to the glaze. After a few minutes of smoking, the ware can be immediately doused with a bucket of water. If, however, the pot has a closed form or varied thicknesses, cooling in the open air for several minutes before dousing is necessary to avoid cracking.

The raku body remains soft and porous, and the glaze is not waterproof. Nevertheless, raku has become quite popular in recent years. The glaze effects are quite varied and, while accidental, have unusual qualities. The speed of the firings, the flame, and the smoke all suggest the character of a "Happening." The oxides used in raku decoration, when reduced, tend to develop a luster with fantastic color combinations. A deep crackle often occurs, which is in keeping with the rather simple form that typifies pots made of a coarse body.

9 Glazes

Calculations and Chemicals

In Chapter 8 a trial-and-error method was suggested by which the novice potter could develop a satisfactory glaze and gain a rudimentary understanding of the properties of the common glaze materials. Despite the long history of ceramics, the scientific formulation of glazes is rather recent. The glazes and techniques evidenced in the historical pieces illustrated in Chapters 1 and 2 were the final results of centuries of such experimentation. But since ceramic techniques are no longer passed from father to son in the traditional manner, it is necessary that we find a quicker and more scientific method of glaze formulation.

CALCULATIONS

All matter composing the earth is made up of approximately one hundred chemical elements in the form of atoms. These elements do not occur in nature in a pure form but in compounds, which are groups of atoms held together by an electrical attraction or bond. The atom is much too small to be weighed, but it is possible to determine the relative weight of one type of atom to that of another. Oxygen, symbolized by the letter O, has been given the arbitrary atomic weight of 16; other atoms are attributed weights corresponding to their proportionate weights in relation to oxygen.

Silica, mentioned frequently in the chapters on clay and glazes, is a major ceramic compound and is found in every clay and glaze. The *molecular formula* for silica (or, more precisely, silicon dioxide) is SiO_2. The atomic weight table in the Appendix (p. 303) lists the weight of silicon as 28. Since two oxygen atoms weigh 32, the total molecular weight of the compound silicon dioxide is 60.

Silica can be added to a clay body or glaze in the silicon dioxide form, but it is most commonly found as part of a more complex compound, such as kaolin ($Al_2O_3 \cdot 2\,SiO_2 \cdot 2\,H_2O$), or potash feldspar ($K_2O \cdot Al_2O_3 \cdot 6\,SiO_2$).

The RO, R₂O₃, RO₂ System

There are three principal components in a glaze. One of these is silica (SiO_2), which gives the glaze its glassy, transparent quality. The second is alumina (Al_2O_3), a refractory element, which contributes toughness and abrasion resistance to the glaze. Since neither of these oxides will melt at temperatures below 3100°F, the potter must add a third ingredient, a flux, such as lead oxide or sodium, that will lower the melting point and combine with both silica and alumina to form, after firing, a hard, glassy coating on the ceramic body.

With rare exceptions, the glaze components are not single refined oxides but complex compounds that are commercially available at reasonable cost. In order to compare glazes or to understand the effects of these varied chemicals, it is necessary to separate the component oxides into the three major parts of the glaze formula. The symbol RO refers to the fluxing agents, which are chiefly metallic or alkaline elements that form their oxides by combining with one atom of oxygen, such as CaO or PbO. Similarly, alumina (Al_2O_3) can be symbolized by R_2O_3 and silica (SiO_2) by RO_2. A table will better illustrate this division of the components of a glaze.

RO	R₂O₃	RO₂
Bases	Neutrals	Acids
Li₂O*	(Amphoteric oxides)	SiO₂
Na₂O*	Al₂O₃	TiO₂
K₂O*	B₂O₃	ZrO₂
CaO	Fe₂O₃	
MgO	Sb₂O₃	Glass formers
BaO	Cr₂O₃	
ZnO	(Refractory	
FeO	elements)	
MnO		
PbO		
CdO		
Fluxing agents		

* One of the few exceptions: 2 atoms of sodium, lithium, or potassium unite with 1 of oxygen to form the oxide.

In the first column are the RO oxides that have the effect of fluxes in either a glaze or a body. They are also called the *base oxides*. Some of the *neutrals* or amphoteric oxides can function as either a base or an acid oxide. However, the major oxide in this group, alumina (Al_2O_3), always has a refractory effect in a glaze. On the other hand, red iron oxide (Fe_2O_3) is an active flux as well as a colorant. Boric oxide (B_2O_3) can react as either a base or an acid. Silica is the major oxide in the acid column. The contribution of TiO_2 and ZrO_2 to a glaze is opacity, not their glass-forming effect. With minor exceptions, the RO, R_2O_3, and RO_2 method of categorizing the main components of a glaze works very well.

The Empirical Glaze Formula

In the interests of simplifying calculations, glaze batches are usually reduced to an *empirical formula*. This is a glaze formula in which the various active ingredients are expressed in molecular proportions. By contrast, the *batch recipe* is a proportion expressed in the actual weights of the raw chemical compounds making up the glaze. Since the materials used in the average glaze batch are rather complex compounds, it is a distinct advantage to be able to define the glaze in terms of single oxides that bear the same proportional relationship to each other as when in their more complex form in the glaze batch. These oxides are grouped into RO, R_2O_3, and RO_2 units.

Before a batch recipe is converted into an empirical formula, it is first necessary to know the chemical formulas of the individual raw materials, as well as their equivalent weights. The molecular formulas and equivalent weights of the molecular compounds for all commonly used ceramic materials are listed in the Appendix (pp. 305–306). The commercial name of the raw material is in the first column, and its molecular formula is in the second. Many compounds are designated by more than one name, such as whiting and calcium carbonate.

The *molecular weight of a compound* is the sum of the atomic weights of its constituent elements. The equivalent weight will often be the same as the molecular weight of the compound, but in many cases it is smaller. This is true of potash feldspar:

Raw material	Formula	Molecular weight	Equivalent weights		
			RO	R_2O_3	RO_2
Feldspar (potash)	$K_2O \cdot Al_2O_3 \cdot 6\,SiO_2$	556.8	556.8	556.8	92.9

According to the given formula, when one molecular unit of potash feldspar is added, the glaze will have one unit of potassium oxide, one unit of alumina, and six units of silica. Since one unit each of potassium oxide and alumina form the compound, their individual equivalent weights are 556.8. And since six units of silica are necessary to form the compound, the equivalent weight of silica is 1/6 of the compound weight, or 92.9. The *equivalent weights* of the oxides of a compound are the same as its molecular weight if the oxide in question appears only once. However, if more than one unit of an oxide occurs, then its equivalent weight will be found by dividing the compound molecular weight by the number of times the oxide in question appears.

These definitions will become clearer in the actual procedure of converting the following glaze batch recipe to an empirical formula.

Glaze recipe	Raw materials	Parts by weight
A lead-borax	White lead	128
glaze maturing	Whiting	15
at cone 04	Borax	103
	Feldspar	
	(potash)	83
	Kaolin	38
	Flint	85

Before we can go into the actual calculations, we must first find the molecular formula of each of the compounds making up the glaze, plus the equivalent weights of the oxides contained in these compounds. It is convenient to put this information in table form, as illustrated (p. 222). By checking over the raw-material formulas, we can determine which of the oxides should be indicated in the spaces to the right of the table.

The batch weights of the raw materials are divided by the equivalent molecular weights of the particular oxides concerned, giving the molecular proportions in the form of single oxides. By arranging these oxides with the amounts calculated into their appropriate RO, R_2O_3, and RO_2 groups, we find that the glaze batch has the following empirical formula:

RO	R_2O_3	RO_2
.495 PbO	.295 Al_2O_3	2.599 SiO_2
.150 CaO	.540 B_2O_3	
.149 K_2O		
.270 Na_2O		

The total of the RO oxides comes to 1.064 instead of the desired unit of one, because round numbers have been used in the batch recipe. By dividing each of the above figures by 1.064 we will have the following empirical formula. The RO is now .998, a figure that is accurate enough for comparative purposes.

RO	R_2O_3	RO_2
.465 PbO	.277 Al_2O_3	2.442 SiO_2
.140 CaO	.507 B_2O_3	
.140 K_2O		
.253 Na_2O		

Considerable research has been done on the properties of ceramic materials, and some reasonable pre-

Batch to Empirical Formula

Raw material and formula	Batch weights		Equivalent weights		PbO	CaO	Na$_2$O	B$_2$O$_3$	K$_2$O	Al$_2$O$_3$	SiO$_2$
White lead [2 PbCO$_3$ · Pb(OH)$_2$]	128	÷	258.5 (RO)	=	0.495						
Whiting (CaCO$_3$)	15	÷	100 (RO)	=		0.15					
Borax (Na$_2$O · 2 B$_2$O$_3$ · 10 H$_2$O)	103	÷	381.04 (RO) / 190.7 (R$_2$O$_3$)	=			0.270	0.540			
Felspar (potash) (K$_2$O · Al$_2$O$_3$ · 6 SiO$_2$)	83	÷	556.8 (RO) / 556.8 (R$_2$O$_3$) / 92.9 (RO$_2$)	=					0.149	0.149	0.890
Kaolin (Al$_2$O$_3$ · 2 SiO$_2$ · 2 H$_2$O)	38	÷	258.1 (R$_2$O$_3$) / 129 (RO$_2$)	=						0.146	0.294
Flint (SiO$_2$)	85	÷	60.06 (RO$_2$)	=							1.415
Totals	452				0.495	0.15	0.270	0.540	0.149	0.295	2.599

dictions can be made about the probable change that a particular chemical will cause in a known type of glaze. There are, however, many variables, such as the length of the glaze grinding time, the thickness of application, the reactions between glaze and body, the kiln atmosphere, and the rate of temperature rise and fall. Since each or all of these conditions can markedly affect a particular glaze, glaze experimentation is something less than a true science. Successful work depends largely upon the overall experience and care of the operator in controlling these factors.

The Batch Recipe

To convert an empirical formula to a batch recipe, it is necessary to reverse the procedure explained in the previous section. As before, the easiest method is to draw up a chart on which to compile the information. This type of conversion will require slightly more familiarity with raw chemical compounds, because we must select those compounds containing the proper oxides without adding any unwanted elements. The parts of compounds that pass off in the kiln as gases or water vapor are ignored. To make the process clearer, let us take the following *empirical glaze formula* and convert it into a batch recipe.

0.40 Na_2O	0.03 Al_2O_3	2.1 SiO_2
0.46 PbO	0.32 B_2O_3	
0.14 FeO		

The general procedure is as follows: First, if any alkaline fluxes are present (Na_2O or K_2O), it is best to include as much as possible in a soda or potash feldspar. This is a cheaper source of the flux, and,

Calculations from Formula to Batch Recipe

Raw material	Oxides in formula Equivalents needed	Na_2O 0.40	PbO 0.46	FeO 0.14	Al_2O_3 0.03	B_2O_3 0.32	SiO_2 2.1
Soda feldspar ($Na_2O \cdot Al_2O_3 \cdot 6\ SiO_2$) 0.03 equivalents		0.03			0.03		0.18
	remainder	0.37	0.46	0.14		0.32	1.92
Borax ($Na_2O \cdot 2\ B_2O_3 \cdot 10\ H_2O$) 0.16 equivalents		0.16				0.32	
	remainder	0.21	0.46	0.14			1.92
Soda ash (Na_2CO_3) 0.21 equivalents		0.21					
	remainder		0.46	0.14			1.92
White lead [$2\ PbCO_3 \cdot Pb(OH)_2$] 0.153 equivalents			0.46				
	remainder			0.14			1.92
Red iron oxide (Fe_2O_3) 0.07 equivalents				0.14			
	remainder						1.92
Flint (SiO_2) 1.92 equivalents							1.92

equally important, it is nonsoluble and not as likely to become lumpy in a glaze as borax will. We then fill out the other single oxides, trying to save the alumina for next to last and taking out the silica at the end. Alumina and silica are often included in other compounds, and the balance can easily be taken care of last in the form of either kaolin or silica. Since silica is always present in larger amounts than alumina and is available in a cheap, pure form, it can safely be saved for the last.

Several of the calculations on page 223 may seem incorrect at first, so perhaps we should point out a few of these seeming inconsistencies. In the first addition, when we take 0.03 equivalents of soda feldspar, we get six times as much SiO_2 as either Na_2 or Al_2O_3, because the formula for soda feldspar is $Na_2O_3 \cdot Al_2O_3 \cdot 6\ SiO_2$. Similarly, borax has twice as much B_2O_3 as Na_2O.

Now that we have the needed molecular equivalents of the chemical compounds, we can find the gram batch weights (or pounds) by multiplying each equivalent by the molecular weights of the chemical compound. Thus we have the following set of calculations:

Raw material	Equivalents		Molecular weights		Batch weights
Soda feldspar	0.03	×	524	=	15.72
Borax	0.16	×	382	=	61.12
Soda ash	0.21	×	106	=	22.26
White lead	0.153	×	775	=	118.58
Red iron oxide	0.07	×	160	=	11.20
Flint	1.91	×	60	=	114.60

Limit Formulas

In the glaze experiments described in Chapter 8 (pp. 206–208), no definite limits were mentioned regarding the ratio between the RO, R_2O_3, and RO_2 parts in a glaze. This is because the major purpose of these glaze tests was to gain familiarity with the qualities of the various glaze chemicals. The forgoing analyses have shown that there are general limits to the amounts of alumina and silica that can be used successfully in relation to a single unit of flux. The firing temperature and the type of flux are also important factors.

In the several limit formulas that follow, a number of possible fluxes are indicated; however, the total amount used must add up to a unit of one. In general, a higher proportion of alumina will result in a mat surface, provided the kiln is cooled slowly. Barium will also tend to create a mat surface. A study of these formulas indicates how the ratio of alumina and silica rises as the temperature increases.

While not intended to take the place of glaze formulas, the listing should be a helpful guide to those seeking to change the temperature range of a favorite glaze. Some glaze chemicals are quite complex, and under certain conditions an addition to a glaze will not have the desired effect. By converting the batch recipes to empirical formulas and comparing them with the suggested limits, one ought to be able to detect the direction of the error.

Variables in Glaze Formulation

Potters are frequently disturbed and disappointed when a glaze obtained from a friend or from a textbook produces quite unexpected results. Several factors may be involved in this problem. Ingredients that are more finely ground than usual will melt at a slightly lower temperature. In the same way fritted glaze additions melt more quickly than do raw compounds of a similar composition. Occasionally the thickness of application or reactions with

Limit Formulas

Cone 08–04   *Lead glazes*

PbO	0.2–0.60	Al₂O₃	0.15–0.20
KNaO	0.1–0.25	B₂O₃	0.15–0.60
ZnO	0.1–0.25		
CaO	0.3–0.60	SiO₂	1.5–2.50
BaO	0 –0.15		

Cone 08–04   *Alkaline glazes*

PbO	0–0.5	Al₂O₃	0.05–0.25
KNaO	.4–0.8		
CaO	0–0.3	SiO₂	1.5–2.5
ZnO	0–0.2		

Cone 2–5   *Lead calcium glaze*

PbO	0.4–0.60	Al₂O₃	0.2–0.28
CaO	0.1–0.40		
ZnO	0 –0.25	SiO₂	2.0–3.0
KNaO	0.1–0.25		

Cone 2–5   *Lead-borax glaze*

PbO	0.2 –0.3	Al₂O₃	0.25–0.35
KNaO	0.2 –0.3	B₂O₃	0.20–0.60
CaO	0.35–0.5		
ZnO	0 –0.1	SiO₂	2.5–3.5

Cone 2–5   *Colemanite glaze*

CaO	0.2–0.50	Al₂O₃	0.2–0.28
ZnO	0.1–0.25	B₂O₃	0.3–0.6
BaO	0.1–0.25		
KNaO	0.1–0.25	SiO₂	2.0–3.0

Cone 8–12   *Stoneware glaze*

KNaO	0.2–0.40	Al₂O₃	0.3–0.5
CaO	0.4–0.70	B₂O₃	0.1–0.3
MgO	0 –0.35		
ZnO	0 –0.30		
BaO	0 –0.30	SiO₂	3.0–5.0

the clay body will produce slightly different results. More distressing and troublesome is the variable nature of such major glaze ingredients as Cornwall stone and the feldspars.

In attempting to alter a glaze that has proved unsatisfactory, the potter has several simple remedies. If the glaze is too runny, he adds flint or kaolin, either of which usually raises the melting point; if it is too dry, he increases the flux to develop a more fluid glaze. Sometimes, however, the effect is quite the opposite, and in such cases the student, quite justifiably, may feel that the instructor who suggested the change doesn't know much about glaze chemistry.

The real culprit in many glaze failures is the chemical phenomenon known as a *eutectic*. A eutectic is the lowest point at which two or more chemicals will combine and melt. It is much lower than the melting point of any of the individual chemicals. For example, lead oxide has a melting point of 1616°F (880°C), and silica melts at 3119°F (1715°C).

One might expect that a 50-50 mixture of lead and silica would melt at the halfway point, 2364°F, yet the actual melting point is much lower, about 1470°F. The lowest melting point of lead and silica (the eutectic point) occurs at about 945°F (510°C), with a mixture of approximately 90 percent lead oxide and 10 percent silica. The line diagram in Figure 429 illustrates the relatively simple reaction between lead oxide and silica and the eutectic point at E.

In an actual glaze—compounded of complex minerals and containing several fluxes, alumina, and even different types of silica—the firing reaction is much more complicated. It is quite possible for there to be two and even more eutectic points.

Figure 430 shows a hypothetical reaction, with two eutectic points, between several fluxes and silica. The vertical movement represents the changing temperature of fusion as a portion of flux is replaced with a like amount of silica. Glazes that fall in areas B and C are most troublesome to

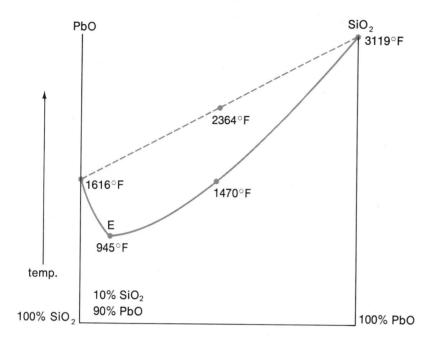

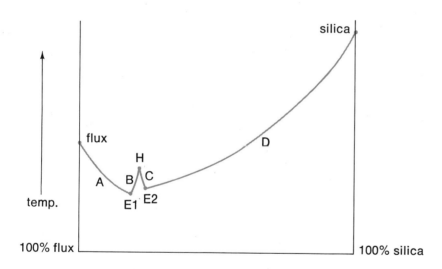

potters, since a slight change in composition or temperature is critical. These are generally high-gloss glazes. In area B a small increase in silica will increase the gloss and raise the melting temperature, but in area C an increase in silica will lower the melting temperature and create a very runny glaze. The points E1, H, and E2 are especially critical, for a very slight temperature rise will change the character of the glaze. The most satisfactory glazes fall in the lower ranges of A and D. Because of the flattened curve in these areas a slight change in temperature or silica is not likely to cause a great variation in the fired glaze. The alumina, calcium, zinc, and dolomite mats fall in the lower area of A.

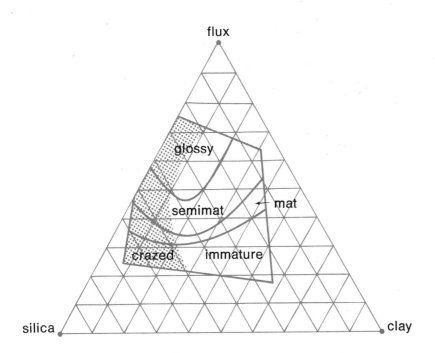

flux

glossy

semimat

mat

crazed

immature

silica

clay

above : 431. This chart shows the glazes obtainable at cone 10 with various amounts of clay, silica, and fluxes.

As the silica is decreased in area A, the glazes become more mat and finally become rough and incomplete with a very low proportion of silica. Transparent and majolica glazes fall in the lower area of D; these become less glossy as the ratio of silica and the temperature are raised. Although the area D glazes can be glossy like the unpredictable glazes in B and C, they are quite stable and little affected by slight changes in silica or temperature. Ash glazes fall in all areas; those in areas B and C are runny and unpredictable.

Figure 430 is a purely theoretical attempt to visualize the reactions between the fluxes and silica. It does not represent an actual glaze, since the function of the alumina is ignored. The more usual method of diagraming a glaze is shown in Figure 431. Here we have the three major components of a glaze: fluxes, silica, and clay (alumina-silica). The small triangle at each apex contains 100 percent of the compound used. As we move along the base line of the silica-clay axis, the ratio becomes 90 percent silica to 10 percent clay (kaolin), then 80 percent

silica to 20 percent clay, and so forth. Progressing vertically, the triangles contain an increasing amount of the third glaze component, the fluxes. The roughly square section in the center covers those glaze tests which at cone 10 fuse to form a glaze. As the gradient indicates, there is a change from mat to glossy as the fluxes are increased and an area of crazed glazes where the alumina content is low. The clay content also has a decisive effect upon whether a glaze is to be glossy or mat. As indicated in both Figures 430 and 431, the mat and semimat glazes cover a much wider range of possible combinations at a given temperature. The sharp gradient of the glossy area in Figure 431 would suggest that the eutectic points for this particular glaze would fall in this range.

The use of a triaxial diagram for planning experiments has many applications in ceramics. It takes much time to complete the entire sequence, and considerable effort can be saved by concentrating on those areas in which meaningful results can be expected. This system is especially helpful in gaining knowledge about the relative fluxing power of various compounds, their effects on colorants, and the blending of colorants and opacificiers.

Calculations   227

CERAMIC CHEMICALS

The chemicals used by the potter are generally not pure single oxides but more complex compounds that are available for industrial uses in a moderately refined form at low cost. Because of differences in either the original mineral or in refining methods, the ceramic chemicals available from different dealers can vary slightly. Even items from the same supplier can change minutely from year to year. Commercial potteries constantly check new shipments of chemicals, but this is seldom done in the small studio. If a favorite glaze reacts strangely, one should consider this factor, provided, of course, there was no deviation from the normal glazing and firing procedure. The feldspars, in particular, vary in their fluxing power. It is for this reason that we have not stressed the importance of a glaze formula but rather the acquisition of an experimental knowledge of the properties of glaze ingredients. The batch glazes listed in the Appendix (pp. 313–319) are mainly for purposes of illustration, and they may have to be adjusted slightly to fit the materials available.

For the convenience of students converting an empirical glaze formula into a batch recipe, a listing follows that gives the major sources of the various oxides in the RO, R_2O_3, and RO_2 groups. A more complete chemical description will be found in the alphabetized section at the end of this chapter.

Sources of Base (RO) Oxides

Barium oxide (BaO) is a very active flux under some conditions. Its glass formation has a brilliancy second only to the lead silicates. Barium's effect on the thermal expansion of the glaze is less than that of the alkalies and calcia. The best source for barium is:

Barium carbonate ($BaCO_3$)

Calcium oxide (CaO), in comparison with the alkaline oxides, produces a glaze more resistant to abrasion, mild acids, and weathering. It also lowers the coefficient of thermal expansion, thereby increasing tensile strength. Although it is often used in small amounts with other fluxes in low-fire glazes, calcium should not be used as the sole flux at temperatures below cone 3. It is the most common flux used at porcelain temperatures. As with alumina, an excess of calcia tends to produce mat textures. Sources of calcium are:

Calcium carbonate ($CaCO_3$)
Calcium borate ($2\,CaO \cdot 3\,B_2O_3 \cdot 5\,H_2O$), more commonly known as colemanite
Dolomite [$CaMg(CO_3)_2$]
Calcium fluoride (CaF_2), better known as the mineral fluorspar
Bone ash, refined, [$Ca_3(PO_4)_2$]
Wollastonite ($CaSiO_3$)

Lead oxide (PbO) has been mentioned frequently as one of the major low-fire fluxes. There are several reasons for its popularity. It combines readily with all other fluxes and has a lower coefficient of expansion than do the alkaline fluxes. Lead gives greater brilliancy to the glaze, although at times this can be a disadvantage. Lead glazes melt and flow well and thus tend to reduce pinholes and other defects of the more viscous type of glaze. The chief drawbacks are the poisonous nature of lead compounds (unless they are fritted) and their weakness to attack by strong fruit acids. Lead tends to blacken or develop a film if slightly reduced. The surface of a lead glaze will scratch easily unless an alkaline flux is added. There are many forms of lead, such as:

Galena (PbS)
Litharge (PbO)
Red lead (Pb_3O_4)
White lead [$2\,PbCO_3 \cdot Pb(OH_2)$]
Lead monosilicate, the fritted lead silicate composed of approximately 16 percent SiO_2 and 84 percent PbO
Lead bisilicate, another commercial lead silicate, with the approximate composition of 65 percent PbO, 33 percent SiO_2, and 2 percent Al_2O_3

Lithium oxide (Li_2O) is more commonly used by glass manufacturers, but it has several important qualities that make its occasional use in glazes valuable. Lithium (the oxide or carbonate) is expensive, because it is present in very small quantities (3–8 percent) in the producing ores. It has a much lower atomic weight than do either sodium or potassium (ratio of 1:3 and 1:5), and therefore a smaller amount of material can be used without lessening the fluxing action. This has the effect of decreasing tensions caused by thermal expansions and contractions and thus promoting a more durable glaze. Sources of lithium are:

Lepidolite ($LiF \cdot KF \cdot Al_2O_3 \cdot 3 SiO_2$)
Spodumene ($Li_2O \cdot Al_2O_3 \cdot 4 SiO_2$)
Lithium carbonate (Li_2CO_3)
Petalite ($Li_2O \cdot Al_2O_3 \cdot 8 SiO_2$)
Amblygonite ($2 LiF \cdot Al_2O_3 \cdot P_2O_5$)

Magnesium oxide (MgO) is frequently found combined with the feldspars and limestones. It lowers the thermal expansion more than do other bases, and it is as satisfactory as the alkaline fluxes in developing a durable glaze. In some combinations it will produce a slight opacity. Used with low-fire glazes, magnesium has a refractory effect; it fluxes easily at higher temperatures and becomes quite fluid. Sources of magnesium are:

Magnesium carbonate ($MgCO_3$)
Dolomite [$CaMg(CO_3)_2$]
Talc (varies from $3 MgO \cdot 4 SiO_2 \cdot H_2O$ to $4 MgO \cdot 5 SiO_2 \cdot H_2O$.) In the solid and more impure form it is also known as steatite or soapstone.
Diopside ($CaO \cdot MgO \cdot 2 SiO_2$)

Potassium oxide (K_2O) is similar in fluxing action to sodium. It has a lower coefficient of thermal expansion, thus increasing the hardness and brilliance of a piece and lowering the fluidity of the glaze. Sources of potassium are:

Potassium carbonate (K_2CO_3), more commonly known as pearl ash
Potash feldspar ($K_2O \cdot Al_2O_3 \cdot 6 SiO_2$)
Cornwall stone, a complex compound of variable composition, roughly similar to a feldspar and having fluxes of calcium, sodium, and potassium ($1 RO \cdot 1.08 Al_2O_3 \cdot 7.79 SiO_2$)
Carolina stone, a domestic product similar to Cornwall stone

Volcanic ash, with a ceramic formula of:
0.660 K_2O 0.899 Al_2O_3 9.59 SiO_2
0.230 Na_2O 0.060 Fe_2O_3 0.05 TiO_2
0.096 CaO
0.014 MgO
Plastic vitrox ($1 RO \cdot 1.69 Al_2O_3 \cdot 14.64 SiO_2$)

Sodium oxide (Na_2O) is one of the more common low-fire fluxes. It has the highest coefficient of expansion of all the bases and generally gives a lower tensile strength and elasticity to the silicates formed than do most other fluxes. The usual ceramic sources of sodium are:

Sodium chloride (NaCl)
Sodium carbonate (Na_2CO_3), more frequently called soda ash
Sodium bicarbonate ($NaHCO_3$)
Borax ($Na_2O \cdot 2 B_2O_3 \cdot 10 H_2O$)
Soda feldspar ($Na_2O \cdot Al_2O_3 \cdot 6 SiO_2$)
Cryolite (Na_3AlF_6)
Nepheline Syenite
($K_2O \cdot 3 Na_2O \cdot 4 Al_2O_3 \cdot 9 SiO_2$)

Zinc oxide (ZnO) can contribute several different qualities to a glaze. It can be used to replace some of the more soluble alkaline fluxes. Zinc is second only to magnesium in reducing the thermal expansion and to calcium in increasing the strength and resistance of a glaze. It contributes some opacity to the glaze and is helpful in reducing crazing defects. The major zinc compound used in ceramics is:

Zinc oxide (ZnO)

Sources of Neutral (R₂O₃) Oxides

Unlike the RO group, which has numerous similar compounds, the R_2O_3 group is almost limited to alumina (Al_2O_3) and a few oxides that have the same oxygen ratio. The greatest difference between a glass and a glaze is the presence of alumina in the glaze. The alumina content is a most important factor in a successful glaze. It controls the fluidity of the melting glaze and enables it to withstand the temperatures needed to mature the body. Greater amounts of alumina increase the hardness of the glaze and its resistance to abrasions and acids.

Crystalline glazes must necessarily be low in alumina, since alumina prevents the devitrification that accompanies the crystal formation.

Alumina (Al_2O_3) in a glaze can vary from 0.1 to 0.9 molecular equivalents, depending upon firing temperatures. The equivalent ratios between the alumina and the silica groups can be from 1:4 to 1:20. For glossy glazes the ratio is about 1:10. As mentioned before, an increase of alumina will tend to produce mat textures. A glossy porcelain glaze firing from cones 10 to 12 will have an alumina-silica ratio of between 1:7 and 1:8, whereas the mats will be 1:3.2 to 1:3.8. Alumina also has an effect on the colors developed. The normal blue of cobalt oxide will become a rose pink in the absence of alumina. Chromium oxide, which usually gives various green tones, will tend to become reddish in the presence of excess alumina. Sources of alumina are:

Alumina hydrate [$Al(OH)_3$]

Feldspar and Cornwall stone (see sections under RO oxides)

Kaolin (china clay) $Al_2O_3 \cdot 2\,SiO_2 \cdot 2\,H_2O$ (see sections under Clay)

Nepheline syenite
    ($K_2O \cdot 3\,Na_2O \cdot 4\,Al_2O_3 \cdot 9\,SiO_2$)

Plastic vitrox (1 RO · 1.69 Al_2O_3 · 14.64 SiO_2)

Pyrophylite ($Al_2O_3 \cdot 4\,SiO_2 \cdot H_2O$)

Antimony oxide (Sb_2O_3) is primarily used as an opacifier and a coloring agent. It is found in:

Antimonious oxide (Sb_2O_3)

Basic antimonate of lead, [$Pb_3(SbO_4)_2$], also known as Naples yellow

Boric oxide (B_2O_3) is one of the neutral oxides (R_2O_3), which, by our previous definition, can react either as bases or acids. The refractory properties of alumina are more like those of acid silica than any of the bases. Boric oxide has a number of characteristics similar to alumina: the alumina of mat glazes can be satisfactorily replaced by boric oxide; color effects do not change by this substitution; both alumina and boric oxide harm underglaze red and green colors; and both can form mixed crystals. On the whole, however, boric oxide functions as a flux, since in comparison with silica it increases the elasticity, lowers the tensile strength, and, in limited quantities, lowers the thermal coefficient of expansion. Like lead, it increases the gloss and refractive index of the glaze. Major compounds containing boron are:

Boric acid ($B_2O_3 \cdot 2\,H_2O$)

Borax ($Na_2O \cdot 2\,B_2O_3 \cdot 10\,H_2O$)

Colemanite (2 CaO · 3 B_2O_3 · 5 H_2O), technically called calcium borate

Chromic oxide (Cr_2O_3) is derived from the mineral chromite ($FeCr_2O_4$). It is used as a colorant in glazes. The fact that the mineral form is a natural spinel would indicate its use as a stain.

Red or **Ferric Iron** oxide (Fe_2O_3) is commonly used as a coloring agent to form brownish-red hues and also to modify copper and cobalt. It would have use as a flux were it not for its strong coloring action. Its presence in many compounds is regarded as an impurity, and considerable effort goes into removing iron flecks from white-ware bodies. It conforms to the R_2O_3 oxide ratio but has none of the refractory qualities that alumina has.

Sources of Acid (RO₂) Oxides

The important oxide in this group, silica, has a refractory effect on glaze, while the others function largely as opacifiers or coloring agents.

Silica (SiO_2) combines readily with the bases to form glassy silicates. It is the most common element in glaze, comprising about 50 percent of it by weight. In a glaze it has the effect of raising the melting point, decreasing fluidity, increasing resistance of the glaze to water and chemicals, increasing hardness and tensile strength, and reducing the coefficients of thermal expansion of the glaze. The amounts of silica used depend upon the flux and the maturing point of the glaze, but it is generally between 1 and 6 molecular equivalents.

Silica (SiO_2) is commonly obtained from sandstone, quartz sands, or flint pebbles. Silica is found combined with many ceramic materials that have been mentioned before. Below are listed a few of the more frequently used silica compounds.

Ball clay $(Al_2O_3 \cdot 2 SiO_2 \cdot 2 H_2O)$
Kaolin $(Al_2O_3 \cdot 2 SiO_2 \cdot 2 H_2O)$
Soda feldspar $(Na_2O \cdot Al_2O_3 \cdot 6 SiO_2)$
Potash feldspar $(K_2O \cdot Al_2O_3 \cdot 6 SiO_2)$
Cornwall stone $(1 RO \cdot 1.16 Al_2O_3 \cdot 8.95 SiO_2)$
Wollastonite $(Ca \cdot SiO_3)$
Petalite $(Li_2O \cdot Al_2O_3 \cdot 8 SiO_2)$

Tin oxide (SnO_2) is used primarily as an opacifier in glazes. Although rather expensive, it has continued in wide use because it has greater covering power than any other opacifier. The chief form of tin is:

Tin oxide (SnO_2), also called *stannic oxide*

Titanium oxide (TiO_2) is probably the only other oxide in the RO_2 group that has some of the refractory qualities of silicon. Its use in glazes, however, is entirely for its effect upon other colors and its action as an opacifier.

Titanium dioxide (TiO_2)
Rutile (TiO_2), an impure form containing iron and vanadium oxides

Characteristics of Ceramic Chemicals

Albany slip is a slip clay, which is a natural clay containing silica, alumina, and fluxes in the correct proportions to function as a glaze. It is mined in the vicinity of Albany, New York. Since it occurs in small pits, its composition and color will vary. Usually it fires to a glossy brown-black at temperatures between cones 8 and 12. Occasionally it may fire to a pale, nearly transparent tan. Slip clays are usually very easy to apply and fire with little, if any, defects. A typical composition and formula follow:

Composition			
	Percent		*Percent*
Silica	56.75	Magnesia	3.23
Alumina	15.47	Titania	1.00
Ferric oxide	5.73	Alkalies	3.25
Lime	5.78		

Formula		
0.195 K_2O	0.608 Al_2O_3	3.965 SiO_2
0.459 CaO	0.081 Fe_2O_3	
0.345 MgO		

Alumina hydrate $[Al(OH)_3]$ is preferred to the calcined form (Al_2O_3) for some uses, since it has better adhesive qualities and remains suspended in the glaze longer. Introduction of alumina for mat effects is considered to be more effective in the hydrate form than in such compounds as clay or feldspar.

Antimonious oxide (Sb_2O_3) is poisonous and slightly soluble in water. For satisfactory effect as an opacifier, it must be used in glazes firing below cone 1. Antimony is also used to produce yellow and orange colors for glazes. The most common mixture, known as *yellow base*, has the following composition:

Red lead	15
Antimony oxide	10
Tin oxide	4

The mixture is calcined to cone 09, then ground and washed.

Barium carbonate $(BaCO_3)$ is usually used in combination with other fluxes, since at lower temperatures it combines very slowly and acts as a refractory to form mat textures. At higher temperatures it reacts strongly as a flux.

Barium chromate $(BaCrO_4)$ is used to produce colors in the pale yellow to light green range. It is generally used in overglaze decoration, since it is fugitive at temperatures over cone 04.

Basic antimonate of lead $[Pb_3(SbO_4)_2]$, also known as *Naples yellow*, is primarily used as a paint pigment. It is a source of low-fire yellows. The presence of lead in Naples yellow is an advantage, since antimony will not produce a yellow unless combined with lead or iron.

Bentonite $(Al_2O_3 \cdot 4 SiO_2 \cdot 9 H_2O)$ is of volcanic origin. This formula is not quite correct since bentonite contains other impurities. South Dakota bentonite has the following analysis:

	Percent		Percent
Silica	64.23	Lime	0.46
Alumina	20.74	Magnesia	2.26
Iron oxide	3.49		

It generally fires to a light cream color and fuses at about 2400°F. Its chief value is its use as a plasticizer for short clays. As such it is about five times as effective as ball clay. Purified bentonite will also make a stronger glaze covering and will help prevent settling in the glaze. An addition of about 3 percent is sufficient.

Bicarbonate of soda ($NaHCO_3$) has some use in casting slips and in forming stains with cobalt sulfate. Soda ash (Na_2CO_3) is the sodium form more commonly used as a flux.

Bismuth subnitrate ($BiONO_3 \cdot H_2O$) generally contains impurities such as arsenic, lead, and silver carbonates. It melts at a low temperature and is used primarily to produce pearly metallic lusters under reducing conditions (see luster glazes, pp. 243–244).

Bone ash in the unrefined state has a formula of $4\,Ca_3(PO_4)_2 \cdot CaCO_3$ with a molecular weight of 1340. The material generally used today is the refined calcium phosphate $Ca_3(PO_4)_2$ with a molecular weight of 310. It is sometimes used as a glaze flux but more commonly as a body ingredient in bone china, chiefly in the kind produced in England. It lowers the firing temperatures required and increases translucency.

Borax ($Na_2O \cdot 2\,B_2O_3 \cdot 10\,H_2O$) is, next to lead, the major low-fire flux. It has a strong action on all ceramic compounds and may even be used in small amounts in the high-fire glazes that tend to be overly viscous in nature. Borax has a different effect than lead upon coloring oxides, and for this reason it is often used either alone or in combination with lead. Borax absorbs moisture and should therefore be kept dry, or weight calculations will be inaccurate. As mentioned earlier, borax is very soluble in water and should not be used on raw ware.

Boric acid ($B_2O_3 \cdot 2\,H_2O$) is a flaky material soluble in water. It is available in a fairly pure state at low price. Although boron is one of the neutral oxides (R_2O_3), it functions more as a flux, since it increases the gloss as does lead. Unlike silica, an acid, boron lowers the expansion coefficient and helps to increase elasticity.

Cadmium sulfide (CdS) is a low-fire yellow colorant. It is usually combined in a stain made of cadmium, selenium, and sulphur frits. Unfortunately it is fugitive above cone 010 and can be used only for overglaze decorations.

Calcium borate (see colemanite).

Calcium carbonate (see whiting).

Calcium fluoride (see fluorspar).

Calcium phosphate (see bone ash).

Calcium zirconium silicate is a commercially produced opacifier with the composition of ZrO_2, 51.12 percent; SiO_2, 25.41 percent; CaO, 22.23 percent. It does not have the strength of tin but is considerably cheaper. It will reduce slightly the maturing temperatures of the lower-fire glazes.

Carolina stone is similar to Cornwall stone.

China clay (see kaolin).

Chromic oxide (Cr_2O_3) and other chromium compounds are commonly used in glazes to produce green colors. Dichromates are preferred because of the greater amounts of chromium per weight. Care must be taken in the glaze composition, for, when combined with tin, a pink will result. Zinc will form a brown, and high-lead glazes may develop a yellow-lead chromate. Reducing conditions in the kiln will blacken the color. In fact, even adjacent tin-glazed and chrome-glazed pieces may affect each other in the kiln. Bright, low-temperature reds (below cone 010) can be produced by chrome oxide in a high-lead and low-alumina glaze.

Clay (see Chap. 4, pp. 139–145) is a decomposed feldspathic-type rock consisting chiefly of silicates of aluminium but often containing numerous other ingredients, such as quartz, micas, feldspars, iron oxides, carbonates of calcium and magnesium, and organic matter.

Cobalt carbonate ($CoCO_3$) is used to introduce a blue glaze color. When it is combined with manganese, iron chromate, or ochre it will produce black colorants.

Cobalt oxide (Co_2O_3) is the major blue colorant. It is extremely strong and therefore is often fritted with alumina and lime or with lead for lower-fire underglaze colors. The frit allows a lighter and more even color dispersion. Color stains made of cobalt, alumina, and zinc are uniform at all temperature ranges. Small amounts of cobalt in combination with MgO, SiO_2, and B_2O_3 will produce a variety of hues in the pink and lavender range.

Cobalt sulfate ($CoSo_4 \cdot 7\ H_2O$), unlike the other cobalt compounds mentioned, is very soluble in water. It melts at a low temperature and is primarily used in decorative work or luster ware.

Colemanite ($2\ CaO \cdot 3\ B_2O_3 \cdot 5\ H_2O$) is a natural hydrated calcium borate, which has the advantage of being only slightly soluble in water. Therefore, it does not develop the granular lumps in the glaze so characteristic of borax. Colemanite has wide use as a low-fire flux, since the boron present melts at a fairly low temperature. It tends to prevent crazing and also functions to some degree as an opacifier. Colemanite can be substituted for calcium in some glazes where calcium would harm the pink or red colors desired. Colemanite, used in both high- and low-fire glazes, tends to develop a milky blue opalescent color. It should be used immediately, since it tends to deflocculate. Gerstley Borate, a type of colemanite, is better in this respect.

Copper carbonate ($CuCO_3$) is a major green colorant used in glazes. The carbonate form is preferred to the oxide form in the production of blue-greens or copper reds under reducing conditions.

Copper oxide is (1) cupric or black copper oxide (CuO) or (2) cuprous or red copper oxide (Cu_2O). The addition of 2 percent or more of copper will decrease markedly the acid resistance of a lead glaze. Lead fluxes tend to produce a blackish green. When copper and tin are used with an alakline flux, a turquoise will result. Potash will induce a yellowish green, while zinc and copper with fluxes of sodium, potassium, and barium will develop a blue tinge.

Cornwall stone is a complex mixture derived from an English deposit of partially decomposed granite rock. It is composed of quartz (flint), feldspar, lepidolite, tourmaline, fluorspar, and small quantities of other minerals. Cornwall stone has characteristics that lie between those of kaolin and feldspar. It is a major ingredient of many English glazes and bodies and is subject to less firing strains than kaolin and feldspar. Because of the more intimate mixture of naturally occuring minerals, a smaller amount of alkali flux is necessary then would otherwise be needed. Since less bulk is required, there is less shrinkage of both the unfired and the fired glaze, thus minimizing glaze defects. Cornwall stone is roughly similar to *petuntze*, the feldspathic powered rock used for centuries by the Chinese as a major ingredient in their porcelain bodies and glazes. Like feldspars, Cornwall stone has variable composition; samples differ in the percentages of silica, potassium, sodium, and so on. If not available, a substitution of 67 parts feldspar, 22 parts flint, and 11 parts kaolin can be made for 100 units of Cornwall stone. However, as previously noted, the new glaze will not have identical characteristics.

A material similar to Cornwall stone, called Carolina stone, is mined in the United States but is not commonly available. An analysis of two samples (p. 234) shows almost identical proportions.

	Cornwall stone Percentage	Carolina stone Percentage
SiO_2	72.6	72.30
Al_2O_3	16.1	16.23
Fe_2O_3	0.23	0.07
CaO	1.4	0.62
MgO	0.1	trace
K_2O	4.56	4.42
Na_2O	3.67	4.14
CaF_2		
TiO_2	0.06	
Ignition loss	2.54	1.06

Formula for Cornwall stone sample

0.185	CaO	1.162	Al_2O_3	8.95	SiO_2
0.359	K_2O	0.0106	Fe_2O_3	0.0055	TiO_2
0.437	Na_2O		*Molecular weight 732.57*		
0.0185	MgO				

Cryolite (Na_3AlF_6) is used primarily as a flux and an opacifier for enamels and glasses. It has a limited use in glazes and bodies as a source of fluxes and alumina. In some glazes, an addition of cryolite will promote crazing.

Dolomite [$CaMg(CO_3)_2$] is a double carbonate of calcia and magnesia. It has a greater use in glass-making than in glazes. It is a cheap method of introducing calcia and magnesia into a glaze. Dolomite will promote a longer and lower firing range in clay bodies. Below cone 4, the addition of a small amount of a lower-firing alkaline flux to the dolomite will greatly increase this effect.

Epsom salts (see magnesium sulfate).

Feldspar is a crystalline rock composed of the aluminum silicates of potassium, sodium, and calcium. These silicates are never found in a pure state but in a mixture with one or the other predominating. For convenience in ceramic calculations, their formulas are usually given as follows:

Potash feldspar (microcline)
$$K_2O \cdot Al_2O_3 \cdot 6\ SiO_2$$
Soda feldspar (albite)
$$Na_2O \cdot Al_2O_3 \cdot 6\ SiO_2$$
Lime feldspar (anorthite)
$$CaO \cdot Al_2O_3 \cdot 6\ SiO_2$$

The feldspars are a major ingredient of porcelain and white-ware bodies and are often the only source of body flux. If the feldspar content of the body is high, the substitution of soda spar for potash feldspar will reduce the vitrification point by as much as 100°F. Feldspars are a cheap source of glaze flux and have the additional advantage of being non-soluble. Because of the presence of Al_2O_3 and SiO_2, the feldspar cannot be considered a flux at low temperature ranges, even though some flux is contributed to the glaze. The fluxing action is increased by the fineness of the particle size. Potash forms a harder glaze than does soda and decreases the thermal expansion. Thus, unless soda is desired for color purposes, potash feldspar should be preferred in the glaze composition (see Appendix, p. 308, for a comparative analysis).

Ferric chloride ($FeCl_3 \cdot 6\ H_2O$) is more commonly called *chloride of iron*. It is very soluble in water and must be stored in airtight containers. Its chief use is as a luster decoration on glass or glazes. It produces an iridescent gold-colored film under proper conditions (see luster glazes, p. 243).

Ferric oxide (see iron oxide).

Ferrous oxide (see iron oxide).

Flint (SiO_2) is also called silica or, in foreign publications, quartz. It is commonly obtained from sandstone, quartz sands, or flint pebbles. True flint is obtained from England, France, and Denmark. It is prepared by calcining and grinding flint beach pebbles. This cryptocrystalline flint has a different specific gravity (2.33) from that prepared from quartz sand or sandstone (2.65). In the United States, all silica is called *flint*. The difference between the two is slight. A "pebble" flint reacts a trifle faster in the glaze. The specific gravity is of importance only if it is used in casting slips.

When used alone, silica melts at the extremely high temperature of 3119°F and forms an unusually hard and stable crystal. It combines under heat, however, with a variety of fluxes at much lower temperatures to form a glass and with the alumina compounds to form the more refractory body structure. An increase in the silica content of a glaze has the effect of raising the maturing temperatures as well as increasing its hardness and resistance to wear. In a glaze, the addition of flint decreases its thermal expansions; in a body it increases them.

Fluorspar (CaF_2), also called *calcium fluoride*, has a limited use as a source of flux in glaze and body compositions. The particle size must be less than 100 mesh when used in the body, or pinholes are likely to form in the glaze. Fluorspar fluxes at a lower temperature than do other calcia compounds. With copper oxides, some unusual blue-green hues can be developed.

Ilmenite ($TiO_2 \cdot FeO$) is the mineral source of titanium and its compounds. Used as a coarse powder-like sand, it produces dark specks in the glaze.

Iron chromate ($FeCrO_4$) is used in combination with manganese and zinc oxide to produce underglaze brown colors or with cobalt to form a black stain. Used alone, it is fugitive above cone 04.

Iron oxides have three forms: (FeO) *ferrous oxide*, (Fe_2O_3) *ferric oxide* or hematite, and (Fe_3O_4) *ferrous-ferric oxide* or magnetite. Iron is the oxide most frequently used to produce tan or brown bodies and glazes. Were it not for its pronounced color, it would have a wide use as a flux. It is responsible for most of the low-firing characteristics and the red color of many earthenware clays. A pink stain can be made with a smaller amount of iron plus alumina, calcium, and flint. When reduced in a suitable glaze, iron will form gray-greens (see celadon, p. 213).

Kaolin ($Al_2O_3 \cdot 2 SiO_2 \cdot 2 H_2O$) is also called *china clay* or *pure clay*. Because of its composition and relative purity, kaolin is the highest-firing clay. It is an important ingredient of all white ware and china bodies, since it fires to pure white. For glazes, kaolin constitutes a major source of Al_2O_3 and SiO_2. The chief residual deposits in the United States are in North Carolina, and sedimentary deposits are found in South Carolina and Georgia. For bodies, the more plastic sedimentary types are preferred. The sedimentary kaolin deposits of Florida are even more plastic and are often termed ball kaolin (see Chap. 4, p. 140).

Lead antimonate (see basic antimonate of lead).

Lead, bisilicate (see lead silicate).

Lead, white (see lead carbonate).

Lead carbonate [$2PbCO_3 \cdot Pb(OH)_2$], more commonly called white lead, is a major low-fire flux that imparts a lower surface tension and viscosity over a wide temperature range. This results in a smooth, brilliant glaze with few surface defects. Lead may comprise all the flux in a low-temperature glaze (Pemco frit #316, p. 308) or, at cone 4, a lesser amount (dinnerware glaze, p. 315). Unless properly compounded, lead glazes can be poisonous, since the harmful lead is released when contacted by acids. Lead should be used only as a silica frit, because otherwise it may be absorbed into the body by inhaling or through a cut in the skin. Toxic lead release is encouraged by the inclusion of more than 2 percent CuO or more than 5 percent combined Fe_2O_3 and MnO_2. However, relatively large amounts of Al_2O_3, SiO_2, CaO, and ZrO_2 increase the acid-resistance of a lead glaze. Additions of Na_2O, K_2O, and BaO all decrease acid resistance (see also pp. 207–8).

Lead oxide as used in ceramics is of two types: (PbO) *litharge* or lead monoxide, and (Pb_3O_4) *red lead* or minium. Litharge is a yellow powder that has greater use in Europe than in the United States. Since litharge occasionally contains impurities and has larger particles than does the carbonate form, the latter is the preferred lead compound. Because of the greater amount of oxygen, the red form is often used in place of litharge. Ceramic grades of red lead are seldom pure but usually contain 75 percent red lead and about 25 percent litharge. Pound for pound, red lead contains more PbO than does the carbonate form.

Lead silicate is a frit made of lead and silica to eliminate the toxic effects of the lead compounds. The two most common types are: *lead monosilicate*, with a composition of 15 percent SiO_2 and 85 percent PbO; and *lead bisilicate*, with a formula of 65 percent PbO, 34 percent SiO_2, and 1 percent Al_2O_3.

Lead silicate, hydrous [$2\,PbSiO_2 \cdot Pb(OH_2)$] has a molecular weight of 807. This material is the basic silicate of white lead. It is used as a substitute for lead carbonate when the CO_2 released by the carbonate forms pinholes or is otherwise objectionable in the glaze.

Lead sulfide (PbS), also called *galena*, is the black powder that is the raw source of all lead compounds. It has a very limited use in glazes.

Lepidolite ($LiF \cdot KF \cdot Al_2O_3 \cdot 3\,SiO_2$), also called lithium mica, contains from 3 to 6 percent of lithia. It has some use as a body ingredient in chinaware and is a source of flux, Al_2O_3, and SiO_2 in higher-temperature glazes. It will tend to brighten most glazes, lower thermal expansions, and reduce brittleness (see lithium carbonate).

Lime (CaO), calcium oxide (see whiting).

Litharge (PbO) (see lead oxide).

Lithium carbonate (Li_2CO_3) is a common source of lithia, which is a strong flux in the higher temperature ranges. With lithia, greater amounts of Al_2O_3, SiO_2, and CaO can be used in alkaline glazes, thus producing a more durable glaze while retaining the unusual copper blues characteristic of the alkaline glazes. It can be used in place of lead in the medium temperature ranges when volitization is a problem.

Magnesium carbonate ($MgCO_3$), magnesite acts as a refractory at lower temperatures, changing to a

flux at higher temperatures. It is valuable to slow down the fluid qualities of crystalline and other runny glazes. It also improves glaze adhesion.

Magnesium sulfate ($MgSO_4 \cdot 7\,H_2O$) is better known as *epsom salts*. Its primary use in glazes is to retard the settling of frits and glazes. Usually 1 percent, dissolved in hot water, will be sufficient and will have no apparent effect on the glaze.

Magnetite (see iron oxides).

Manganese dioxide (see manganese oxide).

Manganese oxide (MnO_2) is used in ceramics as a colorant. It should not be used in concentrations greater than 5 percent in either body or glaze, because blisters may develop. The usual colors produced are in the brown range. With cobalt, a black results; with the proper alkaline fluxes, purple and dark reddish hues can be produced. When fritted with alumina, a pink colorant will be formed.

Nepheline syenite ($K_2O \cdot 3\,Na_2O \cdot 4\,Al_2O_3 \cdot 9\,SiO_2$) is a material roughly similar to a feldspar and has the following composition:

	Percent
SiO_2	60.4
Al_2O_3	23.6
Fe_2O_3	0.08
CaO	0.7
MgO	0.1
Na_2O	9.8
K_2O	4.7
Ignition loss	0.7

Molecular formula			
Na_2O	0.713	Al_2O_3	1.04
K_2O	0.220		
CaO	0.056	SiO_2	4.53
MgO	0.011		

Molecular weight 447

A major use for nepheline syenite is as a substitute for potash feldspar where it lowers the firing temperatures required. It also produces a greater firing range and increased thermal expansion, which in turn will reduce crazing tendencies in the glaze. Its use in a glaze is roughly similar to potash feldspar except for the lowering of the maturing point.

Nickel oxide is used in two forms, (NiO) *green nickel oxide* or nickelous and (Ni_2O_3) *black nickel oxide* or nickelic. The function of nickel in a glaze is almost solely as a colorant. Depending upon the flux used and the ratio of alumina, a variety of colors can be produced: with zinc, a blue is obtained; with lime, a tan; with barium, a brown; and with magnesia, a green. None of these hues are particularly brilliant. In general, nickel is used to soften and alter other coloring oxides. In addition, the use of 5 to 10 percent nickel in a proper glaze results in the formation of a crystalline structure.

Ochre is a term given to clays containing varying amounts of red iron or manganese oxides. Their chief use is in paint manufacturing. However, they can be used as glaze or slip colorants to impart tan, brown, or brick-red hues.

Opax is a standard commercially produced opacifier with the following composition:

	Percent		*Percent*
ZrO_2	90.84	Na_2O	1.11
SiO_2	6.48	Al_2O_3	0.91

Opax does not have the power of tin oxide, but it is considerably cheaper, and for this reason it is often used to replace part of the tin oxide that would otherwise be required.

Pearl ash (see potassium carbonate).

Petalite ($Li_2O \cdot Al_2O_3 \cdot 8\ SiO_2$), lithium-aluminium silicate, is chiefly used as an auxiliary body flux to reduce thermal expansions and increase shock resistance. At about cone 06 it converts into beta spodumene, which has almost no volume change when heated or cooled. It is a source of lithia and silica for medium- and high-temperature glazes.

Plastic vitrox ($1\ RO \cdot 1.69\ Al_2O_3 \cdot 14.64\ SiO_2$) is a complex mineral mined in California that has a use in both glaze and body formulas as a source of silica, alumina, and potash. It is similar to both potash feldspar and Cornwall stone. (See Appendix, p. 307 for comparative analysis.)

Potash feldspar (see feldspar).

Potassium carbonate (K_2CO_3) is more commonly called *pearl ash*. It is used primarily to modify color effects. When pearl ash is substituted for the lead, sodium, or calcium content, the colors resulting from copper oxide can be changed from the usual green to either a yellow-green or a bright blue.

Potassium dichromate ($K_2Cr_2O_7$) is used in glazes as a green colorant. When it is calcined with tin, low-fire stains developing pink and red hues are formed (see chromic oxide).

Praseodymium oxide (Pr_6O_{11}), a black oxide, is a rare earth compound used in ceramics as a yellow colorant. It is commonly combined with zirconium oxide and silica to form a glaze stain that is stable at all normal firing temperatures.

Pyrophyllite ($Al_2O_3 \cdot 4\ SiO_2 \cdot H_2O$) is used primarily in wall-tile bodies, where it decreases thermal expansions, crazing, and moisture expansions to which tile is subjected. Since it is nonplastic, it has limited use in pottery bodies.

Red lead (see lead oxide).

Rutile (TiO_2) is an impure oxide of titanium containing small amounts of iron and vanadium. It is used as a tan colorant.

Selenium (Se) is most often used as a glass colorant. It has a limited use in ceramic glazes and overglaze colors, primarily as cadmium-selenium red frits. These frits, unfortunately, are fugitive at higher temperatures.

Silica (see flint).

Silicon carbide (SiC) has many industrial uses. Its value in ceramics is as the sole or major ingredient in high-temperature kiln furniture and muffles. When added to an alkaline glaze in small amounts ($\frac{1}{2}$ of 1 percent), the carbon will reduce the copper oxides to form localized copper reds.

Sillimanite ($Al_2O_3 \cdot SiO_2$) is similar in many respects to Kyanite. Major uses are in high-temperature refractory bodies.

Silver chloride (AgCl) is the major silver compound used in luster overglaze preparations (see lusters p. 243). When silver chloride is combined with bismuth and with a resin or fat oil as a binder, an overglaze metallic luster with greenish or yellow tints will form.

Soda ash (see sodium carbonate).

Sodium aluminate ($Na_2O \cdot Al_2O_3$) is used to prevent casting slips from setting and to increase the strength of dry ware.

Sodium bicarbonate (see bicarbonate of soda).

Sodium carbonate (Na_2CO_3) is commonly called *soda ash*. It is a very active flux, but because of its solubility it is more commonly used in glazes as a frit ingredient. Small quantities of soda ash, functioning as a deflocculant, will reduce the water of plasticity required in a clay body. This increases workability and strength of the plastic body and reduces the shrinkage when it goes from the wet to the dry state.

Sodium silicate ($Na_2 \cdot XSiO_2$) is a compound that can vary from $1 \, Na_2O \cdot 1.6 \, SiO_2$ to $1 \, Na_2O \cdot 3.75 \, SiO_2$. It usually comes in liquid form and is the major deflocculant used in casting slips. Like soda ash,

it greatly reduces the water required to make the clay into a slip form. In doing so, it lessens the rate of shrinkage, the strains of drying, and breakage in the green and dry states.

Sodium uranate ($Na_2O \cdot UO_3$), more commonly called *uranium yellow*, has unfortunately not been available in the United States since World War II because of restrictions placed on uranium by the Atomic Energy Commission. Uranium yellows are still available, however, in Europe. Uranium compounds formerly were the best source of yellow colorants. When uranium compounds are combined with various fluxes or with tin and zirconium oxide, a variety of hues from bright yellow through orange to vermillion red can be developed (see also uranium oxide).

Spodumene ($Li_2O \cdot Al_2O_3 \cdot 4 \, SiO_2$) is an important source of lithia. The use of litha, which is an active flux, helps to develop unusual copper-blue hues. Spodumene is also added to white ware and porcelain bodies. When used to replace feldspar, it will reduce the vitrification temperature as well as the shrinkage rate. Strange as it may seem, the crystalline form of spodumene expands at about 1700°F (927°C) instead of shrinking. When a mixture of 60 percent spodumene and 40 percent lead bisilicate is used, a nonplastic, press-formed body can be made that at 1970°F (1077°C), will have zero absorption and zero shrinkage.

Steatite, a hydrous magnesium silicate, is a massive variety of talc. Most steatite is used in powdered form for electrical insulators. It has very little shrinkage, and occasionally the rocklike nuggets are turned down in a lathe for special projects. Steatite was used by the Egyptians some 5000 years ago for the creation of beads and small figurines. These were generally covered with a turquoise alkaline copper glaze (see talc).

Talc varies from $3 \, MgO \cdot 4 \, SiO_2 \cdot H_2O$ to $4 \, MgO \cdot 5 \, SiO_2 \cdot H_2O$. In the solid and more impure form, it is also known as *steatite* or *soapstone*. Talc is occasionally used in glazes, but it is more frequently employed as a major ingredient in white-ware bodies firing at moderate temperatures (cones 04–6). Like dolomite, it is used to lower the firing temperatures of kaolin, ball clays, and feldspars, which are often the other body ingredients. Talc will promote a slight opacity in glazes.

Tin oxide (SnO_2), also called *stannic oxide*, is the most effective of all opacifiers. From 5 to 7 percent will produce a completely opaque white glaze. An excess will create a dull surface. Tin also has wide use in stains, since it has considerable effect on the color qualities of most color-forming oxides. Because of its relatively high price, tin substitutes are frequently used (see opacifiers).

Titanium oxide (TiO_2), or more correctly *titanium dioxide*, is a major opacifier when used either alone or in a frit. Like rutile, which is an impure form containing iron, titanium will, if used in any quantity, encourage a semimat surface texture.

Uranium oxide, [U_3O_8 (black)], is a depleted nuclear fuel used as a yellow colorant in low-fire lead glazes. More efficient as colorants are other forms of uranium, such as sodium uranate [$Na_2O \cdot UO_2$ (orange)] and sodium diuranate (yellow). A 5-percent addition of tin oxide aids the color formation, while a reduction fire is detrimental. The tin-vanadium, zirconium-vanadium, and praseodymium yellow stains have greater flexibility and no radiation hazard. They are preferred by most potters.

Vanadium pentoxide (V_2O_5) is a rather weak yellow colorant when used alone. When fritted in the proper composition with tin, it produces a strong yellow color. This stain, known commercially as tin-vanadium stain, has largely replaced the uranium yellows, which are no longer available. It has a wide firing range (cones 06–14), is transparent, and is not affected by a reduction firing.

Volcanic ash occurs in many regions of the American West. It was formed from the dust of volcanic glass erupted in prehistoric times. Since the material often floated through the air many miles before being deposited, it is extremely fine and can be used with little preparation. Its composition is roughly similar to that of a granite-type rock (see the formula under RO oxides, p. 229). An average analysis of Kansas ash is as follows:

	Percent		Percent
SiO_2	72.51	MgO	0.07
Al_2O_3	11.55	K_2O	7.87
Fe_2O_3	1.21	Na_2O	1.79
TiO_2	0.54	Ignition loss	3.81
CaO	0.68		

In most glazes volcanic ash can be substituted for roughly 70 parts of feldspar and 30 parts of flint. A low-fire 04 glaze can be compounded of 60 percent ash and 40 percent borax and lead or just lead.

Whiting ($CaCO_3$) is a *calcium carbonate* produced domestically by processing marble or limestone. European whiting is generally obtained from chalk deposits, such as those at the famous cliffs of Dover. Whiting is the major high-fire flux, although it has a limited use in bodies where a small amount will lower vitrification temperatures and reduce porosity. As a flux, it produces much harder and tougher silicates than will either the lead or alkaline compounds. For this reason, small amounts are often added to the lower-fire glazes. As with other fluxes, calcium has an effect upon the coloring oxides, particularly chrome greens.

Wollastonite ($CaSiO_3$) is a natural calcium silicate. As a replacement for flint and whiting, it reduces firing shrinkage and improves heat shock. It is used in both bodies and glazes.

Zinc oxide (ZnO) is a difficult compound to classify. At high temperatures it is an active flux. When used to excess in a glaze low in alumina and cooled slowly, zinc will produce crystalline structures. Opacity will develop if zinc is used in a high-alumina low-calcium glaze, with no borosilicate fluxes, at cone 1 or higher in amounts of 0.15 equivalents. In general, zinc increases the maturing range of a glaze

Guide to Use of Colorants

Color	Oxide	Percentage	Temperature	Atmosphere
Black				
{ cobalt		1–2	any	either
manganese		2–4		
{ cobalt		1		
iron		8	any	either
manganese		3		
Blue				
cobalt		½–1	any	either
turquoise–copper (alkaline flux)		3–5	low	oxidizing
slate blue–nickel (with zinc)		1–3	low	oxidizing
Brown				
rutile		5	any	reducing
chromium (with MgO, ZnO)		2–5	low	either
iron		3–7	any	oxidizing
manganese		5	any	either
nickel (with zinc)		2–4	any	either
Green				
copper oxide		1–5	any	oxidizing
gray-green–iron		1–4	any	reducing
nickel–magnesia		3–5	low	oxidizing
Red				
pink–chrome and tin (1 to 18)		5	any	oxidizing
coral–chromium (with high PbO)		5	low	oxidizing
purple–manganese (with KNaO)		4–6	any	oxidizing
copper		1	any	reducing
iron (high SiO_2, KNaO), CaO		2–5	low	oxidizing
Tan				
iron		2	any	either
manganese		2	any	either
rutile		2	any	either
Yellow				
antimony yellow stain (with high PbO)		3–5	low	either
praseodymium yellow stain		4–6	any	either
uranium yellow and orange (with high PbO)		5–8	low	oxidizing
zirconium vanadium stain		5–10	any	either
tin vanadium stain		4–6	any	either

and promotes a higher gloss, brighter colors, a reduction of expansions, and, under some conditions, an opacity.

Zirconium oxide (ZrO_2) is seldom used alone as an opacifier in ceramics but is generally combined with other oxides and fritted into a more stable silicate form. Below are listed a few commercial zirconium silicates. None have the strength of tin oxide, but they are considerably cheaper.

Calcium zirconium silicate: 51.12 percent ZrO_2, 25.41 percent SiO_2, and 22.23 percent CaO

Magnesium zirconium silicate: 53.75 percent ZrO_2, 29.92 percent SiO_2, and 18.54 percent MgO

Zinc zirconium silicate: 45.78 percent ZrO_2, 23.08 percent SiO_2, and 30.52 percent ZnO

Zirconium spinel: 39.94 percent ZrO_2, 25.25 percent SiO_2, 19.47 percent ZrO_2, and 19.41 percent Al_2O_3

Most of the above compounds are used in combination with other opacifiers, such as tin or the titanium compounds (see also opax and zircopax).

Zircopax is a standard commercially produced opacifier with the composition of 64.88 percent ZrO_2, 0.22 percent TiO_2, 34.28 percent SiO_2.

Colorants for Glazes and Decoration

Coloring Oxides

Most studio potters obtain their glaze colors from the oxides or carbonates of the more common metals, such as iron, copper, nickel, tin, zinc, and manganese. Other oxides, such as vanadium and cobalt, although rarer and more expensive, are extensively used because of a lack of cheaper substitutes. Most of these compounds have been discussed in previous sections. The list of major colorants (opposite) indicates the oxide necessary and the amount generally used to produce a particular color. However, just because an oxide is listed as producing a green does not mean that it will produce a green in every case. A study of the section on ceramic materials (pp. 231–241) will reveal that generally the particular color that develops from an oxide depends upon the type of flux used, the proportions of alumina or silica, and the firing temperature. In some cases, even the rate of cooling will have an effect upon the glaze. Therefore, the list of oxides and colors on page 240 is merely for convenience in determining color possibilities. Before using the oxide, the potter should be aware of its characteristics and the characteristics of the glaze in which it is to be used.

It is common practice to use two or more colorants in order to modify harsh colors and to obtain subtle variations or mottled color effects. Copper and nickel are often added to soften powerful cobalt hues. Opacifiers are used to brighten colors. Rutile is a frequent addition, since it contributes a runny and slightly specked quality as well as slightly matting a glaze.

Opacifiers

Opacifiers are, for the most part, a group of chemicals that are relatively insoluble in the glaze melt.

Opacifiers

Color	Oxide	Percentage	Temperature	Atmosphere
Pure white	tin	5	any	either
Weak blue white	titanium	8–12	any	either
White	zirconium	8–12	any	either
Weak yellow white	antimony	10–12	low	oxidizing
White	opax (a frit)	10	any	either
White	zircopax (a frit)	10	any	either

Tin oxide and zirconium oxide are the chief examples of this type. As such, they remain suspended in the glaze and, if dense enough, prevent light from penetrating through to the body. Most opacifiers, and of course those of the greatest value, are white. However, some give a slight yellow, pink, or bluish cast to the glaze.

Another type of opacifier is titanium (or zinc under some conditions), which tends to form minute crystalline structures within the glaze. Having a different index of refraction from the major portion of the glaze, it thus breaks up and prevents much light penetration. This is the type of crystal formation associated with mat glazes. It is the reason why all mats must be, necessarily, either wholly or partially opaque.

Spinel Stains

Under certain circumstances, the use of a raw coloring oxide may be objectionable. For example, most metallic oxides are quite soluble in the melting glaze. In the previous section, we noted that the fluxes and other elements of the glaze had considerable effect upon color quality. Overglaze and underglaze decoration with any degree of precision or control is impossible with colorants that diffuse into, or flow with, the glaze. In these cases, a special type of colorant known as a spinel is used.

A spinel stain is a colored crystal that is highly resistant to attack by fluxes in the glaze and to the effects of high temperatures. In strict chemical terms, *spinel* refers to the mineral magnesium aluminate ($MgOAl_2O_3$). However, manganese, iron, and chromium may be present by replacement. The crystal is an octahedron variety of extreme hardness. The ruby gem is a red spinel. By calcining certain oxides together, some very stable colored spinels can be formed. In general, these follow the formula $RO \cdot R_2O_3$. The RO member can be either MgO, ZnO, NiO, CaO, CdO, MnO, or FeO, and the R_2O_3 can be Cr_2O_3, Al_2O_3, or Fe_2O_3.

Preparation of a spinel stain is a long procedure, and it is not recommended unless it is necessary for advanced experimental work. There is a wide range of commercial stains, expertly prepared, available

at reasonable cost. The general idea, however, of the preparation should be understood. Detailed information can be found in the reference texts listed in the Appendix (pp. 329–331).

It is extremely necessary that the chemicals involved are mixed completely and intimately. To this end the raw chemicals should first be passed through an 80-mesh sieve. It is preferable that they be in the form of soluble salts, that is, the nitrates or sulfates of the oxides just listed. These are thoroughly mixed in a liquid solution. After the water has been evaporated, the dry mixture is placed in a crucible or a kiln and calcined. The temperature will vary with the mixture. If the mixture melts into a solid mass, it should be calcined in a pot furnace so that the crucible can be removed with tongs and the contents poured into water, thus preventing the spinel from hardening into a solid crystalline block. Afterwards, the material is broken up with an iron mortar and pestle into a coarse powder, which is then ball milled. For a uniform color without specks, the particle size of the spinel must be extremely small. This may necessitate grinding in the ball mill for well over a hundred hours. When it is sufficiently fine, the stain should be washed several times with hot water to remove any remaining soluble salts. Filters may be necessary at this point to prevent the loss of fine particles.

Other Colored Stains

Besides the spinels, a number of other chemical compounds are calcined to produce stable colorants at certain temperatures. A discussion of a few of the better-known examples will serve to illustrate some of the numerous possibilities in the preparation of colorants.

An ultramarine blue can be formed by a silicate of cobalt. It is made by calcining cobalt oxide and flint, plus a flux such as feldspar.

Green stains can be developed by calcining fluorspar and chromium oxide.

Yellow stains, such as Naples yellow and yellow base, are made from antimony, lead, and tin. Calcium and sodium uranate can also be used, when available, to form various yellow and orange colorants.

Pink and red stains are made by several methods. One of the most unusual is the precipitation of colloidal gold upon kaolin, which is then calcined and ground to form the stain. Other red stains are formed from a mixture of tin, calcium, flint, and chromium. (For further information and specific details, consult the reference texts by Parmelee and Norton and the *Literature Abstracts of Ceramic Glazes* listed in the Appendix, pp. 329–331).

Underglaze Colors

Underglaze colors were briefly mentioned before in the section on decoration (pp. 196–197). As the term indicates, they are colors used under the glaze. Since they will eventually be fired at the same temperature as the glaze, the variety of colors available is less than for overglaze colors. For example, at the hard porcelain range of cone 14, most, if not all, of the delicate hues available in overglaze colors will burn out completely. This leaves only the blues, browns, grays, gold-pinks, reduction reds, and celadon hues available for use at these higher temperatures. It is advisable to run a series of firing tests before attempting any amount of decorative work at such temperatures. The basic reason for employing underglaze rather than overglaze colors is durability. Their greatest use is in the field of dinnerware.

Underglaze colors are made up of a colorant, either a raw oxide or a spinel, a flux such as feldspar to allow the color to adhere to the body, and a diluent like silica, calcined kaolin, or ground bisque ware. The purpose of these last materials is either to lighten the color or to equalize shrinkage. It is rather important that the mixture be adjusted properly to the bisque ware and the final glaze. The glazed surface should show no change in gloss over the decoration. A preliminary firing to red heat is necessary before glazing to burn out the vehicle used to adhere the mixture, which may be either a solution of gun tragacanth or oil of lavender that has been thinned with turpentine. Failure to burn off the carbon formed by the adherent will make the glaze bubble and blister over the decoration.

Overglaze Colors

The major differences between overglaze colors and underglaze colors are the use of a lower melting flux and a wider range of colors. Since the decoration is to be applied to a previously fired glaze, the final firing need be only high enough to allow the flux to melt into the glaze and seal the color. This is usually at a temperature of cone 016, approximately 1470°F (799°C). The flux is made of varying proportions of lead, borax, and flint, depending upon the color to be used with it. The mixture is calcined lightly, ground, and washed. The colorant, and if necessary, an opacifier, is then added, and the whole mixture is ball milled to an adequate fineness. A vehicle such as gum or oil is used to help the mixture to adhere to the glazed surface. In commercial production, where decoration is standardized, printing methods are used. The colors of both types of decoration are applied by decals or silk screen.

Lusters

Since lusters are employed more as decoration than as a glaze, they are included in this section on decorative coloring materials. As was noted earlier in the discussion of glaze types (Chap. 8, p. 214), a luster is nothing more than a thin layer of metal that is deposited and fused upon the surface of the glaze. There are various methods by which this can be accomplished, some of them outlined below. Luster can give a variety of effects, depending upon the transparency or color of the composition and the type of glaze upon which it is applied. In Persian and Hispano-Moresque pieces it is very effectively combined with underglaze decoration. In fact, luster really comes into its own when it is used to enrich other types of decoration. If used alone as an overall glaze, it tends to look like a rather cheap imitation of either glass or metal. The colors available in lusters are a transparent iridescent, a nacreous silver white, and metallic hues in a variety of yellows, greens, browns, and reds.

Preparation of lusters will vary according to the method of firing employed. There are three types of preparation.

1. A mixture composed of a resin, oil of lavender, and a metallic salt is brushed on the glazed ware. The ware is then fired in an oxidizing kiln to a low temperature of between 1100° and 1300°F (593°–704°C), at which point the carbon in the resin reduces the metallic salt to its metal form. Most lusters contain bismuth nitrate, an active flux, as well as the other metal salts. This is used in combination with zinc acetate, lead acetate, and alumina to produce a clear, iridescent luster. The various metal colorants are always used in the form of a salt that decomposes at the lower temperatures needed to form the luster coating. Yellows can be made with chrome alum and bismuth nitrate. Nickel nitrate, cobalt sulphate, manganese sulphate, and iron chloride will produce a variety of browns, shading from yellowish to reddish hues. Uranium nitrate, where available, develops a greenish yellow. Gold is commonly used to produce red hues and platinum to create silvery lusters. Many combinations of these colorants are used and results will be varied, depending in part upon the basic glaze and the firing schedule. In general, the luster mixture will consist of 1 part metallic salt, 3 to 5 parts resin, and 7 to 10 parts oil of lavender. The resin, usually gum dammar, is heated; when it becomes liquid, the nitrate or chloride is added. When the nitrate dissolves, the oil is slowly poured in. The solution is then filtered or cooled and decanted. The experiments in *Literature Abstracts of Ceramic Glazes* (see Appendix, p. 330) will help in creating formulas.

2. The method previously discussed is one that is commonly used today to produce lusters. Another type is similar to that employed many centuries ago by Egyptian and Islamic potters, although it is seldom used today. The ancients developed luster and carried this decorative glaze to its highest level of artistic merit. The chief difference between their method and that described above is the use of a reduction fire to reduce the metal rather than having a reducing agent contained in the resin. The mixture, which is brushed on the glazed ware, consists of 3 parts metal, usually in a carbonate form, 7 parts red ochre, and an adhesive, such as gum tragacanth. Old recipes call for vinegar or wine, but

gum is doubtless more efficient. In the firing cycle, the atmosphere is oxidizing until a low red heat is reached, whereupon reduction is started and continued to the temperature necessary to reduce the metal, usually from 1200° to 1300°F (649–704°C).

3. The third method of developing a luster is also seldom used, but in rare cases it occurs by accident. The color is incorporated into the glaze, preferably in the form of a metallic salt. Various combinations can be used in proportions ranging from 0.5 to 8 percent of the total glaze. As in the resinate type of luster glaze, the use of bismuth, in addition to the other metallic salts, will aid luster development. The kiln is fired oxidizing to the maturity point of the glaze, then cooled to between 1200° and 1300°F (649°–704°C). At this point the kiln is relit and fired for about 15 minutes with a reducing atmosphere. Accurate records should be kept on reduction firings, since variations of temperature and reduction periods will produce quite different results.

Binders

Various materials can be added to either a clay body or a glaze to increase the green or dry strength of the ceramic form, to aid glaze adhesion, and to lessen injury to the fragile glaze coating during the kiln loading. The several blinders and waxes used in industrial production to increase the body strength are not really needed by the studio potter, since his plastic clay body is usually adequate in this regard.

Clay

If the glaze contains an excess of 10 percent kaolin, additional binders may not be needed. However, if the clay content is low, the inclusion of about 3 percent bentonite will increase adhesion. It should be mixed with the dry ingredients.

Gums

Traditionally, gum arabic or tragacanth have been used as glaze binders. The granular gum crystals are soaked overnight in water and stirred vigorously the following day. About one-quarter ounce will make a quart of creamlike mucilage binder. A couple of drops of carbolic acid are needed to prevent decomposition. One or two teaspoons of this solution per quart of glaze is usually adequate.

Methocel

Methocel is a synthetic methylcellulose compound that will not deteriorate as the gums will and which also serves as an agent to prevent setting. The latter is a problem to which colemanite, in particular, is susceptible. Normally 1 to 2 percent methocel by dry weight is sufficient. However, one should not attempt to add the dry powder to a liquid glaze.

Instead, he should sift the powder into hot water in a double boiler, soak the mixture overnight, and then pour the resultant jellylike mass into a larger container of hot water. When all the methocel is dissolved, it can be added to dry glaze ingredients. An electric mixer is useful for this step.

Temporary Binders

In an emergency, sugar, syrup, or wheat flour can be used as a binder. Of course, all of these will ferment, and none of them have the deflocculating action of methocel.

10 The Professional Potter

As the pottery student nears the end of his course of studies, he faces the question of what use he will make of his new knowledge. While pottery making in school can be an exciting experience, a relief from the routine of academic studies, the life of a professional potter is one of hard work and long hours, with compensation often out of proportion to the training required.

For most students the prospect is not encouraging, and ceramics fills the role of an interesting hobby, a relaxation from an industrial or professional livelihood. A few trained potters become teachers, which requires additional work at the graduate level. For the prospective teacher it is useful to have considerable background in other craft media or in sculpture, for beginning positions often include teaching assignments in more than one area. Situations vary widely in terms of facilities, class size, and administrative duties. Ideally, the college or university should provide a studio and sufficient free time to allow the potter to experiment and grow in his field. Unfortunately, many institutions hire a potter because he is creative and productive, only to overwhelm him later with oversize classes and administrative red tape.

THE STUDIO POTTER

In view of the time and energy that must necessarily be expended in teaching, it is natural that many talented students are attracted to the prospect of opening their own studios, and the general affluence of large segments of society has made the idea much more feasible now than it was in years past. The hand-made pot is today truly a luxury item—hardly a necessity.

Perhaps the most difficult task for the potter dreaming of his own studio is to develop a realistic dollars-and-cents approach. The few pots sold during student days seem to represent a great profit. Seldom does the beginner accurately calculate the time he has spent, nor does he realize that, in school,

opposite : 432. DAVID GIL for the Bennington Potters, U.S.A. Tea and coffee pots designed to match Bennington's stacking dinnerware (see Fig. 434).

he had the free use of a kiln worth perhaps $3000, paid nothing for the fuel, and probably purchased his chemicals and clay below cost. All these items, plus the rental of a studio, the expense of utilities, and miscellaneous expenditures such as advertising and mailing, add immeasurably to overhead once the potter is on his own.

The school environment is so unlike that of the producing studio that it would be a great advantage for the student to apprentice himself for a year or so to a professional potter or to find employment in a small pottery. If one plans to have a sales outlet in connection with a studio, location becomes very important. The expense and restrictions of a metropolitan area often make such a situation impractical. For obvious reasons, most potters prefer to live in the country. Setting up shop near a major highway is not really necessary. True pot lovers will seek out an excellent craftsman and return with their friends.

Some potters prefer to sell mainly through outside shops, but since the usual markup in these outlets is 100 percent, it is easy to price oneself out of sales, unless one can produce an attractive line that can be thrown and decorated quickly. Items placed on consignment traditionally have a 50 percent markup. Unfortunately, shops that carry consignment goods often have commercial lines as well and use the consignment pieces primarily as window-dressing, without making much effort to sell them. For some years "craft fairs" have been popular in many parts of the country. A few potters have found these to be an important source of summer sales, although competition has increased in recent years. One potter operating in a rural location near a large city has had good results by holding a "kiln opening" periodically during the summer. Post cards sent to a list of interested customers ensure a good turnout over the weekend.

What to make is perhaps more important than the details of the selling procedure. It is usually a great shock for the beginning potter to realize that the public does not always have the same preferences that he does. While the craftsman may like the mottled brown-glazed bowl, it could sell twice as fast if it were blue. It is not that treasured show pieces will not sell, for indeed they will. But the new customer is more likely to buy, for example, a set of mugs. As he grows to enjoy the feel of the handle and the slight irregularity of form and glaze, he will become interested in something that is more exciting to the craftsman. Unlike the usual retail operation, a very personal relationship develops between the studio potter and his customers. They greet a kiln opening with the same degree of anticipation as does the potter. In fact, one often has the embarrassing problem of cutting short their visits in order to get on with potting.

While the ceramics teacher is to some degree subsidized so that he can make what he pleases, the professional studio potter must sell consistently. This does not mean a lowering of standards, but rather an orientation toward salable items. He is likely to find that the market for the large show piece is limited. Although the average home may have room for a few decorative vases, its capacity for mugs, sugarbowls and creamers, casseroles, pitchers, planters, and so forth, is almost unlimited, and these objects will constitute the major area of sales. To the idealistic beginner the ash-tray-and-candy-dish line may seem like the lowest form of ceramics, and most talented potters would agree. But upon opening a shop, he will discover that the customer who will pay $30 for a vase also wants a hand-made ash tray and will buy anything that could remotely serve this purpose.

In a callous and practically antiesthetic commercial world, which often seems to pander to the lowest taste, the high standards of the student potter are refreshing. However, to make what one pleases and insist that the public take it or leave it can be self-defeating. For example, it is not logical to have only one teapot on the shelf, no matter how attractive it may be. Rather, it is essential to have several styles, colors, and so forth in different price ranges. Some customers will want the most expensive, the best in the house! Others will be bargain hunters. It really makes no difference that all the teapots may represent the same amount of effort on the part of the craftsman. Just as the customer in a clothing store would be distressed to find that all the suits were brown and bore the same price, so the potential buyer of ceramics will hope to find a wide selection.

THE POTTER IN INDUSTRY

The Greek or Chinese potter of two thousand years ago, were he suddenly transported into the studio of today's hand potter, would not find the procedures unfamiliar. But the Industrial Revolution, which began in the mid-eighteenth century, changed drastically the methods in the large commercial pottery (Fig. 433). Today only the few universities that have associations with schools of ceramic engineering offer the courses necessary to an understanding of the problems of ceramic design in industry. In Europe, especially in Scandinavia, there is a much closer contact between industry and the art schools than there is in the United States. In a way it is a pity, for American industry could certainly use a little imagination.

Labor-saving devices were used by the ancients. The Etruscans worked with bisque molds as early as the fifth century B.C., and slip casting was practiced in a limited fashion in T'ang China (A.D. 618–906). But these mechanized processes were limited, and pottery remained largely a handcraft industry. During the eighteenth century the use of steam power to process clay and glaze chemicals and the new plaster of paris for molds made extreme changes in the age-old techniques. Unfortunately, while these and other technical advances made pottery and

433. Loading a double-shuttle car kiln at the Bennington Potters.

above : 434. DAVID GIL for the Bennington Potters, U.S.A. Stacking dinnerware. Press-molded stoneware. (See also Fig. 432, p. 246).

soon even porcelain both cheaper and more accessible to the masses, the quality of design deteriorated rapidly. None of the small hand potteries had the capital, and often not even the business skill, necessary to manage a large commercial enterprise. Furthermore, the importation of oriental porcelains had become very profitable. Although the new porcelain factories were often not successful, they were thought to be immensely profitable, and so were either held as the property of the crown or parceled out among close retainers.

The great tragedy in the industrialization of ceramics was not so much the change in technique, but rather the fact that design decisions were no longer made by the potter, who could draw on centuries-old ceramic tradition, but were imposed by the new factory manager, an entrepreneur whose major desire was to show a profit by whatever means possible. The potter became merely a hired hand. European ceramics of the eighteenth and nineteenth centuries thus became a weird assemblage of borrowed Greek forms decorated in the Chinese or Italian fashion. The flexibility of plaster as a mold material made feasible the easy copying of forms and decoration conceived in metal, glass, and even basketry. As discussed in Chapter 2, Colonial American potters were soon overwhelmed by the

mass-produced import, with the result that a native pottery tradition was never truly established in the United States.

In time American potteries became as industrialized as those abroad. With few exceptions they have continued to reflect the influence of foreign wares. (The borrowing is, of course, reciprocal, for there are European cars with Detroit styling and Japanese versions of many Scandinavian designs.)

The opportunities in contemporary dinnerware and "art gift ware" ceramics are not great. There is much competition from imports made in England, Germany, and Japan, countries that have long had important ceramics industries. The higher wages typical of American industry are also a factor, for in spite of mechanization there are still many hand operations that require training and skill. Price is not the only element in this competition, for Americans still retain to some degree a Colonial mentality that equates an import with a certain aura of superiority. Many foreign factories have larger design staffs and are more innovative than their American counterparts, which may well be another reason for the success of the import. This is largely explained by the fact that, in the United States, too many decisions are made by the advertising department, rather than by the design staff. Huge budgets are allocated to research in what will sell most profitably, so that very little time or money is left for creative projects aimed at developing a more useful and attractive product.

left : 435. JERRY ROTHMAN for Interpace Corporation, U.S.A. *Madeira* dinnerware. Earthenware.

below : 436. LONDA WEISMAN for the Bennington Potters, U.S.A. Candelabrum. Wheel-thrown clay, height 3′.

Although they represent the exception, there are several potteries with design staffs composed of producing potters and with managements that try to channel their ideas into production. Figures 434 to 436 illustrate examples of both unique pieces and production ware from two of these potteries, which have more imaginative design programs than most. The cost of design per item in mass production is extremely small. There is no doubt that most factories could do a better job in improving standards.

In all fairness it must be acknowledged that well-designed and reasonably priced objects have not always sold well. This must be attributed to the low level of taste that is prevalent in the buying public and is also characteristic of many wholesalers, store buyers, and sales clerks. It is surprising how many people are intimidated by sales personnel, especially in stores purporting to carry "quality" merchandise. Even a well-designed item is not likely to sell if poorly displayed or regarded in a deprecating manner by the sales clerk. In addition, decorator consultants often encourage the purchase of whatever industry decides will be the fashionable style of the season.

Were it not for the fact that there are numerous stores abroad and a few in the United States that consistently display an attractive line of excellently designed products, the future of the handcrafts would seem grim indeed. Unfortunately, these few shops will remain exceptions, unless American industry as a whole experiences a change of heart. The widespread availability of quality merchandise in Scandinavia is made possible by the close cooperation of the schools, the government, and industry over a period of many years.

Though few people would question the desirability of progress, one must be careful not to confuse progress with mere change. It may well be that the materialism of American industrial society rules out any improvement in public sensitivity. Typical "art appreciation" courses in the public schools and colleges are aimed more at developing "culture" than at seeking true critical analysis. Little direction can be expected from government agencies, which tend to serve industrial rather than public needs. Only industry as a whole has the widespread resources and influence to promote a genuine improvement in design, and, with this in mind, the prospects for the future are not hopeful.

Against this rather bleak background, it is encouraging to note that there are a few large and several small potteries that are "bucking the tide" and are attempting to furnish the public with ceramics designed with originality and with a true feeling for clay (Figs. 437–439). It is fashionable among some of today's theorists to deride the relationship

437. Studio workshop at the Bennington Potters. PAT GILMAN *(foreground)* creates a mirror frame, while LONDA WEISMAN throwns on the wheel.

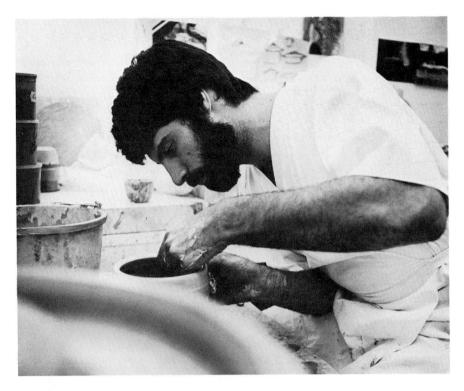

left : 438. Jeffrey Toussley throwing in the design studios of the Interpace Corporation.

below : 439. Craig Holmes throwing bottles on a constant-speed, heavy-production wheel at Pacific Stoneware, Inc.

The Potter in Industry   253

above : 440. Workshop at the Bennington Potters. Casseroles are molded on a hydraulic press using the Ram Process.

right : 441. Designer FRANCIS CHUN decorates a dish at the Interpace studios.

between material and form. This may be the direction that our plastic world is taking. But it will certainly lead to an impoverishment of our senses if the unique and authentic qualities of both material and form in the various craft media lose their identities. There is no more logic in attempting to reproduce a metal or glass form in clay than there is in making marmalade taste like mustard.

Both the Interpace Corporation and the Bennington Potters, whose work is illustrated (Figs. 432, 434–436), are noteworthy in having pottery studios attached to their factories (Figs. 440–443).

right : 442. DAVID GIL, manager of the Bennington Potters, creates a decorative tile, part of a divider screen for the Catamount Bank in Vermont.

below : 443. Design conference at the Interpace Corporation includes designers, glaze chemists, and production managers. *Clockwise from left foreground* : GEORGE TAYLOR, JEFFREY TOUSSLEY, SABERO GUZMAN, MINEO MIZUNO (standing), ELLIOTT HOUSE (director), FRANCIS CHUN, MARY J. WINANS, HENRY TAKEMOTO (standing), ROBERT CHAUSSE, AL BRUNT, OTTO LUND, and GEORGE JAMES.

Pacific Stoneware is operated by a professional potter, Bennett Welsh, who employs several trained ceramists for the creation of a production line that includes thrown ware and many hand-decorating methods (Figs. 444-445). Thus, designs can evolve from a clay prototype in a more natural and satisfying fashion, as distinguished from the usual drafting board industrial design concept.

DESIGNING FOR PRODUCTION

While the prototype for a mass-produced piece may evolve on the potter's wheel, it is essential that the ceramic designer have a working knowledge of the techniques of slip casting and jiggering. The long process that finally results in placing a pattern in production requires close cooperation between the designer, the mold maker, the glaze chemist, and the production engineer. The prototype usually is thrown on the wheel, but the mold maker most often works from a scale drawing (Fig. 446).

The designer first works up a variety of designs and then gradually eliminates those that are obviously nonfunctional, too commonplace, or too difficult to reproduce. Since the cup is the most-used item in a dinner set, it is often the starting point. When its shape has been roughly determined, other pieces are designed to relate to it. It is essential that the designer have a feeling for the clay form and a knowledge of how it can deform in firing. Heavy dinnerware is not very popular. Therefore, the foot rim and wall thickness must be of a dimension only sufficient to support the form.

After the cross sections are determined (Fig. 447), a plaster model is made. A metal template made from the profile drawing (Fig. 448) is placed

444. DON MCPHERSON of Pacific Stoneware loading a car kiln with the daily output of decorative mugs.

above : 445. BENNETT WELSH, Director of Pacific Stoneware, correcting details in a master model of a ceramic owl-bell.

446–448. Three steps in designing for production.

top right : 446. Scale drawings are made from the thrown prototype.

above right : 447. Cross sections are used to prepare the plaster model.

right : 448. A metal template is fashioned from the profile drawing.

449–451. The plaster model is prepared for jiggering.

above : 449. Minor refinements in the form of the model are made with cutting tools.

above right : 450. The mold is trimmed to fit the wheel head of the jigger machine.

right : 451. The top and bottom sections of the case mold.

below : 452. Steel template and plaster cup mold.

on the turning rig. Plaster is poured around the pin in small amounts until the form is completed. A circular movement of the template trims off the excess and develops a solid plaster study model.

Because of shrinkage that will occur in firing, the final model is oversize. Minor refinements in form can be made with cutting tools as the final model is developed on the wheel head (Fig. 449). After the plaster cup model is complete, it is coated with a plaster separator. A retaining collar is put in place, and fresh plaster is poured over the cup model to form the original jigger mold. Figure 450 shows the trimming of the mold to fit the wheel head of the jigger machine. It is necessary to have a mold for each cup to be made in the day's production, which may be thousands. Figure 451 illustrates the top and bottom sections of the case mold used to make the jigger block mold. The ball-and-socket projections allow for an accurate positioning of the sections prior to pouring the block mold. The case molds are made of a harder and denser plaster mix than that used for the jigger cup mold, which must readily absorb water from the clay after it is jiggered.

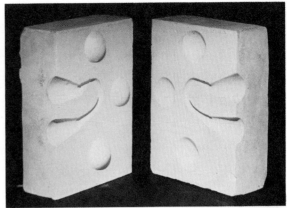

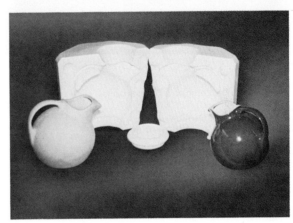

In jiggered ware, only one surface is shaped by the plaster form. The inner cup surface is formed by the jigger template. Figure 452 shows the steel template being checked for clearance, and Figure 453 illustrates a half section of the cup handle on a plaster or marble base. After the retaining walls are in place and the surface has been shaped, a layer of plaster is poured in, forming one half of the mold. Keys are carved out of the fresh plaster, and the complete handle section is put in place. English Crown soap is commonly used as a mold separator. If the plaster mold is dry, it must be moistened before soaping and casting, for otherwise the soap would be drawn into the dry cast, causing the two sections to stick. After the cast is finished, it is a simple matter to carve pouring openings into the damp plaster (Fig. 454). Before pouring a clay handle, however, the mold sections must be dry. For the pilot design

top left : 453. Half section of a cup handle on a plaster base.

top right : 454. Two halves of a plaster mold for a cup handle.

above left : 455. A template is cut to form the bottom surface of a saucer.

above right : 456. The three sections of a plaster mold used in slip casting.

project, a single handle mold is adequate; in production, a dozen handles normally are cast at one time.

Designing a plate or saucer is a somewhat different operation from designing a cup. In this case, the plaster mold is shaped to form the inside, or upper contour, of the plate. The template is cut to form the bottom surface (Fig. 455). The mold for slip casting is not quite the same as that used in jiggering, since it usually consists of three sections (Fig. 456). However, simple, tapered tumbler shapes

above : 457. The completed place settings.

below right : 458. Hollow, absorbent molds are filled with liquid slip clay.

can be cast in a single mold. The process from the initial sketches to the completed line (Fig. 457) is long, and several years may elapse before marketing can begin.

Mixing Plaster

There are available a variety of plasters of different hardnesses and setting rates, for use in model making, block molds, or case molds. Theoretically, 18.6 pounds of water will set up 100 pounds of plaster; in practice, at least 60 pounds of water will be needed to achieve the proper flow. The less water used, the stronger the cured plaster will be. Plaster normally sets in about twenty minutes, but it must be poured before it hardens. This time will depend upon the amount of mixing. The plaster must be sieved into the water (to avoid large lumps) until the water will absorb no more. It is then allowed to set from three to four minutes until it is thoroughly wet. Small batches can be mixed by hand or larger ones with a power mixer. After a few minutes of mixing, the plaster will begin to thicken. It must be

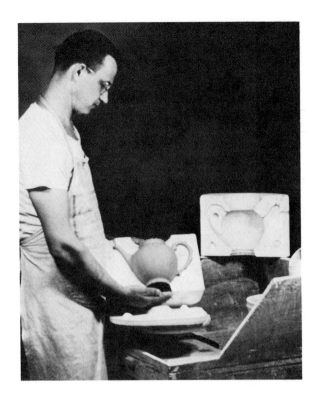

left : 459. A slip-cast creamer is removed from a three-piece mold.

above : 460. Cup handles are joined to the cup with slip.

poured at this point. Once it begins to set, it is useless and must be discarded. (It cannot be poured down the sink, for it will clog the drains.) Plaster manufacturers can furnish tables giving strength and porosity for various mixtures. For production it is most important that all molds have a similar porosity.

Slip-casting Techniques

Slip casting is a method of making ceramics in which liquid clay is poured into a hollow, absorbent mold (Fig. 458). Within a few minutes after pouring, a film of firm clay appears on the inner surface of the mold. As water is absorbed, the clay becomes thicker. When the desired thickness develops, the mold is upended and the center portion, which is still liquid, is poured out. The remaining clay coating continues to harden and eventually shrinks away from the mold. Simple cup forms can be made in a single piece mold, while undercut and more complicated shapes require two, three, or occasionally more pieces in the mold (Fig. 459).

When multiple sections are used, they are keyed together with ball-and-socket projections and are held together during pouring with heavy rubber bands, such as one might cut from an automobile inner tube. As the water soaks into the plaster mold, the level of slip in the cavity falls, and a small amount must be added. To avoid frequent slip additions during casting, a collar is added to the top of the original model to serve both as a funnel for the slip and as a clay reservoir. The angle of the collar is used as a guide in trimming the top edge of the formed piece. This is done with a fettling knife when the cast piece has hardened sufficiently. At this stage the mold sections are carefully removed, and the casting seams on the piece are scraped off and sponged to create a smooth surface.

In order to avoid uneven shrinkage or air pockets, some pieces must be cast in sections and luted together with slip. This is particularly true of small handles, which are cast solid rather than drain cast (Fig. 460). Depending upon the character of the clay, this type of joining can be done at either the

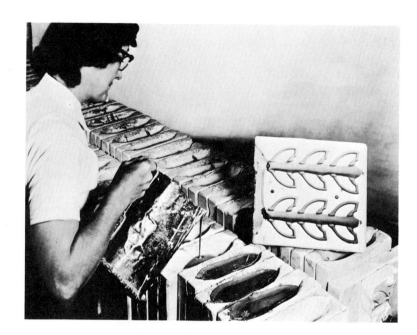

461. Cup handles are cast twelve to a mold and removed and separated when they are leather hard.

leather-hard or the dry stage (Fig. 461). The procedure is quite different from that used for thrown objects, in which case sections should be joined as soon as they can be handled without distortion.

Casting Slips

Unlike a clay used in throwing, a clay body for jiggering and casting need not be very plastic. In fact, the plastic clays are often avoided, since their greater water absorption means more shrinkage, which is usually accompanied by warping. Various types of binders are used to impart greater green and dry strength to the ware. This more than compensates for the substitution of less-plastic ingredients.

Of great importance in a casting slip is the use of *deflocculants*, such as sodium silicate and soda ash. The addition of about 1 percent of either of these chemicals to the dry weight of the clay will reduce considerably the amount of water needed to make a fluid slip. A properly deflocculated casting slip is easily pourable but has a clinging, syrupy consistency that substantially retards the settling of the heavier slip particles. Georgia kaolin, which has a uniform particle size, is the major porcelain clay used in casting slips. One negative feature of the slip

body is that its bland smoothness is relatively uninteresting when compared to the color and texture of a throwing clay. Some typical casting slips for various temperatures are:

Talc body (cones 06–05)	
Plastic vitrox	16
Ball clay	35
Talc	49

Parian body (cones 3–4)	
Feldspar	60
Kaolin	30
Ball clay	10

Porcelain body (cones 8-9)	
Flint	20
Feldspar	36
Kaolin	30
Ball clay	14

A common name for sodium silicate is water glass. It is, in fact, a solution of sodium silicate in water. The sodium silicate is made by fusing a mixture of soda ash and silica sand. The term is a general one, since the proportion of sodium to silica may vary greatly. N-brand solution is the trade name given to the type commonly used as a deflocculant in ceramics. Soda ash (sodium carbonate), either alone or in combination with sodium silicate, is a more effective deflocculant than sodium silicate alone in casting slips having organic matter, such as is found in ball clay. Slip should not be stored for long periods, especially in warm weather, because fermentation occurs, and this may cause pinholes in the cast ware.

A standard practice is to use about three parts N-brand sodium silicate by weight to one part soda ash. The proportions depend on the body formula.

If it includes a large amount of clay, a one-to-one mixture of soda ash and N-brand silicate solution may prove more satisfactory. After weighing, the soda ash should be dissolved in hot water and then both deflocculants added to the water. As a beginning one might take 100 pounds of slip body and slowly add it to a large crock containing 50 pounds of water, which is about six gallons (8.3 pounds to the gallon). More or less of the slip body may be needed, depending upon the ingredients and the deflocculant action. The resulting slip should have a thick, syrupy consistency. A blunger is helpful in mixing the ingredients (Fig. 462), although a large wire whisk can be used for test batches. Slip should always be screened before using, for any lumpy particles will settle and give a poor casting. Care must be taken in screening and filling the mold in order not to trap air bubbles in the slip.

462. A large blunger is used to mix the ingredients in a clay body.

It is better not to use more than 1 percent deflocculant, even less if possible, in relation to the dry ingredients' weight, since an excess will sometimes cause the slip to become pasty and nonpourable. It will also gradually seal the pores of the plaster mold with an insoluble film of calcium silicate, making it difficult to remove the casting and eventually spoiling the mold completely. Soda ash is more troublesome in this regard than silicate. Drying the molds from the outside by inverting them or covering the mouths will help to prevent this accumulation on the inner mold surface.

Jiggering Methods

As every novice potter soon learns, it is impractical to throw large, flat shapes on the potter's wheel. Countless generations of potters have used bisque molds to shape one surface of flat dishes and to support the soft clay while drying. With the use of plaster molds, the forming process is quite rapid and accurate. In addition, the plaster mold produces a smoother surface than would be possible with a bisque mold.

The composition of the clay used for jiggering is different from that of the throwing clay used by the hand potter. Since the ware is supported by the mold during the initial drying period, it need not be so plastic. In fact, since plastic clay shrinks more in drying, thus increasing the likelihood of warpage, it is used in limited amounts. To compensate for this loss in green and dry strength, various binders—such as lignin extract and methocel—are added to the clay body.

The body ingredients are weighed and mixed in a blunger as in the preparation of a casting slip. The resultant liquid is screened and pumped into a filter press, which is an accordianlike machine of metal and canvas that squeezes excess water from the slip, leaving plastic clay. The clay comes from the filter press in slabs about 1 to 1 ½ inches thick and 16 to 24 inches square. These slabs are then placed in the hopper of a pug mill, which operates much like a meat grinder. At one end is a vacuum attachment, which, combined with the compressing action of the screw blades, removes even the smallest air

pockets from the clay. This feature not only eliminates possible body defects but also renders the clay more plastic. Though not as crucial as in throwing, the absence of air bubbles in clay used for jiggering is still important.

Sections of clay can be extruded from the pug mill in different diameters, depending upon the use to which they will be put (Fig. 463). The size used for the plate shown in the jigger machine (Fig. 464) would be 6 to 8 inches. A slice about 1 inch thick is cut off the pugged clay with a wire and placed over a square of canvas on the bench. The clay slice is then hit with a malletlike weight that compresses it to half this thickness. This clay bat is in turn slapped down over a plaster plate mold resting on the jigger head. The next step is to force out any air remaining between the clay and the plaster mold. This is usually done with the moistened hand as the jigger head revolves slowly. The operator then brings the steel template down toward the mold, further compressing the clay and cutting away the excess to form the bottom contours of the plate and the foot rim. The mold bat and plate are placed on a conveyor belt that carries them through a dryer. Finally, the plate is removed from the mold, and the seam that is created where the template and mold meet is trimmed away.

It is difficult to obtain a perfectly uniform thickness in slip casting. Heavy cups with attached handles are often slip cast, but thinner porcelain cups are jiggered, since even the slightest variation would be noticeable. The procedure in jiggering cups and bowls is slightly different: the mold is a hollow form, and the template is shaped to the inside surface of the piece. One method of jiggering cups is to throw a wad of clay into the mold and allow the template to force the clay downward and outward to form the walls of the cup. Another way begins with the throwing of a rough cup form on a potter's wheel (Fig. 465). This form is placed into the mold and jiggered as in the other procedure (Fig. 466). The particular method used would depend largely upon the characteristics of the clay body and to some extent upon the shape desired. The latest machines are completely automatic and produce a fantastic hourly output.

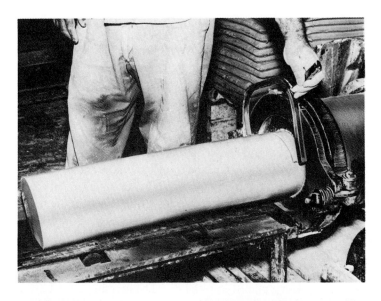

below and bottom : 465–466. A rough cup shape is thrown on the wheel and later expanded in a mold by the action of the jigger template.

top : 463. A section of clay is cut off after extrusion from the pug mill.

above : 464. The jigger trims off the bottom profile of a dinner plate.

Designing for Production   265

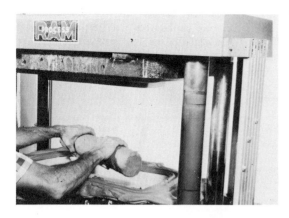

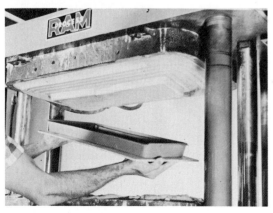

Press Forming

Certain forms can be duplicated very economically by the use of molds in hydraulic presses. Most electrical insulators are made in such a fashion, using a nearly dry body with wax as a forming lubricant. The process illustrated (Figs. 467–470) is more adaptable to pottery production, provided the shapes are simple and have no undercuts. Male and female dies shape the form and, under great pressure, squeeze out the excess clay. An unusual feature is that the hard but porous gypsum plaster die has a tubular grid embedded in the plaster. Compressed air flowing from the tubes into the die allows the clay form to be released immediately after pressing. Figure 467 shows a wad of stiff but plastic clay being placed into the die. The pressing operation is very rapid (Fig. 468). Compressed air released into the lower die breaks the clay suction, and the press rises (Fig. 469). The operator removes the newly formed tray on a supporting panel after the compressed air releases it from the upper die (Fig. 470).

Production Kilns

The term *commercial production* covers a wide range of activities from the manufacture of huge tonnages of building bricks to the forming of minute electrical insulators. Special kilns have been developed to fire the ever-increasing volume of commercial ware. Industrial kilns are not merely larger versions of the small pottery kiln, since a larger kiln is difficult to fire uniformly and has a long cycle of firing, cooling, and loading. Instead, part of the kiln is made movable, as in the car kiln (see p. 277). The car kiln is easy to load and unload and does not lose as much heat in the process as do standard kilns. By placing

left, top to bottom : 467–470. Four steps in press forming.

467. A wad of stiff clay is placed into the die.

468. The press is lowered, and the clay is squeezed between the two sections.

469. The suction is released, and the press rises.

470. The operator removes the finished piece.

a door at each end of the kiln, the loading cycle is speeded up even more. This type of construction is called a shuttle kiln.

As lightweight, high-temperature refractories became common, an envelope type of kiln was developed (Fig. 471). In this design, two permanent kiln beds are built, and the kiln moves back and forth over them. Its advantages are the smaller floor area required and the fact that lighter kiln furniture can be used, since there is not even the vibration of a moving kiln car. These kilns are available in many sizes, but they are primarily intended for small-size pottery or special-order production.

The huge production of the larger potteries would not be possible without the tunnel kiln, which has continuous operation, with no stoppage for cooling or loading. Figure 472 shows a loaded kiln car entering the tunnel. The chamber is approximately 5 by 9 feet and 200 feet long. The cars, fitted tightly together, move through the kiln at a slow but constant speed, taking seventy to ninety hours to heat, fire, and cool. The entering temperature is 300°F, which gradually increases to 2300°F in the center section, and then tapers off as the cars move away from the burners. The kiln cars have a heavily insulated floor. A channel iron on the car side usually projects into a sand seal on the kiln wall,

above : 471. An envelope kiln about to be rolled over a load of freshly glazed pottery.

left : 472. A car entering the kiln with a load of cups stacked lip to lip.

which protects the undercarriage from a direct flow of heat. Hot air escaping toward the end sections is piped back to preheat the burner-port air. This factor, plus the possibility of continuous operation for months on end, provides a most economical system.

As would be imagined, loading of this kiln is quite different from that of a small studio kiln. Because of the long firing cycle and the great number of duplicate shapes, a very tight load is possible. However, thin dinnerware pieces must be supported to prevent warpage. Cups are loaded in pairs, lip to lip, with a weak cement to prevent accidental slippage. Dry refractory clay is shot into openings between stacked dinner plates for support (Fig. 473). A coaster of high alumina content is placed under each stack to prevent its sticking to the shelves. It is common practice in dinnerware manufacture to fire the bisque to the maturity of the body while it is well supported.

After glazing, the ware is fired at a lower temperature, so that there is no shrinkage and less chance

right : 473. Removing bisque plates from the kiln car.

below : 474. A sagger of cups after the glaze fire.

of warping. A potter can keep a small kiln relatively clean and need not worry about dust and brick particles in an open glaze fire. However, this is not true of large kilns firing continuously for long periods. To protect the ware in the glaze fire, it is loaded into boxlike forms made of fireclay, called saggers.

Figure 474 shows a sagger load of cups after the glaze fire. A layer of bitstone (coarse silica sand), which does not adhere easily to the thin glaze on the foot rim, covers the sagger bottom. High-fire porcelains are always fired on the foot rim in the individual sagger. The foot rims will be unglazed but smoothly polished. High-fire china ware, such as the sagger load of saucers shown in Figure 475, is completely glazed. The individual pieces rest on dowels of porcelain that are inserted into the sagger wall as the pieces are loaded. This porcelain spur will cause a tiny blemish in the glaze, but it does provide a great economy in loading and firing. Figure 476 shows the loading of saggers containing glazed cups and dinner plates.

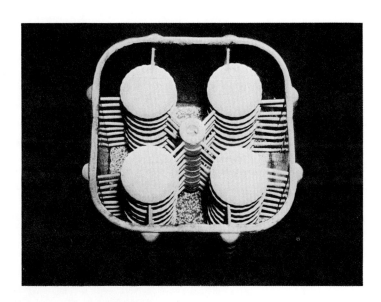

right : 475. A sagger load of saucers.

below : 476. The loading of saggers containing glazed pieces.

11 Kilns
Operation and Construction

At some remote period in time (c. 8000 B.C.) man discovered that clay, when baked in a fire, would become hard and durable. For thousands of years he fired his pottery in a shallow pit on a bed of twigs (Figure 478). Broken shards covered the heaped-up pottery to provide protection from the fuel above and to retain the heat. With a continual application of dry twigs and grass a red heat could be achieved, after which the coals were covered with soil and allowed to cool. Smothered with ash, the red-clay body was usually black from carbon. Burnished and incised surfaces were the only decoration possible. All early black ware was fired in this manner, as is the pottery of some aboriginal tribes in modern times. A pit firing is an interesting project for a summer-camp ceramics class.

In time early potters learned to dig a chamber into a hillside to provide heat insulation, a better draft, and a fire pit, with a resulting higher fire. Finally, clay bricks with a straw binder were used to construct a circular kiln chamber, a combustion area, a fire grate, and an ash pit (Fig. 479). The ware was loaded from the top, covered with shards, and basted with a clay and straw mixture leaving a few exhaust openings. Such a kiln was used to fire the slip-decorated ware made in the Middle East about 3500 B.C.

As technical proficiency increased, a kiln was developed that had a permanent dome-shape roof, a short chimney, and a door opening from the side. The Greeks, who needed controlled conditions of oxidation and reduction to achieve their red- and black-figure ware, used such a kiln. The chambers were not large—probably no more than 4 to 6 feet in diameter. This design evolved into the beehive and the taller bottle-neck updraft kiln, which, with multiple fireboxes, were used throughout Europe until the development of large commercial kilns during the Industrial Revolution.

The higher-fire stoneware and porcelain achieved early by the Chinese and Koreans was due as much to their kiln design as to their use of kaolin bodies. These early kilns were long and narrow and

opposite : 477. DOROTHY PERKINS, U.S.A. Bottle. Stoneware, squared after throwing, with sgraffito decoration; height 11″.

271

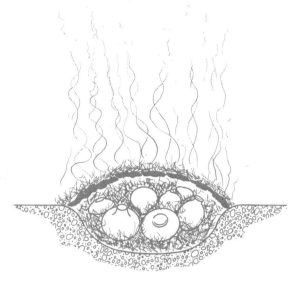

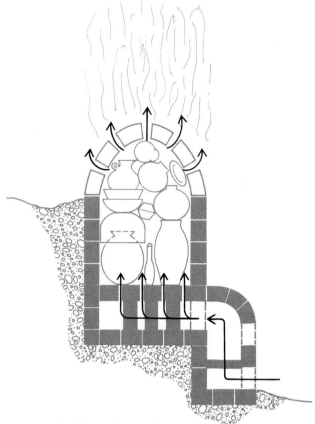

built on a sloping hillside for increased draft. A large firebox was at the base, but since the kiln might be 150 feet in length, additional stoking holes were needed to increase the heat in the upper portion. The ash that fell on many of the pieces was responsible for their glazelike surface. In order to better control the heat, the long, climbing kiln was divided into chambers, first in China and later—about 1600—in Japan. Partly because of the space taken up by saggars (fireclay boxes to contain glazed ware), the Chinese kiln chambers were sometimes 15 feet high. The Japanese were smaller, usually about 6 feet high, but had as many as twenty chambers (Fig. 480). Although wood kilns are efficient at high temperatures, their use is declining because of the cost of fuel and the excess smoke they produce.

above left : 478. Primitive shallow-pit kiln.

above : 479. Early wood-burning kiln.

below: 480. Japanese wood-burning climbing kiln.

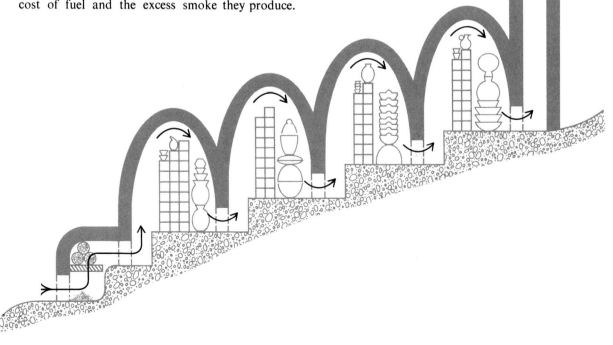

MODERN KILNS

The kiln types employed by the ancients are still in use today, but they have been modified to accommodate new fuels, new materials, and, in the case of industry, the need for expanded and efficient large-scale production. Perhaps the most drastic change in kiln design in recent times was caused by the development of a new source of power—electricity. Since the electric kiln needs no chimney or fuel lines and is comparatively portable, simple, and safe to operate, it has played a large part in the current popularity of ceramics. It is especially convenient for the potter whose studio might be relatively temporary or for the school whose original design provided for neither a chimney nor a source of fuel.

Fuel Kilns

Whether wood, coal, oil, or gas is used as a fuel, the basic kiln design is much the same. A combustion area is needed either below or to one side of the kiln chamber. Wood or coal requires a larger area equipped with a grate and an ash pit (see Figs. 479–480). Saggers, which protect the glazed ware from flying ash, take up much space. In time, small kilns were constructed with an inner muffle chamber that served the same purpose. Both fuel oil and manufactured gas contain sulphur, which is injurious to lead glazes. The updraft muffle kiln shown in Figure 481 was designed to eliminate this

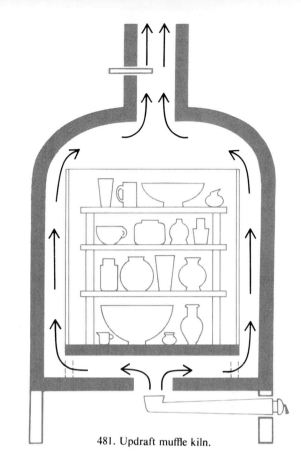

481. Updraft muffle kiln.

problem. The design, however, creates extra heat in the floor area, making an even firing difficult. Placing burners closer to the side wall will alleviate the problem to some extent. Most portable gas kilns are of this type.

The downdraft kiln illustrated in Figure 482 provides a more even heat distribution and has come

482. Downdraft kiln.

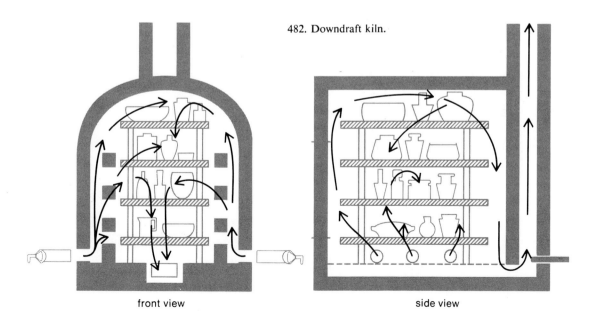

front view   side view

273

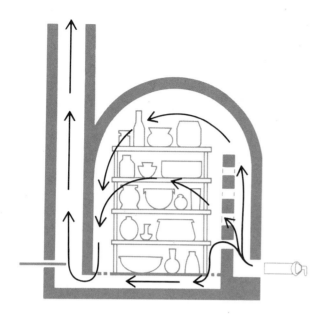

to be the standard design used by most potters. This is especially true since the advent of cleaner natural gas, which has eliminated the need for a muffle. In this downdraft kiln the heat enters from multiple burners on each side, is deflected upward by the bag wall, and then is drawn down through the ware to a channel under the floor by the suction of the chimney. If the fuel supply and draft are adequate, adjustments to the bag wall height and damper can ensure a heat deviation of no more than one cone, and usually less, from top to bottom.

left: 483. Arch kiln with burners on one side.

below and opposite page: 484–487. Kilns with alternate arrangements of burners.

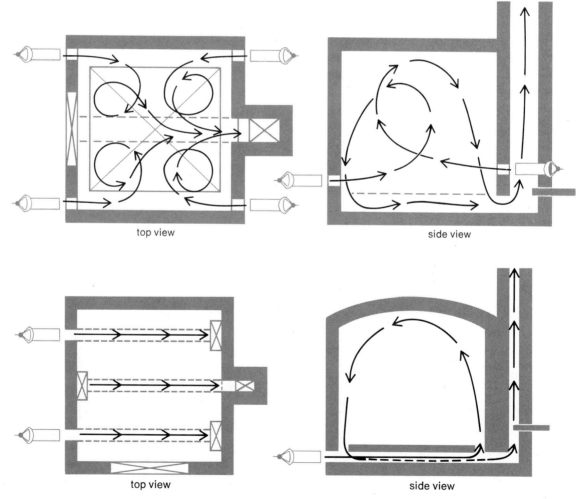

top view

side view

top view

side view

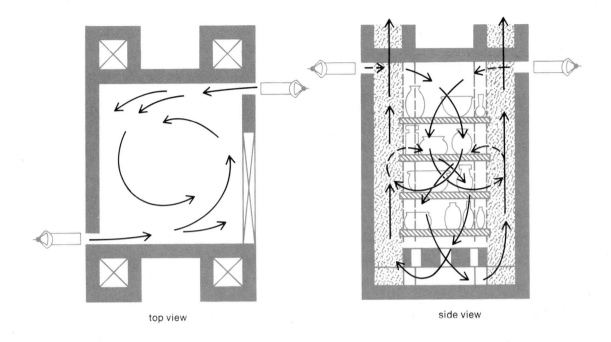

top view   side view

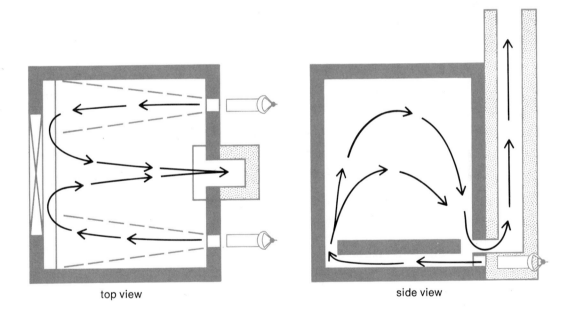

top view   side view

For a smaller-size kiln, a layout such as that illustrated in Figure 483, with the burners placed to one side, may prove equally satisfactory. Numerous other burner arrangements have been tried, despite the fact that the design sketched in Figure 482 is most efficient. Some of these alternate plans are shown in Figures 484–487. In some installations a burner or a fan at the base of the stack is desirable to induce a draft in the early stages of firing. This addition may also be needed in the case of a tall chimney, such as is found on kilns in many classroom studios.

The kiln illustrated in Figure 488 is essentially the same as the one in Figure 482, except that the

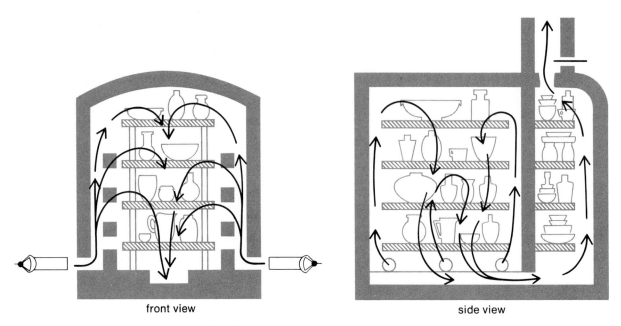

front view   side view

488. Kiln with bisque chamber in the chimney.

chimney area is enlarged to provide a separate bisque chamber. Unless the glaze temperature in the main area is unusually high, this chimney chamber will bisque at between cone 010 and cone 06. While most schools have an ample supply of both pots and kilns to ensure a full load for each firing, the individual potter may experience firing delays. The double chamber permits a more even flow of work and simultaneous bisque and glaze firings at no extra cost.

A kiln that is fired with fuel oil requires a slightly larger combustion area than does one using natural gas. The catenary arch kiln shown in Figure 489 is ideal for fuel oil, since the flare at the bottom provides the extra combustion area needed. Except for the arch construction, the design is similar to that of a gas kiln. The curve is established by suspending a chain from two points, thus forming a natural, self-supporting arch. A proportion in which the base equals the height is the most stable and provides excellent heat distribution. Because the arch is self supporting, no tie rods or steel frame are needed. Oil is a satisfactory fuel, cheaper than gas, but it has some drawbacks. A separate shedlike installation is desirable, since the fumes that are

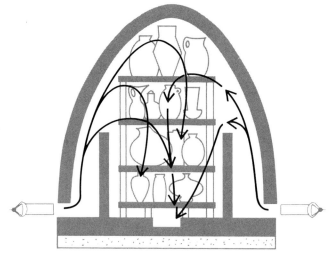

489. Catenary arch kiln.

given off, together with the noisy blowers, make an oil-burning kiln impractical for use in the studio or classroom.

Square kilns are more likely to fire evenly, and a slightly wider door width is preferable to a deep chamber for loading convenience. It is assumed that the chambers of the kilns discussed have a loading area of about 10 to 20 cubic feet. However, many schools need a larger capacity. The physical strain incurred in stretching to load the heavy shelves and ware at the far end of a 30-cubic-foot chamber is too much for many students. In such cases a car kiln (Fig. 490) may be a good solution. This, again, is essentially the Figure 482 design, but the floor section is built on steel frame and wheels, so that it can be rolled in and out of the kiln on a track. The door becomes an integral part of the car, instead of being bricked up in the usual fashion. There must be a close fit between the floor and the side walls, with a channel iron in the floor extending into a sand trough in the side wall to form a heat seal. In the car kiln the ware can be loaded from either side without undue strain.

Electric Kilns

The gas kiln, because of its cheaper operation, greater size, and ability to reduce, is preferred by most studio potters and university ceramics departments in the United States. In the Scandinavian countries, however, where electricity is cheap and gas is not common, the electric kiln is almost universally used by the studio potter. The electric kiln has many advantages for the public school. It is as simple to operate as turning on a light switch, and there are no problems of burner adjustment or draft control. The kiln, normally weighing about three hundred pounds, can be wheeled anywhere. It requires only a 220-volt electrical outlet—a minor consideration compared to the gas kiln's demand of a high-temperature chimney or large-size gas lines.

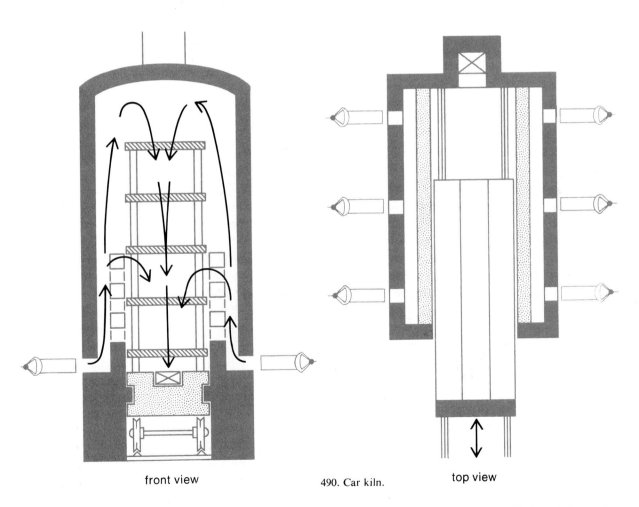

front view   490. Car kiln.   top view

Room ventilation is not a problem, provided the clay body contains no sulphur or unusual impurities.

The electric kiln comes in two basic styles—the top loader and the front loader. In either type, a kiln with less than an 18 × 18-inch interior should not be considered, for it is too small to be other than a toy. Since the heat comes from radiation produced by coiled elements recessed in the side walls, a kiln chamber bigger than 24 × 24 inches requires a large coil or strip element, which greatly increases the cost of the kiln. Because they must have a stand and a heavy frame to carry the door, plus flexible connections to the door elements, front-loading kilns are much more expensive. The top loader is not only cheaper but easier to load, and it is therefore a more logical purchase.

There are three types of electric heating elements. Suitable for a low fire (up to 2000°F) are those made of coiled nickel-nichrome wire. The Kanthol type is constructed of a different alloy and will produce temperatures up to cone 8 (2300°F), although some types will go higher. Larger and higher-firing industrial kilns use carbon compounds in the form of a rod from $\frac{1}{4}$ inch to 2 inches in diameter. Unfortunately, the special transformers needed are more expensive than the kiln itself, which places this kiln at a price disadvantage compared with the more inexpensive gas or oil kilns.

KILN LOADING AND FIRING

The final step in the potter's art—the loading and firing of the kiln—is most important, for carelessness can easily ruin one's previous efforts. It can also do permanent damage to the kiln. With the exception of salt-glazed ware and commercial high-fire porcelain (see Chap. 10, pp. 268–269), all pottery is usually fired first at a low bisque temperature. Some clay bodies can be successfully glazed in the raw state, but the fragility of unfired clay and the difficulty of glazing some shapes make a double firing desirable, especially in schools, where techniques of glazing and loading are being taught.

The bisque fire temperature is generally between cone 010 and cone 06, depending upon the clay body used.

The fired bisque ware must be hard enough to endure normal handling in the glazing operation, yet sufficiently absorbent to permit glaze adhesion. Although the stacking of a bisque kiln is quite different from that required for a glaze fire, in each case at least one inch of free space must be left between the electrical elements and the ware. In a gas kiln 2 or 3 inches is a desirable margin to allow free passage of heat and to avoid hot spots.

Raw ware must be completely dry before it is loaded in the bisque kiln. Since there is no problem of glaze sticking, kiln wash is not needed, and pieces may touch each other. It is possible to stack one piece inside or on top of others, building to a considerable height. Care must be taken to make foot rims coincide for support and to avoid placing heavy pieces on more fragile ones. Large shallow bowls, which might warp, are better fired upside down on the rim. Several smaller sizes can be placed beneath. Covers should be fired in place to prevent warping, and tall knobbed covers can be reversed to save space.

Even though apparently dry, the raw clay contains much moisture, and the firing should proceed at a low heat for several hours. Kiln doors should be left ajar or peepholes left open for an hour or so to allow this moisture to escape. Large, heavy pots or sculptural pieces must be fired at a slow speed to prevent the moisture contained in hidden air pockets from being converted into steam, which would cause the piece to explode.

Chemical changes in the body during firing are slight at first (Fig. 491). When the temperature reaches 350° to 400°F (175°–200°C), all atmospheric moisture should have left the ware, causing little or no shrinkage. Most of the chemically combined water will leave the ware at temperatures between 950° and 1300°F (510°–705°C). During this "water smoking" period considerable shrinkage occurs as both the chemically combined water and gases from organic material leave the body. The firing should not be too rapid, for the body is very weak. As the temperature approaches 1750°F (955°C) and continues to 1850°F (1010°C), needlelike crystals of alumina-silica ($3 Al_2O_3 \cdot 2 SiO_2$), called mullite, begin to form, but they are not fully developed until stone-ware temperatures are reached. These give toughness to the body, and as the temperature increases, additional free silica forms a glass around these crystals. Because of impurities and varying compositions, clay bodies achieve maximum hardness at different temperatures. Earthenware clay matures at about 2000°F (1090°C), stoneware at about 2350°F (1290°C), and pure clay (kaolin) at about 3000°F (1650°C). (See also Chap. 4, pp. 139–145.)

Most potters use cones to measure the cone 06 to cone 010 bisque fire, but some judge maturity by the bright red color of the ware. A uniform bisque temperature is necessary to create the proper absorbency for glazing. When the correct temperature is reached, the electric kiln is simply turned off and allowed to cool. In the fuel-burning kiln, the chimney damper must be closed immediately to prevent a cold draft of air from being sucked into the burner ports, which might crack both the ware and the shelves. Just as the kiln must be fired slowly, so must it be allowed to cool naturally. The damper can be opened after cooling overnight, and the peephole plugs can be removed, but the door must not be opened more than a crack until the temperature is down to 400°F. An even slower cooling may be desirable for extremely large or heavy pieces. An expensive kiln, which should give at least 10 years' service before repairs are needed, may be ruined after a short time by careless firing and cooling.

The glaze fire differs in several respects from the bisque fire: the loading is different, the kiln atmosphere may be varied, and the final temperature must be carefully controlled. Since mishaps may occur from runny glazes, all kiln shelves must be coated with a *kiln wash*. This is made of equal parts of silica (flint) and kaolin in a creamy mixture. Each coat is applied before the last is completely dry. A new shelf can be sprayed with aluminum paint before the kiln wash is painted on. Additional protection can be obtained by dusting on a thin layer of coarse silica sand. The shelf edges must be cleaned to prevent this sand from sifting down on the ware below. All glazed ware should be "dry footed" —that is, all glaze cleaned off the base and about

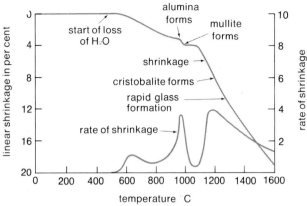

491. Linear shrinkage and rate of shrinkage for kaolin. (F. H. Norton, *Elements of Ceramics*, Addison-Wesley, 1952.)

¼ inch up the foot rim. Glazes that are runny, such as crystalline and copper reds, can be placed on a slice of insulating brick to soak up the excess.

A uniform load without tight spots will produce an even firing. One should never try to fire a half load, since uneven temperatures are almost certain to occur. Staggering the shelves in a large kiln will create a better heat flow. In the typical electric kiln shelves should not be placed close to the bottom or the top, for a cold spot will develop in the center area. Test tiles must always be stacked in a middle position, since there is usually some temperature variation from top to bottom. A center support is desirable for larger shelves. Damp clay pads used to level uneven posts should be dusted first with dry flint to avoid sticking. If the shelves are of moderate size, three posts will eliminate leveling problems. As in the bisque fire, covers are best fired in place, but one must make certain that the contact areas are clear of glaze. Placing glazed ware too close to the upper bag wall often results in shiny spots, although gaps in the bricks may even out the heat in this area. Glazed pieces should be at least ¼ inch apart, because heat radiation can also cause shininess.

Reduction firing means that part of the firing cycle is conducted with an inadequate amount of air and oxygen to burn up all the fuel. As a result, the free carbon in the air unites with, and thus reduces, the oxygen content of the metallic oxides in both the body and the glaze, thereby altering their color. In a forced-draft burner this is accomplished by cutting down on the air, while in a natural-draft burner the flue damper is cut back slightly, so that less air is sucked into the kiln. Excessive reduction is undesirable. Not only does the temperature drop rapidly, but the body may erupt with blisters or even bloat, and the glaze becomes a dirty gray. In a natural-draft kiln a slight backing up of the flame at the burner ports will occur. This is all that is necessary for a reduction, not the belching of flame and smoke that some students seem to enjoy —until the blistered pots come out. Because of atmospheric pressure built up during reduction, one should not pull out the peep plugs with his face near the opening, for the flame will shoot out at least a foot. In a tall, bricked-up door a section of curved sheet metal under the tie rod and pressing against the top bricks is helpful, since the door bricks may lean outward.

The atmosphere should be an oxidizing one during the first part of the firing cycle, in order to ensure the most efficient heat rise. The reduction needed to produce a rich body color is most effective between cones 016 and 010. When the maximum temperature is reached, the damper can be adjusted to provide a neutral or slightly reducing fire. The usual practice is to cut back the burners slightly after the cones go over to allow a half hour or so of an oxidizing *soaking heat* in which temperature variations can stabilize and glazes become smooth.

The term *reduction fire* must not be confused with *reduction glazes*. The latter are glazes especially compounded to produce copper-red and celadon colors (see p. 213). In the firing of these glazes there is no real change in body color but rather a reduction of the coloring oxides in the glaze from an oxidic to a metallic form. Thus, copper green becomes a rich red, and the iron brown-red is transformed into a gray-green. In a reduction fire the glaze reduction begins later than the body reduction, but it must occur before the glaze begins to melt. Since the reduction causes the heat rise to diminish, there is usually an alternation of reduction and oxidation. Too much oxidation will bleach out the color. Copper-red color variations range from a mottled blue, green, and red to a deep purple-red

or a pale pink, depending upon the reduction sequence, the glaze thickness, and the body color.

A *localized reduction* can be obtained by adding ½ of 1 percent of silicon carbide (carborundum, forty-mesh or finer) to a suitable copper alkaline glaze. The result is usually a speckled red-and-purple color. Its only real advantage is its adaptability to the electric kiln. An electric kiln can be reduced by popping a few moth balls through the peephole. The kiln should have heavy elements, which have a good oxidized coating from many previous firings. Continuous reductions will eat away the elements, but an occasional one will do little harm to the kiln.

The single-fire *salt glaze* is fired to the maturity of the body. Coarse rock salt, soaked in water and placed in small paper cups, is inserted by a wire loop into the burner ports over a two-hour interval. New kilns use more salt—about $1/3$ pound per cubic foot of kiln area. Clay draw rings hooked from the peephole indicate the salting progress.

Pyrometric cones provide the potter with his most accurate method of measuring the *work heat* in the kiln. The name is inaccurate, for the pyrometric "cone" is actually a tetrahedron or pyramid shape 1 ¾ inches high, with a base that is ½ inch across. Cones are compounded of a material similar to a glaze. When softened by the heat they bend, and when a complete arc is formed the temperature in the kiln is that of the cone number (see Appendix, pp. 310–311). The base is beveled to indicate the proper angle at which to press them into a pad of clay. The usual practice is to use three cones, for example, 6, 8, and 9 if the firing is to reach cone 8. The bending of cone 6 warns the potter that the kiln is approaching the proper temperature, and burner or damper adjustments to stabilize the heat are made at this point. In a large kiln the cones are placed near both top and bottom, not too close to the door. As cone 8 bends, the burners can be cut back for a soaking period. A softening of cone 9 indicates an overfiring. Kilns usually fire slightly hotter at the bottom, so a dryer glaze can be used there. If the cones are difficult to see, blowing into the peephole through a tube or inserting a metal rod near the cones will reveal them more clearly.

A slower rise in temperature, and the resulting longer period of chemical reaction, will permit a glaze to mature at a lower temperature than if the heat rise is rapid. This relationship between time and temperature is called the *work heat ratio*, and it is recorded by the pyrometric cone but not by the *pyrometer*. The pyrometer consists of a pair of welded wires of dissimilar metals, called a thermocouple, which is inserted into the kiln. When the kiln is heated, a minute electrical current indicates temperature change on a millivolt meter callibrated in degrees F or C. A pyrometer is convenient to have when the potter is making adjustments to produce the most efficient heat rise, or when he wishes to determine the proper time to begin a reduction. However, unless one has an exact and unvarying firing schedule, it is not completely dependable. In time corrosion of the thermocouple tips affects the accuracy of the reading, but this can be adjusted to the proper cone by moving a tiny screw on the meter face. Thermocouples and pyrometers are available in both low- and high-fire models. The rather inexpensive ones used by potters are seldom reliable over a wide range of temperatures; that is, if the cone 8 reading is correct, the cone 04 may be inaccurate. Optical pyrometers are also available; these are quite accurate but rather expensive. Glazed draw rings, which were common before the introduction of cones, can also be used to measure the kiln temperature. Such clay rings are the only method of determining glaze buildup in a salt kiln.

KILN MATERIALS

Because of the industrial market most kiln materials are available in any large city, but prices may vary. Even in a small town a building-supply dealer can generally provide firebrick and other materials.

Firebrick is made in a number of special compositions, but the common alumina-silica *hard refractory firebrick* is satisfactory for most purposes. Different grades are produced for operating temperatures of 1600°, 2000°, 2300°, 2600°, and 2800°F (870°, 1093°, 1260°, 1427°, and 1538°C), and some can be used at temperatures as high as 3000° and 3200°F (1649° and 1742°C). The bricks used for higher operating temperatures are denser and lose much of their insulating ability. They are also more expensive. Therefore, one should not purchase a higher-grade brick than is needed. A 2600°F brick is generally used for kilns firing from cones 8 to 10. Special arch- and wedge-shape bricks can be ordered for the curve of the kiln roof. A kiln constructed entirely of hard firebrick will consume a lot of fuel, since the bricks absorb and conduct a considerable amount of heat. Fortunately, porous *insulating firebrick* is also made, which has an insulating value from three to five times as great as the hard brick. Insulating firebricks are available in a similar temperature range as hard brick, but the cost is much higher. They are most often used as a backup layer next to the hard brick, although kilns made entirely of insulating bricks are common. Although more expensive, they require less fuel, and the insulating brick can be cut easily with a coarse-tooth saw, such as an inexpensive pruning or bow-saw.

Castable refractories of varying compositions for several operating temperatures are also available. These can be mixed and poured like concrete. Although more expensive than brick, castable refractories are useful for forming odd shapes, such as burner ports or small arches. They are dense and conduct heat much as a hard brick does. A castable calcium-alumina refractory can be used as liner for a dual-purpose salt kiln, so that salt will not accumulate on the firebrick interior. With this arrangement a bisque or glaze kiln can safely be used for an occasional salt-glaze firing. Over a long period the door bricks will have to replaced several times, and the combustion area near the burner ports will require chipping out and recasting due to the salt action, but the rest of the kiln will remain unaltered.

Other insulating materials of a lower heat tolerance but of great insulating value can also be used for a backup layer. Even common soft red brick will serve this purpose. Kilns of more than 30 cubic feet are commonly built with a hard firebrick core, a middle portion of insulating firebrick, and an outer layer of red brick.

Asbestos sheets and blocks of various sizes provide a good insulation. If the outer walls rise to a height of several courses, loose granular vermiculite poured to a depth of 6 to 8 inches can be used to give further insulation to the roof crown, which in most cases tends to be rather cool. To insulate a high, curved roof, such as a catenary, vermiculite can be mixed with fireclay and water, with sodium silicate as a binder, and this mixture troweled on to a depth of several inches.

Transite, a rigid cement-asbestos sheet material, comes in several sizes and thicknesses. It is useful for the outer panels of a small kiln having an angle iron frame, for it protects and dresses up the brickwork and can serve as a retainer for loose insulation poured between the brick wall and the transite. Transite is also available in tubular form, and in this guise it makes a quite satisfactory chimney, provided sufficient air space surrounds the pipe. A thickness of ½ inch is usually sufficient; thicker sections tend to spall and flake off due to the great difference in heat to which the inner and outer surfaces are exposed.

Kiln furniture includes the shelves, posts, and other props used in the kiln. The heavy fireclay shelves that were formerly used have disappeared as better materials have replaced them. Sillmanite shelves are suitable for earthenware temperatures, but the more expensive *silicon carbide* shelves give longer service and are compounded for use at various temperatures. A ¾-inch thickness is adequate for standard loads. A center post is necessary to avoid sagging and possible breakage in spans of 24 inches or more. Since it is less subject to strain in cooling and heating, a rectangular shelf gives longer service than a square one. A slow heating and cooling cycle not only minimizes damage to the pots but will prolong the life of the kiln furniture, especially the shelves.

Posts made of fireclay are available in various sizes. They often have a center opening to promote a more even expansion. High-temperature insulating bricks can be cut to make satisfactory posts. Dipping the ends of the fireclay posts into aluminum paint will lessen their tendency to stick to the bottoms of the silicon carbide shelves. This problem does not arise with triangular slip-cast posts made of porcelainlike material. Triangular porcelain stilts having pointed contact areas and often a nickel-nichrome wire insert, can be used for some covers or for small pieces that must be glazed all over. The small contact blemishes are not noticeable. (See Chap. 10, pp. 268–269, for a description of saggers and industrial setting methods.)

KILN CONSTRUCTION

Twenty-five years ago few potters were building their own kilns, but with the burgeoning interest in ceramics and with increased knowledge, this practice is now quite commonplace. The beginner, who has little experience in the principles of kiln design, had best attempt to duplicate a proven design, rather than to experiment on his own. Not counting the value of his time, the potter may save 50 percent over the cost of a prefabricated model. Moreover, larger heavy-duty downdraft kilns are seldom available ready made.

The Electric Kiln

The electric kiln, which needs no chimney or gas lines, presents the least challenge to the novice (Fig. 492). Unless one is quite technically inclined, it is best to forgo the problems of calculating length of element wire, size, resistance, and ohms necessary to obtain the desired heat in the kiln chamber. It is easier to purchase replacement elements for a standard kiln made by a reputable manufacturer. The electrical switches might be quite difficult to locate, for the best type is not commonly available. Kiln manufacturers carry replacements.

The angle-iron frame with supporting angles can be fabricated easily, but it must be quite square and accurate. Quarter-inch-thick transite, cut a bit small to allow for heat expansion, can be used for the floor base and outer walls. The standard insulating firebrick straight (9 × 4 ½ × 2 ½ inches), laid "on the flat," is used for the side wall; the 2300°F grade is used for a cone 04 kiln, the 2300° or 2600°F for a cone 6 to 8 kiln. No cutting of the

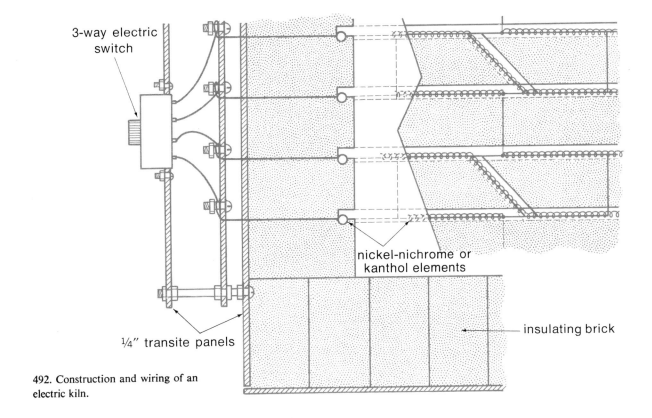

3-way electric switch

nickel-nichrome or kanthol elements

¼″ transite panels

insulating brick

492. Construction and wiring of an electric kiln.

bricks is required for an 18 × 18-inch interior. The bricks must be staggered as the courses are built up. They can be prevented from shifting by driving long finishing nails through the bricks or by applying a thin coat of fireclay and sodium silicate after first moistening with water. No cement should be used within 1 ½ inches of the elements, in case the elements are placed in the joint.

The element recess can be cut with a coarse saw (a Swedish pruning saw, for example) and a round rasp or with a simple cutting tool in a drill press. To retard possible contamination the recesses can be coated with aluminum paint or with a thin kiln wash before inserting the elements. Low-fire nickel-nichrome replacement elements come in a coil like a screen-door spring. They can be stretched to fit the kiln by driving four nails into a section of plywood at a distance comparable to the size of the element recess and a fifth at the point where the element end enters the kiln from the control box. Most elements go twice around the kiln and need a dia-

gonal slot to complete the circle. The coils must not touch at any point, or a hot spot will develop.

Unless one has some electrical experience, it is advisable to have an electrician hook up the wiring. Bolts in the transite to hold the control panel should be inserted before the bricks are laid in place. A piece of transite can serve as the base. Brass bolts should be used as connecting posts between the elements and the insulated switch wires. The usual switch has three positions, low, medium, and high, which are hooked up on 110 volts, 210 volts in series, and 210 volts in parallel to give the needed current. After repeated firings the nickel-nichrome elements will contract, but they can be carefully stretched again and put back in place. A ventilated cover with adequate clearance must enclose the exposed connections.

The cover on a top-loading kiln presents little problem, for ¼-inch bolts—two in each brick, running through an angle iron on each side—will provide adequate support. If the angle is continued

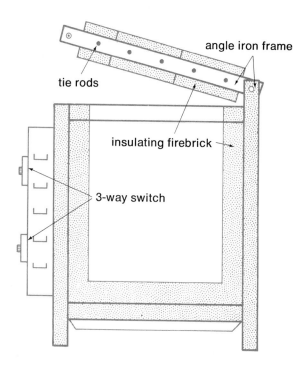

tie rods

angle iron frame

insulating firebrick

3-way switch

493. Electric kiln, lid and switches.

to the rear and the back frame angle is elevated 2 inches, a hinge can be contrived by drilling a hole and inserting a rod. Similarly, an extension in front and a rod inserted in a pipe will provide a lifting handle (see Fig. 493).

The high-fire (cone 8) electric kiln can also use bricks 4 ½ inches thick. However, in this case, an extra 1-inch backing of asbestos would be desirable. Unless a porcelain insert channel is used, greater care must be exercised in selecting firebricks. Because of the higher heat any iron impurities in the firebricks will melt and in turn will cause the element to flux and burn out. The hard Kanthol elements become brittle after use, but their tendency to contract is diminished if they are first fired to cone 8, even though subsequent firings are lower.

The Gas Kiln

Thanks to the uniformity of the insulating firebricks, one can build a small gas kiln using no cement (Fig. 494). This is particularly true of raku kilns, which are small and temporary in nature. A single

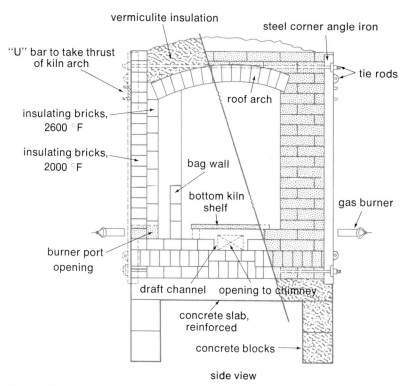

vermiculite insulation

steel corner angle iron

"U" bar to take thrust of kiln arch

tie rods

roof arch

insulating bricks, 2600 °F

insulating bricks, 2000 °F

bag wall

bottom kiln shelf

gas burner

burner port opening

draft channel   opening to chimney

concrete slab, reinforced

concrete blocks

side view

494. Construction of a gas kiln.

burner can be placed in a simple box, with the pots set on a few bricks. A flat roof with a small hole for exhaust is sufficient. Either a bolted top or a similar side section can be used, since the ware is inserted and removed from the hot kiln with tongs.

A single 4 ½-inch wall of insulating brick may be adequate for a small kiln, such as the single-bag-wall design illustrated in Figure 483. A 4- or 5-cubic-foot kiln can be fired easily with two atmospheric burners. The square kiln is most likely to have uniform heat; deep kilns are hard to load, and a tall chamber will allow a temperature variation from top to bottom. Insulating bricks are not hard to cut, but it is easier to plan a design based on the uncut unit.

After the desired size has been established (as close to a cube form as possible), a calculation should be made to determine the burner capacity needed. Manufacturers supply information on the B.t.u. (British thermal units) of their various burners. Unless the kiln is quite small, several burners are preferable to one large unit, in order to avoid a concentration of heat. Generally about 6000 or 7000 B.t.u. are required in a stoneware kiln for each cubic foot of capacity, including the combustion area. For the average Bunsen or aspirating burner, a 3-inch opening is sufficient. The chimney size should be at least equal to the area of all burner ports, even slightly larger if possible, especially if there are angles in the flue connection or if the chimney is unusually high (both of which result in friction loss).

The opening through which the depressed floor flue exhausts into the chimney should be smaller than the chimney itself to prevent a too-rapid heat loss. However, it should be constructed in such a way as to allow easy enlargment, if necessary. Unless the kiln is unusually large, a bag wall constructed of firebrick laid on edge is sufficient. Only the first few courses of bricks need be permanent. The function of the bag wall is to force the flames and heat upward in the kiln. Its height will depend upon the kiln size, the chimney draft, and other factors. Additional bricks can be laid without cement if more heat is needed in the upper kiln area. About 4 or 5 inches of combustion area between the kiln and the bag wall is sufficient in the average gas kiln. A slightly larger area is needed if oil is used for fuel.

Refractory mortar cements are available for bonding the bricks, either in dry or wet form. A cheaper and essentially similar material can be mixed from two parts fireclay and one part fine grog. An even stronger bond can be made by adding one gallon of sodium silicate to 100 pounds of the dry mix. Unless the bricks are first moistened, they will soak up too much mortar, so it is best to immerse them in water and then allow them to drain. Only the thinnest layer of mortar is needed, since the bricks are very uniform and do not require a thick layer of cement for leveling purposes. The best method is to dip the edges of the bricks in a soupy mortar and tap them into place immediately with a hammer on a wood block. Because of their porosity, the insulating bricks expand very little in heating and can be placed very close together. The dense firebricks, however, expand considerably under heat; therefore, about ¼ inch of space with no mortar should be left between every third or fourth brick, for otherwise the outside layer of cooler brick will be forced open in firing.

It is especially advisable to plan on a unit brick size when using hard bricks. They can be cut by tapping a groove on each side with a mason's hammer, then split by hitting a solid blow on a mason's chisel with a heavy hammer. No such procedure is possible with the wedge-shaped bricks needed for the kiln arch. The usual arch rises at the rate of 1 ½ inches per foot. Placing the bricks on edge for a 4 ½-inch thickness provides sufficient strength for the average-size kiln. The #1 arch brick tapers from 2 ½ to to 2 ⅛ inches. By drawing two curves 4 ½ inches apart on a large board and using a 1 ½-inch rise per foot over the desired span, the required number of #1 arch bricks can be calculated. Some straights will be needed, but they should be kept to a minimum, as should the mortar.

These calculations present no problem in an insulating brick arch, since the softer bricks can be trimmed to a wooden pattern using a coarse rasp. A sharply angled skewback brick is needed where the arch meets the side wall. The kiln will require a 2 ½-inch angle-iron support at each corner, with ½-inch take-up rods at top and bottom. While these give a slight rigidity to the kiln, their main purpose is to hold the heavy angle iron brace, which is needed on the outer wall to take up the thrust of the kiln arch.

A supporting form to hold the arch can be made easily by cutting several boards to the arch curve and covering them with a masonite sheet. It is wise to leave a bit of slack and to place wedges under the uprights so that the form can be removed easily after the steel angles and rods are in place. The catenary-arch kiln is self supporting and needs no metal bracing. Its curve can be established by suspending a chain from two nails at the desired floor width. The result will be a rather pointed curve. The structure will be most stable if the height approximates the width of the base. This design is perhaps best suited to an oil-burning kiln, since the flare at the base provides the extra combustion area needed for oil fuel.

The weight of a kiln is considerable, and it requires at least a 4-inch concrete base. In order to avoid leaning over and bumping the head in loading, it is a good idea to build the kiln on a reinforced concrete slab elevated to the necessary height with concrete blocks. Such a kiln can be moved later, if necessary, with little or no damage. In arranging the brick structure one should always plan to stagger the joints and occasionally have a tie brick to bind two courses together. The corner bricks are laid first, making certain the plan is perfectly square. A level and a guide line are essential, since the eye is not dependable. Common red bricks can be used as backup for that part of the floor area not depressed for the exhaust channel. The kind of brick to be used and the wall thickness are determined by size and general use. For the usual salt kiln and the oil-fueled kiln an inner course of 4 ½-inch hard firebrick is necessary, backed up by a 2000°F insulating firebrick. If the size approaches 30 cubic feet, an additional outer layer of common red brick would be desirable.

A properly constructed kiln will give many years of service and require few repairs. A stoneware kiln with a 15- to 25-cubic-foot capacity can be built with a 2600°F insulating brick on edge and a 2000°F brick on the flat, thus creating a 7-inch wall. Although the initial cost is high, the construction is easier and the fuel cost lower. However, insulating bricks retain little heat and cool more rapidly; therefore, a 30-cubic-foot or larger kiln should be equipped with a hard inner liner as mentioned earlier. The kiln door jambs should be built of the same brick as the inner liner, whatever the type used. Kilns that are covered by only a simple roof have been built for summer schools. To provide protection from driving rains and snow during the off season, the procedures described above are reversed, and the hard durable firebrick is placed on the outside with the insulating brick as an inner liner. The results are apparently satisfactory.

It is obvious from all these examples that there is no one way to build a kiln. The illustrations show a variety of burner placements. Most potters find the downdraft layout (Figs. 482, 489) to be the most satisfactory for the 10- to 25-cubic-foot size. A smaller kiln might use the crossdraft design shown in Figure 483. Although the updraft muffle kiln (Fig. 481) is a common design for commercial kilns, neither this nor the open-flame updraft are recommended for construction by the potter.

The Chimney

Because of the extreme temperatures involved, the kiln cannot exhaust into an ordinary household chimney. For a shedlike studio, a simple transite pipe may be sufficient to carry the exhaust. In the classroom, however, an insulated fireclay Van Packer unit may be necessary, especially for the portion within the building. The exterior section can have the usual fireclay liner and brick construction. Small kilns can exhaust into a metal hood above the kiln, thus sucking the cooler room air to the stack and eliminating some of the temperature problem.

A short, direct connection from kiln to chimney is just as important for a proper draft as is the height of the stack. If needed, overhead connections can be made with transite or a metal fireclay-lined pipe. Undue length or angles in this connection will require a much higher and larger stack size than normal. Tall stacks with unusual connections will probably need a burner or a fan in the stack base to induce an initial draft. If there are no surrounding buildings to cause a downdraft, a 15- to 20-foot chimney should be sufficient. A 6- ×-6-inch flue is usually adequate for a 10-cubic-foot kiln and a 9- ×-9-inch flue for a 20-cubic-foot design. However, an even larger size is recommended, especially in a taller stack which has some friction loss. A slot must be left in the draft flue at the point where it leaves the kiln for a damper. It can be made of a small or a broken kiln shelf.

Burners

There are many types of burners available, both oil and gas, and some can be improvised with simple materials. The smoke produced by the drip-type oil burner normally relegates its use to an isolated location. In some cases vacuum cleaner units can be used for added draft. The blowers needed to provide additional air and the fumes from oil fuel are disturbing factors if the kiln area is adjoining a classroom. An outdoor location in a warm climate creates no problem, but the kiln must be watched, for the burners can become clogged, and this is a fire hazard.

Although more expensive, natural gas or liquid butane are both convenient and relatively safe. For a medium-size kiln one needs a natural-gas line at least two inches in diameter, with several pounds of pressure at the meter, even though the large regulator that is needed will reduce the pressure to about 6 ounces at the kiln. A large kiln using liquid gas requires a 500-gallon tank, which usually can be rented. There is a drop of pressure when the tank is less than half full, because of the cooling that occurs as the gas is being used rapidly. Gas pressure is also calculated in terms of the amount of pressure needed to raise a column of water in a glass tube.

According to this system, 1 ounce of gas pressure equals 1.73 inches of water pressure.

For a controlled and even firing, several simple aspirating or Bunsen burners are preferable to one or two large forced-draft burners. A solenoid safety valve should be connected near the burner in case of a temporary gas interruption. All gas lines must be absolutely tight, since even the slightest leak is dangerous. In selecting a burner size one ought to allow for some excess capacity. As mentioned earlier, about 6000 or 7000 B.t.u. are required for each cubic foot of the kiln interior, including the combustion area. This figure assumes that the insulation is adequate and that the general design, draft, and so forth are efficient.

FIRING LEAD GLAZES

When any glaze is fired, a small percentage of the more active flux compounds volatilize. In a gas kiln these vapors pass out the chimney, but with most electric kilns the chemical vapors tend to be deposited on the glaze surface during the cooling period. Normally, this is no problem, but in the case of a lead glaze it creates a potential danger. Excess lead on a glaze surface is unstable, since it lacks sufficient silica and alumina to form a durable crystalline structure. Under these conditions even a correctly compounded lead glaze can leach toxic lead particles when exposed to acid liquids or food. The solution is to drill several small holes near the base of the kiln and in the upper walls. These holes should not be as large as the usual peephole, for otherwise too much heat would be lost. Vents of this kind will provide a natural flow in the kiln atmosphere and will clear the kiln of lead vapors. Unless the kiln is in an open, ventilated area, it is further advisable to equip it with a small hood and exhaust fan.

12 Studio Equipment

This chapter presents a selection of the necessary items of studio equipment available to the potter. The addresses of specific manufacturers, together with a schedule of typical prices, are listed in the Appendix (pp. 324–328).

CERAMIC KILNS

The prospective kiln buyer should first study Chapter 11 (pp. 271–287), which discusses in more detail the characteristics of various kiln designs. Since it requires neither gas lines nor a special chimney, the small electric kiln of a 3- to 5-cubic-foot size is adequate for the amateur or for the average public school (Figs. 496–497). For the college ceramics program a gas kiln is necessary (Figs. 498–501), not only for its larger size but because of the higher temperatures and the possibility of reduction firing. In an instructional situation, as opposed to a production effort, several small kilns are preferable to one large kiln. Frequent firings are needed to experiment with glazes and decorative techniques, as well as to gain experience with loading and firing procedures. Typical equipment for a university ceramics program might include two electric kilns of 3 cubic feet each and three gas kilns in the 8-, 10-, and 12-cubic-foot sizes. Dimensions refer to the shelf-loading area. In comparing kilns for purchase, care must be taken to determine the actual loading area and to exclude both the combustion area and the space needed for the flow of heat around the shelves. An excess kiln capacity is desirable to accommodate an increasing number of students. Colleges with graduate programs might well consider a car kiln for greater capacity and ease in loading (Figs. 502–503).

Although most public schools fire their ceramics to about cone 04, a higher-firing kiln is useful, for the kiln rated at only 2000°F will not stand up under continued use. The kanthal elements in a 2300°F kiln will contract from their recesses, unless the kiln is first fired to about 2300°F. After this the elements will be brittle but will remain in place.

opposite : 495. WALTER HYLECK, U.S.A. *Phoney Ringtail Cat Under Large Black Beret.* Stoneware with low-fire black and silver luster glazes, height 18″.

above : 496. Paragon top-loading electric kiln for temperatures to cone 8. Chamber $17 \times 17 \times 18''$.

right : 497. Unique front-loading electric kiln for temperatures to cones 8–10. Chamber $17 \times 17 \times 17''$, weight 600 lbs.

498. West Coast open-fire updraft gas kiln for temperatures to cones 10–12. Chamber $24 \times 24 \times 36''$.

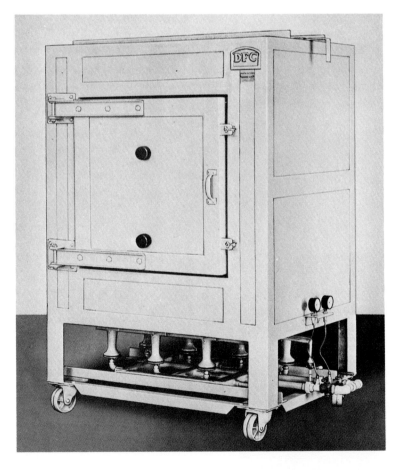

above : 499. Alpine open-fire updraft gas kiln for temperatures to cones 8–10. Capacity 24 cubic feet.

left : 500. Denver Fire Clay updraft muffle gas kiln for temperatures to cone 6. Capacity 12 cubic feet.

left : 501. Unique heavy-duty downdraft gas kiln for temperatures to cones 8–12. Force draft with automatic cutoff controls. Capacity 30 cubic feet.

below : 502. Unique heavy-duty downdraft gas car kiln for temperatures to cone 11. Force draft with automatic shutoff controls. Capacity 30 cubic feet.

above : 503. Denver Fire Clay updraft shuttle-car gas kiln for temperatures to cone 6. Car area 24 × 60 × 25″, overall length 24′, capacity 20 cubic feet, shipping weight 7000 lbs. The double-door construction makes possible the use of an additional car for faster loading and operation.

right : 504. Unique pyrometer with insulated leads and thermocouple.

All gas kilns should be equipped with a simple automatic cutoff in case of a gas interruption. The elaborate controls and regulating pyrometer used in industrial ceramics are not only very expensive and unnecessary on a small kiln, but they often make operation more difficult. Although pyrometric cones are essential to gauge final temperatures accurately, a portable pyrometer (Fig. 504) and thermocouple are most helpful in regulating heat rise and in determining temperatures for a reduction firing.

There are several devices on the market that employ a cone and a sliding spring mechanism to turn off the power in an electric kiln, but these cannot be recommended, because all too often the metal parts become corroded, and this can lead to malfunction and possible overfiring of the kiln.

POTTER'S WHEELS

Because of their somewhat limited production, good potter's wheels are rather expensive. While an expert can throw on any wheel, a beginner will have difficulty achieving satisfactory results on poor equipment. The cheap wheels advertised in hobby magazines should be strictly avoided! It is far better to confine oneself to hand-built pottery than to settle for such an inferior wheel.

Potters usually prefer to use the kind of wheel on which they first learned to throw, and, as the illustrations reveal, there is no consensus about the perfect type. Many teachers prefer the simple kick wheel (Figs. 505–508) for beginners; when in difficulty, they forget to kick, thus slowing down the wheel at the proper time. A wheel with an integral and adjustable seat, a splash pan, and foot rests is

top left : 505. Oak Hill traditional kick wheel. Waterproof plywood frame; 31″ flywheel, iron weight 80 lbs.; 14″ aluminum wheel head; overall shipping weight 170 lbs.

center left : 506. Soldner kick wheel. Welded-pipe frame; reinforced concrete flywheel, weight 90 lbs.; 14″ aluminum wheel head; 20×38″ work table. Available with ½-horsepower 5–100 rpm motor attachment.

below left : 507. Randall kick wheel. Welded steel frame, 9″ recessed aluminum wheel head, 19″ aluminum splash pan, adjustable bucket seat; 28″ flywheel, standard weight 115 lbs. (adjustable if desired); overall shipping weight 200 lbs. Available with ½-horsepower motor attachment.

above : 508. Denton Vars side-treadle wheel designed by Bernard Leach. Hardwood frame, weighted flywheel, fiber glass pan, 13″ aluminum wheel head.

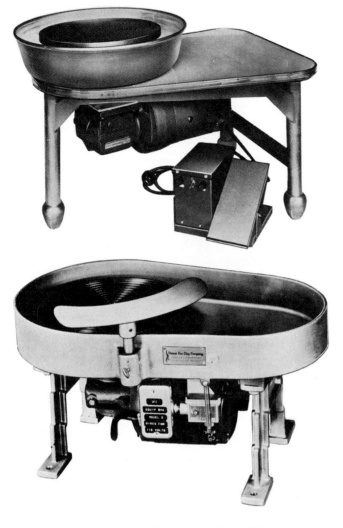

below : 511. Skutt bench-type electric wheel. One-third-horse-power variable-speed motor with adjustable belts at speeds of 35–125 or 50–165 rpm; 12″ wheel head; cast-aluminum frame.

bottom : 512. Randall special wheel. Three-quarter-horse-power 110-volt D.C. motor, variable speed 0–175 rpm, with foot control; height 19 ½″, 18 ¼″ aluminum wheel head; shipping weight 275 lbs. This wheel is designed for the production potter. It can also be used for stand-up throwing of large forms.

top : 509. Alpine heavy-duty wheel. One-half-horsepower variable-speed motor with foot controls, 0–160 rpm; platform height 16″, 13″ wheel head.

above : 510. Denver Fire Clay bench-type electric wheel. One-quarter-horsepower variable-speed motor, 48–200 rpm; 12″ wheel head.

undoubtedly the most convenient. A few of these have motorized attachments.

The choice of an electric wheel (Figs. 509–512), given the varying motor sizes available, may well depend upon the size of the pieces to be thrown. In any case, the single-speed motor should be avoided, as should motors not capable of variable and quite slow speeds. Speeds in excess of 100 rpm are not needed if the motor has adequate torque.

CLAY MIXERS

Preparing plastic clay for the classroom or active studio can require much effort. The practice of buying bagged plastic clay at high prices is not economically feasible when one uses more than 3 tons of dry clay during the school year. The blunger and filter press mixing process seems unnecessarily involved for the small studio, especially when many pounds of dry trimmings and discarded pots must be reclaimed. The three machines illustrated (Figs. 513–515) allow these clay scraps, after proper soaking, to be mixed into a plastic state. Dry powdered clay can be added if necessary. The action of the Randall and Soldner machines is not unlike that of commercial bakery dough machines. In fact, dough mixers can be used for clay, and second-hand models are occasionally available at low price. The Walker pug mill discharges clay at a container height and with a slightly stiffer consistency.

right : 513. Soldner clay mixer with reinforced concrete tub. Unit dimensions 48×48×31″, weight 450 lbs.; 2-horsepower 115/220 volt motor. Available with stainless-steel blades, improved starter, and fan-cooled motor.

below left : 514. Walker pug mill, shown with mixing and compression screw flight blades, all operating parts stainless steel. Overall dimensions 63×33×36″, hopper opening 16×20″, weight 270 lbs.; ¾-horsepower 110-volt motor with 150:1 reduction gear; automatic overload switch and knee cut-off bar.

below right : 515. Randall clay mixer. Overall dimensions 56×36×34″, capacity 100 lbs. dry clay; 3-horsepower motor with heavy reduction unit, 220 or 440 volts; safety switch and overload fuse; shipping weight 600 lbs.

top : 516. Porcelain mortar and pestle. Available in 16 oz. and 32 oz. sizes.

above : 517. Craftools porcelain ball mill jars. Available in gallon, half-gallon, and quart sizes.

top : 518. Craftools ball mill. Length 20″, ¼-horsepower motor.

above : 519. Craftools brass glaze sieve. Available in 8 to 100 mesh sizes.

GLAZE-ROOM EQUIPMENT

Commercial chemicals today are so finely ground that a simple mixing with a wire whisk is usually sufficient. However, certain coarse materials, such as calcined ingredients or volcanic ash, may require the use of a mortar and pestle (Fig. 516) or, for larger amounts, a ball mill (Figs. 517–518). A portable kitchen food mixer or a paint mixer in an electric drill are quite efficient for mixing moderate quanti-

ties of glaze. A variety of brass sieves (Fig. 519) in mesh sizes of 80, 60, 30, 15, and 8 are useful. The finer sizes are for sifting glazes and the coarser for grog.

As a rule, glazes are most conveniently applied by pouring, dipping, or brushing. The sprayed glaze is very fragile and can easily be damaged in loading. Nevertheless, certain glaze and decorative effects can best be achieved by spraying (Fig. 520). Since the amount of sprayed work is likely to be small,

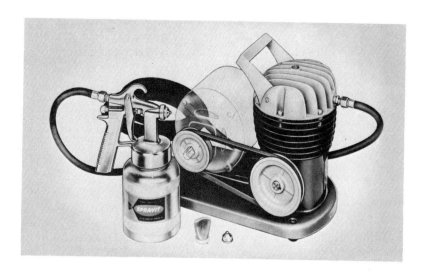

left : 520. Craftools portable paint sprayer suitable for glazes. One-quarter-horsepower motor, gun hose, and nozzles.

right : 521. Craftools portable spray booth. Exhaust fan and fiber glass filters, inside dimensions 30 × 24″.

far right: 522. Craftools glaze spray booth. Exhaust fan and turntable. Available with air filter and regulator.

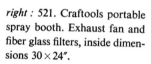

523. Ohaus triple-beam gram scales. Several models available from local dealers.

524. Craftools cast-iron banding wheel. Ball-bearing movement, 8″ head.

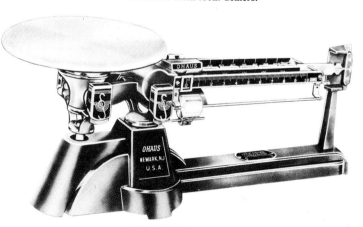

a booth with filters (Figs. 521–522) rather than a permanent exhaust system will be less expensive and usually adequate. Gram scales (Fig. 523), large pound scales, and decorating wheels (Fig. 524) are necessary in every glaze room. Dipping tongs are desirable for glazing small pieces.

SPECIAL EQUIPMENT

In view of the amount of heavy material that must be moved in the studio—bagged clay and chemicals, fire bricks, plastic clay in large cans—a shop lift on rollers is an essential item (Fig. 525). Bagged clay and chemicals should be placed on pallets upon delivery. Large sculptural pieces are best constructed on a plywood base resting a pallet. By means of the lift, the transference into the kiln is relatively easy. Sand or small wooden rollers between the pallet and the base allow the piece to be skidded into place. The plywood base is left to burn out.

Ware racks (Fig. 526) are invaluable in loading and unloading kilns, as well as in storing and moving ware from the glazing area to the kilns. Draped with plastic they can serve as extra damp-room storage. Thrown pieces cut off the wheel can be put on 6-inch boards that fit the ware rack. Overhead racks to accommodate pots on these short boards are also common, especially in the private studio

left : 525. Big Joe hydraulic shop lift. Capacity 1000 lbs., lifting height 54″; dimensions 44 ¾ × 29″, weight 380 lbs.

above : 526. Unique welded-steel ware rack on casters. Dimensions 65 × 22 × 28″.

which is likely to have limited space. The damp room can have a similar provision to hold boards of thrown pots. A damp room is a necessity in schools because of the time lapse between classes.

A plaster bat with a hollowed center section is convenient for drying small batches of clay. One or two large bats, which may hold up to 50 pounds of slip, are also helpful for drying special mixtures. While clay slabs can be rolled out on a sanded table, large flat plaster-of-paris slabs are useful, especially if the clay is a bit moist. In the classroom it is best to have wedging tables at two different heights to accommodate both shorter and taller students. Because of their continued use a welded-steel base frame is recommended for plaster-faced wedging tables. The plaster must be scraped periodically to remove the colloidal clay particles that would otherwise seal up the surface.

THE CERAMIC STUDIO

The general layout of the studio is quite important for both the individual potter and the teacher. The various work areas should be laid out in such a way that interference and unnecessary traffic are avoided. Raw materials and clay mixing should be concentrated near the delivery entrance and this area provided with adequate ventilation. A good arrangement is a rather open studio with drop panels from the ceiling to concentrate the kiln fumes and heat, which can then be exhausted from the studio. The throwing, modeling, and decorating areas should be spacious and well lighted.

Ware racks have been mentioned before as an aid to moving thrown pots from the wheel area to the kilns. Bisque ware can also be unloaded from the kilns onto such racks for transference to the glaze area and finally back to the kilns for the glaze firing. Sinks should be conveniently located in the several work areas. Plaster work is best concentrated in a single area, and the sink used for this purpose should drain into a large open tank with several baffles to trap plaster particles, which would otherwise certainly stop up the drains.

A duplicate set of clearly labeled glaze chemicals is desirable in the glaze area. Odd lots of glaze, instead of being discarded, can be poured into a crock for use as a shop glaze for interiors. Large cans on rollers, some containing water, should be placed in the wheel area for clay trimmings and throwing water, as well as to provide a place to wash tools and hands. (This ought not be done in the sinks, for eventually the drains will become clogged.) The aged clay can be reclaimed to serve as a base for new powdered clay in the pug mill or clay mixer.

The classroom-studio is really rather like a small commercial pottery. It should be an airy, clean, and enjoyable place in which to work. Unless the studio is organized efficiently, both student and teacher can suffer many frustrations. Each student must develop the habit of cleaning up as he goes along. All students should participate in the loading of the kilns, with the firing entrusted to the advanced students, for these are skills that are as important to master as throwing. Clay preparation is a real problem in most studios, for it is laborious and time consuming regardless of the equipment. Ideally, a rotating team of students can periodically make up clay as it is needed. In practice some use more than their share, while others fail to knead clay from failed pots or thoughtlessly allow it to harden in the drying bats. As a solution many schools pay a few students to make up clay and place it in 25-pound plastic bags, which are sold at cost to the individual student. While this entails a certain amount of bookkeeping, it does help to eliminate some careless studio practices.

Appendix

Reference
Tables

Atomic Weights of Common Elements

Element	Symbol	Atomic number	Atomic weight
Aluminum	Al	13	26.97
Antimony	Sb	51	121.76
Barium	Ba	56	137.36
Bismuth	Bi	83	209.00
Boron	B	5	10.82
Cadmium	Cd	48	112.41
Calcium	Ca	20	40.08
Carbon	C	6	12.01
Chlorine	Cl	17	35.457
Chromium	Cr	24	52.01
Cobalt	Co	27	58.94
Copper	Cu	29	63.54
Fluorine	F	9	19.00
Gold	Au	79	197.20
Hydrogen	H	1	1.008

Atomic Weights of Common Elements—*continued*

Element	Symbol	Atomic number	Atomic weight
Iridium	Ir	77	193.10
Iron	Fe	26	55.84
Lead	Pb	82	207.21
Lithium	Li	3	6.94
Magnesium	Mg	12	24.32
Manganese	Mn	25	54.93
Molybdenum	Mo	42	95.98
Neon	Ne	10	20.183
Nickel	Ni	28	58.69
Nitrogen	N	7	14.008
Oxygen	O	8	16.00
Palladium	Pd	46	106.70
Phosphorus	P	15	30.98
Platinum	Pt	78	195.23
Potassium	K	19	39.096
Silicon	Si	14	28.06
Silver	Ag	47	107.88
Sodium	Na	11	22.997
Sulphur	S	16	32.066
Tin	Sn	50	118.70
Titanium	Ti	22	47.90
Uranium	U	92	238.07
Vanadium	V	23	50.95
Zinc	Zn	30	65.38
Zirconium	Zr	40	91.22

Common Ceramic Raw Materials

Material	Raw formula	Compound molecular weight	Equivalent weight	Fired formula
Aluminum hydroxide	$Al_2(OH)_6$	156	156	Al_2O_3
Antimony oxide	Sb_2O_3	292	292	Sb_2O_3
Barium carbonate	$BaCO_3$	197	197	BaO
Bone ash (calcium phosphate)	$Ca_3(PO_4)_2$	310	103	CaO
Boric acid	$B_2O_3 \cdot 3\,H_2O$	124	124	B_2O_3
Borax	$Na_2O \cdot 2\,B_2O_3 \cdot 10\,H_2O$	382	382	$Na_2O \cdot 2\,B_2O_3$
Calcium borate (colemanite)	$2\,CaO \cdot 3\,B_2O_3 \cdot 5\,H_2O$	412	206	$2\,CaO \cdot 3\,B_2O_3$
Calcium carbonate (whiting)	$CaCO_3$	100	100	CaO
Chromic oxide	Cr_2O_3	152	152	Cr_2O_3
Cobalt carbonate	$CoCO_3$	119	119	CoO
Cobalt oxide, black	Co_3O_4	241	80	CoO
Copper carbonate	$CuCO_3$	124	124	CuO
Copper oxide, green (cupric)	CuO	80	80	CuO
Copper oxide, red (cuprous)	Cu_2O	143	80	CuO
Cornwall stone[a]	$(1\,RO \cdot 1.16\,Al_2O_3 \cdot 8.95\,SiO_2)$	732	652	same
Cryolite	$Na_3 \cdot AlF_6$	210	420	$3\,Na_2O \cdot Al_2O_3$
Dolomite	$CaCO_3 \cdot MgCO_3$	184	184	$CaO \cdot MgO$
Feldspar, potash	$K_2O \cdot Al_2O_3 \cdot 6\,SiO_2$	557	557	same
Feldspar, soda	$Na_2 \cdot Al_2O_3 \cdot 6\,SiO_2$	524	524	same
Kaolin (china clay)	$Al_2O_3 \cdot 2\,SiO_2 \cdot 2\,H_2O$	258	258	$Al_2O_3 \cdot 2\,SiO_2$
Kaolin (calcined)	$Al_2O_3 \cdot 2\,SiO_2$	222	222	$Al_2O_3 \cdot 2\,SiO_2$
Iron chromate	$FeCrO_4$	172	172	$FeCrO_4$
Iron oxide, red (ferric)	Fe_2O_3	160	160	Fe_2O_3
Iron oxide, black (ferrous)	FeO	72	72	FeO
Flint (quartz, silica)	SiO_2	60	60	SiO_2
Fluorspar (calcium fluoride)	CaF_2	78	78	CaO
Lead carbonate (white lead)	$2\,PbCO_3 \cdot Pb(OH)_2$	775	258	PbO
Lead monosilicate	$3\,PbO \cdot 2\,SiO_2$	789	263	same
Lead oxide (litharge)	PbO	223	223	PbO
Lead oxide, red	Pb_3O_4	685	228	PbO

Common Ceramic Raw Materials—*continued*

Material	Raw formula	Compound molecular weight	Equivalent weight	Fired formula
Lepidolite	$LiF \cdot KF \cdot Al_2O_3 \cdot 3\ SiO_2$	356	356	same
Lithium carbonate	Li_2CO_3	74	74	Li_2O
Magnesium carbonate	$MgCO_3$	84	84	MgO
Manganese carbonate	$MnCO_3$	115	115	MnO
Manganese dioxide (black)	MnO_2	87	87	MnO
Manganese oxide (greenish)	MnO	71	71	MnO
Nepheline syenite[b]	$1\ RO \cdot 1.04\ Al_2O_3 \cdot 4.53\ SiO_2$	447	447	same
Nickel oxide, green	NiO	75	75	NiO
Nickel oxide, black	Ni_2O_3	166	83	NiO
Petalite	$Li_2O \cdot Al_2O_3 \cdot 8\ SiO_2$	197	197	same
Plastic vitrox[c]	$1\ RO \cdot 1.69Al_2O_3 \cdot 14.64\ SiO_2$	1139	1139	same
Potassium carbonate (pearl ash)	K_2CO_3	138	138	K_2O
Pyrophyllite	$Al_2O_3 \cdot 4\ SiO_2 \cdot H_2O$	360	360	$Al_2O_3 \cdot 4\ SiO_2$
Sodium bicarbonate	$NaHCO_3$	84	168	Na_2O
Sodium carbonate (soda ash)	Na_2CO_3	106	106	Na_2O
Spodumene	$Li_2O \cdot Al_2O_3 \cdot 4\ SiO_2$	372	372	same
Talc (steatite)	$3\ MgO \cdot 4\ SiO_2 \cdot H_2O$	379	126	$3\ MgO \cdot 4\ SiO_2$
Tin oxide (stannic oxide)	SnO_2	151	151	SnO_2
Titanium dioxide (rutile impure TiO_2)	TiO_2	80	80	TiO_2
Wollastonite	$Ca \cdot SiO_3$	116	116	same
Zinc oxide	ZnO	81	81	ZnO
Zirconium oxide	ZrO_2	123	123	ZrO_2

[a] Formula for Cornwall stone

K_2O	0.4453	Al_2O_3	1.0847	SiO_2	7.796
Na_2O	0.2427	Fe_2O_3	0.0065		
CaO	0.1873				
MgO	0.0821	*Mol. weight 652*			
CaF_2	0.0421				

[b] Formula for Nepheline syenite

Na_2O	0.713	Al_2O_3	1.04	SiO_3	4.53
K_2O	0.220				
CaO	0.056	*Mol. weight 447*			
MgO	0.011				

[c] Formula for Plastic vitrox

CaO	0.045	Al_2O_3	1.693	SiO_2	14.634
MgO	0.058	Fe_2O_3	0.005		
Na_2O	0.054				
K_2O	0.842	*Mol. weight 1139.40*			

Analysis of Common Clays and Chemicals

Material	SiO$_2$	Al$_2$O$_3$	Fe$_2$O$_3$	TiO$_2$	CaO	MgO	K$_2$O	Na$_2$O	Li$_2$O	Ignition loss
Red Dalton clay	63.2	18.3	6.3	1.3	0.3	0.5	1.6	1.2		6.4
Barnard clay	41.4	6.7	29.9	0.2	0.5	0.6	1.0	0.5		8.4
Monmouth stoneware	56.8	28.5			0.3	0.3	0.3	1.3		12.2
Jordon stoneware	69.4	17.7	1.6	1.3	0.1	0.5	1.5	1.39		6.4
Albany slip	57.6	14.6	5.2	0.4	5.8	2.7	3.2	0.8		9.5
Ball clay	51.9	31.7	0.8	1.5	0.2	0.2	0.9	0.4		12.3
Sagger clay	59.4	27.2	0.7	1.6	0.6	0.2	0.7	0.3		9.4
Fireclay	58.1	23.1	2.4	1.4	0.8	1.1	1.9	0.3		10.5
Georgia kaolin	44.9	38.9	0.4	1.3	0.1	0.1	0.2	0.2		14.21
English kaolin	47.25	37.29	0.84	0.05	0.03	0.28	1.8	0.04		12.21
Petalite	77.0	17.5					(0.5)		4.3	0.7
Pyrophyllite	73.5	20.0	0.5		0.1		1.4	1.2		3.3
Bentonite	64.32	20.7	3.47	0.11	0.46	2.26	2.9			5.15
Volcanic ash	72.51	11.55	1.21	0.54	0.68	0.07	7.87	1.79		3.81
Plastic vitrox	75.56	14.87	0.09		0.22	0.20	6.81	0.29		2.04
Feldspar, potash	68.3	17.9	0.08		0.4		10.1	3.1		0.32
Cornwall stone	72.6	16.1	0.23	0.06	1.4	0.1	4.56	3.67		2.54
Nepheline syenite	60.4	23.6	0.08		0.7	0.1	9.8	4.6		0.7
Lepidolite	55.0	25.0	0.08				9.0	1.0	4.0	0.92[a]
Spodumene	62.91	28.42	0.53		0.11	0.13	0.69	0.46	6.78	0.28

[a] plus 5 percent Fluorine.

Water of Plasticity of Various Clays

Washed kaolin	44.48–47.50
White sedimentary kaolin	28.60–56.25
Ball clays	25.00–53.30
Plastic fireclays	12.90–37.40
Flint fireclays	8.89–19.04
Sagger clays	18.40–28.56
Stoneware clays	19.16–34.80
Brick clays	13.20–40.70

$$\text{Water of plasticity} = \frac{\text{weight of plastic sample} - \text{weight of dry sample}}{\text{weight of dry sample}} \times 100$$

Analysis of Several Standard Feldspars[a]

Material	SiO$_2$	Al$_2$O$_3$	Fe$_2$O$_3$	CaO	MgO	K$_2$O	Na$_2$O	Ignition loss
Spruce Pine # 4	67.9	19.01	0.05	1.54	trace	4.98	6.22	0.08
Bell	68.3	17.9	0.08	0.4	trace	10.1	3.1	0.32
Eureka	69.8	17.11	0.1	trace		9.4	3.5	0.2
Kingman	66.0	18.7	0.1	0.1		12.0	2.8	0.2
Oxford	69.4	17.04	0.09	0.38		7.92	3.22	0.3
Chesterfield	70.6	16.33	0.08	0.3		8.5	3.75	0.4
Buckingham	65.58	19.54	trace	0.16	0.2	12.44	2.56	0.32

[a] The variable quality of the feldspar fluxes is a major reason why glaze recipes may need alteration unless materials are identical.

Oxide Equivalents of Selected Commercial Frits[a]

Company		K$_2$O	Na$_2$O	CaO	PbO	Al$_2$O$_3$	B$_2$O$_3$	SiO$_2$	Formula weight
Pemco	54		0.32	0.68			0.64	1.47	191
	67	0.12	0.19	0.69		0.37	1.16	2.17	311
	926	0.01	0.31	0.68		0.11	0.61	1.90	225
	83		0.28		0.72	0.20	0.26	2.43	276
	316[b]				1.00	0.25		1.92	364
	349	0.09	0.09	0.58	0.24	0.19	0.36	2.80	313
Ferro	3124	0.02	0.28	0.70		0.27	0.55	2.56	279
	3134		0.32	0.68			0.63	1.47	210
	3211			1.00			1.11		133
	3223		1.00				2.00	5.00	502
	3419		0.28		0.72		0.57	0.89	276
	3386	0.02	0.08		0.90	0.13	1.77	4.42	499
	3396		0.50		0.50		1.00	2.00	332
Hommel	285	0.10	0.90			0.21	0.94	2.72	315
	267	0.13	0.31	0.56		0.29	1.24	2.05	301
	266		0.32	0.68		0.32	1.10	1.31	245
	22			0.47	0.53		0.98	2.88	385
	240		0.28		0.72		0.56	0.90	271
	13		0.30		0.70		0.39	0.41	227

[a] In most cases the above frits will constitute a complete glaze at cone 06.

[b] Cone deformation eutectic for PbO · Al$_2$O$_3$ · SiO$_2$ system; a highly acid-resistant frit in powder form.

Color Scale for Temperatures

Color	Degrees C	Degrees F
Lowest visible red	475	885
Lowest visible red to dark red	475–650	885–1200
Dark red to cherry red	650–750	1200–1380
Cherry red to bright cherry red	750–815	1380–1500
Bright cherry red to orange	815–900	1500–1650
Orange to yellow	900–1090	1650–2000
Yellow to light yellow	1090–1315	2000–2400
Light yellow to white	1315–1540	2400–2800
White to dazzling white	1540 and higher	2800 and higher

Average Temperatures to Which Various Ceramic Products are Fired

Products	Degrees F
Heavy clay products	
Common brick—surface clay	1600–1800
Common brick—shale	1800–2000
Face brick—fireclay	2100–2300
Enamel brick	2100–2300
Drain tile	1700–1900
Sewer pipe	2030–2320
Roofing tile	1960–2140
Terra cotta	2070–2320
Pottery	
Flower pots	1580–1850
Stoneware (chemical)	2650–2700
Stoneware (once fired)	2318–2426
Semivitreous ware	2282–2354
Pottery decalcomanias	1400–1500
Refractories	
Firebrick—clay	2300–2500
Firebrick—silica	2650–2750
Silicon carbide	3236–3992
White wares	
Electrical porcelain	2390–2500
Hotel china—bisque	2390–2436
Hotel china—glaze	2210–2282
Floor tile	2318–2498
Wall tile—bisque	1886–2354
Wall tile—glaze	1186–2246

Temperature Equivalents—Orton Standard Pyrometric Cones[a]

Cone number	Large cones		Small cones		Seger cones (used in Europe) Degrees C
	150°C[b]	270°F[b]	300°C[b]	540°F[b]	
020	635	1175	666	1231	670
019	683	1261	723	1333	690
018	717	1323	752	1386	710
017	747	1377	784	1443	730
016	792	1458	825	1517	750
015	804	1479	843	1549	790
014	838	1540			815
013	852	1566			835
012	884	1623			855
011	894	1641			880
010	894	1641	919	1686	900
09	923	1693	955	1751	920
08	955	1751	983	1801	940
07	984	1803	1008	1846	960
06	999	1830	1023	1873	980
05	1046	1915	1062	1944	1000
04	1060	1940	1098	2008	1020
03	1101	2014	1131	2068	1040
02	1120	2048	1148	2098	1060
01	1137	2079	1178	2152	1080

[a] From the Edward Orton, Jr., Ceramic Foundation, Columbus, Ohio.

[b] Temperature rise per hour.

Temperature Equivalents—Orton Standard Pyrometric Cones—*continued*

| Cone number | Large cones | | Small cones | | Seger cones (used in Europe) |
	$150°C^b$	$270°F^b$	$300°C^b$	$540°F^b$	Degrees C
1	1154	2109	1179	2154	*1100*
2	1162	2124	1179	2154	*1120*
3	1168	2134	1196	2185	*1140*
4	1186	2167	1209	2208	*1160*
5	1196	2185	1221	2230	*1180*
6	1222	2232	1255	2291	*1200*
7	1240	2264	1264	2307	*1230*
8	1263	2305	1300	2372	*1250*
9	1280	2336	1317	2403	*1280*
10	1305	2381	1330	2426	*1300*
11	1315	2399	1336	2437	*1320*
12	1326	2419	1335	2471	*1350*
13	1346	2455			*1380*
14	1366	2491			*1410*
15	1431	2608			*1430*

Conversion formula

Centigrade to Fahrenheit

example: $100°C \times \dfrac{9}{5} = 180 \quad 180 + 32 = 212°F$

Fahrenheit to Centigrade

example: $212°F - 32 = 180 \quad 180 \times \dfrac{5}{9} = 100°C$

Melting Points of Selected Compounds and Minerals

	Degrees C	Degrees F
Alumina	2050	3722
Barium carbonate	1360	2480
Bauxite	2035	3695
Borax	741	1365
Calcium oxide	2570	4658
Cobaltic oxide (O_2)	905	1661
Copper oxide (CuO)	1064	1947
Corundum	2035	3695
Cryolite	998	1830
Dolomite	2570–2800	4658–5072
Ferric oxide	1548	2518
Fireclay	1660–1720	3020–3128
Fluorspar	1300	2372
Kaolin	1740–1785	3164–3245
Lead oxide (litharge)	880	1616
Magnesium carbonate (dissociates)	350	662
Magnesium oxide (approx.)	2800	5072
Mullite	1810	3290
Nepheline syenite	1223	2232
Nickel oxide (O_2)	400	752
Orthoclase feldspar (potash)	1220	2228
Potassium oxide	red heat	
Rutile	1900	3452
Silica	1715	3119
Silicon carbide (decomposed)	2200	3992
Sillimanite	1816	3301
Sodium oxide	red heat	
Tin oxide	1130	2066
Titanium oxide	1900	3452
Whiting (dissociates)	825	1517
Zircon	2550	4622

Glaze and Stain Recipes

In the past ceramic glaze formulas were discussed with much secrecy. Fortunately, this attitude has changed. What is done with a glaze is much more important than how it is made. It is hoped that the reference tables in this text will allow more time to be spent on actual studio projects.

Regardless of the variety of glazes and decorative devices described, the student should not be too impressed by technique. Many of the finest potters use only a few standard glazes and stains and a minimum of decoration. Techniques are important and should be studied, but they should never overshadow the search for ideas.

The list of glazes in this section will supplement the general discussion of glaze types and the function of the various glaze chemicals (Chap. 9, pp. 231–241). For convenience, the glazes are listed in the form of batch recipes. Because of variations in local chemicals, firing procedures, and so forth, adjustments may have to be made to some of these recipes. Temperatures given are for large-size cones.

Low-fire Lead[a] and Alkaline Glazes

	Cones 05–03, Lithium blue		*Cones 08–09, Chromium red*
27.0	Lithium carbonate	70.04	Red lead
14.1	Kaolin	18.80	Flint
55.9	Flint	2.13	Soda ash
3.0	Bentonite	9.03	Kaolin
4.0	Copper carbonate	5.00	Potassium bichromate

	Cones 04–02, Barium mat glaze		*Cones 04–02, Alumina mat*
6.4	Whiting	48.0	White lead
41.6	White lead	12.0	Whiting
21.0	Potash feldspar	21.8	Potash feldspar
12.5	Barium carbonate	13.7	Calcined kaolin
6.7	Calcined kaolin	4.1	Kaolin
11.8	Flint		

[a] For information about toxic qualities of lead glazes, see *Lead Glazes for Dinnerware*, published by the International Lead Zinc Research Organization, Inc., 292 Madison Avenue, New York.

Low-fire Lead and Alkaline Glazes—*continued*

Cone 04, Lithium semiopaque (from K. Green)

18.5	Lithium carbonate
17.6	White lead
8.2	Bone ash
6.0	Soda feldspar
10.7	Kaolin
37.1	Flint
1.9	Bentonite

Cone 04, Semigloss rutile (from K. Green)

66.00	White lead
5.03	Plastic vitrox
15.68	Kaolin
13.29	Flint
5.70	Rutile

Cone 06, Acid-resistant lead

14.80	White lead
38.17	Soda feldspar
6.24	Kaolin
16.16	Gerstley borate
2.18	Whiting
21.16	Silica
1.27	Zirconium oxide

Cone 04, Lead-borax turquoise, fluid

12.0	Whiting
26.0	Borax
1.5	Soda ash
19.5	White lead
27.5	Potash feldspar
13.0	Flint
0.5	Kaolin
10.5	Tin oxide
2.8	Copper carbonate

Cone 04, Colemanite crackle glaze

33.5	Potash feldspar
41.5	Colemanite
14.0	Barium carbonate
11.0	Flint

Cone 04, Burnt-red glaze

48.2	White lead
7.3	Whiting
11.5	Kaolin
3.0	Zinc oxide
30.0	Flint
6.0	Tin oxide
4.0	Red iron oxide

Cone 04, Volcanic-ash mat (from A. Garzio)

22.7	Colemanite
5.8	Whiting
3.0	Barium carbonate
7.0	White lead
5.0	Borax
30.0	Volcanic ash
20.0	Kaolin
3.5	Zinc oxide
6.8	Tin oxide

Cone 04, Volcanic ash

60	Volcanic ash
20	Colemanite
10	White lead
10	Borax

Medium-fire Glazes, Cones 2–4

Cones 1–2, Clear glaze

52.60	White lead
15.70	Soda feldspar
3.36	Whiting
2.84	Zinc oxide
9.90	Flint
15.60	Cornwall stone
0.2	Gum tragacanth

Cone 4, Dinnerware glaze

51.5	Ferro frit #3124
25.1	Pemco frit #316
4.0	Whiting
4.7	Kaolin
14.7	Flint

(resistant to food acids containing 0.233 equivalents of PbO.)

Cone 2, Plastic vitrox

29.0	White lead
16.7	Potash feldspar
44.3	Plastic vitrox
10.0	Whiting

Cone 2, Colemanite

8.20	Calcined zinc oxide
38.50	Potash feldspar
17.55	Colemanite
6.80	Barium carbonate
6.45	Steatite (talc)
22.50	Flint

Medium-fire Glazes, Cone 6

Cone 6, Barium blue

55.5	Potash feldspar
41.5	Barium carbonate
3.0	Zinc oxide
2.0	Copper carbonate
1.0	Methocel or gum

Cone 6, Ash

38	Wood ashes
20	Potash feldspar
20	Whiting
13	Talc
9	Kaolin

Cone 6, Mat

63.6	Potash feldspar
18.3	Whiting
9.1	Kaolin
4.5	Talc
4.5	Zinc oxide

Cone 6, Mat

46.15	Nepheline syenite
17.70	Kaolin
10.60	Talc
3.55	Whiting
18.45	Flint
3.55	Zinc oxide

Porcelain and Stoneware Glazes, Cone 8

Cone 8, Semimat

36.5	Potash feldspar
25.7	Kaolin
17.5	Whiting
12.0	Flint
8.2	Rutile

Cone 8, Feldspar

44.5	Soda feldspar
12.0	Whiting
7.3	Kaolin
36.2	Flint

Cone 8, Lepidolite (crackle glaze)

18.8	Lepidolite
43.4	Potash feldspar
6.3	Cryolite
6.3	Bone ash
12.6	Whiting
12.6	Colemanite

Cones 7–8, Semimat volcanic-ash glaze (from A. Garzio)

26.7	Volcanic ash
7.5	Colemanite
19.7	Nepheline syenite
6.1	Whiting
7.5	Magnesium carbonate
7.2	Kaolin
5.3	Flint

Porcelain and Stoneware Glazes, Cones 8-13

Cones 9–10, White mat (from R. Eckels)

43.0	Feldspar, potash
18.3	Whiting
11.2	Flint
22.8	Kaolin
4.7	Zinc oxide
3.0	Rutile
2.0	Tin oxide

Cones 8–11, White opaque

45.35	Feldspar (potash)
12.85	Kaolin (Florida)
17.50	Whiting
1.45	Borax
20.50	Flint
2.35	Zinc oxide
30.20	Zircopax

Cones 10–13 (from A. Garzio)

53.8	Feldspar (potash)
19.2	Whiting
19.2	Ball clay
4.6	Kaolin
3.2	Zinc oxide

Cones 10–12, Mat

40.0	Feldspar (potash)
22.3	Whiting
21.0	Kaolin
16.7	Silica
4.4	Titanium oxide

Crystalline Glazes

Cones 07–05, Aventurine

45.7	Borax
2.6	Borium carbonate
3.3	Boric acid
1.7	Kaolin
46.7	Flint
17.7	Red iron oxide

(Grind and use immediately or frit without the clay.)

Cones 03–04, Aventurine

94	Ferro frit #3304
19	Red iron oxide
6	Kaolin (Florida)

Cones 3–4, Zinc crystal

13.4	Soda ash
15.5	Boric acid
22.2	Zinc oxide
42.8	Flint
6.1	Ball clay
6.7	Rutile

(Grind and use immediately or frit without the clay.)

Cone 8, Zinc crystal (pale green)

11.6	Sodium carbonate
6.6	Whiting
18.2	Kaolin (Florida)
42.2	Silica
21.4	Zinc oxide
3.1	Copper carbonate
5.3	Titanium (rutile)

(Grind and use immediately or frit without the clay.)

Cone 11, Zinc crystal

45.5	Feldspar
15.9	Whiting
15.9	Flint
22.7	Zinc oxide

Cone 11, Titanium crystal

25	Soda ash
50	Flint
25	Zinc oxide
10	Titanium oxide

Cones 9–10, Zinc crystal (from M. Hansen)

74	Pemco frit #283
21.5	Zinc oxide
4.5	Flint
1.0	Bentonite

#1

plus MnO_2 5 percent

$CuCO_3$ 5 percent

Rutile 4 percent

#2

$CuCO_3$ 3 percent

Rutile 5 percent

#3

NiO   1 percent

$CuCO_3$ 3 percent

Reduction Glazes

Cone 04, Celadon

20.5	White lead
1.6	Whiting
52.5	Godfrey spar (soda)
25.4	Soda ash
1.5	Red iron oxide
2.5	Tin oxide

(Grind dry, use immediately if wet. Fire: reduction, cone 012–07; oxidizing, cone 07–04.)

Cone 2, Local copper-red reduction (from Harder)

34.00	Soda feldspar
28.40	Borax
0.75	Soda ash
6.60	Fluorspar
12.45	Kaolin
17.80	Flint
2.00	Tin oxide
0.50	Copper carbonate [plus .5 percent silicon carbide (180 mesh carborundum)]

Cone 6, Copper-red reduction (from Curtis)

11.8	White lead
11.8	Red lead
5.9	Whiting
2.9	Kaolin
29.4	Flint
29.4	Borax
4.4	Boric acid
4.4	Soda ash
1.7	Tin oxide
0.5	Copper oxide

Cone 04, Copper luster

66.3	White lead
24.5	Cornwall stone
9.2	Flint
1.94	Cobalt oxide
1.15	Copper oxide
9.6	Manganese oxide

(Black when thin, copper when thick. Fire: reduction cone 012–07; oxidizing cone 07–04.)

Cone 8, Copper-red reduction

27.9	Cornwall stone
32.5	Flint
4.0	Zinc oxide
9.3	Barium carbonate
4.3	Soda ash
22.0	Borax
2.0	Copper carbonate
2.0	Tin oxide

Cones 6–8, Celadon reduction

62.2	Potash feldspar
7.6	Whiting
5.0	Kaolin
25.2	Flint
1.5	Red iron oxide

Cones 8–10, Celadon

79.5	Feldspar (potash)
6.2	Whiting
14.3	Flint
2.0	Red iron oxide

Reduction Glazes—*continued*

Cone 8, Local copper reduction (from Baggs)

32.8	Soda feldspar
1.9	Soda ash
28.0	Borax
7.3	Whiting
12.3	Kaolin
17.7	Flint
1.8	Tin oxide
0.3	Copper carbonate
0.65	Silicon carbide

Cones 9–10, Copper red

13.0	Ferro frit #3191
44.0	Feldspar (soda)
14.0	Whiting
3.0	Kaolin (Florida)
25.0	Flint
1.0	Tin oxide
0.2	Copper carbonate

(Add .2 silicon carbide for local reduction.)

Ceramic Stains[a]

(For preparation, see Chap. 9)

#1 Pink stain

50	Tin oxide
25	Whiting
18	Flint
4	Borax
3	Potassium dichromate

(Calcine to cone 8; stain is lumpy and must first be broken up in iron mortar, then ground.)

#2 Pink stain

50.5	Tin oxide
19.0	Whiting
7.5	Fluorspar
20.5	Flint
7.5	Potassium dichromate

(Calcine to cone 8 and grind.)

#3 Crimson stain

22.9	Whiting
6.6	Calcium sulfate
4.4	Fluorspar
20.8	Flint
43.7	Tin oxide
1.6	Potassium dichromate

(Calcine to cone 8 and grind.)

#4 Ultramarine stain

50	Chromium oxide
12	Flint
38	Cobalt oxide (CoO, cobaltous)

(Calcine to cone 8 and grind.)

[a] These stains must be finely ground to obtain the desired color.

Ceramic Stains—*continued*

#5 Blue-green stain

41.8   Cobalt oxide (CoO)
19.3   Chromium oxide
39.0   Aluminium oxide

(Calcine to cone 8 and grind.)

#7 Black stain

43   Chromium oxide
43   Red iron oxide
10   Manganese dioxide
 4   Cobalt oxide

(Calcine to cone 8 and grind.)

#9 Red-brown stain

22   Chromium oxide
23   Red iron oxide
55   Zinc oxide

(Calcine to cone 8 and grind.)

#11 Yellow stain

33.3   Antimony oxide
50.0   Red lead
16.7   Tin oxide

(Calcine to cone 6 and grind.)

#6 Orange stain

29.8   Antimony oxide
12.8   Tin oxide
14.9   Red iron oxide
42.5   Red lead

(Calcine to cone 6 and grind.)

#8 Turquoise stain

56   Copper phosphate
44   Tin oxide

(Calcine to cone 6 and grind.)

#10 Brown stain

64.6   Zinc oxide
9.7   Chrome oxide
9.7   Red iron oxide
8.0   Red lead
8.0   Boric acid

(Calcine to cone 8 and grind.)

#12 Black stain

65   Chromium oxide
35   Red iron oxide

(Calcine to cone 8 and grind.)

Clay Bodies

The clay body preferred by the studio potter is quite different from that used by a commercial pottery. For slip casting or jiggering a uniformity of texture is necessary, for obvious technical reasons. Similarly, any impurities imparting color to the body are undesirable. Therefore, bodies used in commercial production are carefully selected, ground, and refined. Plasticity is of minor importance, and, since it is associated with high shrinkage rates, it is avoided.

Local supplies of earthenware and plastic fireclays are available in the United States, particularly in the Midwest. Since they are widely used in cement, plaster, and mortar mixtures, they are competitively priced and generally quite reasonable.

Because the volume of clay used in the school studio will normally be between one and five tons per year, both the initial cost and the shipping charges are important. Thus, clay that can be bought locally has a decided advantage, even if it needs a certain amount of sieving or small additions. Occasionally, a truckload of raw clay can be purchased reasonably from a local brick or tile works.

Earthenware bodies present no real problem of supply in the Midwest, since there are many brick and tile factories which also sell bagged clay. Shale clays with coarse particles will cause trouble unless they are run through a sieve of from 15 to 20 meshes per inch. Some earthenware clays contain soluble sulfates, which will form a whitish scum on the fired ware; however, the addition of ¼ to 2 percent barium will eliminate this fault. Many such clays will not be very plastic unless they are aged. Adding about 5 percent bentonite, which is extremely plastic, will usually render a short clay workable. Often two clays that alone are not suitable can be mixed together to form a good body. Only experimentation will indicate the necessary changes.

Occasionally, the body will lack sufficient flint to fuse with the fluxes it contains. Cream-colored clays can be rendered more plastic by the addition of ball clays. Talc has some plasticity and is often used in low-fire white ware bodies as a source of both flux and silica. Feldspar, nepheline syenite, and plastic vitrox are also added to various bodies to contribute fluxing qualities.

Stoneware and porcelain bodies are usually compounded from several ingredients. In fact, it is quite rare for a single clay to satisfy all throwing and firing requirements. There is no clay that, by itself, will make a porcelain body. Oriental porcelain is made from one or two claylike minerals which are fairly plastic. Since nothing in the Western world compares with petuntze, porcelain bodies must be compounded from clay and various minerals.

Both stoneware and porcelain will form hard, vitrified bodies at cone 10. The major difference between the two is that stoneware contains some impurities, chiefly iron, which give it a gray or tan color. Both stoneware and porcelain bodies are compounded for varying temperatures and, in the case of porcelain, for different degrees of translucency. Greater translucency is usually obtained by increasing the feldspar ratio, which has the accompanying disadvantage of an increase in warpage when the ware is fired.

Fireclay and stoneware clays differ from pure clay (kaolin) chiefly in that they contain various

Suggested Clay and Porcelain Bodies

Cone 2, Light red clay body	
60	Red clay
25	Flint
15	Kaolin

Cone 2, Cream clay body	
43	Ball clay
7	Kaolin
25	Soda feldspar
18	Flint
7	Red clay

Cones 2–8, Stoneware body	
20	Jordan clay or Monmouth
25	Ball clay
30	Plastic fireclay
10	Nepheline syenite
5	Flint
12	Grog (fine size for wheel work)

Cones 8–10, Stoneware body	
32	Jordan or Monmouth
32	Fire clay
18	Grog (fine, 60-mesh)
18	Flint

Cone 8, Stoneware body	
40	Ball clay
40	Fireclay
20	Earthenware (for color and texture)

Cones 8–10, Porcelain body	
45	Kaolin
25	Feldspar (potash)
16	Ball clay
14	Flint

Cones 8–12, Porcelain body	
27	Ball clay
27	Kaolin
27	Feldspar (potash)
19	Flint

Cones 10–15, Porcelain body	
25	Ball clay
25	Kaolin
25	Feldspar (potash)
25	Flint

fluxes and impurities which lower the fusion point and impart a gray, tan, or buff color.

The familiar crocks and old-fashioned jugs that we occasionally still see were made of stoneware clays. Since manufacturers today want completely white bodies, not many items are made of stoneware. Therefore, local sources of stoneware clays may be scarce, and transportation costs may be excessive. Fireclays, which have a more universal industrial use, can be substituted for stoneware. Some fireclays are very plastic and fine enough for throwing. They often contain some iron impurities, which give the body a flecked appearance. Depending upon the firing temperature and the effect desired, it may be necessary to blend in an earthenware or stoneware clay or ingredients such as feldspar, talc, or silica.

The table on page 322 lists several types of clay and porcelain bodies. They are included merely as suggestions, since it usually will be necessary to vary these recipes depending upon the raw materials available locally.

Engobes are essentially clay slips, with the significant difference that some engobes are intended for use on either dry or bisque ware, thus necessitating additions of flint, feldspar, and occasionally a flux to the slip in order to adjust the varying shrinkage rates. The general purpose of an engobe is to provide a smoother surface and usually a different-colored base for glaze or brushed decoration.

If the engobe is to be used on a damp piece, a sieved slip of the throwing body can be used, pro-vided the color is not objectionable. The usual colorants can be added, except for the chrome oxides, which react unfavorably with tin. One percent of a strong oxide, such as cobalt, is sufficient, although from 5 to 7 percent of iron or vanadium may be needed. Blistering will result if over 7 percent manganese is used. Five percent of an opacifier is often needed to lighten the color.

Engobes used on leather-hard ware must be adjusted to reduce shrinkage by calcining part of the clay and by additions of flint and feldspar. On dry ware the clay content of the engobe can rarely be more than 40 percent, with the balance composed of flint and feldspar. A 5-percent addition of borax will toughen the surface and aid adhesion.

When used on bisque ware, an engobe must have a clay content of less than 25 percent, or it will shrink excessively and flake off the pot. Furthermore, it must contain sufficient fluxes to fuse with the bisque surface. Its characteristics resemble those of an underfired glaze. In view of the low clay content, a binder may be necessary.

Too thick an application of an engobe on any surface, whether leather-hard clay or bisque ware, will crack or flake off. On the other hand, a thin coating will allow the body color to show through. In addition to the usual finely ground coloring oxides, one may add coarsely ground ores, ilmenite, rust chips, chopped copper scouring pads, and other materials to the engobe. Such additions melt out into the covering glaze with interesting effects that are limited to the area of the applied engobe.

Schedule of Representative Equipment Prices *

	From	To
electric kiln, top loading, cone 8, chamber $17 \times 17 \times 17''$	$ 300	$ 350
electric kiln, front loading, cones 8–10, chamber $17 \times 17 \times 17''$	450	600
gas kiln, updraft, high fire, chamber $24 \times 24 \times 36''$	1,400	1,600
gas kiln, updraft, high fire, capacity 24 cubic feet	2,500	3,000
gas kiln, updraft muffle, high fire, chamber $29 \times 24 \times 30''$	2,000	2,500
gas kiln, downdraft, high fire, capacity 30 cubic feet	3,000	3,500
gas car kiln, capacity 20–30 cubic feet	4,000	4,500
pyrometer	35	50
kick wheel	115	350
electric wheel	250	600
clay mixer, pug mill	700	1,200
mortar and pestle	3	10
ball mill	100	150
ball mill jars	15	75
sieves	5	15
glaze sprayer	60	75
spray booth	75	85
gram scales	20	45
decorating wheels	14	25
shop lift	250	300
ware rack	75	100

* Prices of heavy equipment are F.O.B. city of manufacture.

Sources of
Materials
and Equipment

The cost of materials is an important factor in developing a school or college ceramics program, especially if it is to be paid out of the general budget for the course. A rough estimate of the amount per student per semester is $10 to $15, depending upon shipping costs, which may be considerable. For advanced students, who produce more pottery, the price is even higher. In addition, the firing charges, which may also be applied to the departmental budget, must be considered. Replacement of kiln shelves is another continuing expense.

A businesslike approach to the problem of purchasing materials will do much to keep the costs as low as possible. The smaller figure of $10 per student reflects the saving possible by purchasing in quantity. Supplies bought from a hobby-shop dealer will cost much more than $10 per student.

The price of clay, which seems so cheap by the pound, can be deceiving, for an enormous amount is consumed in the studio classroom. For most types of clay the shipping fees are greater than the cost of the clay itself. Of course, local clays can be dug, but the trouble and labor of processing them may make this solution undesirable. Fortunately, clay is commonly used in mortar and cement, so it is available from most building-supplies dealers in 50-pound bags, usually priced at about $1.00 per bag. These clays are generally shale earthenware, which requires sieving. Often bentonite or flint or talc must be added to render the shale clay suitable for throwing, but even so these clays represent considerable savings. Many fireclays can be procured from local dealers, who sell them for repairing furnaces or industrial ovens. With minor modifications these fireclays can be converted into satisfactory stoneware bodies.

Coloring oxides, which are used sparingly, can be purchased in small quantities. However, even a small ceramics department should buy the more common chemicals—lead, flint, borax, and the feldspars—in 100-pound lots. They may not be used up during a single semester, but the saving is so great that the larger purchase is warranted.

When ordering materials it is occasionally advisable to buy a few bulky but cheap items, so that the shipment can be sent by freight or motor truck, thus avoiding the expensive parcel-post rate.

SUPPLY DEALERS

East Coast

CLAYS

Hammill & Gillespie, Inc.
O. W. Ketcham Architectural Tile Co.
Langley Ceramic Studio
Mandl Ceramic Supply Co.
Newton Pottery Supply Co.
Pottery Arts Supply Co.
Roder Ceramic Studio
Rowantree Pottery
Stewart Clay Co.
United Clay Mines
Jack D. Wolfe, Inc.

KILNS

W. H. Fairchild (electric)
L. & L. Manufacturing Co. (electric)
Roder Ceramic Studio (electric)
Unique Kilns (gas and electric)

KILN BURNERS

Flynn Burner Corp. (gas)
Hauck Mfg. Co. (oil)
Johnson Gas Appliance Co. (gas)

MISCELLANEOUS EQUIPMENT

Craftools, Inc.
B. F. Drakenfeld, Inc.
Roder Ceramic Studio
Walker Jamar Co.

CERAMIC CHEMICALS

Ceramic Color & Chemical Mfg. Co.
B. F. Drakenfeld
Gare Ceramic Supply Co.
Ernest Hanzlicek (volcanic ash)
Langley Ceramic Studio
Newton Pottery Supply Co.
Standard Ceramic Supply Co.
Whittaker, Clark and Daniels, Inc.

POTTER'S WHEELS

Clay Art Center (electric)
Craftools, Inc. (kick and electric)
Randall Wheel (kick & electric)
Standard Ceramic Supply Co.

FRITS

Ferro Corp.
Pemco Corp.

REFRACTORY MATERIALS

Armstrong Cork Co.
Babcock and Wilcox Co.
A. P. Green Fire Brick Co.
Johns-Manville Co.
New Castle Refractories
Remey Refractories

Midwest and South

CLAYS

Cedar Heights Clay Co.
Christy Firebrick Co.
General Refractories Co.
A. P. Green Fire Brick Co.
Hammill & Gillespie, Inc.
V. R. Hood, Jr.
Kentucky-Tennessee Clay Co. (ball)
La Mo Refractory Supply Co.
Spinks Clay Co.
Trinity Ceramic Supply Co.
Western Stoneware Co. (Monmouth)
Zanesville Stoneware Co.

KILNS

Allied Engineering Corp. (gas)
American Art Clay Co. (electric)
DFC Corporation (gas and electric)
Harrop Ceramic Service Co. (electric)
Paragon Industries, Inc. (electric)

KILN BURNERS

DFC Corporation (gas)
Flynn Burner Corp. (gas)
Hauck Mfg. Co. (oil)
Johnson Gas Appliance Co. (gas)

CERAMIC CHEMICALS

Ceramic Color & Chemical Mfg. Co.
George Fetzer
General Color and Chemical Co.
Ernst Hanzlicek (volcanic ash)
Harshaw Chemical Co.
Illini Ceramic Service
Kraft Chemical Co.
Minnesota Clay Co.
Trinity Ceramic Supply Co.

FRITS

Ferro Corp.
Harshaw Chemical Co.

POTTER'S WHEELS

American Art Clay Co. (kick and electric)
H. B. Klopfenstein & Sons (kick)
Nils Lou (electric)
Oak Hill Industries Inc. (kick)
Randall Wheel (kick and electric)
Denton M. Vars (Leach wheel)

MISCELLANEOUS EQUIPMENT

American Art Clay Co.
Archie Bray Foundation (decorating wax)
Big Joe Mfg. Co.
De Vilbiss Co. (spray equipment)
Illini Ceramic Service
Minnesota Clay Co.
Tepping Ceramic Supply Co.
U.S. Stoneware Co. (ball mills)

REFRACTORY MATERIALS

A. P. Green Fire Brick Co.
Johns-Manville Corp.
La Mo Refractory Supply Co.
New Castle Refractories
Walsh Refractories Corp.

West and Pacific Coast

CLAYS

L. H. Butcher Co.
Cannon Co.
Denver Fire Clay Co.
Garden City Clay Co.
Hy-Land Mfg. & Supply Co.
Interpace Corp.
Spinks Clay Co.
Van Howe Co.
S. Paul Ward, Inc.
Western Ceramic Supply Co.
Westwood Ceramic Supply Co.

KILNS

A. D. Alpine, Inc. (gas and electric)
J. J. Cress Co. (electric)
Denver Fire Clay Co. (gas and oil)
E. W. Mendall (gas)
Nordstrom Kiln Co. (gas)
Skutt & Sons (electric)
West Coast Kiln Co. (gas)

CERAMIC CHEMICALS

Braun Corp.
L. H. Butcher Co.
Hy-Land Mfg. & Supply Co.
Leslie Ceramic Supply Co.
Van Howe Co.
S. Paul Ward, Inc.
Western Ceramic Supply Co.
Westwood Ceramic Supply Co.

POTTER'S WHEELS

A. D. Alpine, Inc. (electric)
Robert Brent (kick & electric)
Denver Fire Clay Co. (electric)
Oscar-Paul Corp. (electric)
Shimpo-West (electric)
Skutt & Sons (electric)
Paul Soldner (kick and electric)

REFRACTORY MATERIALS

B. & B. Refractories
Interpace Corp.
Pyro-Engineering

MISCELLANEOUS EQUIPMENT

L. H. Butcher Co.
Van Howe Co.
S. Paul Ward, Inc.
Westwood Ceramic Supply Co.

ADDRESSES OF LISTED DEALERS

Allied Engineering Corp. (division of Ferro Corp.), 4150 E. 56 St., Cleveland, Ohio 44105

A. D. Alpine, Inc., 353 Coral Circle, El Segundo, Calif. 90245

American Art Clay Co., 4717 W. 16 St., Indianapolis, Ind. 46222

Armstrong Cork Co., Lancaster, Pa. 17604

Babcock and Wilcox Co., 161 E. 42 St., New York, N.Y. 10017

Big Joe Mfg. Co., 7225 M. Kostner Ave., Chicago, Ill. 60646

B. & B. Refractories Corp., 11927 Rivira Rd., Santa Fe Springs, Calif. 90670

Archie Bray Foundation, P.O. Box 344, Helena, Mont. 59601

Braun Corporation, 13635 Bonnie Beach, Los Angeles, Calif. 90054

Robert Brent, 1101 Cedar St., Santa Monica, Calif. 90405

L. H. Butcher Co., 15 & Vermont Sts., San Francisco, Calif. 94107

Cannon & Co., Box 802, Sacramento, Calif. 95804

Cedar Heights Clay Co., 50 Portsmouth Rd., Oak Hill, Ohio 45656

Ceramic Color and Chemical Mfg. Co., P. O. Box 297, New Brighton, Pa. 15066

J. J. Cress Co., Inc., 1718 Floradale Ave. S., El Monte, Calif. 91733

Christy Firebrick Co., 3144 N. Broadway, St. Louis, Mo. 63147

Clay Art Center, 40 Beech St., Port Chester, N.Y. 10573

Craftools, Inc., 1 Industrial Rd., Woodridge, N.J. 07075

DFC Corporation, P. O. Box 5507, Denver, Colo. 80217

De Vilbiss Co., 300 Phillips Ave., Toledo, Ohio 43601

B. F. Drakenfeld, Inc., Washington, Pa. 15301

W. H. Fairchild, 712 Centre St., Freeland, Pa. 18224

Ferro Corp., 4150 E. 56 St., Cleveland, Ohio 44105

George Fetzer, 1205 17 Ave., Columbus, Ohio 43211

Flynn Burner Corp., 425 Fifth Ave., New Rochelle, N.Y. 10802

Garden City Clay Co., Redwood City, Calif. 94064

Gare Ceramic Supply Co., 165 Rosemont St., Haverhill, Mass. 01830

General Color and Chemical Co., P. O. Box 7, Minerva, Ohio 44657

General Refractories Co., 7640 Chicago Ave., Detroit, Mich. 48204

A. P. Green Fire Brick Co., Mexico, Mo. 65265

Hammill & Gillespie, Inc., 225 Broadway, New York, N.Y. 10007

Ernest Hanzlicek, Wilson, Kan. 67490

Harshaw Chemical Co., 1945 E. 97 St., Cleveland, Ohio 44106

Harrop Ceramic Service Co., 35 E. Gay St., Columbus, Ohio 43215

Hauck Mfg. Co., P. O. Box 26, Westchester, Ill. 60153

O. Hommel Co., P.O. Box 475, Pittsburgh, Pa. 15230

V. R. Hood, Jr., Box 1213, San Antonio, Tex. 78206

Hy-Land Mfg. & Supply Co., 4990 E. Asbury St., Denver, Colo. 80222

Illini Ceramic Service, 439 N. Wells St., Chicago, Ill. 60610

Interpace Corp., 2901 Los Feliz Blvd., Los Angeles, Calif. 90039

Johns-Manville Co., 22 E. 40 St., New York, N.Y. 10016

Johnson Gas Appliance Co., Cedar Rapids, Iowa 52405

Kentucky-Tennessee Clay Co., Mayfield, Ky. 42066

O. W. Ketcham Architectural Tile Co., 125 N. 18 St., Philadelphia, Pa. 19103

H. B. Klopfenstein & Sons., Rt. 2, Crestline, Ohio 44827

Kraft Chemical Co., 917 W. 18 St., Chicago, Ill. 60608

L & L Mfg. Co., Box 348, Twin Oaks, Pa. 19104

La Mo Refractory Supply Co., 323 Iris Ave., New Orleans, La. 70121

Langley Ceramic Studio, 413 S. 24 St., Philadelphia, Pa. 19146

Leslie Ceramic Supply Co., 1212 San Pablo Ave., Berkley, Calif. 94706

Nils Lous, 1501 Asbury Rd., St. Paul, Minn. 55108

Mandl Ceramic Supply Co., RR 1, Box 369A, Pennington, N.J. 08534

L. W. Mendall, 12330 E. Rush St., El Monte, Calif. 91733

Minnesota Clay Co., 2310 E. 38 St., Minneapolis, Minn. 55406

Newton Pottery Supply Co., Newton, Mass. 01432

Nordstrom Kiln Co., 9046 Garvey, S. San Gabriel, Calif. 91777

Oscar-Paul Corp., 522 W. 182 St., Gardena, Calif. 92247

Oak Hill Industries, RR 4, Davenport, Iowa 52804

Paragon Industries, Inc., Box 10133, Dallas, Tex. 75207

Pemco Corp., 5601 Eastern Ave., Baltimore, Md. 21224

Pottery Arts Supply Co., 2554 Greenmount Ave., Baltimore, Md. 21218

Pyro Engineering Corp., 200 S. Palm Ave., Alhambra, Calif.

Randall Wheel, Box 774, Alfred, N.Y. 14802

Remey Refractories, Hedley and Delaware Aves., Philadelphia, Pa. 19137

Roder Ceramic Studio, 500 Broadway, Clifton Heights, Pa. 19018

Rowantree Pottery, Blue Hill, Maine 04614

Shimpo-West, P.O. Box 2315, La Puente, Calif. 91746

Shutt & Sons, 2618 S.E. Steele St., Portland, Ore. 97202

Paul Soldner, Box 917, Aspen, Colo. 81611

Spinks Clay Co., Box 829, Parris, Tenn. 38242; or Box 578 Wrightwood, Calif. 92397

Standard Ceramic Supply Co., P. O. Box 4435, Pittsburgh, Pa. 15205

Stewart Clay Co., 133 Mulberry St., New York, N.Y 10013

Tepping Ceramic Supply Co., 3517 Riverside Dr., Dayton, Ohio 45405

Trinity Ceramic Supply Co., 9016 Diplomacy Row, Dallas, Tex. 75235

Unique Kilns, 530 Spruce St., Trenton, N.J. 08638

United Clay Mines Corp., Trenton, N.J. 08606

U. S. Stoneware Co., Akron, Ohio 44309

Van Howe Co., 1185 S. Cherokee Ave., Denver, Colo. 80223; and 4216 Edith N.E., Albuquerque, N.M. 87107

Denton M. Vars, 825 West Minnehaha Ave., St. Paul, Minn. 55104

Walker Jamar Co., 365 S. First Ave., E. Duluth, Minn. 55802

Walsh Refractories, 101 Ferry St., St. Louis, Mo. 63147

S. Paul Ward, Inc., 601 Mission St., South Pasadena, Calif. 91030

West Coast Kiln Co., 635 Vineland Ave., La Puente, Calif. 91746

Western Ceramic Supply Co., 1601 Howard St., San Francisco, Calif. 94103

Western Stoneware Co., Monmouth, Ill. 61462

Westwood Ceramic Supply Co., 14400 Lomitas Ave., City of Industry, Calif. 91744

Whittaker, Clark, and Daniels, Inc., 100 Church St., New York, N.Y. 10017

Jack D. Wolfe Co., Inc., 724 Meeker Ave., Brooklyn, N.Y. 11222

Zanesville Stoneware Co., Zanesville, Ohio 43701

SOURCES OF MATERIALS AND EQUIPMENT IN CANADA

CLAYS

A. P. Green Firebrick Co., Rosemount Ave., Weston, Ont.

Baroid of Canada, Ltd., 5108 Eighth Ave., S.W., Calgary, Alta.

Jean Cartier, 1029 Bleury St., Montreal, P.Q.

Clayburn Harbison, Ltd., 1690 W. Broadway, Vancouver, B.C.

Magcobac Mining Co., 510 Fifth St., S.W., Calgary, Alta.

Mercedes Ceramic Supply, 8 Wallace St., Woodbridge, Ont.

Pembena Mountain Clay, 945 Logan, Winnipeg, Man.

Pottery Supply House, 491 Wildwood Rd., P.O. Box 192, Oakville, Ont.

Saskatchewan Clay Products, P.O. Box 970, Estevan, Sask.

GLAZE MATERIALS

Barrett Co., Ltd., 1155 Dorchester Blvd., W. Montreal 2, P.Q.

Blyth Colors, Ltd., Toronto, Ont.

Greater Toronto Ceramic Center, 167 Lakeshore Rd., Toronto 14, Ont.

E. Harris & Co. of Toronto, Ltd., 73 King St., East Toronto, Ont.

Lewiscraft Supply House, 28 King St., West Toronto, Ont.

Mercedes Cermic Supply, 8 Wallace St., Woodbridge, Ont.

Pottery Supply House, 491 Wildwood Rd., P.O. Box 192, Oakville, Ont.

KILNS

Ferro Enamels, 26 Davis Rd., P.O. Box 370, Oakville, Ont.

Hurley Bennett, 1497 Pierre Ave., Windsor, Ont.

Mercedes Ceramic Supply, 8 Wallace St., Woodbridge, Ont.

Pottery Supply House, 491 Wildwood Rd., P.O. Box 192, Oakville, Ont.

POTTER'S WHEELS

Hurley Bennett, 1497 Pierre Ave., Windsor, Ont.

Mercedes Ceramic Supply, 8 Wallace St., Woodbridge, Ont.

Pottery Supply House, 491 Wildwood Rd., P.O. Box 192, Oakville, Ont.

C.W. Ride, North Hatley, P.Q.

W. H. Williams, 144 Westwood Ave., Hamilton, Ont.

SOURCES OF MATERIALS AND EQUIPMENT IN ENGLAND

CLAYS

English China Clay Ltd., 18 High Cross St., St. Austell, Cornwall

Fulham Pottery, London, S.W. 6

Pike Bros., Wareham, Dorset

Potclays, Ltd., Wharf House, Copeland St., Hanley, Stoke-on-Trent

Price Bros., Burslem, Stoke-on-Trent

Watts Blake & Bearn Ltd., Newton Abbot, Devon

GLAZE MATERIALS

Blythe Color Works, Ltd., Cresswell, Stoke-on-Trent

E. W. Good & Co., Ltd., Barker St., Longton, Stoke-on Trent

George Goodwin & Son, Ltd., Westwood Mills, Lichfield St., Hanley, Stoke-on-Trent

W. Podmore & Sons, Ltd., Caledonian Mills, Shelton, Stoke-on-Trent

Reeves & Sons, Ltd., Enfield, Middlesex

Wengers Ltd., Etruria, Stoke-on-Trent

ELECTRIC KILNS

Applied Heat Co., Ltd., Elecfurn Works, Otterspool Way, Watford-by-Pass, Watford, Herts.

British Ceramic Service Co., Ltd., Park Ave., Wolstanton, Newcastle, Staffs.

Cromartie Kilns, Dividy Road, Longton, Staffs.

Kilns & Furnaces Ltd., Keele St. Works, Tunstall, Stoke-on Trent

GAS KILNS

Dowson & Mason Gas Plant Co., Ltd., Alma Works, Levenshulme, Manchester 19

Bernard W. E. Webber Ltd., Alfred St., Fenton, Stoke-on-Trent

POTTER'S WHEELS

Corbic, Gomshall, Surrey

Judson & Hudson Ltd., Keighley, Yorks.

Potters Equipment Co., 73/77, Britannia Rd., London, S.W. 6

Alec Tiranti Ltd., 72 Charlotte St., London, W. 1

Bernard W. E. Webber Ltd., Alfred St., Fenton, Stoke-on-Trent

MISCELLANEOUS EQUIPMENT

Fulham Pottery, London, S.W. 6

Fred Nettleship, 84 New College Close, Gorliston, Norfolk (cane handles)

Oxshott Pottery, Potters Craft, Oakshade Rd., Oxshott, Surrey (plans, kilns, wheels)

References

REFERENCES FOR THE STUDENT POTTER

Leach, Bernard. *A Potter's Book*. London: Faber and Faber, 1940. Leach is perhaps the best-known independent studio potter today, and he has written an extremely readable book. From the creative point of view, it cannot be recommended too highly. Illustrated.

Norton, F. H. *Ceramics for the Artist Potter*. Reading, Mass.: Addison-Wesley, 1956. Norton covers the entire range of ceramics from the forming processes to the chemistry of glazes, with numerous illustrations.

Rhodes, Daniel. *Clay and Glazes for the Potter*. Philadelphia: Chilton, 1957. An extremely clear treatment of clays, glazes, and calculations.

————. *Kilns*. Philadelphia: Chilton, 1968. The most complete book on kilns available.

————. *Stoneware and Porcelain*. Philadelphia: Chilton, 1959. A companion book to *Clay and Glazes for the Potter*. In addition to a discussion of stoneware and porcelain, the book contains much useful studio information. Well illustrated.

Sanders, Herbert H. *The World of Japanese Ceramics*. Palo Alto, Calif: Kodansha International, 1967. A very informative and beautifully illustrated volume.

SUPPLEMENTAL TEXTS

Andrews, A. T. *Ceramic Tests and Calculations*. New York: Wiley, 1928. A standard text for ceramic glaze, clay, and frit calculations.

Billington, Dora M. *The Technique of Pottery*. London: B. T. Batsford, 1962. A very readable and complete ceramic text by an experienced English potter and teacher.

Casson, Michael. *Pottery in Britain Today*. New York: Transatlantic Press, 1967. Fine photographs, very short text.

Eley, Vincent. *A Monk at the Potter's*. Leicester, Eng.: Ward, 1952. This interesting account of a young monk who decided to start a pottery at his monastery contains some very practical information.

Green, David. *Pottery, Materials and Techniques*. New York: Praeger, 1967. This text is particularly oriented toward materials available in England, but it is of interest to all students.

Hettes, Karel, and Rada Pravoslav. *Modern Ceramics*. London: Drury House, 1965. A survey of contemporary ceramics throughout the world, with a short text and many color illustrations.

Hetherington, A. L. *Chinese Ceramic Glazes*. Los Angeles: Commonwealth Press, 1948. A small, very readable volume, dealing primarily with Sung iron and copper glazes.

Home, Ruth M. *Ceramics for the Potter*. Peoria, Ill.: Bennett, 1953. This volume contains some very useful information about clays and glazes from both the historical and the contemporary viewpoint. There is also a section on native Canadian clays.

Koenig, J. H., and W. H. Earhart. *Literature Abstracts of Ceramic Glazes*. Ellenton, Fla.: College Institute, 1951. A series of condensations—with formulas—of all important articles about glazes appearing in American trade magazines, ceramic society publications, and British, German, and other foreign journals.

Leach, Bernard. *A Potter in Japan*. London: Faber and Faber, 1960. An account of Leach's return to Japan, his visits with potter friends from his early years in that country.

Norton, F. H. *Elements of Ceramics*. Reading, Mass.: Addison Wesley, 1952. An introductory text for ceramic engineers, containing technical information about minerals, clays, and glazes, plus various commercial refining and production processes.

Parmelee, Cullen W. *Ceramic Glazes*. Chicago: Industrial Publications, 1951. A very complete and comprehensive text on ceramic glaze materials, slips, glazes, chemical reactions, and glaze calculations.

Rosenthal, Ernst. *Pottery and Ceramics*. Harmondsworth, Eng.: Pelican, 1949. A complete survey of the ceramic field, primarily from an industrial viewpoint.

Wildenhain, Marguerite. *Pottery, Form and Expression*. New York: American Craftsmen's Council, 1959. This beautifully illustrated book by one of America's foremost potters contains a moving expression of the art of living, as well as the art of ceramics.

MAGAZINES AND PROFESSIONAL JOURNALS

Ceramic Data Book, Industrial Publications, 5 S. Wabash Avenue, Chicago, Ill. 60603. Published annually, covering supplies, manufacturers, and equipment.

Ceramics Monthly, 4175 N. High Street, Columbus, Ohio 43214. Oriented toward the amateur; many useful articles.

Craft Horizons, 16 East 52 Street, New York, N.Y. 10022. Covering all craft fields, with many articles dealing with contemporary American and foreign ceramics. Well illustrated.

Design Quarterly, Walker Art Center, 1710 Lyndale Avenue S., Minneapolis, Minn. 55403. A well-illustrated periodical covering contemporary design, often ceramics.

Journal of the American Ceramic Society, Columbus, Ohio. Technical articles, usually slanted toward industrial ceramics but occasionally of interest to the studio potter.

FOREIGN PUBLICATIONS

Dansk Kunstaandvaerk, Palaegade 4, Copenhagen, Denmark. Covers the entire Danish design field; well illustrated. Many sections are in English.

Designed in Finland, Finnish Foreign Trade Association, E. Esplanaadik 18, Helsinki. Illustrated booklet on Finnish design published each year, with English text.

Domus, via Monte di Pieta 15, Milan, Italy. Covers the decorative arts fields, emphasizing architecture; beautifully illustrated.

Form, Svenska Slöjdföreningen, Nybrogatan 7, Stockholm, Sweden. This journal of the Swedish Design Society covers all design fields; well illustrated. Contains a short English section.

Kontur, Svenska Slojdforeningen, Nybrogatan 7, Stockholm, Sweden. Beautifully illustrated booklet published once a year on Swedish design and crafts. Text in English.

Kunst + Handwerk, Arnold-Heise Str. 23, Hamburg 20, Germany. Industrial design and handcrafts in Germany and Europe. Well illustrated, German text.

La Ceramica, via F. Corridoni 3, Milan, Italy. Although an industrial publication, many articles concern studio potters and sculptors. English summary very short.

Pottery Quarterly, Northfields, Tring, Herts, England. A variety of articles, both historical and contemporary, as well as critiques. Well illustrated.

Pottery in Australia, 30 Turramurra Avenue, Turramurra, N.S.W. Biannual journal of the Potters' Society, well illustrated.

Vrienden van de Nederlandse Ceramik, Paulus Potterstraat, Amsterdam—Z 1. Illustrated journal of the Dutch ceramic society. English summary.

SELECTED HISTORICAL BIBLIOGRAPHY

General Texts

Charleston, Robert J. *World Ceramics*. New York: McGraw-Hill, 1968.

Cox, Warren E. *The Book of Pottery and Porcelain.* New York: Crown, 1944.

Savage, George. *Porcelain Through the Ages.* Baltimore: Penguin, 1954.

Ancient, Mediterranean, and Classical Ceramics

Alexion, Styliaros, Nickolaos Platon, and Hanni Gunanella. *Ancient Crete.* New York: Praeger, 1968.

Arias, P. E. *Greek Vase Painting.* New York: Abrams, 1961.

Boardman, John. *Pre-Classical, from Crete to Archaic Greek.* Baltimore: Penguin, 1967.

Chamoux, François. *Greek Art.* Geenwich, Conn.: New York Graphic, 1966.

Childe, Gordon. *What Happened in History.* Baltimore: Penguin, 1962.

Demargne, Pierre. *The Birth of Greek Art.* New York: Golden Press, 1964.

Hutchinson, R. W. *Prehistoric Crete.* Baltimore: Penguin, 1962.

Martinatos, Spyridon. *Crete and Mycenae.* New York: Abrams, 1960.

Noble, Joseph Veach. *The Techniques of Painted Attic Pottery.* New York: Watson-Guptill, 1965.

Petrie, Flinders. *The Making of Egypt.* London: Sheldon Press, 1939.

Platon, Nickolaos. *Crete.* Cleveland, Ohio: World Publishing, 1966.

Raphael, Max. *Civilization in Egypt.* New York: Pantheon, 1947.

———. *Prehistoric Pottery.* New York: Pantheon, 1947.

Richardson, Emeline Hill. *The Etruscans.* Chicago: University of Chicago Press, 1964.

Swedish Institute in Rome. *Etruscan Culture.* New York: Columbia University Press, 1962.

Far Eastern Ceramics

Beurdeley, Michel. *The Chinese Collector Through the Centuries.* Rutland, Vt: Tuttle, 1966.

Griffing, Robert P. *The Art of the Korean Potter.* New York: Asia Society, 1968.

Hazashiza, Seizo, and Gakuji Hasebe. *Chinese Ceramics.* Rutland, Vt.: Tuttle, 1966.

Honey, William Bowyer. *The Ceramic Art of China.* London: Faber and Faber, 1944.

Kidder, J. Edward. *The Birth of Japanese Art.* New York: Praeger, 1964.

Kim, Chewon. *Korean Art,* Vol. II, *Ceramics.* Seoul: Ministry of Foreign Affairs, 1961.

Kim, Chewon and Won-Yong. *Treasures of Korean Art.* New York: Abrams, 1966.

Koyama, Fugio, and John Figgess. *Two Thousand Years of Oriental Ceramics.* New York: Abrams, 1960.

Leach, Bernard. *Kenzan and His Tradition.* London: Faber and Faber, 1966.

Miki, Fumio. *Haniwa.* Rutland, Vt.: Tuttle, 1960.

Munsterberg, Hugo. *The Ceramic Art of Japan.* Rutland, Vt.: Tuttle, 1964.

Prodan, Mario. *The Art of the T'ang Potter.* London: Thames and Hudson, 1960.

Islamic, Hispano-Moresque, and African Ceramics

Davidson, Basil. *The Lost Cities of Africa.* Boston: Little, Brown, 1959.

Frothingham, Alice Wilson. *Lusterware of Spain.* New York: Hispanic Society of America, 1951.

Lane, Arthur. *Early Islamic Pottery.* New York: Van Nostrand, 1948.

———. *Later Islamic Pottery.* London: Faber and Faber, 1957.

Leuzinger, Elsy. *Africa.* New York: Crown, 1960.

Meauzé, Pierre. *African Art.* Cleveland: World Publishing, 1967.

Wassing, René S. *African Art.* New York: Abrams, 1968.

Wilkinson, Charles K. *Iranian Ceramics.* New York: Abrams, 1963.

Wilson, Ralph Pinder. *Islamic Art.* New York: Macmillan, 1957.

Medieval through 19th-century European Ceramics

Honey, William B. *European Ceramic Art.* London: Faber and Faber, 1949.

Liverani, Giuseppe. *Five Centuries of Italian Majolica.* New York: McGraw-Hill, 1960.

Rackham, Bernard. *Medieval English Pottery.* New York: Van Nostrand, 1949.

Vydrova, Jirina. *Italian Majolica.* London: Spring House, 1960.

Pre-Columbian and Colonial American Ceramics

Anton, Ferdinand, and Frederick J. Dockstader. *Pre-Columbian Art.* New York: Abrams, 1968.

Bushnell, G. H. S. *Ancient Arts of the Americas.* New York: Praeger, 1965.

Disselhoff, H. D., and S. Linne. *The Art of Ancient America*. New York: Crown, 1960.

Dockstader, Frederick, J. *Indian Art in South America*. Greenwich, Conn., New York Graphic, 1967.

Haberland, Wolfgang. *The Art of North America*. New York: Crown, 1964.

Kubler, George. *The Art and Architecture of Ancient America*. Baltimore: Penguin, 1962.

Ramsay, John. *American Potters and Pottery*. New York: Tudor, 1947.

Spargo, John. *Early American Pottery and China*. New York: Century Library of American Antiques, 1926.

Willey, Gordon, R. *An Introduction to American Archaeology*. Englewood Cliffs, N. J., Prentice-Hall, 1966.

Glossary of Ceramic Terms

See Chapter 9
for more complete coverage of ceramic chemicals

absorbency The ability of a material (clay, plaster of paris, and so forth) to soak up water.

acid One of three types of chemicals that constitute a glaze, the other two being the bases and the intermediates or neutrals. The acid group is symbolized by the radical RO_2. The most important acid is silica (SiO_2).

Albany slip A natural clay containing sufficient fluxes to melt and function as a glaze. It develops a dark brown-black glaze at cones 8 to 10 without any additions. Since it is mined in several localities in the vicinity of Albany, N. Y., its composition may vary slightly from time to time. Similar clays, found in various sections of the United States, were much used by early American stoneware potteries.

alkali Generally, the base compounds of sodium and potassium but also the alkaline earth compounds lime and magnesia. They function as fluxes, combining easily with silica at relatively low temperatures.

alumina (Al_2O_3) A major ingredient found in all clays and glazes. It is the chief oxide in the neutral group (R_2O_3) and imparts greater strength and higher firing temperatures to the body and glaze. When added to a glaze, it will assist in the formation of mat textures, inhibit devitrification, and increase the viscosity of the glaze during firing.

ash Generally, the ashes of trees, straw, leaves, and so forth. It is commonly used in the Far East to provide from 40 to 60 percent of high-temperature glaze ingredients. Depending upon the type, it will contain from 40 to 75 percent silica, from 5 to 15 percent alumina, and smaller amounts of iron, phosphorus, lime, potash, and magnesia.

aventurine A glaze composed of a soda, lead, or boric oxide flux often with an excess of iron oxide (more than 6 percent). If it is cooled slowly, iron crystals will form, and these crystals will sparkle and glisten beneath the surface of the glaze.

bag wall A baffle wall in a kiln, separating the chamber from the combustion area.

ball clay An extremely fine-grained, plastic, sedimentary clay. Although ball clay contains much organic matter, it fires white or near white in color. It is usually added to porcelain and white-ware bodies to increase plasticity.

ball mill A porcelain jar filled with flint pebbles and rotated with either a wet or dry charge of chemicals. It is used to blend and to grind glaze and body ingredients.

barium carbonate (BaCO₃) Used in combination with other fluxes to form mats in the low-temperature range. A very small percentage (¼ to 2) added to a clay body will prevent discoloration caused by soluble sulphates, such as the whitish blotches often seen on red bricks and earthenware bodies.

basalt ware A hard, black, unglazed stoneware body developed about 1775 by the Wedgwood potteries in England in an effort to imitate classical wares.

bat A disk or slab of plaster of paris on which pottery is formed or dried. It is also used to remove excess moisture from plastic clay.

batch Raw chemicals comprising a ceramic glaze that have been weighed out in a specific proportion designed to melt at a predetermined temperature.

bentonite An extremely plastic clay, formed by decomposed volcanic ash and glass, which is used to render short clays workable and to aid glaze suspensions.

binders Various materials; gums, polyvinyl alcohol, methylcellulose used to increase glaze adherence or to impart strength to a cast or pressed clay body.

bisque or biscuit Unglazed ware.

bisque fire Preliminary firing to harden the body, usually at about cone 010, prior to glazing and subsequent glaze firing.

bistone Coarse crushed quartz used in saggers to support thin procelain in the bisque.

blowing The bursting of pots in a kiln caused by a too-rapid temperature rise. The water content of the clay turns into steam and forces the body to expand and explode.

blunger A mixing machine with revolving paddles used to prepare large quantities of clay slip or glazes.

bone china A hard, translucent china ware produced chiefly in England. The body contains a large amount of bone ash (calcium phosphate), which allows it to mature at cone 6 (2232°F). It is not very plastic and is therefore difficult to form; it also tends to warp.

calcine To heat a ceramic material or mixture to the temperature necessary to drive off the chemical water, carbon dioxide, and other volatile gases. Some fusion may occur, in which case the material must be ground. This is the process used in the production of plaster of paris, Portland cement, and ceramic stains.

casting (or slip casting) A reproductive process of forming clay objects by pouring a clay slip into a hollow plaster mold and allowing it to remain long enough for a layer of clay to thicken on the mold wall. After hardening, the clay object is removed.

chemical water Water (H₂O) chemically combined in the glaze and body compounds. At approximately 450°C (842°F) during the firing cycle this water will begin to leave the body and glaze as water vapor. Little shrinkage occurs at this point, although there is a loss in weight.

china A loosely applied term referring to white-ware bodies fired at low porcelain temperatures. They are generally vitreous, with an absorbency of less than 2 percent, and may be translucent.

china clay *See* kaolin.

clay A decomposed granite-type rock. To be classed as a clay the decomposed rock must have fine particles so that it will be plastic. Clays should be free of vegetable matter but will often contain other impurities, which affect their color and firing temperatures. They are classified into various types, such as ball clays, fireclays, and slip clays. Pure clay is expressed chemically as $Al_2O_3 \cdot 2SiO_2 \cdot 2H_2O$.

coefficient of expansion The ratio of change between the length of a material mass and the temperature.

coiling A hand method of forming pottery by building up the walls with ropelike rolls of clay and then smoothing over the joints.

combing A method of decoration developed by dragging a coarse comb or tip of a feather over two contrasting layers of wet clay slip or glaze.

Cornwall stone (also Cornish stone) A feldsparlike material found in England and widely used there for porcelain-type bodies and glazes. Compared to American feldspar, it contains more silica and a smaller amount, though a greater variety, of fluxes. It comes closest to approximating the Chinese *petuntze*, which is a major ingredient of Orient porcelain bodies and glazes.

crackle glaze. A glaze containing minute cracks in the surface. The cracks are decorative and are often accentuated by coloring matter that is rubbed in. They are caused in cooling by the different rates at which the body and the glaze contract after firing.

crawling Separation of the glaze coating during firing, which exposes areas of unglazed clay caused by too heavy application. The glaze cracks upon drying or from uneven contraction rates between glaze and body.

crazing An undesirable and excessive crackle in the glaze, which penetrates through the glaze to the clay body. It should be remedied by adjusting the glaze or body composition to obtain a more uniform contraction ratio.

crocus martis Purple red oxide of iron, used as a red-brown glaze colorant.

crystal glazes Glazes characterized by crystalline clusters of various shapes and colors embedded in a more uniform and opaque glaze. The crystals are larger than in aventurine and may on occasion cover the entire surface. The glaze ingredients generally used are iron, lime, zinc, or rutile with an alkaline flux, high silica, and low alumina ratio. A slow cooling cycle is necessary for the development of the crystals.

cupric and **cuprous oxides** Copper oxides (CuO, Cu_2O), the major green colorants. They will also produce red under reducing conditions, with an alkaline flux.

damp box A lined metal cabinet in which unfinished clay objects are stored to prevent them from drying.

deflocculant Sodium carbonate or sodium silicate used in a casting slip to reduce the amount of water necessary and to maintain a better suspension.

Delft ware A light-colored pottery body covered with a lead-tin glaze, with overglaze decoration in cobalt on the unfired glaze. Delft was first made in Holland in imitation of Chinese blue-and-white porcelain.

della Robbia ware Ceramic sculpture of glazed terra cotta, generally in relief, produced in Florence by Lucca della Robbia or his family during the fifteenth century. The glaze used was the lead-tin majolica type developed in Spain.

dipping Glazing pottery by immersing it in a large pan or vat of glaze.

dryfoot To clean the bottom of a glazed piece before firing.

dunting Cracking of fired ware in a cooling kiln, the result of opening the flues and cooling too rapidly.

earthenware Low-fire pottery (below 2000°F), usually red or tan in color with an absorbency of from 5 to 20 percent.

eggshell porcelain Translucent, thin-walled porcelain.

empirical formula A glaze formula expressed in molecular propositions.

engobe A prepared slip that is halfway between a glaze and a clay; contains clay, feldspar, flint, a flux, plus colorants. May be used on bisque ware.

equivalent weight A weight that will yield one unit of a component (RO or R_2O_3 or RO_2 in a compound). This is usually the same as the molecular weight of the chemical compound in question. In ceramic calculations, equivalent weights are also assigned to the RO, R_2O_3 and the RO_2 oxide groups that make up the compound. If one of these oxide groups contains more than one unit of the oxide, its equivalent weight

would be found by dividing the compound molecular weight by this unit number. (*See* Chap. 9.)

eutectic The lowest melting point of the mixture of materials composing the glaze. This is always lower than the melting points of the individual materials.

faience Earthenware covered with a lead-tin glaze; a French term for earthenware derived from the Italian pottery center at Faenza, which, during the Renaissance, produced this ware partially in imitation of Spanish majolica. (*See* also majolica and Delft ware.)

fat clay A plastic clay such as ball clay.

ferric and **ferrous oxides** (Fe_2O_3 and FeO) Red and black iron oxide. As impurities in clay, they lower the firing temperature. They are the chief source of tan and brown ceramic colors and, under reducing conditions, the various celadon greens (*see* reduction).

fire box Combustion chamber of a gas, oil, or wood-fired kiln, usually directly below the kiln chamber.

fireclay A clay having a slightly higher percentage of fluxes than pure clay (kaolin). It fires tan or gray in color and is used in the manufacture of refractory materials, such as bricks, muffles, and so forth for industrial glass and steel furnaces. It is often quite plastic and may be used by the studio potter as an ingredient of stoneware bodies.

flues Passageways around the kiln chamber through which the heating gases pass from the firebox to the chimney.

flux Lowest-melting compound in a glaze, such as lead, borax, soda ash, or lime, and including the potash or soda contained in the feldspar. The flux combines easily with silica and thereby helps higher-melting alumina-silica compounds eventually to form a glass.

foot The ringlike base of a ceramic piece, usually heavier than the surrounding body.

frit A partial or complete glaze that is melted and then reground for the purpose of eliminating the toxic effects of lead or the solubility of borax, soda ash, and so forth.

frit china A glossy, partly translucent chinaware produced by adding a glass frit to the body.

galena Lead sulphide, used as a flux for earthenware glazes, more common in Europe than in the United States.

glaze A liquid suspension of finely ground minerals that is applied by brushing, pouring, or spraying on the surface of bisque-fired ceramic ware. After drying the ware is fired to the temperature at which the glaze ingredients will melt together to form a glassy surface coating.

glaze fire A firing cycle to the temperature at which the glaze materials will melt to form a glasslike surface coating. This is usually at the point of maximum body maturity, and it is considerably higher than the bisque fire. However, delicate porcelain, subject to warping, is often fired high in the bisque with a lower glaze fire. To prevent warping in the high bisque fire, the ware is placed upside down on its rim or with protective disks on the lips. Some pieces may be embedded in a layer of flint sand.

glost fire An older term for a glaze firing.

greenware Pottery that has not been bisque fired.

grog Hard fired clay that has been crushed or ground to various particle sizes. It is used to reduce shrinkage in such ceramic products as sculpture and architectural terra-cotta tiles, which, because of their thickness, have drying and shrinkage problems. From 20 to 40 percent grog may be used, depending upon the amount of detail desired and whether the pieces are free standing or pressed in molds.

gum arabic or **gum tragacanth** Natural gums used in glazes as binders to promote better glaze adherence to the body. Binders are necessary for fritted glazes containing little or no raw clay. They are also useful when a bisque fire accidentally goes too high, or in reglazing. The gum, of course, burns out completely during the fire.

hard paste True porcelain that is fired to cone 12 or above (2420°F); also called *hard porcelain.*

ilmenite (TiO$_2$·FeO) An important source of titanium. In the granular form it is used to give dark flecks to the glaze. It is often sprinkled upon the wet glaze without previous mixing.

iron oxide *See* ferric oxide.

jiggering, jollying An industrial method of producing pottery. A slab of soft clay is placed upon a revolving plaster mold of the object to be formed. As the wheel head turns, a metal template on a moving arm trims off the excess clay and forms the reverse side of the piece.

kanthal A special metal alloy produced in Sweden for wire or strip elements in electric kilns firing from 2000° to 2400°F.

kaolin Al$_2$O$_3$·2SiO$_2$·2H$_2$O) Pure clay, also known as china clay. It is used in glaze and porcelain bodies and fires to a pure white. Sedimentary kaolins found in Florida are more plastic than the residual types found in the Carolinas and Georgia.

kiln A furnace made of refractory clay materials for firing ceramic products.

kiln furniture Refractory shelves and posts upon which ceramic ware is placed while being fired in the kiln.

kiln wash A protective coating of refractory materials applied to the surface of the shelves and the kiln floor to prevent excess glaze from fusing the ware to the shelves. An inexpensive and effective wash can be made from equal parts of flint and kaolin.

kneading Working clay with the fingers or the heel of the hand in order to obtain a uniform consistency.

lead White lead [basic lead carbonates, 2PbCO$_3$·Pb(OH)$_2$], red lead (Pb$_3$O$_4$), and galena (lead sulphide, PbS) are among the most common low-fire fluxes.

leather hard The condition of the raw ware when most of the moisture has left the body but when it is still soft enough to be carved or burnished easily.

limestone A major flux in the medium- and high-fire temperature ranges when it is powdered in the form of whiting (calcium cabonate). If a coarse sand is used as a grog, it should not contain limestone particles. Calcined lime will expand in the bisque and cause portions of the body to pop out.

luster A type of metallic decoration thought to have been discovered in Egypt and further developed in Persia during the ninth and fourteenth centuries. A mixture of a metallic salt, resin, and bismuth nitrate is applied to a glazed piece and then refired at a lower temperature. The temperature, however, must be sufficient to melt the metal and leave a thin layer on the decorated portions.

luting A method of joining together two pieces of dry or leather-hard clay with a slip.

majolica Earthenware covered with a soft tin-lead glaze, often with a luster decoration. The ware originally came from Spain and derived its name from the island of Majorca, which lay on the trade route to Italy. Faenza ware was greatly influenced by these Spanish imports. All Renaissance pottery of this type is now generally called majolica ware.

mat glaze A dull-surfaced glaze with no gloss but pleasant to the touch, not to be confused with an incomplete fired glaze. Mat surfaces can be developed by the addition of barium carbonate or alumina, and a slow cooling cycle.

maturity The temperature or time at which a clay or clay body develops the desirable characteristics of maximum nonporosity and hardness; or the point at which the glaze ingredients enter into complete fusion, developing a strong bond with the body, a stable structure, maximum resistance to abrasion, and a pleasant surface texture.

mold A form or box, usually made of plaster of paris, containing a hollow negative shape. The positive form is made by pouring either wet plaster or slip into this hollow. (*See* casting.)

muffle A lining, made of refractory materials, forming the kiln chamber, around which the hot gases pass from the firebox to the chimney. The purpose is to protect the ware from the direct flames of the fire and the resulting combustion impurities. Some of these panels may be removed for a redution fire.

muffle kiln A kiln with muffle features in contrast to a kiln using saggars. (*See* saggars.)

mullite Interlocking needlelike crystals of aluminum silicate ($3Al_2O_3 \cdot 2SiO_2$) which begin to form in high-temperature bodies between 1850° and 2200°F. This formation is responsible for much of the greater toughness and hardness of stoneware and porcelain, and in particular for the closer union developed between the glaze and the body.

neutral fire A fire that is neither oxidizing nor reducing. Actually this can be obtained only in practice by a slight alternation between oxidation and reduction.

opacifier A chemical whose crystals are relatively insoluble in the glaze, thereby preventing light from penetrating the glass formation. The color most sought is white, although for some purposes others may be as effective. Tin oxide is by far the best opacifier. Zirconium and titanium oxides are also used. Many other oxides are effective in certain combinations and within limited firing ranges. These are commercially available in frit forms under trade names, such as Zircopax, Opax, and Ultrox.

overglaze Decoration applied with overglaze colors on the glaze and fired ware. The third firing of the overglaze ware is at a lower temperature than the glaze fire.

overglaze colors Colors containing coloring oxides or ceramic stains, a flux, and some type of binder. The fluxes are necessary to allow the colors to melt into the harder glaze to which they are applied. The lower temperatures at which most underglazes are fired (about cone 016–013) allow the use of colorants that are unstable at higher temperatures.

oxidizing fire A fire during which the kiln chamber retains an ample supply of oxygen. This means that the combustion in the firebox must be perfectly adjusted. An electric kiln always gives an oxidizing fire.

paste The compounded bodies of European-type porcelains.

peach bloom A Chinese copper-red reduction glaze with a peachlike pink color.

peeling Separation of the glaze or slip from the body. Peeling may be caused when slip is applied to a body that is too dry, or when a glaze is applied too thickly or to a dusty surface.

peep hole A hole placed in the firebox, kiln chamber, or muffle flues of a kiln, through which one can observe the cones or the process of combustion.

petuntze A partially decomposed feldspar-type rock found in China, roughly similar in composition to Cornwall stone. With kaolin it forms the body of Oriental porcelains.

plaster of paris Hydrate of calcium sulphate, made by calcining gypsum. It hardens after being mixed with water. Because it absorbs moisture and it can be cut and shaped easily, it is used in ceramics for drying and throwing bats, as well as for molds and casting work.

plasticity The quality of clay that allows it to be manipulated and still maintain its shape without cracking or sagging.

porcelain (Chinese) A hard, nonabsorbent clay body, white or gray in color, that rings when struck.

porcelain (hard) A hard, nonabsorbent clay body that is white and translucent. In both types of hard porcelain the bisque is low fired and the glaze is very high (generally cone 14–16).

pottery Earthenware; a shop in which ceramic objects are made.

pressing Forming of clay objects by pressing soft clay between two plaster molds, such as in the production of cup handles.

pug mill A machine for mixing plastic clay.

pyrometer An instrument for measuring heat at high temperatures. It consists of a calibrated dial connected to wires made of two different alloys, the welded tips of which protrude into the kiln chamber. When heated, this welded junction sets up a minute electrical current, which registers on the indicating dial.

pyrometric cones Small triangular cones ($1^1/_8$ and $2^5/_8$ inches in height) made of ceramic materials that are compounded to bend and melt at specific temperatures, thus enabling the potter to determine when the firing is complete.

quartz Flint or silica (SiO_2).

raku A soft, lead-glazed, hand-built groggy earthenware made in Japan and associated with the tea ceremony. Raku ware is unique in that the glazed preheated bisque is placed in the red-hot kiln with long-handled tongs. The glaze matures in 15 to 30 minutes, and the ware is then withdrawn.

reducing agent Glaze or body material such as silicon carbide, which combines with oxygen to form carbon monoxide during the firing.

reduction fire A firing using insufficient oxygen; carbon monoxide thus formed unites with oxygen from the body and glaze to form carbon dioxide, producing color changes in coloring oxides.

refractory The quality of resisting the effects of high temperatures; also materials, high in alumina and silica, that are used for making kiln insulation, muffles, and kiln furniture.

rib A tool of wood, bone, or metal that is held in the hand while throwing to assist in shaping the pot or to compact the clay.

RO, R_2O_3, RO_2 The symbols or radicals for the three major groups of chemicals that make up a ceramic glaze. The RO radical refers to the base chemicals, such as the oxides of sodium, potassium, calcium, and lead which function in the glaze as fluxing agents. The R_2O_3 radical refers to the intermediate or amphoteric oxides, some of which may on occasion function either as bases or acids. The chief oxide of interest in this group is alumina (Al_2O_3), which always reacts as a refractory. The third radical RO_2 stands for the acid group, the glass formers, such as silica (SiO_2).

rouge flambé A type of Chinese copper-red reduction glaze (*sang de bœuf*) which is a mottled deep red with green and blue hues, also called a transmutation glaze.

rutile An impure form of titanium dioxide (TiO_2) containing much iron. It will give a light yellow or tan color to the glaze, with a streaked and runny effect. Used in large amounts it will raise the maturing temperature.

saggars Round boxlike containers of fireclay used in kilns lacking muffles. The glazed ware is placed in saggars to protect the glaze from the combustion gases.

salt glaze A glaze developed by throwing salt (NaCl) into a hot kiln. The salt vaporizes and combines with the silica in the body to form sodium silicate, a hard glassy glaze. A salt kiln is of a slightly different construction and is limited in use to the salt glaze.

sang de bœuf The French term for oxblood, which describes the rich, deep-red hues produced by the Chinese in their copper-red reduction glazes.

sgraffito Decoration achieved by scratching through a colored slip to show the contrasting body color beneath.

shard A broken fragment of pottery.

short A body or clay lacking in plasticity.

shrinkage Contraction of the clay in either drying or firing. In the firing cycle the major body shrinkage for stoneware clays begins at approximately 900°C (1652°F). Earthenware clays will begin to fuse and shrink at slightly lower temperatures.

siccative Agent for drying the oils used in underglaze decoration.

silica Flint (SiO_2) produced in the United States by grinding almost pure flint sand.

silicate of soda A deflocculant. A standard solution of sodium silicate (commercial N brand) has the ratio of 1 part soda to 3.3 parts silica. Specific gravity 1.395.

single fire A firing cycle in which the normal bisque and glaze firings are combined. The advantages are a great saving of fuel and labor, and development of a stronger bond between the body and the glaze. These are partially offset by the need for greater care in handling the ware, plus the danger of cracking if in glazing the raw pieces absorb too much moisture. In a salt glaze, however, these disadvantages do not occur.

sintering A firing process in which ceramic compounds fuse sufficiently to form a solid mass upon cooling but are not vitrified. An example is low-fire earthenware.

slip A clay in liquid suspension.

slip clay A clay such as Albany and Michigan containing sufficient fluxes to function as a glaze with little or no additions.

spinel Chemically, magnesium aluminate ($MgAl_2O_3$), an extremely hard crystal arranged in an octahedron atomic structure. In ceramics, a spinel is a crystal used as a colorant in place of the metallic oxides because of its greater resistance to change by either the fluxing action of the glaze or the effects of high temperatures.

spray booth A boxlike booth equipped with a ventilating fan to remove spray dust, which, whether toxic or not, is harmful.

spraying Applying glazes with a compressed-air spray machine, the chief commercial method.

sprigging Applying clay in a plastic state to form a relief decoration.

stain Sometimes a single coloring oxide, but usually a combination of oxides, plus alumina, flint, and a fluxing compound. This mixture is calcined and then finely ground and washed. The purpose is to form a stable coloring agent not likely to be altered by the action of the glaze or heat. While stains are employed as glaze colorants, their chief use is as overglaze and underglaze decorations and body colorants.

stilt   A ceramic tripod upon which glazed ware is placed in the kiln. Tripods with nickel-nichrome wire points are often used to minimize blemishes to the glaze. They are never used for high-fire porcelain, which must be dry footed for greater support.

stoneware   A high-fire ware (above cone 8) with slight or no absorbency. It is usually gray in color but may be tan or slightly reddish. Stoneware is similar in many respects to porcelain, the chief difference being the color, which is the result of iron and other impurities in the clay.

stoneware clays   Clays more plastic than a porcelain body, firing above cone 8 to a gray color.

talc ($3MgO \cdot 4SiO_2 \cdot H_2O$)   A compound used in most white-ware bodies in the low to moderate firing ranges as a source of silica and flux. It is slightly plastic and can be used to lower the firing range, if need be, of a stoneware or fireclay body.

terra cotta   An earthenware body, generally red in color and containing grog. It is the common body type used for ceramic sculpture.

terra sigillata   The red slip glaze of the Romans, similar to the Etruscan *bucchero* and Greek *black varnish*. It was made of fine decanted particles of red clay, and was normally oxidized to form a red body.

throwing   Forming pottery of plastic clay on a potter's wheel.

tin enamel   A term used incorrectly by many older historians to describe the tin-lead majolica type glaze. An enamel is a very low-fire glaze used as an overglaze decoration. It was extensively used by the Turks and the late Ming and Ch'ing potters.

tin-vanadium stain   A major yellow colorant produced by a calcined mixture of tin and vanadium oxides.

trailing   A method of decorating, using a slip trailed out from a rubber syringe.

translucency   The ability of a thin porcelain or white-ware body to transmit a diffused light.

turning   Trimming the walls and foot of a pot on the wheel while the clay is in a leather-hard state.

underglaze   Colored decoration applied on the bisque ware before the glaze is applied.

viscosity   The nonrunning quality of a glaze, caused by glaze chemicals that resist the flowing action of the glaze flux.

vitreous   Pertaining to the hard, glassy, and nonabsorbent quality of a body or glaze.

volatilization   Action under influence of extreme heat of the kiln in which some glaze elements turn successively from a solid to a liquid, and finally into a gaseous, state.

ware   Pottery or porcelain in the raw, bisque, or glazed state.

warping   Distortion of a pot in drying because of uneven wall thickness or a warm draft of air, or in firing when a kiln does not heat uniformly.

water glass   Another term for a liquid solution of sodium silicate that is used as a deflocculant.

water smoking   The initial phase of the firing cycle up to a dull red heat ($1000°$ to $1100°F$). Depending upon the thickness of the ware, this may take from two or three hours for thin pottery, to twelve hours for sculpture. The heat rise must be gradual to allow atmospheric and chemical water to escape. In some cases there will be organic impurities which will also burn out, releasing carbon monoxide.

wax resist   A method of decorating pottery by brushing on a design with a hot melted wax solution or a wax emulsion. This will prevent an applied stain or glaze from adhering to the decorated portions. The wax may be applied to either the raw or bisque ware, over or between two layers of glaze.

weathering   The exposure of raw clay to the action of rain, sun, and freezing weather, which breaks down the particle size and renders the clay more plastic.

wedging   Kneading plastic clay with the fingers and heel of the hands in a rocking spiral motion, which forces out trapped air pockets and develops a uniform texture.

white lead [$2PbCO_3 \cdot Pb(OH)_2$]   A major low-fire flux.

white ware   Pottery or china ware with a white or light cream-colored body.

whiting   Calcium carbonate ($CaCO_3$), similar chemically to limestone and marble; a major high-fire flux.

yellow base   A glaze stain produced by a calcined mixture of red lead, antimony, and tin oxides.

Zircopax   Trade name of a commercial frit used as an opacifier. It is composed primarily of zirconium oxide and silica. It is about half as strong as tin oxide, but its price is much lower regardless of the quantity used.

Index

For ceramic terms, see Glossary, pp. 333–339;
for ceramic chemicals, see pp. 228–241.
References are to page numbers, except for
color plates and black-and-white illustrations,
which are identified by figure and plate numbers.

Kusube, Yaichi, vase, 116, Fig. 240

Lakofsky, Charles, porcelain jar, 168, Fig. 359
Leach, Bernard, 67, 72, 75–76, 121; plate, 72, Fig. 129; vase, 75, Fig. 130
Leach, David, casseroles, 76, Fig. 133
Leach, Richard, jug, Pl. 20, p. 211; salt glaze details, Pls. 21–22, p. 212
lead, compounds, 228, 231; glazes, 208, 225; eutectic fusion of lead and silica, 226, 313–314, Fig. 429
leather hard, 195–196
Leonardo da Vinci, *Ginevra de' Benci,* 31, Fig. 59
lepidolite, 213, 236, 307
Leslie, Bailey, bottles, 127, Fig. 264
Leuchovius, Sylvia, wall plaque, 106, Fig. 212
Levine, Marilyn, vase, 130, Fig. 274
Lewis, Marion, sculptural form, 129, Fig. 269
Lichtenstein, Roy, *Head with Black Shadow,* Pl. 16, p. 193
lime, 209, 239 (*see also* whiting)
limit formulas, 224–225
Lindberg, Stig, 104; *Ting,* 105, Fig. 207; mural (detail), 105, Fig. 208; *People Bottles,* Pl. 12, p. 125
Lindh, Francesca, vase, 113, Fig. 234; plaque, Pl. 13, p. 126
Lion Gate, Mycenae, 6, Fig. 10
lithium compounds, 228–229, 236
Liukko-Sundström, Heljätuulia, *Torpedo,* 112, Fig. 230
Lund, Otto, in Interpace studios, 255, Fig. 443
luster glazes, 214, 243–244
luster ware, Alhambra vase, 28, Fig. 49; armorial plate, 29, Fig. 51; drug jar, 28, Fig. 50; Italian, 29; Middle Eastern, 24, 26; plate, 30, Fig. 56; plate, 29, Fig. 52; preparation of glaze, 243–244; Spanish, 27–28; vase, 27, Fig. 48,; wall tile, 24, Fig. 42

MacKenzie, Warren, *Four Vases (for a Gynecologist's Office),* 182, Fig. 386; vase, 146, Fig. 292; vase, 210, Fig. 425
Madsen, Sten Lykke, *Fantastic Animal,* 99, Fig. 191; *Fantasy Hen,* 100, Fig. 195
magnesium compounds, 229, 236
magnetite, 235 (*see also* iron compounds)
Magnussen, Erik, *Abstract Sculpture,* 100, Fig. 194; casserole, 99, Fig. 190
majolica, 29, 35, 87, 98
manganese compounds, 236
Markson, Mayta, planter, 128, Fig. 266
Martz, Karl, bowl, Pl. 18, p. 194
Mason, John, *Cross,* Pl. 15, p. 160; sculptural form 178, Fig. 380; wall mural, 175, Fig. 375
mass production, design for, 256–260, Figs. 446–457; forming methods, 261–266, Figs. 458–470; kilns, 266–269, Figs. 471–476
mat glazes, 210, 213, 315–316
materials and supplies, 324–328
Mayan ceramics, 52–53; figure, 52, Fig. 96; jar, 53, Fig. 97
McConnell, Carl, wine jug, 121, Fig. 252
McIntosh, Harrison, bottle, Pl. 17, p. 194; compote, 167, Fig. 355; jar, 188, Fig. 394
McPherson, Don, in Pacific Stoneware studios, 256, Fig. 444
melting points of minerals, 312
methocel, 245 (*see also* binders)
Mexican ceramics, 48–54, Figs. 87–95, 99–100, 104
Midanik, Dorothy, vases, 130, Fig. 272
Middle Eastern ceramics, 23–26, Figs. 41–47
Mimbres ceramics, 54–55; bowl, 55, Fig. 103
Mingei, 114
Minoan ceramics 4–7; jar, 5, Fig. 8; *Snake Goddess,* 6, Fig. 9
mishima, 59–60, 195, Figs. 409–410
Mississippi Valley, 54; bottle, 54, Fig. 101
Mizuno, Mineo, in Interpace studios, 255, Fig. 443

Mochica ceramics, 44–46; bottles, 45, Fig. 80–81; jar, 46, Fig. 82
molds, design of, 256–260; historical uses, 249; slip casting, 261–264
molecular weight, 220; table of ceramic materials, 305–306
Møller, Dorthe, mug and teapot, 102, Fig. 199
Mongol invasions of China, 11, 60; in the Middle East, 25, 27
Morino, Hiroaki, slab sculpture, 118, Fig. 245; vase, 120, Fig. 250
Morino, Kako, vase, 117, Fig. 242
Morris, William, 72, 87, 94
mullite, 209, 278–279, Fig. 491
Munch-Petersen, Ursula, vase, 100, Fig. 192
Murray, William Staite, 72
Museum of Contemporary Crafts, New York, 134
Mycenaean ceramics, 6–7; amphora, 7, Figs. 11–12

Naples yellow, 231
Naske, Sabine, *Garden Cock,* 97, Fig. 188; *Tree of Life,* 97, Fig. 187
Natzler, Gertrud and Otto, 134
Nayarit ceramics, 50–52; *Seated Ball Player,* Pl. 4, p. 39; seated figure, 51, Fig. 94
Naxca ceramics, 45; bottle, 45, Fig. 78; bowl, 45, Fig. 79
Neolithic ceramics, 1–2, 7, Figs. 3–4, 13
nepheline synenite, 236–237, 306–307
neutral oxides, 229–230
Newman, Bryan, pitchers, jar, bowl, plate, 78, Fig. 137
nickel oxides, 237
nickel-nichrome elements, 278
Norman, William, bottle, 131, Fig. 276
Norwegian ceramics, 108–109, Figs. 218–224; Dubourgh, teapots, 108, Fig. 218; Hald, bowl, 109, Fig. 222; Hansen, bowl and vases, 109, Fig. 220; deep bowl, 109, Fig. 223; Pløen, vases, 108–109, Figs. 219, 221, 224

ochre, 237
Oestreicher, Helly, *Cylinders and Arcs,* 80, Fig. 145
Olmec ceramics, 48–49; seated figure, 49, Fig. 88
Onda folk potters, 114; teapot, 114, Fig. 236
opacifiers, 241–242
opax, 237, 241
Orton cones, 310–311
overglaze colors, 243
oxygen, 219

Paak, Carl, sculptural pot, 180, Fig. 282
Pacific Stoneware, 256, Figs. 444–445
Panopoulos, Kostas, bottle, 90, Fig. 171; vase, 93, Fig. 174
Papavgeris, Athanase, panels, 93, Figs. 175–176
Parian pitcher, 57, Fig. 108
Patel, Narendra, 174; styrofoam used in sculpture, 172–174, Figs. 369–374
pearl ash, 237 (*see also* potassium compounds)
Peeler, Richard, *Beautiful Love,* 71, Fig. 128; bottle, 192, Fig. 407
Perkins, Dorothy, bottle, 270, Fig. 447; vase, 190, Fig. 396
Perkins, Lyle N., vase, 138, Fig. 289
Persson, Inger, vase forms, 106, Fig. 210
Persson, Britt Ingrid, *Line Drawings,* 107, Fig. 217
Persian ceramics, 23, 25–26; wall tile, 24, Fig. 42; jug, 25, Fig. 43
Peruvian ceramics, 43–48, Figs. 78–83, 85–86
petalite, 144, 237, 307
Picasso, Pablo, 85; *Le faune barbre,* 84, Fig. 155; *Red and White Owl,* 84, Fig. 156
pinch pot, 149, Figs. 295–298
plaster of paris, first use of, 36, 58; mixing proportions, 260–261; molds, 256–262, Figs. 447–456

Photographic Sources

References are to figure numbers unless indicated Pl. (plate).

Aistrup, Inga, Vedbaek, Denmark, and Den Permanente, Copenhagen, 197; Alinari–Art Reference Bureau, Ancram, N.Y., 27, 34, 36, 40, 49, 59; Bach, Larry, 387; Barrows, George, New York, 87; Beaudin, J. P., and Canadian Guild of Potters, Toronto, 279; © Beata Bergström, Stockholm, 217; Boesch, Ferdinand, New York, 286; Borchi, Florence, 164, 167; Calder, Sam, Los Angeles, 355; Canadian Guild of Potters, Toronto, 264, 266–267, 270, 272–275, 277; Den Permanente, Copenhagen, 194, 198, 200–202; Department of Technical Education, New South Wales, and *Pottery in Australia*, Turramurra, N.S.W., 263; Dutch Ceramic Society, Amsterdam, 145, 147, 149–154; Elisofon, Eliot, New York, 70; Fredericton Photo, N.B., and Canadian Guild of Potters, Toronto, 265, 276, 278; Frund, J. L., and Canadian Guild of Potters, Toronto, 280; Galerie Louise Leiris, Paris, 155; Gobbels, Bernd, 177; Hicks, Alan, Portland, Ore., 511; Hirmer Fotoarchiv, Munich, 7, 9, Pl. 2; Howard, Bob, and Canadian Guild of Potters, Toronto, 269; Industrial Photo Service, Trenton, N.J., 526; Jones, Edward C., Danville, Va., 409, 414; Jorgensen, Ole H., Naestred, Denmark, and Den Permanente, Copenhagen, 203; Karlsson, Stig T., Vauxholm, Sweden, 213; King, John, New Canaan, Conn., Pl. 5; La Nory, Armour, Montreal, and Canadian Guild of Potters, Toronto, 271; Leigh, Trenton, N.J., 497, 504; Lyttle, Douglas, Kalamazoo, Mich., 501; Maspono, Oriol, Barcelona, 159; Moore, Peter, New York, 88; Nordness, Lee, Gallery, New York, 287–288; Norwegian Society of Arts and Crafts and Industrial Design, Oslo, 218–224; Olivier Pictures, Amsterdam, and Dutch Ceramic Society, Amsterdam, 146, 148; Olsson, Jan, Göteborg, 205; Pedersen, Peer, and Den Permanente, Copenhagen, 199; *Pottery in Australia,* Turramurra, N.S.W., 252, 254–258, 260–261; *Pottery Quarterly,* Herts, England, 129, 131–133, 137, 141; Quiresi, Ezio, Cremona, 163, 168; Ram, Inc., 467–470; Robert, Sten, 215; Robinson, James, and *Pottery in Australia,* Turramurra, N.S.W., 253; Slusarski, Peter A., 446–457; Sowden, Harry, Mosman, N.S.W., and *Pottery in Australia,* Turramurra, N.S.W., 262; Storr, James, Höhr-Grenzhausen, Germany, 183, 186; Stournaras, N., Athens, 32; Strizic, Mark, Australia, and *Pottery in Australia,* Turramurra, N.S.W., 259; Strüwing, Copenhagen, and Den Permanente, Copenhagen, 204; Syracuse China Corporation, 458–466, 471–476; Uht, Charles, New York, 72, 74–77, 79–86, 89, 91–95, 97–100, 102–103, 156; Title, Robert, and Canadian Guild of Potters, Toronto, 268; van den Berg, Amsterdam, and Dutch Ceramic Society, Amsterdam, 143; van Veelen, Cees, Amsterdam, and Dutch Ceramic Society, Amsterdam, 144; Vine, David, New York, 388; Wheeler, Dan W., New York, 290.